iPad® and iPhone® Tips and Tricks

Jason R. Rich

800 East 96th Street,
Indianapolis, Indiana 46240 USA

iPAD® AND iPHONE® TIPS AND TRICKS

ISBN-13: 978-0-7897-4912-3

ISBN-10: 0-7897-4912-2

Library of Congress Cataloging-in-Publication data is on file.

Printed in the United States of America

First Printing: December 2011

TRADEMARKS

WARNING AND DISCLAIMER

BULK SALES

Que Publishing offers excellent discounts on this book when ordered in quantity for bulk purchases or special sales. For more information, please contact

U.S. Corporate and Government Sales
1-800-382-3419
corpsales@pearsontechgroup.com

For sales outside the United States, please contact

International Sales
international@pearson.com

EDITOR-IN-CHIEF
Greg Wiegand

ACQUISITIONS EDITOR
Laura Norman

DEVELOPMENT EDITOR
Robin Drake

MANAGING EDITOR
Sandra Schroeder

SENIOR PROJECT EDITOR
Tonya Simpson

COPY EDITOR
Cheri Clark

INDEXER
Tim Wright

PROOFREADER
Water Crest Publishing

TECHNICAL EDITOR
Jennifer Ackerman-Kettell

PUBLISHING COORDINATOR
Cindy Teeters

BOOK DESIGNER
Anne Jones

COMPOSITOR
Bumpy Design

CONTENTS AT A GLANCE

TABLE OF CONTENTS

ABOUT THE AUTHOR

Jason R. Rich (www.JasonRich.com) is the bestselling author of more than 49 books, as well as a frequent contributor to a handful of major daily newspapers, national magazines, and popular websites. He's also an accomplished photographer and an avid Apple iPad, iPhone, Apple TV, and Mac user.

Jason R. Rich is also the author of the books *Your iPad 2 at Work* and *Using iPhone iOS 5 Edition*, as well as the *iPad 2 Essentials* video course, all published by Que Publishing.

More than 50 feature-length how-to articles by Jason R. Rich, covering the Apple iPhone and iPad, can be read free online at the Que Publishing website. Visit www.iOSArticles.com and tap on the Articles tab. You can also follow Jason R. Rich on Twitter (@JasonRich7).

DEDICATION

I am honored to dedicate this book to Steve Jobs (1955–2011), a true visionary, entrepreneur, and pioneer who forever changed the world. My condolences to his family, friends, and coworkers at Apple, and to those whose lives he touched. Thank you, Mr. Jobs…for everything.

ACKNOWLEDGMENTS

Thanks to Laura Norman at Que Publishing for inviting me to work on this book, and for all of her guidance as I've worked on this project. My gratitude also goes out to Greg Wiegand, Tonya Simpson, Robin Drake, Cindy Teeters, Todd Brakke, Jennifer Ackerman-Kettell, and Paul Boger, as well as everyone else at Que Publishing/Pearson who contributed their expertise, hard work, and creativity to the creation of *iPad and iPhone Tips and Tricks*.

I'd also like to acknowledge everyone at Apple, and congratulate them on the incredible innovations made to the iOS 5 operating system and on the ongoing worldwide success of the iPhone and iPad.

Thanks also to my friends and family for their ongoing support. Finally, thanks to you, the reader. I hope this book helps you fully utilize your iOS device in every aspect of your life, and take full advantage of the power and functionality your iPhone and/or iPad offers.

WE WANT TO HEAR FROM YOU!

As the reader of this book, *you* are our most important critic and commentator. We value your opinion and want to know what we're doing right, what we could do better, what areas you'd like to see us publish in, and any other words of wisdom you're willing to pass our way.

As an editor-in-chief for Que Publishing, I welcome your comments. You can email or write me directly to let me know what you did or didn't like about this book—as well as what we can do to make our books better.

Please note that I cannot help you with technical problems related to the topic of this book. We do have a User Services group, however, where I will forward specific technical questions related to the book.

When you write, please be sure to include this book's title and author as well as your name, email address, and phone number. I will carefully review your comments and share them with the author and editors who worked on the book.

Email: feedback@quepublishing.com

Mail: Greg Wiegand
Editor-in-Chief
Que Publishing
800 East 96th Street
Indianapolis, IN 46240 USA

READER SERVICES

Visit our website and register this book at quepublishing.com/register for convenient access to any updates, downloads, or errata that might be available for this book.

Introduction

Whether you're a new iPhone or iPad user who just purchased an Apple mobile device that runs iOS 5, or you're a veteran iPhone and/or iPad user who has upgraded your device to run the latest and greatest of Apple's mobile device operating systems, you're in for an amazing experience.

Apple's iOS 5 not only enables your iPhone, iPad, or iPod touch to be a powerful mobile device that's capable of handling a wide range of tasks simultaneously, it also is an operating system that enables you to utilize an incredibly fast-growing library of apps.

Between the customizability of iOS 5 and your ability to utilize your mobile device with preinstalled and optional apps, you can personalize your phone or tablet so that it's perfectly suited to meet your unique needs.

Like Microsoft Windows for PC-based computers or Apple's OS X Lion for the Mac, for example, iOS is an operating system created by Apple that works with its mobile devices, including the various iPhone, iPad, or iPod touch models. Just like any

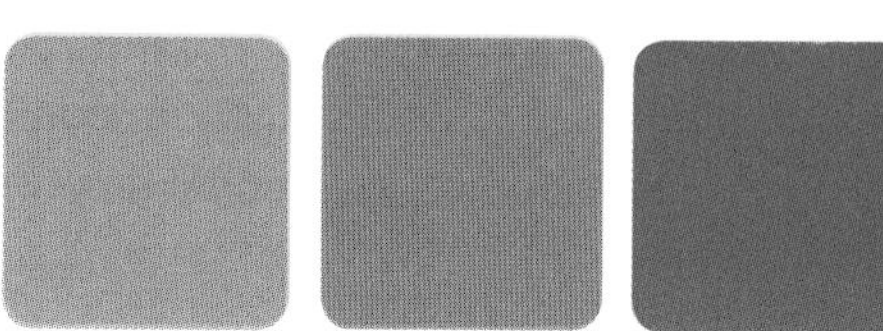

operating system, iOS manages and controls the device's hardware and software resources, and handles every task it ultimately carries out.

Apple first introduced the world to the original Apple iPhone in early 2007. Since then, the phone hardware, as well as the iOS operating system, has quickly evolved. Each updated version of Apple's iOS has introduced users to new features and functionality, ultimately making the iPhone, and later the iPad and iPod touch, among the bestselling and most versatile mobile devices on the planet—not to mention that they're among the most technologically advanced in terms of what's available to consumers.

WHY YOU NEED iOS 5 ON YOUR APPLE MOBILE DEVICE

The introduction of iOS 5 for the iPhone, iPad, and iPod touch marks a significant advancement and improvement, not just in the operating system itself, but in how we can utilize and interact with Apple's mobile devices. If these advancements and innovations could be summarized in a single world, the term used to describe all that's new in iOS 5 would be "integration."

> **! CAUTION** iOS 5 refers to the version of the operating system, and should not be confused with the model number of your device, such as the iPhone 4S. The Apple iPhone 3Gs, iPhone 4S, iPod touch, iPad, and iPad 2 are among the devices that have the capability to run the iOS 5 operating system.

As soon as you begin using iOS 5 on your device, you'll discover that your favorite apps, as well as many of the features and functions built in to the operating system, now nicely integrate with each other, making it easier for you to fully utilize, access, manipulate, and share all sorts of data and content, not just on the device you're using, but across multiple devices and your primary computer.

NEW AND MODIFIED APPS AND FEATURES

Using the familiar Photos app, not only can you view the digital images stored on your iPhone or iPad, you also can now crop, rotate, enhance, and edit them from within the Photos app, and then share them via email, Twitter, or iCloud.

Likewise, when using Safari to surf the Web, you can now experience tabbed browsing, which helps you keep track of and quickly switch between multiple web pages. In addition to bookmarking web pages, you can create Reading Lists, which can be viewed later, or use Reader to view web pages without other onscreen clutter.

Other popular apps, such as Mail, Calendar, iPod (now called Music), and iTunes, also offer new features that you'll soon be wondering how you lived without.

WHICH DEVICES USE iOS 5?

To fully utilize all the features and functionality of iOS 5, you'll need to use it with an iPhone 4 or iPhone 4S, or with an iPad 2. However, many (but not all) of the functionalities of this newly revised operating system also work fine with the iPhone 3Gs, the original iPad, and the iPod touch. Keep in mind that certain features work only with the latest iPhone 4S or exclusively with the iPad 2.

You'll soon discover how to use many of the more than 200 new features built in to iOS 5, plus learn how to quickly and easily share data and content between apps and various devices, and with other people. Not only will this book help you get the most out of your Apple mobile device, it also will help you stay connected and more easily manage the data stored on your phone or tablet.

NEW AND IMPROVED INTERACTIVITY

One of the many things that originally set the iPhone apart from its competition, and later made the iPad the world's most sought-after tablet, was the touchscreen built in to these devices. Using a series of onscreen taps, swipes, and finger movements, it's possible to interact with all of your device's apps and handle a wide range of tasks—without needing a traditional keyboard or a stylus.

NEW AND IMPROVED TOUCHSCREEN TECHNIQUES

From the moment you turn on your iPhone or iPad (or take it out of Sleep mode, which is also referred to as Standby mode), aside from pressing the Home button to return to the Home screen at any time, virtually all of your interaction with the tablet is done through the following finger movements and taps on the device's highly sensitive touchscreen:

- **Tap:** Tapping an icon or a link that's displayed on your device's screen serves the same purpose as clicking the mouse when you use your main computer. And, just as when you use a computer, you can single-tap or double-tap, which is equivalent to a single or double click of the mouse.
- **Hold:** Instead of a quick tap, in some cases, it is necessary to press and hold your finger on an icon or onscreen command option. When a hold action is required, place your finger on the appropriate icon or command option and hold it there. There's never a need to press down hard on the touch screen.
- **Swipe:** A swipe refers to quickly moving a finger along the screen from right to left, left to right, top to bottom, or bottom to top, to scroll to the left, right, down, or up, respectively, depending on which app you're using.

- **Pinch:** Using your thumb and index finger (the finger next to your thumb), perform a pinch motion on the touchscreen to zoom out when using certain apps. Or "unpinch" (by moving your fingers apart quickly) to zoom in on what you're looking at on the screen when using most apps.

TIP Another way to zoom in or out when looking at the device's screen is to double-tap the area of the screen on which you want to zoom in. This works when you're surfing the Web in Safari or looking at photos using the Photos app, as well as within other apps that support the zoom in/out feature.

- **Pull-Down:** Using your index finger, swipe it from the very top of the iPhone or iPad quickly downward onto the screen. This will cause the new Notification Center window to appear, alerting you of incoming email messages, text messages, alarms, or other time-sensitive actions that need to be dealt with. You can be holding the device in portrait or landscape mode for this to work. To make this window disappear, tap anywhere on the screen outside the Notification Center window, or on the iPhone, place your finger on the icon with three horizontal lines and use a swipe up movement.
- **Finger Pinch (iPad Only):** To exit any app and return to the Home Screen, place all five fingertips of one hand on the screen so that they're spread out, and then draw your fingers together, as if you're grabbing something. Be sure, however, that the new multitasking features are turned on from within the Settings app (found under the General heading).
- **Swipe-Up (iPad Only):** Make the multitasking bar appear at the bottom of the screen by using several of your fingers and swiping them upward, from the very bottom of the screen toward the top. (Or press the Home button twice in quick succession.)
- **Multi-Finger Horizontal Swipe (iPad Only):** When multiple apps are simultaneously running, swipe several fingers from left to right or from right to left on the screen to switch between active apps.

You can also use several of your fingers together and swipe left or right when looking at the multitasking bar to switch between active apps.

TIP To wake up your iPhone when it is in Sleep mode, typically you would tap on the Home button once. However, now that you're running iOS 5, when you double-tap on the Home button, the Lock Screen reveals a Camera icon and Music Control icons. Tap on the Camera icon to launch the Camera app, and then use the Volume Up (+) button on the side of the iPhone to quickly snap a photo. Or, use the music controls to play, pause, fast forward, or rewind music from an active playlist.

On the iPad, when you double-tap on the Home button when the tablet is in Sleep mode, the music controls appear at the top of the Lock Screen.

HOW TO MAKE THE BEST USE OF THE VIRTUAL KEYBOARD

Whenever you need to enter data into your iPhone or iPad, you almost always use the virtual keyboard that pops up on the bottom portion of the screen when it's needed. The virtual keyboard typically resembles a typewriter or computer keyboard; however, certain onscreen keys have different purposes, depending on which app you're using.

For example, when you access the iPhone or iPad's main Spotlight Search screen, notice the large Search key on the right side of the keyboard. However, when you use the Pages word processor app, the Search key becomes the Return key (see Figure I.1). When you surf the Web using the Safari web browser app, the Search key becomes the Go key in certain situations.

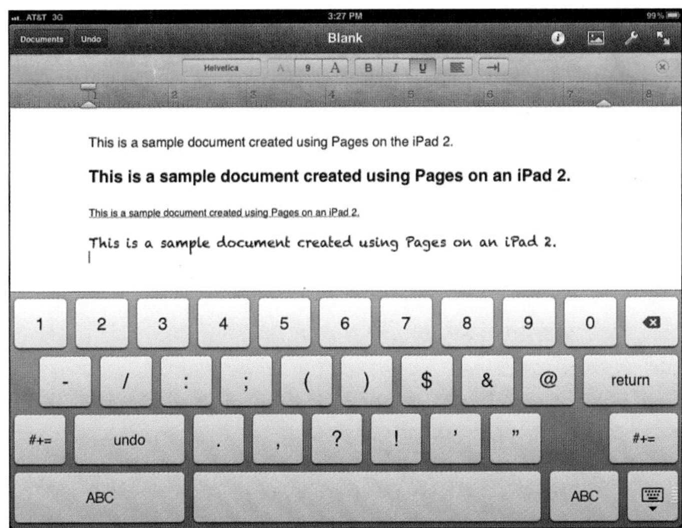

FIGURE I.1

The appearance of the virtual keyboard changes based on which app you're using and the type of data you need to enter. Pages, running on the iPad 2, is shown here.

When you're using an app that involves numeric data entry, such as Numbers (see Figure I.2), the layout and design of the virtual keyboard change dramatically.

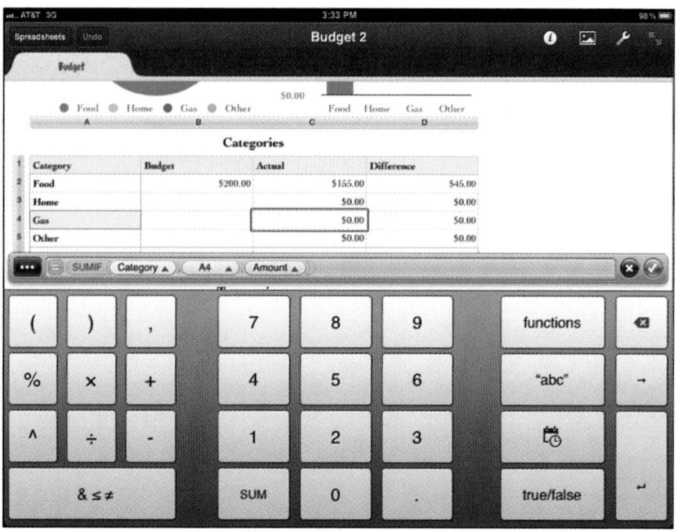

FIGURE I.2

When you're doing numeric data entry into the Numbers app, the layout of the virtual keyboard changes dramatically. Shown here is Numbers running on an iPad 2.

As part of the iOS 5 upgrade, using your index fingers on your right and left hand simultaneously, place them in the center of the iPad's virtual keyboard and move them apart quickly to divide the onscreen keyboard into two sections, as shown in Figure I.3. Some people find this virtual keyboard format more convenient for typing while they're holding their device. When the virtual keyboard appears, use your fingers to tap the keys and type.

> **TIP** From the Settings app, you can turn off the keyboard click noise that's otherwise heard when you're tapping the virtual keyboard keys. You also can turn off the Auto-Capitalization, Auto-Correction, Check Spelling, and Enable Caps Lock features that, when turned on, automatically fix what you're typing when the iOS deems the change appropriate.

To make the keyboard disappear, you can often tap anywhere on the screen except on the virtual keyboard itself, or you can tap the Hide Keyboard key, which is typically located in the lower-right corner of the virtual keyboard.

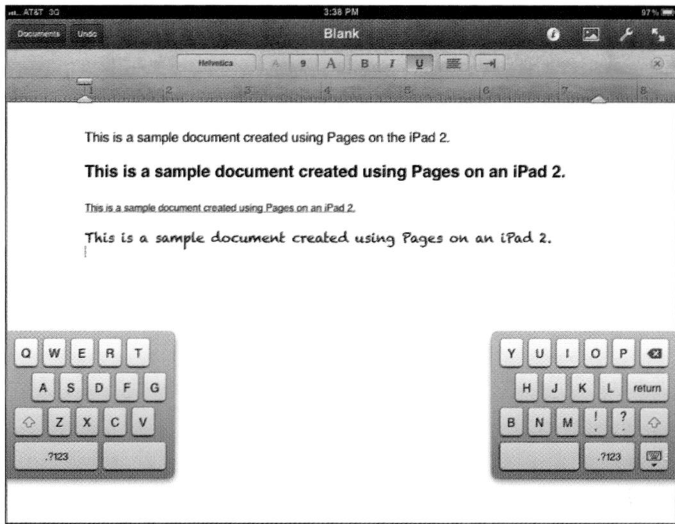

FIGURE I.3

Splitting the virtual keyboard in half is a new iOS 5 option.

Whenever data entry is required when you're using an app, the virtual keyboard automatically displays as it's needed. However, if you need to fill in a data field when using a particular app, for example, and the virtual keyboard is not visible, simply tap the blank onscreen field where data needs to be entered, and the appropriately formatted virtual keyboard will appear.

In terms of the iPad's hardware (the device itself), from the Settings app, you can decide how the tablet's side switch (located above the volume control buttons) will work. Your options include Lock Rotation and Mute button. Chapter 2, "Tips and Tricks for Customizing Settings," explains how to personalize this feature. Otherwise, the power button, home button, and volume buttons on your iPhone or iPad continue to serve the same purposes as they did in the past.

When using the Camera app to snap photos, however, you'll discover that iOS 5 has added some new functionality to your iPhone and iPad's buttons.

WHAT THIS BOOK OFFERS

iPad and iPhone Tips and Tricks will help you to discover all the important new features and functions of iOS 5, easily update your mobile device, and transform your iPhone, iPad, or iPod touch into the most versatile, useful, and fun-to-use tool possible.

Each chapter of this book focuses on a different aspect of Apple's newly revised operating system and how it should be used with your iPhone, iPad, or iPod touch. For example, you'll discover how to personalize your iPhone or iPad by adjusting the various options within the Settings app. You'll learn strategies for protecting your privacy and maximizing the capabilities of your device's security options. You'll explore the possibilities of two of the most sought-after new features on the iPhone 4S: the rear-facing 8MP digital camera, and the cutting-edge Siri feature, which allows you to control your iPhone with voice commands.

TIP Most of this book focuses on using iOS 5 with an iPhone or iPad; however, some of the content also relates directly to using this operating system with an iPod touch, especially if it's connected to the Web via a Wi-Fi connection.

Apps created for the iPhone will work flawlessly on the iPad. However, iPhone-specific apps that are not hybrid iPhone/iPad apps will not fully utilize the iPad's larger display. iPad-specific apps will not work on an iPhone

Much of this book focuses on the core apps preinstalled with iOS 5, including Notification Center, Messages, Newsstand, and Reminders. The chapters that cover these apps are chock-full of tips and strategies for getting the most out of these apps. We also explore how to utilize the App Store to find, purchase (if applicable), download, install, and use the optional apps that best address your unique needs.

ATTENTION, PLEASE...

Throughout this book, look for Tip, Note, Caution, What's New, and More Info boxes that convey useful tidbits of information relevant to the chapter you're reading.

The What's New boxes, for example, highlight new features or functionality introduced in iOS 5, while the More Info boxes provide website URLs or list additional resources you can use to obtain more information about a particular topic.

IN THIS CHAPTER

- How to upgrade your iPhone or iPad to iOS 5 using iTunes Sync
- How to configure iOS 5 on your device
- How to set up a free Apple iCloud account
- How to update your existing apps

1

UPGRADING TO iOS 5

If you've had your iPhone or iPad for a while and it's currently running an older version of the iOS operating system, such as iOS 4.3.4, now that Apple has made the iOS 5 operating system available, you'll definitely want to upgrade your device. Keep in mind that some of the very early iPhone and iPod touch models cannot be upgraded to iOS 5.

Whether you're using an iPhone or iPad, making the transition from iOS 4.3.4 (or earlier) to iOS 5 will require you to use the iTunes sync process. However, after iOS 5 has been installed on your new iPhone or iPad, all future iOS and app upgrades can be done wirelessly.

NOTE *iPad and iPhone Tips and Tricks* applies to the iOS 5 operating system, which is compatible with the iPhone 3Gs, iPhone 4, iPhone 4S, iPad, iPad 2, iPod touch third generation, and iPod touch fourth generation, as well as any later versions of these devices. Throughout this book, these iPhone, iPad, and iPod touch models are referred to often as "iOS devices" or "Apple mobile devices." Unless otherwise indicated, the tips, strategies, and how-to information in this book also apply to the iPod touch (third- and fourth-generation models), even if they're not specifically listed.

HOW TO UPGRADE FROM IOS 4.3.4 (OR EARLIER) TO iOS 5

If you have an iPhone or iPad that currently has iOS 4.3.4 (or an earlier version) installed, follow the directions in this section to download and install the iOS 5 operating system onto your device.

FIND OUT WHICH VERSION OF iOS YOUR DEVICE USES

To determine which version of the iOS operating system your device currently has installed, from the Home Screen, tap on the Settings app, and then tap on the General option. Next, tap on the About option, found under the General heading, and look at the Version information. Figure 1.1 shows this on an iPhone 4 that is currently running iOS 4.3.4.

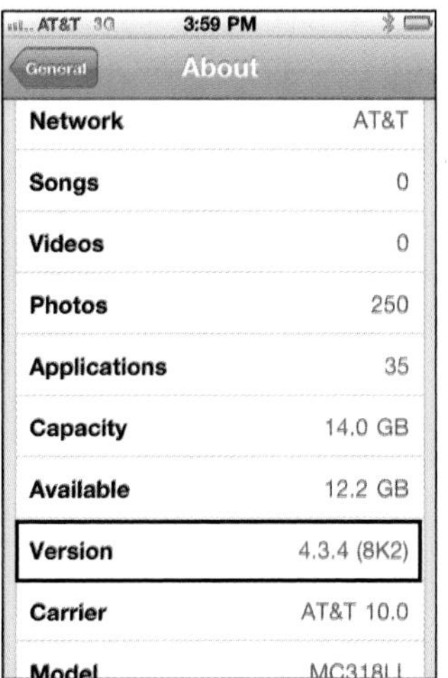

FIGURE 1.1

From the Settings app on your device, you can easily determine which version of iOS it's running.

TIP To upgrade from iOS 4.3.4 (or earlier) to iOS 5, your primary computer must be running the most current version of iTunes (version 10.5 or later). From the iTunes pull-down menu, click the Check for Updates option to ensure you're running the latest version of this software on your Mac or PC. If you're informed that a more up-to-date version of the iTunes software is available, download and install it before upgrading your mobile device to iOS 5.

If you need to download and install iTunes for the first time on your PC or Mac, visit www.apple.com/itunes/download.

AVOIDING iTUNES CONFUSION

You have an iTunes app on your computer and you have an iTunes app on your Apple mobile device, but these apps have different purposes. The iTunes app on your computer is for syncing and backing up content, managing applications, listening to or viewing your purchased content (such as movies, music, or podcasts) on your computer, and so on.

The iTunes app on your mobile device is used to purchase and download content directly to that device, as well as to access Apple's Ping service from the device. Other applications on your mobile device enable you to play your purchased content. For example, you can use the Music app to listen to your downloaded music.

HOW TO UPGRADE TO iOS 5 USING iTUNES

After the latest version of iTunes (version 10.5 or later) is running on your PC or Mac, use the iTunes sync procedure to create a current backup for your iPhone or iPad before starting the iOS 5 download and install process. To do this, iTunes must be running on your primary computer, and your mobile device should be connected to your computer via the white USB cable that came with your iOS device. If you're using an optional dock, your iPhone or iPad should be inserted into the dock, and the dock should be connected to your primary computer (or a USB hub that's connected to your primary computer) via the supplied USB cable.

From this point forward, your primary computer must be connected to the Internet to continue with the iOS 5 upgrade procedure. After completing the backup process, click the Summary tab for your iPhone, iPad, or iPod touch that's displayed at the top of the iTunes screen (on your primary computer). In the Version box, click the Check for Update icon.

iTunes will determine what the most recent version of iOS 5 is. If your iOS device is running an older version of the operating system, a message appears stating that you should download and install the latest version of the iOS operating system, which will be iOS 5.0 or later.

Follow the onscreen prompts on your primary computer to begin downloading iOS 5. During this procedure, do not disconnect your iPhone, iPad, or iPod touch. Depending on the speed of your Internet connection, the iOS 5 download process could take a while, so be patient.

When iOS 5 has been downloaded, it will automatically be transferred to your iPhone or iPad and installed. Again, this process could take up to 30 minutes, so be patient and do not disconnect your iOS device from the primary computer during this process or attempt to use the device.

After iOS 5 is installed on your Apple mobile device, it will reset. At this point, it will be necessary to configure iOS 5 on your device, and then restore your saved apps and data.

HOW TO CONFIGURE iOS 5 ON YOUR iPHONE OR iPAD

After iOS 5 is installed on your iPhone or iPad, you'll see the new Welcome screen when the device is turned on for the first time. Plan on spending about 5 minutes configuring the new operating system and then, if applicable, restoring your previously backed up data, personal settings, and apps, which could take an additional 15 to 30 minutes or longer.

This part of the process can be done with your device connected to your primary computer using the iTunes sync process, or it can be done wirelessly. Configuring iOS 5 wirelessly on your iPhone or iPad requires that the device have access to the Web via a Wi-Fi connection.

From the initial iOS 5 setup screen, move the slider from left to right to proceed to the next Welcome screen. From this screen, select a language. English is the default, but Spanish and 19 other options are available. Tap on your selection so that a check mark appears on the screen next to it, and then tap on the blue-and-white Next icon.

Next, from the Country or Region screen, select where you'll be primarily using your iOS device. The default option is United States, but the pull-down menu lists almost every other country on the planet. Tap on your selection so that a check mark appears next to it, and then tap on the Next icon.

The Location Services screen appears next. Your iPhone or iPad has the capability to pinpoint and track its exact location using GPS, crowd-sourced Wi-Fi hotspots, and cell-tower locations. From this screen, you can turn on this feature or disable it. However, after iOS 5 is operational, you can customize this feature from the Settings app, which is discussed in Chapter 2.

For now, tap on either the Enable Location Services or the Disable Location Services option. When a check mark appears next to your selection, tap on the Next icon.

When the Wi-Fi Networks screen appears (shown in Figure 1.2), under the Choose a Network heading, any available Wi-Fi hotspots will be listed.

TIP If no Wi-Fi hotspots appear, your device will not be able to connect to a Wi-Fi hotspot, so to continue, you'll need to keep your iPhone or iPad connected to your primary computer via the supplied USB cable, and select the Connect to iTunes option by tapping it.

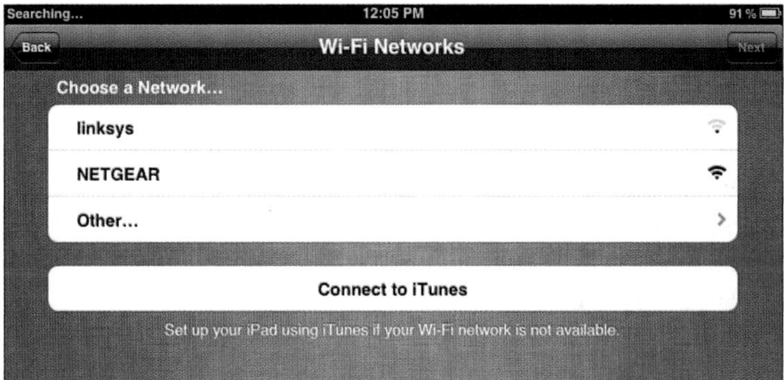

FIGURE 1.2
From the Wi-Fi Networks screen, determine how your iPhone or iPad will connect to the Internet to continue the iOS 5 setup process.

After an Internet connection method has been selected, tap on the Next icon. You'll see the Set Up iPhone or Set Up iPad screen displayed next. From this screen, you can choose one of three options:

- Set up a new iPad (or iPhone)
- Restore from iCloud Backup
- Restore from iTunes

If you're setting up a brand-new iPhone or iPad, tap on the Set Up As New iPhone/iPad option. However, if you're upgrading your existing iPhone or iPad, tap and select the Restore from iTunes option to continue. This will allow you to restore your data, personalized preferences, cellular phone number, and Internet account data (if applicable), as well as your apps.

In the future, after you have set up iOS 5 and an iCloud account, you'll be able to restore your device wirelessly from backup data stored on iCloud by selecting the Restore from iCloud Backup option. Or, if your backup data is stored on your primary computer, you'll be able to restore data wirelessly (or using the supplied USB cable) from your primary computer using iTunes sync. For now, however, depending on your situation, tap on the Set Up As New iPad (iPhone) or Restore from iTunes option, and then tap on the Next icon to continue.

HOW TO SET UP A NEW iPHONE OR iPAD

If you opted to continue the iOS 5 setup procedure by selecting the Set Up As New iPhone or Set Up As New iPad option, the next screen enables you to create an Apple ID account and/or continue the process using your existing Apple ID and password.

From the Apple ID screen, tap either the Sign In with an Apple ID or Create a Free Apple ID option. Or you can tap on the Skip This Step option and complete this step later.

> **TIP** If you already own any Apple equipment, such as a Mac, an iPhone, an iPad, or an iPod, chances are you have already created a free Apple ID account. Enter this existing Apple ID account username and password when prompted. This information will ultimately allow you to use the App Store, iBookstore, and iTunes to make purchases and to set up a free iCloud account.

Assuming that you have an Apple ID account and password, select the Sign In with an Apple ID option by tapping it and, when prompted, use the virtual keyboard to enter your Apple ID and corresponding password (as shown in Figure 1.3). Tap on the Next icon to continue.

When the Terms and Conditions screen appears, tap on the blue-and-white Agree icon to continue. You will be prompted to confirm this decision when a pop-up Terms and Conditions window appears. Once again, tap on the Agree icon.

You'll now be given the opportunity to set up an iCloud account using your Apple ID and password. iCloud is an online-based file-sharing service that has been designed to be used with iOS 5 and your favorite apps. Thus, you can use this free service to wirelessly transfer and synchronize files, contacts, calendars, photos, music, eBooks, and other content.

Near the bottom center of the Set Up iCloud screen, you'll see a virtual switch that allows you to turn on or off the iCloud functionality within your iPhone or iPad. If you turn on this switch and then tap on the Next icon, your free iCloud account will be set up, and your device will configure itself to begin using the iCloud service. You can fully customize how your iPhone or iPad interacts with iCloud later.

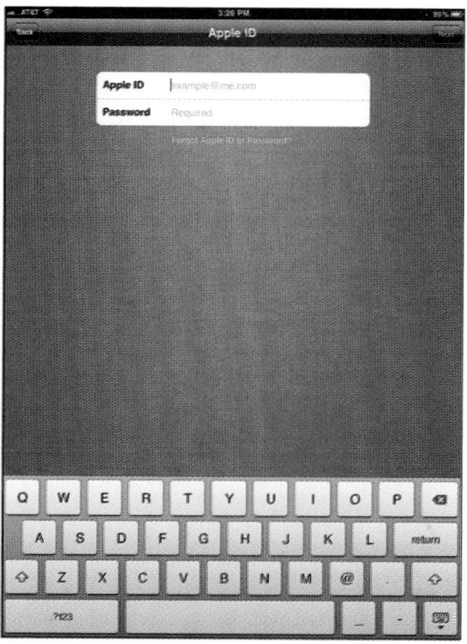

FIGURE 1.3

When prompted, enter your Apple ID and password.

Assuming that you have access to a Wi-Fi connection on an ongoing basis, you can configure your iPhone or iPad to automatically and wirelessly back itself up once per day and store the backup data on iCloud. During this setup procedure, when the iCloud Backup screen appears (shown in Figure 1.4), you can choose to maintain a wireless backup of your mobile device using iCloud, or choose to maintain a backup of your device on your primary computer (using the iTunes sync process).

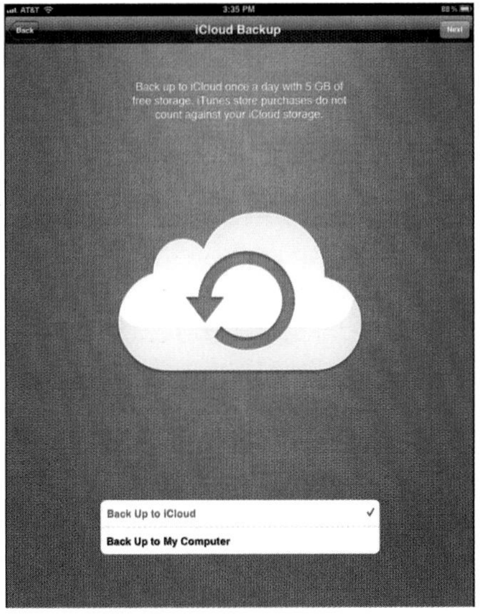

FIGURE 1.4

Decide whether your iOS device will store its backup data files on iCloud or on your primary computer's hard drive.

> **TIP** Should you store your backup files on iCloud or your hard drive? Each option offers benefits:
>
> - The benefit to storing your iPhone or iPad's backup data files on iCloud is that as long as a Wi-Fi Internet connection is available to your mobile device, you can wirelessly create a backup file or, if necessary, restore data from that backup from virtually anywhere. However, a Wi-Fi Internet connection must be present to create or restore from a backup that's stored on iCloud, and during the backup (or restore) process, your iOS device must be connected to an external power source. Your device will automatically be backed up once per day. However, from within the Settings app, you can also initiate the backup process manually whenever you wish.
> - The benefit to storing your iPhone or iPad's backup data files on your primary computer's hard drive via iTunes Sync is that its always available to you, regardless of whether a Wi-Fi Internet connection is available. However, to create or restore from the backup, your iPhone or iPad must be connected to your primary computer via the supplied USB cable, or you must be able to establish a wireless connection within a Wi-Fi network between your computer and your mobile device. Whenever the iTunes sync connection is made between your primary computer and your iOS device, a new backup will be created. You can manually initiate this connection as often as you wish.

Tap on the Next icon to continue. Now, you'll have the option to set up the free Find My iPhone or Find My iPad feature. This feature enables you to pinpoint the exact location of your device if it gets lost or stolen. To use it, however, you must set up and activate this feature. (See the later section, "Where's My Device? How to Use the Find My iPhone or Find My iPad Feature," for details on this useful feature.)

When the Find My iPhone or Find My iPad screen appears, you'll see the virtual on/off switch (as shown in Figure 1.5). Make sure this virtual switch remains in its default On position; then tap on the Next icon to automatically activate this feature using your Apple ID account information, and continue the setup procedure.

FIGURE 1.5

As you're setting up iOS 5 on your iPhone or iPad, you can turn on and activate the Find My iPhone or Find My iPad feature. Or you can do this later from the Settings app.

Again tap on the Next icon when you see the Diagnostics screen. This is the final step in the initial iOS 5 setup process. The Thank You screen will appear next. To begin using your iPhone or iPad, simply tap on the Start Using iPhone or Start Using iPad icon that appears near the bottom center of this screen.

The Home Screen will now be displayed on your iPhone or iPad (see Figure 1.6). The Home Screen contains icons for all the preinstalled (core) apps: Messages, Calendar, Notes, Reminders, Maps, YouTube, Videos, Contacts, Game Center, iTunes, App Store, Newsstand, FaceTime, Camera, Photo Booth, Settings, Safari, Mail, Photos, and Music (formerly iPod). If you're using an iPhone, the Phone app will also be displayed on the Home Screen.

FIGURE 1.6

The iOS 5 Home Screen on an iPad 2.

HOW TO RESTORE FROM iTUNES

If you're upgrading your iPhone or iPad from iOS 4.3.4 (or earlier) to iOS 5, and previously created a backup with your device before starting the iOS 5 installation procedure, you can continue the iOS 5 installation process and restore all your data, personal settings, cellphone number/Internet account information, and apps by selecting the Restore from iTunes option during the iOS 5 setup procedure.

With your iPhone or iPad still connected to your primary computer via the USB cable, iOS 5 automatically installs on your device, and your backup data, apps, and preferences are restored. When the process is completed, you'll be ready to use your iPhone or iPad, which will now be running iOS 5.

Depending on how much data, how many apps, and what content needs to be restored to your iPhone or iPad from a previously stored backup, the process of finalizing the iOS 5 install and then restoring your content could take up to 30 minutes, so be patient.

WHERE'S MY DEVICE? HOW TO USE THE FIND MY iPHONE OR FIND MY iPAD FEATURE

If turned on, the Find My iPhone (or Find My iPad) feature is now fully integrated into the iOS 5 operating system. During the initial iOS 5 setup procedure, you had the option to automatically set up and activate this feature. However, you can modify this setting at any time by tapping the Settings app, tapping the iCloud option, and then selecting the Find My iPad option.

With the release of the iOS 5 operating system, the Find My iPhone/iPad feature was made a free, standalone service, as opposed to being part of Apple's now obsolete MobileMe online service. This feature enables you to access the Web from any device, have Apple locate the exact location of your iPhone or iPad, and then display its whereabouts.

Even when Find My iPhone/iPad is set up and active, the device must be turned on (or in Sleep mode but not turned off) and must have a connection to the Internet via 3G or Wi-Fi for the feature to work. There is an option, however, that will notify you when the device gets turned back on, if it's turned off when you initially attempt to locate it.

After Find My iPhone/iPad is activated, if you misplace the device or it gets stolen, from any computer or wireless Internet device, you can access www.icloud.com/find and have the website service quickly pinpoint the location of your device and display its location on a map. From this website, you can also type a message that will instantly appear on your missing device's screen (asking for it to be returned, for example), or you can force the device to emit a sound (so that you can find it easier if it's lost in your office, for example).

It's also possible to lock the device using a password or wipe out and delete the contents of your iPhone/iPad remotely, which ensures that your sensitive data doesn't fall into the wrong hands. You can always restore your data using your iCloud or iTunes sync backup files after the unit has been retrieved. A free Find My iPhone app can also be downloaded from the App Store and used with the Find My iPhone or Find My iPad feature.

Find My iPhone/iPad isn't a perfect solution for finding a lost or stolen device, but it can be useful in certain situations. However, if someone knows your Apple ID and password, he or she can easily track your exact whereabouts at any time using the www.icloud.com/find website. Later, we focus more on security measures you can implement on your iPhone or iPad to help protect your privacy.

iOS 5 WHAT'S NEW With the launch of iCloud, in addition to the Find My iPhone/iPad feature, Apple launched the Find My Friends app. When given permission, this optional app (which is available from the App Store) enables others to track your whereabouts in real time. Although this feature has many practical real-world applications, to ensure your privacy, it can be turned on or off quickly and at your discretion. Plus, you can choose exactly who has the ability to "follow" you.

You can also set up the ability for others to follow you for only a specific period of time. Using the enhanced Restrictions features of iOS 5, parents can keep tabs on their kids who use an iPhone or iPad, for example, but prevent them from being able to turn off the Find My Friends feature. Again, for the Find My Friends feature to work, the iOS device must have access to the Web via a Wi-Fi or 3G connection.

INTEGRATE YOUR DATA, APPS, AND MORE WITH APPLE'S iCLOUD

In the past, if you wanted to send a file or data between your primary computer and your iPhone or iPad, it needed to be done via email or using the iTunes sync process (which involves connecting the devices using the supplied USB cable). However, some types of data and files could also be transferred using a compatible online-based file-sharing service, such as Dropbox or WebDAV. This capability was limited to certain types of data and could be used with only a handful of apps.

One of the new features of iOS 5 is its integration with Apple's iCloud service. iCloud is an online-based file-sharing service. If you opt to turn on and use this initially free service, you'll quickly discover that it makes synchronizing data, transferring files and content, and sharing information between your iPhone, iPad, Mac, and/or PC a simple process, plus it allows you to maintain a wireless backup of your iOS device.

iOS 5 WHAT'S NEW Using iOS 5 on your iPhone or iPad, you can decide whether you want to back up your device whenever you manually connect it to your primary computer using the iTunes sync process, or whether you want your device to automatically create a backup of its contents wirelessly and store the data on iCloud. If you opt for the once-daily wireless backups to be created, you must keep this feature turned on, and your device needs to be within a Wi-Fi hotspot to connect to iCloud. To use the wireless backup feature, a 3G connection will not work.

Initially, when used with your iPhone or iPad, iCloud automatically handles a handful of tasks because it's fully compatible with many of the core apps that come preinstalled on your device, as well as other popular apps, such as Pages, Numbers, and Keynote. Many third-party app developers have also implemented iCloud compatibility into their apps (or will soon be doing so).

When you set up a free iCloud account using your existing Apple ID and password (which can also be established for free), you're immediately given 5GB of free online storage space, plus an unlimited amount of additional online storage space to store the content you purchase from iTunes, the App Store, and Apple's iBookstore (including music, movies, TV show episodes, apps, and eBooks).

TIP For an additional annual fee, you can purchase extra online storage space for your iCloud account. Plus, you can upgrade to Apple's premium iTunes Match service for $24.99 per year. (See the later section, "Upgrade to the Premium iTunes Match Service," for details.)

Especially when you use a Wi-Fi Internet connection, content, files, and data can quickly be transferred between your iPhone or iPad and iCloud. The process takes a bit longer if you're using a 3G connection (which excludes the capability to transfer files over 20MB in size).

iCloud really becomes useful when you consider that it can be used as a hub in cyberspace for wirelessly and quickly sharing data, files, and content between your iPhone or iPad and your primary computer. So, using iCloud, you can transfer a Microsoft Office file from your computer to iCloud, for example, and then retrieve it from iCloud and store it on your iPhone or iPad. Depending on the type of file, you can then use it with Pages, Keynote, Numbers, or another app installed on your device.

When you begin using iCloud, you'll quickly discover that it is more than just a remote hard drive in cyberspace that allows you to wirelessly share content and data among multiple computers and devices. iCloud also provides an easy way to instantly and wirelessly synchronize photos, music, emails, contacts, scheduling data, Safari bookmarks, eBooks, and other information between your primary computer and your iPhone and/or iPad.

SYNCHRONIZE YOUR DIGITAL PHOTOS

You've probably discovered how much fun it is to take digital photos using the cameras built in to your iPhone or iPad, or even with your standalone digital camera. Using iOS 5, not only can you now edit and then share these images via email or quickly post them on Twitter, Facebook, or Google+, for example, you also can keep your digital images wirelessly synchronized between your iOS mobile device(s) and your primary computer using iCloud.

After it's set up, iOS 5 enables you to create a Photo Stream. Thus, when you snap a new photo on your iPhone or iPad, for example, it will automatically be transferred (uploaded) to iCloud, and then downloaded to your other computer(s) or other iOS devices. There's no longer a need to manually sync your devices to share your favorite digital images on all of your devices and computers (both Macs and PCs).

As with some of the other file-sharing features offered using iCloud, to create and manage a Photo Stream and keep large numbers of digital images synchronized among your devices, your iPhone and/or iPad must have access to a Wi-Fi web connection as opposed to a 3G Internet connection.

After setting up the Photo Stream feature once, you'll discover that it can also be used to automatically stream your favorite digital images to your Apple TV device. Your Photo Stream can include up to 1,000 of your most recent digital images. iCloud stores all new images for 30 days, during which time you can arrange to download them to any or all of your computers and/or devices and store them in Albums.

TIP Beyond the 30-day period during which a photo is automatically saved on iCloud, you can transfer your favorite images from the Photo Stream to a specific Photo Album, where it will be stored indefinitely. However, you never need to worry about images being erased accidentally. An archival copy of every digital image added to your Photo Stream (and temporarily stored on iCloud) is also automatically stored indefinitely on your primary computer's hard drive until you delete it manually.

TRANSFER FILES AND DOCUMENTS

iCloud is fully compatible with the optional Pages, Numbers, and Keynote apps, allowing you to easily transfer Microsoft Office–compatible files between your iPhone, iPad, and primary computer (Mac or PC). It also works with PDF files, photos, and other types of data files that can be utilized on both your primary computer and your mobile device.

Pages is a full-featured word processor for the iPhone and iPad that is compatible with Microsoft Word. Numbers is a spreadsheet management program for the iPhone and iPad that is compatible with Microsoft Excel, and Keynote is a digital slide presentation tool compatible with Microsoft PowerPoint.

iOS 5 WHAT'S NEW Not only will iCloud enable you to wirelessly transfer data files and documents between devices, but it also will ensure that your documents are kept up to date on each device and computer; so, as long as you have access to the Web, you will also always have access to the most current version of your files or data as changes are made to them.

If set up to do this, all of your files are automatically uploaded to iCloud, so you never have to worry about manually transferring documents or figure out which version of which document you saved in a particular location. This same capability is also being incorporated into other apps and software packages offered by third-party developers.

SYNC YOUR APPS, EBOOKS, BOOKMARKS, AND OTHER CONTENT

In addition to automatically keeping track of and making important documents available to you via iCloud, when they work together (which they were designed to do), iOS 5 and iCloud also keep track of your apps, eBooks, and other content, and make them available on any of your devices at any time (as long as an Internet connection is present).

For smaller files, this feature works with both a 3G and a Wi-Fi Internet connection. So, if you purchase and begin reading an eBook on your iPad, you can also download that eBook file (and your current digital eBook bookmarks) to your iPhone or primary computer, and continue reading on another device.

You'll also discover that iCloud can be used to automatically and wirelessly sync your web browser bookmark data. Thus, as you're surfing the Web on your primary computer, you can store a bookmark using your browser, and that bookmark will almost instantly appear when you use Safari to surf the Web on your iPhone or iPad. Or you can save a Safari bookmark on your iOS mobile device and have it transferred to the web browser on your primary computer.

iOS 5 WHAT'S NEW When you set up an iCloud account, Apple offers you a free [*username*]@me.com email account as well. The benefit to using this optional email account is that it automatically remains synchronized on all your devices via iCloud.

SYNC YOUR CONTACTS AND SCHEDULING DATA

Before the release of iOS 5, it was possible to synchronize contact and schedule data between your iPhone, iPad, and/or primary computer using the iTunes sync process or via Apple's now-defunct MobileMe service.

When iCloud is used with the Contacts and Calendar apps on your iPhone and/or iPad, all of your contacts and scheduling data can automatically be synchronized in real time, between your mobile device(s) and primary computer, as long as a web connection is available to each device.

As a result, if you're out and about and add an important appointment to the Calendar app on your iPhone, that new appointment will also appear on your compatible calendar program on your Mac or PC, your compatible online-based scheduling application, and/or your Calendar app on your iPad. Your Contacts and Calendar information is also always accessible via the web from any computer or mobile device. Just point your web browser to www.icloud.com, and sign in to your iCloud account using your Apple ID and password.

MAINTAIN A RELIABLE REMOTE BACKUP OF YOUR iPHONE OR iPAD

Both the iPhone and the iPad are technologically advanced and extremely reliable devices, but they're not flawless. Occasionally, problems can occur that could result in the loss or corruption of data. Thus, it's an extremely smart strategy to maintain a reliable backup of the complete contents of your iPhone or iPad. Prior to the release of iOS 5, the iTunes sync process was used to create a backup of your iOS mobile device, allowing the data, apps, and files to be archived on your primary computer.

This backup method is still available to you using the iTunes sync process. However, with iOS 5, if you have access to Wi-Fi in your home or office, you can use a wireless iTunes sync process to back up your iPhone or iPad.

A third option is to use your iPhone or iPad running iOS 5 with iCloud and maintain an automatic daily backup via iCloud. This feature can be initially set up from within the Settings app. When it's activated, a Wi-Fi connection is required for your iPhone or iPad to access the Web and maintain a daily backup of the device. The data, files, and pertinent information stored on your iPhone or iPad will be saved on the iCloud service in a secure format.

NOTE When you create a backup of your iPhone or iPad that's stored on iCloud, it's accessible only via your secure Apple ID account and password.

Using the iOS 5/iCloud backup feature, all the music, apps, and eBooks stored on your iPhone or iPad—as well as your photos and video files, personalized device settings, app data (including data from the Calendar, Contacts, iBooks, and Safari apps), home screen and app organization settings, text and MMS messages, and custom ringtones—will automatically be backed up each day.

After a backup of your device is stored on iCloud, you can later restore content to your device wirelessly by retrieving the necessary backup data from iCloud and reinstalling it on your iPhone or iPad.

SHARE iTUNES PURCHASES WITH ALL YOUR DEVICES

After your iCloud account is set up, whenever you purchase a new song on iTunes, for example, that song will instantly be available to you on your primary computer, as well as on all of your iOS mobile devices (including your iPhone, iPad, and/or iPod touch with Internet compatibility). Plus, all your past iTunes purchases become accessible on any device from which you can access iCloud because those purchases automatically get stored on iCloud.

> **TIP** You can connect to iCloud from your iPhone or iPad using a 3G or Wi-Fi connection to transfer music or eBook files. A Wi-Fi connection is required to transfer TV show episodes, movies, or large files.

UPGRADE TO THE PREMIUM iTUNES MATCH SERVICE

Whenever you make a music purchase on iTunes, that purchase automatically gets stored in your iCloud account, but the storage space required for this does not count against your free 5GB of online storage space. However, beyond the music you've purchased from iTunes, perhaps you've built up your digital music library by ripping music from your personal audio CD collection, or you've downloaded music from other online sources, such as Amazon.com. If you want to make your entire digital music collection available to all of your computers and devices via iCloud, you'll need to upgrade your iCloud account and sign up for the iTunes Match service for $24.99 per year.

This service analyzes your entire digital music collection and compares it to the entire music library available from iTunes (which encompasses well over 20 million songs). All matches immediately become available from your iCloud account and can be accessed by all of your compatible devices, anytime and from anywhere your iPhone, iPad, iPod (with Internet connectivity), or primary computer has an Internet connection.

Any songs from your personal digital music library that can't automatically be matched up by iTunes Match need to be uploaded to iCloud only once, regardless of where they were purchased, and those songs will also become available wirelessly on all of your iCloud-compatible devices.

Using this service, all your music, as well as your personal playlists, will be automatically synced between devices. So, a playlist you create on your iPhone can be listened to on your iPad or on your primary computer at any time.

HOW TO UPDATE YOUR APPS WIRELESSLY

After you've upgraded to iOS 5, you'll probably discover that the developers of your favorite apps have also released updated versions. If you want to check whether you're running the most current versions of the apps already installed on your iPhone or iPad, you can do so wirelessly using a 3G or Wi-Fi connection.

From the Home Screen, tap on the App Store app, and then tap on the Updates icon. If the message All Apps Are Up to Date is displayed, you're in good shape; otherwise, you'll be given the option to upgrade any out-of-date apps.

After you initially acquire an app from the App Store, all subsequent updates to that app are free of charge. Plus, now that you're running iOS 5 on your device, you'll be able to easily share your app purchases among multiple iOS devices that you own. For example, if you own an iPhone and an iPad, you'll be able to purchase an iPhone or hybrid iPhone/iPad app once and then install and use it on both devices.

A hybrid app is one that is designed for use on both an iPhone and an iPad. Some apps are iPad-specific, for example, and will run only on the iPad or iPad 2. Meanwhile, apps designed specifically for the iPhone will run on iPads, but these apps will not take advantage of the tablet's larger display or advanced capabilities.

Although it's often easier to update apps directly from the device itself, you can also download app updates using your primary computer and iTunes, and then use the iTunes sync process to transfer the updated app(s) to your iPhone and/or iPad.

> iOS 5 **WHAT'S NEW** When you create an iCloud account and begin using iCloud with your iPhone or iPad, all your app purchases (and free app downloads) will be stored on iCloud. If you delete an app from your phone or tablet, you can reinstall it anytime, free, from iCloud. When you return to the App Store, tap on the Purchased icon that's displayed at the bottom of the screen. All the apps you've purchased (and the free apps you've downloaded) will be displayed. Tap on the cloud icon displayed in each app's description to reinstall it on your phone or tablet.

IN THIS CHAPTER

- How to personalize your iPhone or iPad by adjusting the Settings app
- How to protect your privacy by adjusting the Location Services and Passcode options
- How to move app icons around on the Home Screen and create Folders

2

TIPS AND TRICKS FOR CUSTOMIZING SETTINGS

Many of the core preinstalled apps in iOS 5 offer new functionality that enables them to work together seamlessly. If you're active on Twitter, you can create and send tweets from within several apps, including Photos and Safari, without launching the Twitter app. You can send a file via email from within many apps, all without launching the Mail app. Do you receive attachments in email? Compatible apps can launch by themselves to display the incoming content.

The new Notification Center app in iOS 5 tracks all alarms, alerts, missed phone calls or FaceTime calls, incoming text messages or email messages, and other events or tasks that require your attention, displaying them in a central location for easy reference and one-touch access.

Many apps on your iPhone or iPad use the built-in GPS and Location Services capabilities to pinpoint the device's exact location and then utilize and sometimes share that information. For example, the Maps app uses Location Services to determine where you are and provide directions to your intended destination. Photos uses Location Services to add geo-tagging information to digital photos (and videos) you shoot, so that later you can tell exactly where they were shot.

You can communicate with and control an iPhone 4S by using your voice, thanks to Siri. Press and hold down the Home button for several seconds (or hold down the button on your wireless Bluetooth headset); then speak to the iPhone using normal sentences. To fulfill your verbal requests, your iPhone 4S will automatically access any apps and data it needs.

Before using Siri for the first time, you'll need to activate this feature in two places in the Settings app.

To turn on Siri's functionality, launch the Settings app, tap on the General option, and then tap on the Siri app. Make sure the virtual on/off switch for the Siri option is turned on. Then scroll down on that screen, customizing the related options as needed.

Because many of Siri's tasks depend on knowing your current location, you also must turn on Location Services for the Siri app. On the main Settings menu, tap on the Location Services option; then make sure the main Location Services option and the Siri option are both turned on.

For your iPhone or iPad to handle all of these tasks and integrate functionality between apps, iOS 5 makes a lot happen automatically behind the scenes. However, you can use the Settings app on your device to personalize a variety of options that give you better control over how your device responds to you while managing your apps, files, content, and data. After iOS 5 is installed and fully operational on your iPhone or iPad, you should adjust some of these settings rather than rely on their default settings.

TIP If you install additional apps on your iPhone or iPad, and those apps have customizable features, the customization options will likely appear in the Settings app.

USING THE SETTINGS APP

To access the Settings app, from the Home Screen tap on the Settings app icon. On your iPhone, the main Settings menu will appear (shown in Figure 2.1). You can then use your finger to scroll downward, and view all the options and submenus available from within Settings.

FIGURE 2.1

The main Settings menu displayed on an iPhone 4 running iOS 5.

On your iPad, the main Settings menu will appear on the left side of the screen (shown in Figure 2.2). When you tap on an option from the Settings menu on the left, the initial submenu that is associated with the selected menu option is displayed on the right side of the screen.

> iOS 5 **WHAT'S NEW** Although the main layout and interface of the Settings app is the same as in older versions of the iOS, you'll discover many new Settings options, as well as submenus in the iOS 5 version of Settings, many of which offer you controls over your device's operation that were not previously offered. The user-customizable options available from the Settings app will also vary based on what model iOS device you're using.

After you launch the Settings app, you'll discover that the menus and submenus are displayed in a hierarchical structure. Under the main Settings heading, you'll see a handful of main menu options relating to various apps and functions offered by your iPhone or iPad. By tapping on many of these options on the iOS device, a submenu is displayed. From that submenu, additional but related options, some of which will have submenus themselves, will become accessible.

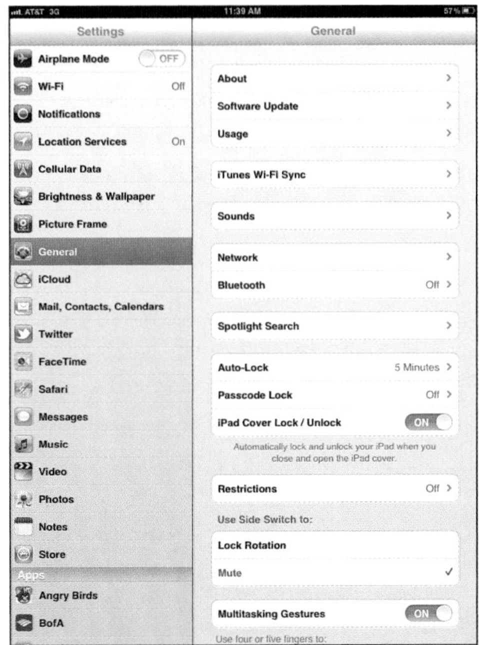

FIGURE 2.2

The main Settings menu displayed on an iPad 2 running iOS 5.

> **TIP** From anywhere within the Settings app, you can instantly return to the Home Screen by pressing the Home button on your iPhone or iPad, or on the iPad also by using the hand-grab motion that involves placing all five fingers from one hand on the screen simultaneously, such that your fingers are spread out slightly, and then moving your fingers together (dragging them quickly on the screen) as if you're grabbing something.
>
> Or you can access multitasking mode and switch to another app by pressing the Home button twice in quick succession, or on the iPad also by dragging three or four fingers (held closely together) from the very bottom of the screen in an upward direction toward the top of the screen.

MAIN OPTIONS AVAILABLE FROM THE SETTINGS APP

When you launch the Settings app, the first thing you'll see is the main Settings menu. The following is a comprehensive summary of the main options available from this menu, which will vary slightly based on whether you're using an iPhone, an iPad, or another iOS device.

AIRPLANE MODE (iPHONE/iPAD WI-FI + 3G MODELS)

This Settings option has no submenu but offers a virtual on/off switch. It's used to switch your device to Airplane Mode. Ideal for when you're on an airplane or traveling overseas, putting your device in Airplane Mode shuts down its capability to access the 3G wireless web and keeps the unit from sending or receiving wireless transmissions. However, all its other features and functions remain fully operational.

Even while your device is in Airplane Mode, you can still turn on Wi-Fi mode and/or Bluetooth, allowing the iOS device to access the Web via a Wi-Fi hotspot (to utilize the wireless web access available on some commercial aircraft, for example), and also communicate with a Bluetooth-enabled wireless keyboard or headset.

In Airplane Mode, a small airplane icon appears in the upper-left corner of the screen (see Figure 2.3). This iPhone is also connected to a Wi-Fi network. You can see the Wi-Fi signal strength icon displayed in the upper-left corner of the screen, near the Airplane Mode icon. In addition, this iPhone has Bluetooth turned on and a Bluetooth-compatible headset connected. You can tell this from the Bluetooth icons displayed in the upper-right corner of the screen, next to the battery indicator icon and percentage meter.

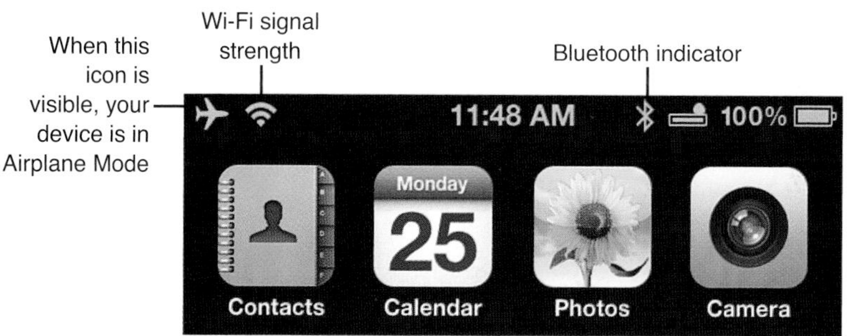

FIGURE 2.3

In Airplane Mode, a small airplane icon will appear in the upper-left corner of the screen.

WI-FI (iPHONE/iPAD)

Located directly below the Airplane Mode option is the Wi-Fi option. On the iPhone, when you tap on this option, a submenu containing a virtual on/off switch is displayed. When it's turned on, a listing of available Wi-Fi networks is listed directly below the Choose a Network heading. Tap on the Wi-Fi network you want to connect to.

On an iPad, when you tap on the Wi-Fi option in the left column of the main Settings screen, the right side of the screen will immediately display the various options available to you for choosing and connecting to a Wi-Fi hotspot.

On the right side of the screen are the Wi-Fi Networks options. At the top, the first user-selectable option is labeled Wi-Fi. It's accompanied by a virtual on/off switch to its right. When this option is turned on, your device will immediately begin looking Wi-Fi hotspots in the vicinity.

If one or more Wi-Fi hotspots are available, they are listed in a few seconds under the Choose a Network heading.

To choose any Wi-Fi hotspot listed, simply tap on it. In a few seconds, a check mark appears to the left of your selected Wi-Fi hotspot, and a Wi-Fi signal indicator appears in the upper-left corner of your device's screen, indicating that a Wi-Fi connection has been established.

If you select a Wi-Fi network that is password protected (showing a lock icon), an Enter Password window appears on your screen. Using the iPhone or iPad's virtual keyboard, enter the correct password to connect to the Wi-Fi network you selected. You will often have to do this when connecting to a Wi-Fi hotspot offered in a hotel, for example.

BENEFITS OF ACCESSING THE WEB VIA WI-FI HOTSPOT

Connecting to the Internet via Wi-Fi rather than 3G (on an iPhone or iPad Wi-Fi + 3G model) offers several benefits:

- A Wi-Fi connection is much faster than a 3G connection.
- You can send and receive data, stream content from the Web, and upload/download large files—all without using the monthly wireless data allocation associated with your service provider's 3G wireless data plan.
- You can use the FaceTime app for videoconferencing, download movies and TV show episodes from iTunes directly onto your device, and store wireless backups of your iPhone or iPad on iCloud.
- With the Wi-Fi option and the Ask to Join Networks option turned on, your iPhone or iPad can automatically find and connect to an available Wi-Fi hotspot, with or without your approval.

The main drawback of accessing the Internet via Wi-Fi connection is that your iPhone or iPad must stay within the radius of the connecting Wi-Fi hotspot or your Internet connection will be lost. The signal of most Wi-Fi hotspots extends for only a few hundred feet from the wireless router.

NOTIFICATIONS (iPHONE/iPAD)

This Settings option (shown in Figure 2.4) enables you to determine which apps will function with iOS 5's new Notification Center app, plus allows you to determine how your other apps that generate alerts, alarms, or notifications will notify you.

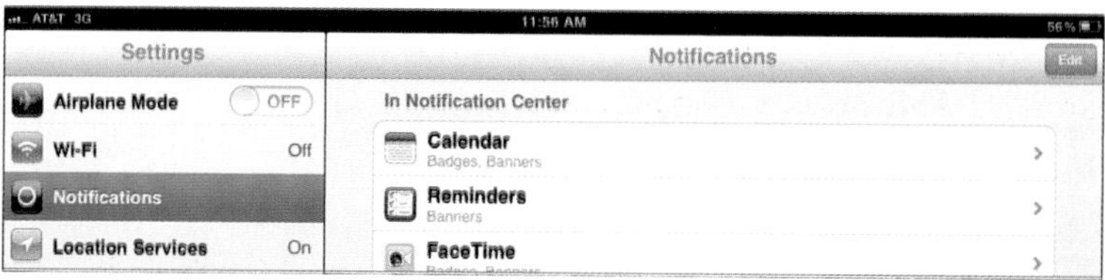

FIGURE 2.4

Apps that are set to exchange data with Notification Center (shown here on the iPad 2).

When you tap on the Notifications option, a submenu under the heading In Notification Center will list apps currently installed on your iPhone or iPad that are compatible with Notification Center, and that are set to automatically share data with Notification Center.

These apps include Phone (iPhone only), Calendar, Reminders, Game Center, FaceTime, Messages, and Mail, which all come preinstalled with iOS 5. However, additional apps that you install later might also be compatible with Notification Center, and will ultimately be listed here as well. On your iPhone, additional listings found on this menu are for the Weather and Stock Widget, which can be turned on or off.

Below the In Notification Center heading is another heading, labeled Not in Notification Center. Here, apps that are capable of generating alerts, alarms, badges, or notifications are listed. However, the apps listed here are not currently set to exchange data with the Notification Center app.

As you review each app listed under the In Notification Center or the Not in Notification Center heading, you can tap on it to reveal a secondary submenu pertaining specifically to that app. For example, when you tap on Calendar, displayed under the In Notification Center heading, the submenu that's revealed offers a handful of additional options for customizing how alerts, alarms, badges, and notifications that are generated by the Calendar app will be handled. To avoid being bombarded by excessive alarms, alerts, and notifications from apps that aren't important to you, turn off those apps in Notification Center.

At the top of the Calendar submenu (shown in Figure 2.5) is the Notification Center option that's accompanied by a virtual on/off switch. When turned on, it allows the Notification Center app to alert you when alerts, alarms, badges, or notifications are generated by this app. The second option, labeled Show, allows you to determine how many related alerts, alarms, or notifications generated by the Calendar app are listed at any given time in the Notification Center app. Your options include 1, 5, 10, or 20 recent items. As you're first starting to use this new iOS 5 feature, keep the number of alerts manageable by selecting just five per app. You can always add more for specific apps that are more important to you.

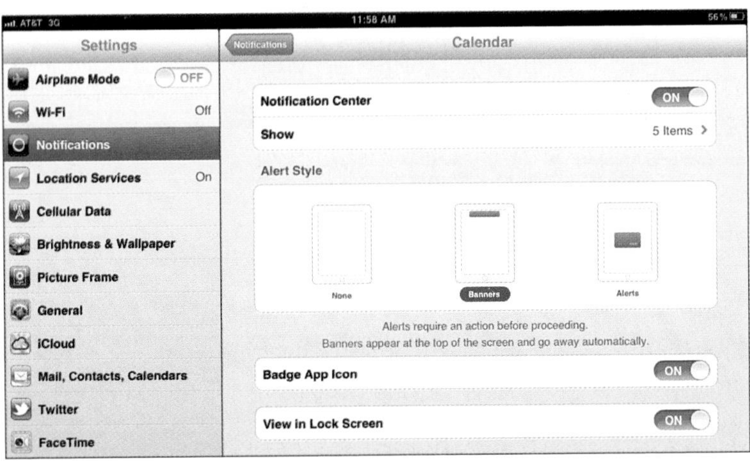

FIGURE 2.5

You can determine how any app that is capable of generating alerts, alarms, notifications, or badges will act from within the Settings app.

In addition to determining whether the Notification Center app will pay attention to and exchange data with a particular app, in this case Calendar, you can also select an additional Alert Style by tapping on one of the three Alert Style options, which include None, Banners, and Alerts.

- If you select None but have the Notification Center virtual switch for the app turned on, alerts, alarms, and notifications generated by that particular app will appear only in the window that's displayed by the Notification Center app, for example, when you swipe your finger downward from the very top of your iPhone or iPad's display.
- If you tap on the Banners option, in addition to alerts, alarms, and notifications generated by the app appearing in the Notification Center, a banner is displayed at the top of the iPhone or iPad screen to alert you. However, the banner disappears after several seconds.
- If you tap on the Alerts icon, an alert window will appear on your iPhone or iPad's screen whenever the app you're customizing from within Settings generates an alarm, an alert, or a notification. To make this alert window

disappear, you'll need to tap on a specific icon in the window to confirm receipt of each alert. This feature is useful for getting your attention if the alert or notification is extremely important to you, such as an appointment in the Calendars app.

Some apps also utilize Home Screen badges. A badge is a small red-and-white circle that appears in the upper-right corner of an app icon on your iPhone or iPad's Home Screen (see Figure 2.6). If you turn on the Badge App Icon feature for a specific app, that app's icon can alert you with a badge, such as a number, when something related to the app needs your attention. For example, your Mail app icon will display a number in its Home Screen badge to tell you how many new email messages you've received. Likewise, the App Store's icon badge may indicate the number of apps that need you to download updates.

FIGURE 2.6

This App Store app icon from an iPad 2's Home Screen shows an example of a Home Screen badge. In this case, it indicates that two apps currently installed on the iPad need to be updated.

Finally, you can determine whether alarms, alerts, or notifications generated by a particular app will be displayed on the Lock Screen when your device is otherwise in Sleep Mode.

LOCATION SERVICES (iPHONE/iPAD)

Also found under the main Settings menu in the Settings app is an option labeled Location Services. When this option is turned on, it allows the iPhone or iPad to automatically utilize the GPS functionality built in to the device with various apps. Certain apps and services, such as Maps or Find My iPhone (or Find My iPad), for example, take advantage of the capability to pinpoint your exact location.

> **TIP** If you'll be utilizing the optional Find My Friends app, which allows authorized people to track your whereabouts in real time, you'll definitely want to customize the Location Services options related to Find My Friends, and from within the app, determine who can "follow" you and when. You can turn on or off this functionally quickly and whenever you'd like, but you must remember to turn it off when you want your privacy.

When the Location Services option is turned on, your iPhone or iPad can fully utilize its GPS capabilities, in addition to crowd-sourced Wi-Fi hotspots and cell towers, to determine your exact location. When it's turned off, your device will not be able to determine (or broadcast) your location. However, some of your apps will not function properly.

iOS 5 gives you even greater control over when your iPhone or iPad will share your location. Under the Location Services submenu in Settings, tap on the System Services option. This will reveal an additional submenu that's new in iOS 5. The options here include Cell Network Search, Diagnostics & Usage, Location-Based iAds, Setting Time Zone, and Traffic. You can turn any of these options on or off by tapping on the corresponding virtual switch.

Also from this submenu screen, you can adjust the virtual on/off switch associated with the Status Bar icon. When it's turned on, anytime your iPhone or iPad is sharing your location, an optional diagonal-pointing arrow-shaped icon will appear and change color in the upper-right corner of the iPhone or iPad's screen, near the battery indicator.

From elsewhere in the Settings app, you can customize settings for individual apps that may utilize Location Services, and in some cases turn on or off this feature on an app-specific basis.

> **TIP** When the Location Services option is turned on and you snap a photo or shoot video using the Camera app, the exact location where that photo or video was shot will be recorded and saved. This feature is deactivated if you turn off the Location Services option.

CELLULAR DATA (iPAD)

This feature applies to iPad models that have Wi-Fi + 3G. When the Cellular Data option is turned on, your tablet is able to access the wireless data network from the wireless service provider that you're subscribed to. When this option is turned off, your device is able to access the Internet only via a Wi-Fi connection, assuming that a Wi-Fi hotspot is present.

The Data Roaming option appears below the Cellular Data option. When turned on, Data Roaming allows your iPad to connect to a 3G network outside the one you subscribe to through your wireless service provider. The capability to tap in to another wireless data network might be useful if you must connect to the Internet, there's no Wi-Fi hotspot present, and you're outside your own service provider's coverage area (such as when traveling abroad).

! CAUTION When your iPhone or iPad is permitted to roam and tap in to another 3G wireless data network, you will incur hefty roaming charges, often as high as $20 per megabyte (MB). Refrain from using this feature unless you've prepurchased a 3G data roaming plan through your service provider, or be prepared to pay a fortune to access the Web.

When your device can't find a compatible 3G network, it will seek out an older 2G network, which is much slower. For example, when your AT&T iPhone or iPad (with 3G capabilities) is connected to the Edge network, the letter "E" will appear instead of the "3G" label in the upper-left corner of the screen.

Based on the 3G wireless data plan you subscribe to, you can view or modify your account details by tapping on the View Account option. Once you log in using the username and password you created when the account with your service provider was set up, you can change your credit card billing information, or modify your monthly data plan, for example.

TIP Unless specifically instructed by a technical support person representing Apple or your wireless data service provider, don't change the default setting of the SIM PIN option at the bottom of the Cellular Data screen.

SOUNDS (iPHONE)

This option allows you to control the speaker of your iPhone. When it's in Silent mode, for example, you can turn on the Vibrate mode so that the handset shakes, instead of playing a ringtone. You can also control the Ringer Volume using an onscreen slider, and adjust the custom ringtones and audio alerts associated with various features and functions of your iPhone. Your iPhone has a library of different audio alarms and alerts, as well as ringtones built in, plus you can download additional ringtones from iTunes.

BRIGHTNESS & WALLPAPER (iPHONE/iPAD)

The Brightness and Wallpaper options, which are listed separately in the main menu of the Settings app on the iPhone (shown in Figure 2.7) but listed together on the iPad (shown in Figure 2.8) allows you to control the brightness of your iPhone or iPad's screen, and also customize the wallpaper of your device's Lock Screen and Home Screen.

FIGURE 2.7

On the iPhone, the Brightness and Wallpaper options are listed separately in the main Settings menu of the Settings app. The functionality of these options is the same, however, on the iPhone and iPad.

FIGURE 2.8

Use the brightness slider to control how light or dark your iPhone or iPad's screen will appear. Shown here is the Brightness & Wallpaper submenu found in the Settings app of the iPad 2.

When you tap on this option, the Brightness & Wallpaper submenu appears. At the top of this submenu is a brightness slider. Place your finger on the white dot that appears in the slider, and drag it to the right to make the screen brighter, or to the left to make the screen darker. This will override the Auto-Brightness option, if you have that feature turned on.

The Auto-Brightness option has an associated virtual on/off switch. When it's turned on (the default setting), your device will take into account the surrounding lighting where you're using your Phone or iPad, and then adjust the screen's brightness accordingly.

NOTE On the iPhone, Brightness and Wallpaper are separate menu options in Settings. On the iPad, they're listed together as Brightness & Wallpaper.

Customize Your Lock Screen and Home Screen Wallpaper

One of the ways you can customize the appearance of your iPhone or iPad is to change the wallpaper displayed on the device's Lock Screen and behind your app icons on the Home Screen.

From the Brightness & Wallpaper option available from the Settings app, you can quickly change the wallpapers that are displayed on your device. As you'll discover, your iPhone or iPad has more than two dozen preinstalled wallpaper designs built in, plus you can use any digital images stored on your device (in the Photos app) as your Lock Screen or Home Screen wallpaper.

When you tap on the Brightness & Wallpaper option, the Brightness & Wallpaper submenu options appear. On the iPhone, tap on the Wallpaper option, which is listed separately. Below the brightness slider is the Wallpaper option. Here, you see a thumbnail graphic of your iPhone or iPad's Lock Screen (left) and its Home Screen (right).

Tap on either of these thumbnail images to change its appearance. When you do this, the Settings screen will change, and two options are listed. On top is the Wallpaper option. Below it is the Camera Roll option (where photos shot with your iPhone or iPad are stored) and/or Photos option (where digital images transferred into your iPhone or iPad are stored).

Tap on the Wallpaper option to display thumbnails for the preinstalled wallpaper graphics you can choose from (as shown in Figure 2.9), and then tap on your selection.

Next, on the iPhone or iPad's screen, the graphic you select is displayed in full-screen mode. On the iPad, in the upper-right corner of the screen are three command icons, labeled Set Lock Screen, Set Home Screen, and Set Both. This is shown in Figure 2.10. On the iPhone, you will see a Cancel icon and a Set icon; when you tap on the Set icon, the additional Set Lock Screen, Set Home Screen, and Set Both icons are displayed.

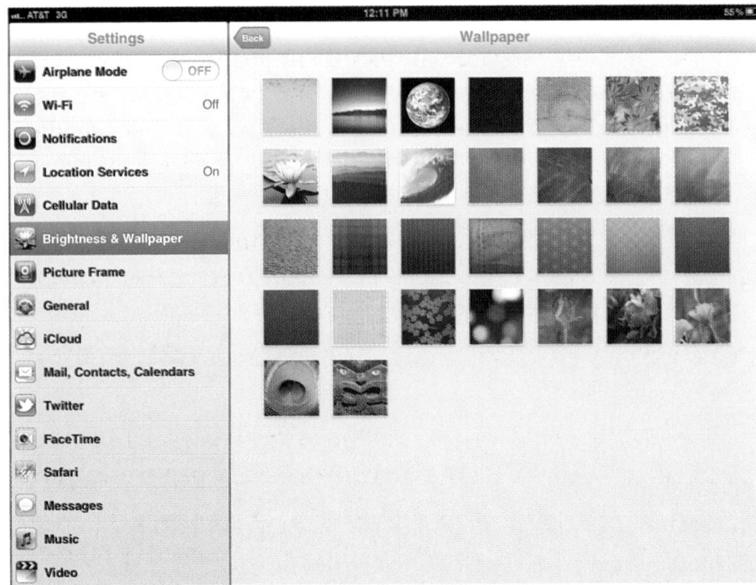

FIGURE 2.9

When looking at the collection of wallpaper graphics, tap on the one you'd like to use.

FIGURE 2.10

After selecting a custom graphic to use as a wallpaper, tap on one of three icons to determine where the graphic is displayed—on your Lock Screen, Home Screen, or on both of these screens.

Choose one of these options by tapping on its icon:

- Tap on the Set Lock Screen icon to change just the wallpaper graphic of your iPhone or iPad's Lock Screen. As a reminder, this is the screen you see when you first turn on your phone or tablet, or wake it up from Sleep Mode. From the Lock Screen, you must swipe your finger along the Slide to Unlock slider to unlock the tablet and access the Home Screen.
- Tap on the Set Home Screen icon to change just the wallpaper graphic of your iPhone or iPad's Home Screen. This is the graphic that will appear behind your app icons on each of your Home Screen pages.
- Tap on the Set Both icon to use the same wallpaper graphic as both your Lock Screen and your Home Screen wallpaper.

After making your selection, when you return to the iPhone or iPad's Lock Screen or Home Screen, you'll now see your newly selected wallpaper graphic displayed.

Instead of choosing one of the preinstalled wallpaper graphics, you also have the option to use any of your own digital images, including photos you've transferred to your iOS device and have stored within the Photos app, or photos you've shot using the Camera app.

To select one of your own photos to use as your Lock Screen or Home Screen wallpaper, tap on the Brightness & Wallpaper option of the Settings app on the iPad (or the Wallpaper option on the iPhone), and then tap on the thumbnails that appear showcasing your iPhone or iPad's Lock Screen and Home Screen.

This time, located below the Wallpaper option, tap on the folder that contains the image you want to use as your wallpaper. This might include a photo you've shot using your iPhone or iPad (found in the Camera Roll folder), or a photo you've imported into the Photos app.

Tap on the folder name that contains the image you want to use. When all the image thumbnails appear, tap on the image thumbnail you want to use as your wallpaper for your Lock Screen and/or Home Screen. When the photo you selected appears in full-screen mode, tap on one of the three command icons that appear. Again, your options include Set Lock Screen, Set Home Screen, and Set Both.

After you've made your selection, your newly selected wallpaper graphic will appear on your Lock Screen and/or Home Screen, as you can see in Figure 2.11 and Figure 2.12.

FIGURE 2.11

A newly selected Lock Screen graphic, chosen from a photo stored on the iPhone 4 in the Photos app, is shown.

FIGURE 2.12

The image you selected from the Settings app will now be displayed as your Home Screen wallpaper, behind your app icons.

PICTURE FRAME (iPAD)

When your iPad isn't in use or on the go with you, perhaps it sits idly on your desk. If this is the case, instead of looking at a dark screen while the unit is in Sleep Mode awaiting its next use, you can transform the tablet into a digital picture frame and have it display an animated slideshow of your favorite images.

Every time you turn on your iPad, or awaken it from Sleep Mode, the Lock Screen appears. In the lower-right corner of this screen is a picture frame icon. It's used to transform your tablet into a digital picture frame.

However, to personalize the settings of this Picture Frame app, you'll need to access the Picture Frame options from the Settings app. When you tap on the Picture Frame option in the Settings app, the Picture Frame options are displayed.

From the Picture Frame menu in Settings, you can adjust the animated transition shown in between images. Your choices are Dissolve or Origami.

Moving down on this settings screen, you can determine how long each image is displayed (your choices are 2, 3, 5, 10, or 20 seconds) and whether you want the app to automatically zoom in on each person's face as your images are displayed.

The Zoom In on Faces option and the Shuffle option (which determines whether the images are displayed in order or randomly) both have virtual on/off switches associated with them. Tap on each switch to move it from on to off, or vice versa.

In the bottom area of the Picture Frame screen in the Settings app, you can choose which images are displayed as part of your slideshow. Choose either All Photos, or a specific Album or Event folder.

When you launch the Picture Frame app from the Lock Screen, how the slideshow is presented will be based on the settings you've selected and/or personalized using the Settings app.

GENERAL (iPHONE/iPAD)

The General option is found about halfway down on the main Settings option screen. When you tap this General option, various suboptions become available. Unless otherwise noted, each option is available using an iPhone or iPad. The General options found in the Settings app include the following:

- **About**—Tap on the About option to access information about your iPhone or iPad, including its serial number, which version of the iOS it's running, its memory capacity, and how much memory is currently available on the device. This is purely an informative screen with no options to customize or adjust.

- **Software Update**—Use this option to update the iOS operating system wirelessly, without having to connect your iPhone or iPad to your primary computer and use the iTunes sync procedure. To do this, however, a Wi-Fi Internet connection must be present. This is a new feature added to iOS 5.
- **Usage**—Tap on this option to see how the storage capacity of your iPhone or iPad is being utilized, as well as how your available online-based iCloud storage is being utilized. From the Battery Usage option displayed on this screen, you can decide whether you'll display your device's battery life as a numeric percentage (for example, 73%), as opposed to just as a battery icon graphic.

  Also, from this screen, you can see how much data the iPhone or iPad has sent or received using the wireless data network it's connected to.

  Tap on the Reset Statistics option to reset the Sent and Received settings. When you add the Sent and Received figures together, you'll be able to determine your total data usage since you last tapped the Reset Statistics icon. This feature is particularly useful if you're overseas and roaming, to determine how much you'll be billed, or for making sure you don't go beyond your monthly allocated data usage based on the wireless data plan you've signed up for.
- **Siri (iPhone 4S Only)**—Turn on or off Siri functionality on the iPhone 4S, and adjust specific settings related to this feature. One of the important options you'll want to set from the Siri menu within Settings is related to My Info. When you tap on this menu feature, select your personal contact entry from the All Contacts listing. You'll also want to ensure your personal contact entry contains properly labeled details about your addresses (home, work, and so on), phone numbers, email addresses, and so on. This is information Siri will refer to often.
- **Sounds (iPad)**—Tap on this option to adjust the overall volume of iPad 2's built-in speaker (or the volume of the audio you hear through headsets), as well as to turn on or off various audible tones and alarms your phone or tablet generates.

  From this menu, you can also assign specific audio tones, sounds, or ringtones to specific types of alerts and alarms, plus turn on or off the click noise associated with pressing keys on the iPad's virtual keyboard.
- **Network**—This option allows you to select and connect your iPhone or iPad to either a VPN (Virtual Private Network) or a Wi-Fi network, assuming that one is present. For help connecting to a VPN, contact the IT department in your company.

- **Bluetooth**—If you plan to use any type of Bluetooth device with your phone or tablet, such as a wireless headset, wireless external speakers, a printer, or a wireless keyboard, you'll first need to turn on the Bluetooth feature on your iPhone or iPad, and then pair that device with your iOS device.

  After a device or an accessory has been paired with your iPhone or iPad, it will automatically be detected and become usable whenever Bluetooth on your iPhone or iPad and the accessory are turned on, and they're in close proximity. The Bluetooth device is listed under the Devices heading on the Bluetooth settings screen. Yes, you can have multiple Bluetooth devices wirelessly connected to your tablet simultaneously.

> **TIP** If you're using your iPhone or iPad without having a Bluetooth device connected, you can turn off the Bluetooth feature altogether. This will help extend the battery life of your iOS device. When you turn on this feature, your iPhone or iPad will automatically seek out any Bluetooth-compatible devices in the vicinity. The first time you use a particular Bluetooth device with your iOS mobile device, you will need to pair it. Follow the directions that came with the device or accessory for performing this initial setup task. (The pairing process should take only about a minute or two.)

- **iTunes Wi-Fi Sync**—Another new feature of iOS 5 is the capability to wirelessly sync and back up your iPhone or iPad so that the backup data is stored on your primary computer's hard drive. This feature works just like the familiar iTunes sync process that involves connecting your iOS device to your computer via the supplied USB cable; however, with this feature, the connection can be established wirelessly if both devices have access to the same Wi-Fi network.
- **Spotlight Search**—Upon tapping this option, you can determine which portions of your iPhone or iPad are searched when you use the Spotlight Search feature built in to the device. From the Home Screen, if you scroll to the left (swipe your finger from left to right), the Spotlight Search screen appears. Search fields also appear in some other apps.

  From the Spotlight Search setup screen (from within the Settings app), you can determine whether the Contacts, Applications, Music, Podcasts, Videos, Audiobooks, Notes, Mail, Events, Mail, Reminders, Messages, and/or other app-specific databases are searched. On the iPhone, you can also select Voice Memos, for example.

- **Auto-Lock**—Anytime your iPhone or iPad is turned on, if you don't do anything for a predetermined about of time, it can be set to automatically switch to Sleep Mode to conserve battery life.

  From the Auto-Lock option, you can determine whether Sleep Mode is activated after 2, 5, 10, or 15 minutes of non-use. Or you can choose the Never option so that the iPhone or iPad will never automatically switch into Sleep Mode, even if it's left unattended for an extended period.
- **Passcode Lock**—Use this feature to set and then turn on or off the Passcode option built in to iOS 5. This is just one level of security you can use to keep unauthorized people from using your phone or tablet.
- **iPad Cover Lock/Unlock (iPad 2 Only)**—This feature places the tablet into Sleep Mode when a Smart Cover is placed over the screen, and then wakes up the device when the Smart Cover is removed.
- **Restrictions**—Upon tapping the Restrictions icon, you will have the option to Enable Restrictions, and then manually set those restrictions. For example, you can block certain apps from being used, keep the user from deleting or adding apps to the device, keep someone from making in-app purchases, or keep someone from accessing certain types of iTunes or app content (including TV shows, movies, music, and podcasts). Basically, this is a way to "childproof" your iPhone or iPad, by allowing a user to gain access to only specific apps or content. If you choose to utilize this feature, make sure you don't forget the password you associate with it. Once a password is set and activated, if you forget it, it might be necessary to erase your entire iOS device and reload everything from scratch.
- **Use Side Switch To (iPad)**—Located on the right side of your iPad is a tiny switch. You'll find it just above the volume up/down button. From the General Settings screen, you can determine what the primary function of this switch will be. You can use it as either a Lock Rotation switch or a Mute switch.

  When it's used as a Lock Rotation switch, when it's turned on, you can physically rotate your iPad but the screen will not automatically switch between landscape and portrait mode.

  Or when it's used as a Mute switch, this will turn off the iPad's built-in speaker so that no sounds are heard, such as alarms. This is useful when using your iPad in a meeting, or in a quiet area (such as a library), for example.

TIP On the iPhone, the Mute button, which silences all sounds your iPhone is capable of generating, is located on the left side of the handset, above the Volume Up and Volume Down buttons.

- **Multitasking Gestures (iPad)**—iOS 5 introduces several new finger gestures for interacting with your iPad's touchscreen. You can opt to turn on or off recognition of these gestures by adjusting the virtual on/off switch that's associated with the Multitasking Gestures option.
- **Date & Time**—These settings allow you to switch between a 12- and a 24-hour clock, and determine whether you want your iPhone or iPad to automatically set the time or date (when it's connected to the Internet). To ensure that the time and date remain correct, based on whatever time zone you travel to, leave the Set Automatically option under the Date & Time screen turned on.
- **Keyboard**—You can make certain customizations from the Setting screen that impact how your virtual keyboard responds as you're typing. Tap on the Keyboard option when using the Settings app, and you'll discover several customizable settings, such as whether Auto-Capitalization, Auto-Correction, and Check Spelling are turned on.
- **International**—By default, if you purchased your iPhone or iPad in the United States, the default Language and keyboard options are for English; however, you can adjust these settings by tapping on the International option.
- **Accessibility**—Designed to make the iPhone or iPad easier to use by people with various sight or hearing difficulties, as well as physical limitations, you can personalize various settings found under the Accessibility option to take advantage of certain features, like Voice Over or Large Text on the screen. Unless you need to utilize any of these options, simply leave them at their default settings.
- **Reset**—Every so often, you might run in to a problem with your iPhone or iPad such that the system crashes or you need to reset specific settings. For example, to restore your iPhone or iPad to its factory default settings and erase everything stored on it, tap on the Reset option, and then tap on the Erase All Content and Settings option. In general, you'll want to refrain from using any of these settings unless you're instructed to do so by an Apple Genius or a technical support person.

! CAUTION Before using any of the options found under the Settings Reset option, which will potentially erase important data from your iPhone or iPad, be sure to perform an iTunes sync or back up your device wirelessly to iCloud and create a reliable backup of your device's contents.

Several of the options found under the General heading you'll probably never need to tinker with or adjust. Leave them at their default settings. Others you'll need to utilize often as you use your iPhone or iPad for different tasks.

iCLOUD (iPHONE/iPAD)

From the Settings menu in the Settings app, tap on the iCloud option to customize the settings associated with Apple's online file-sharing and data-backup service.

Using the Settings app, you can adjust which types of data automatically get wirelessly backed up and/or synced with the iCloud service, including Mail, Contacts, Calendars, Reminds, (Safari) Bookmarks, Notes, and Photo Stream. You can also turn on or off the Find My iPhone (or Find My iPad) and Find My Friends service. On the iPhone, you'll see an option labeled Documents and Data as well.

Your free iCloud account comes with 5GB of online storage space. Tap on the Storage & Backup tab near the bottom of the iCloud screen to manage your existing online storage space or purchase additional online storage space. From the Storage & Backup screen within Settings, you can also turn on or off the Back Up to iCloud feature. This determines whether your iPhone or iPad will automatically and wirelessly back up your device on a daily basis and store the backup files on iCloud.

MAIL, CONTACTS, CALENDARS (iPHONE/iPAD)

If you use your iPhone or iPad on the job, three apps you probably rely on heavily are Mail, Contacts, and Calendars. From the Settings app, you can customize a handful of options pertaining to each of these apps, and you can actually set up your existing email accounts to work with your iPhone or tablet.

iOS 5 **WHAT'S NEW** Under the Calendars heading of the Mail, Contacts, Calendars option, one new feature added to iOS 5 is Default Alert Time. Tapping on this option within Settings reveals a new Default Alert Times menu screen, from which you can automatically set advance alarms for birthdays, events, and all-day events stored in your Calendar app.

If you fill in the Birthday or Event field as you create contacts entries in the Contacts app, these dates can automatically be displayed in the Calendars app to remind you of birthdays, anniversaries, or other special occasions. By setting the Default Alert Times feature within Settings once, you will automatically be reminded of each upcoming birthday, event, or all-day event at 9:00 on the morning of the event, one day before the event, two days before the event, or one week before the event, based on your preference.

The advance warning of a birthday or (anniversary) event, for example, gives you ample time to send a card (using the optional new Cards app, for example) or send a gift.

TWITTER (iPHONE/iPAD)

The Twitter online social networking service has now been fully integrated into iOS 5, and is accessible from within several iPhone and iPad core applications, as well as the actual official Twitter app.

From the Settings app, tap on the Twitter heading that's displayed under the main Settings menu in Settings. First install the official (free) Twitter app onto your iPhone or iPad, and then customize the settings so that you can send Tweets from various core apps, including Photos and Safari.

The Twitter features built in to iOS 5 will work with your existing Twitter account.

There are many third-party apps for the iPhone and iPad available from the App Store that allow you to access Twitter. However, only the official Twitter app (that can be downloaded from within the Settings app) allows you to utilize all the Twitter-related features integrated into iOS 5. Using this app, you can also manage multiple Twitter accounts.

PHONE (iPHONE)

From the submenu associated with this Settings option, you can view your mobile phone number, and adjust calling features, like Call Forwarding and Call Waiting. You can also turn on or off International Assist, which is useful if you're calling overseas or making calls from overseas, plus you can access features associated with managing your wireless service account.

TIP One of the easiest ways to manage your wireless account associated with your iPhone is to download the free app offered by your wireless service provider that's available from the App Store. The company-specific app enables you to monitor your monthly usage, pay your monthly bill, and handle a variety of other tasks associated with your account. For example, if you're an AT&T Wireless customer in the U.S., you'll want to download the myAT&T app.

FACETIME (iPHONE/iPAD)

In Settings, you can set up a free FaceTime account and associate an email address, an Apple ID, or your iPhone's phone number with your FaceTime account, which is how others will be able to find and call you to initiate a live video conference.

SAFARI (iPHONE/iPAD)

Safari is the web-browsing app built in to the iPhone and iPad. It's very similar to the Safari web browser available on all Mac computers. You'll discover that with the iOS 5 upgrade, a handful of new and useful web-surfing features have been added to the Safari app, which now has a handful of new settings you can customize using the Settings app.

MESSAGES (iPHONE/iPAD)

iMessage is a new online-based text-messaging service introduced by Apple with iOS 5. This service works very much like the text-messaging capabilities of your cellphone, but with this service, you can send and receive an unlimited number of messages for free. The service is currently compatible with only iOS devices, including the iPad, iPad 2, iPhone 3Gs, iPhone 4, iPhone 4S, and iPod touch.

At least initially, the iMessage service must be accessed using the iPhone or iPad's Messages app, which comes preinstalled with iOS 5. Tap on the Messages option in Settings to set up an iMessage account using your Apple ID, and to manage your account.

On the iPhone, the Messages app is also used to send, receive, and manage text messages sent or received via your wireless service provider. Text messages utilize the cellular network to be sent and received, and text messaging is a paid feature offered by your wireless service provider. Using your iPhone, you can send a text message to any other cellphone or smartphone user, regardless of which network the person uses.

MUSIC (iPHONE/iPAD)

One of the apps built in to your iPhone or iPad is the Music app (which replaced the iPod app that was part of iOS 4.3.4 and earlier versions of the iOS). Basically, this app transforms your phone or tablet into a full-featured digital music player and enables you to experience the music and audio files you have stored on your iOS device or on iCloud. This includes music, podcasts, and audiobooks acquired from iTunes, or similar content from other services.

Using the Settings app, you can customize a handful of options relating to the Music app. From the main Settings app menu, tap the Music option. Using a series of virtual on/off switches, you'll then be able to adjust the Sound Check, EQ, Volume Limit, and Lyrics & Podcast Info options.

VIDEO (iPHONE/iPAD)

You use the Videos app that comes preinstalled on your iPhone or iPad to watch TV show episodes and movies you've purchased or rented. From the Settings app, you can adjust how the Videos app functions by turning on or off various settings and features.

From the Settings app, tap the Videos option. When the Video submenu options appear, you can adjust four main settings, starting with the Start Playing feature. The default option for this feature is to resume playing a video where you last left off; however, you can change this option to make videos always start at the beginning. You can also turn on or off closed captioning, for example. If you have a wireless home network and an Apple TV or Mac, you can set up Home Sharing to wirelessly transfer content between computers and devices.

PHOTOS (iPHONE/iPAD)

In the past, the Photos app was used mainly for viewing and sharing digital images stored on your iPhone or iPad. With the additional features added to the Photos app with iOS 5, you now can edit your digital images and share them in an even greater number of ways.

The Photos app also now takes advantage of iCloud, and allows you to create a Photo Stream. However, in the Settings app, you can turn on or off the capability to create and manage a Photo Stream with iCloud. You can also customize the Slideshow settings used to display photos on your iPhone or iPad's screen when it's in Slideshow mode.

NOTES (iPHONE/iPAD)

Whereas the optional Pages app gives you full word processing capabilities on your iPhone or iPad, and the new Reminders app (which comes preinstalled on your iOS 5 device) can be used as a powerful to-do list manager and organizational tool, the Notes app can be used as a basic text editor to jot down notes and then store and/or share them.

In the Settings app, you can set the default onscreen font used in the Notes app. The options include Noteworthy, Helvetica, and Marker Felt.

STORE (iPHONE/iPAD)

The App Store app is used to find, purchase (if applicable), download, and install new apps onto your iPhone or iPad. From the Settings app, you can associate your Apple ID with the App Store app, which allows you to make purchases using the credit card that's associated with your Apple ID account.

By adjusting the virtual on/off switches associated with the Automatic Downloads options available in the Store submenu of Settings, you can determine whether all new music and app purchases will automatically be downloaded onto the device you're using, and whether the cellular data network can be used for downloading these purchases (as opposed to a Wi-Fi connection).

TIP If you have a preset amount of wireless data usage per month (through your wireless service provider), you should avoid streaming Internet content to your iPhone or iPad and refrain from uploading or downloading large files, because this will use up your monthly data allocation much faster. There is no limit to how much data you can send/receive, however, using a Wi-Fi Internet connection.

USER-INSTALLED APPS

By scrolling toward the bottom of the main Settings menu in the Settings app, you'll discover a listing of individual apps that you have installed on your iPhone or iPad and that have user-adjustable options or settings available from within the Settings app. Tap on one app listing at a time to modify these settings. Remember, as you install new apps in the future, additional app listings will be added to this section of the Settings menu and will need to be adjusted accordingly.

KEEP YOUR DEVICE AND DATA PRIVATE: HOW TO ACTIVATE AND USE THE PASSCODE LOCK FEATURE

As you'll discover, there are several simple ways to protect the data stored on your iPhone or iPad, and keep it away from unauthorized users. If you want to keep data on your phone or tablet private, the first thing to do is set up and activate the Passcode Lock feature that's built in to iOS 5.

From the Settings app, tap on the General option. Next, tap on the Passcode Lock option to turn on this feature. (By default, the Passcode option is turned off.)

When the Passcode Lock screen appears, tap on the icon located at the top of the screen that's labeled Turn Passcode On to activate this security feature.

When the Set Passcode window appears on the phone or tablet's screen (shown in Figure 2.13), use the virtual numeric keypad to create a four-digit security passcode for your device. This code is requested every time the iPhone or iPad is turned on or woken up from Sleep Mode.

FIGURE 2.13

From the Passcode Lock screen, you can set and then activate the Passcode Lock feature built in to the iPhone or iPad. Use it to keep unauthorized people from using your tablet or accessing your sensitive data. This feature is shown here on an iPhone 4.

> **NOTE** If you're using an iPhone 4S, you'll discover the Passcode Lock menu screen in Settings has an extra Siri option.

You can enter any four-digit code. Input one digit at a time when the Set Passcode window appears. When prompted, type the same code a second time. When you've done this, the Set Passcode window disappears and the feature becomes active.

Now, from the Passcode Lock screen in the Settings app, you can further customize this feature. For example, tap on the Require Passcode option to determine when the iPhone or iPad will prompt the user to enter the passcode. The default option is Immediately, meaning between when the Lock Screen and Home Screen appears each time the phone or tablet is turned on or woken up.

If you don't believe that a four-digit passcode is secure enough, turn off the Simple Passcode option. When you do this, a Change Passcode window appears, along with the full virtual keyboard. You can now create a more complicated, alphanumeric passcode to protect your device from unauthorized usage. Anytime you have the option to create a password or passcode on an iOS device, or on your computer or for accessing a website, for example, avoid using something obvious, such as "1234" or your birthday. When possible, mix and match numbers and letters to create your password.

From this screen, if you're using an iPad, you can also determine whether the Picture Frame app option will be displayed on your Lock Screen. This option has a virtual on/off switch associated with it. When it's turned on, the Picture Frame app icon will appear on the Lock Screen. When it's turned off, you will not be able to turn on the Picture Frame app from the Lock Screen. The app icon to do so will not be displayed.

Also on the Passcode Lock screen is the Erase Data option. If an unauthorized user enters the wrong passcode 10 consecutive times, the iPhone or iPad will automatically erase all data stored on it, if this feature is turned on.

! CAUTION Activating the Erase Data feature gives you an added layer of security if your tablet falls into the wrong hands. However, to recover the data later, you must have a reliable backup created and stored. Otherwise, that data will be lost forever.

ORGANIZE APPS ON YOUR HOME SCREEN WITH FOLDERS

If you're like most iPhone and iPad users, you'll probably be loading a handful of third-party apps onto your device. After all, there are several hundred thousand third-party apps to choose from. To make finding and organizing your apps easier from the iPhone or iPad's Home Screen, and to reduce onscreen clutter, you can place app icons in folders.

Utilizing the Folders feature is easy. From the Home Screen, press and hold down any app icon until all the app icons begin shaking on the Home Screen. Using your finger, drag one app icon on top of another, to automatically place both of those apps into a new folder.

You can organize your apps in folders based on categories, like Games, Travel, Finance, Productivity, Social Networking, or Bookmarks (shown in Figure 2.14), plus choose your own folder names (or use what's suggested), and then drag and drop the appropriate app icons into the folders you create. After your app icons are organized, simply press the Home button again on the iPhone or iPad to save your folders and display them on your Home Screen.

If you later want to remove an app icon from a folder, so that it appears as a standalone app icon on your Home Screen, simply press and hold any of the folder icons until all the onscreen icons start to shake. The folder's contents are displayed.

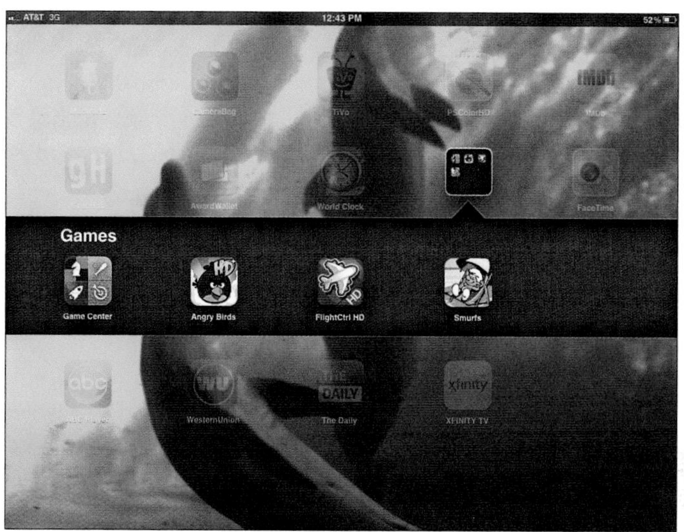

FIGURE 2.14

You can create folders on your device's Home Screen to reduce clutter and better organize your apps.

Using your finger, when the app icons are shaking, simply drag the app icons, one at a time, back onto the Home Screen. Each will then be removed from the folder. Press the Home button to finalize this action.

TIP One feature that's not new to iOS 5, but that's very useful, is the capability to move app icons around on your iPhone or iPad's Home Screen. From the Home Screen, press and hold down any app icon with your finger. When the app icons start to shake, you can use your finger to drag one app icon at a time around on the Home Screen.

Your iPhone or iPad can extend the Home Screen up to four pages. (Switch pages by swiping your finger from left to right, or right to left when viewing the Home Screen.)

To move an app icon to another Home Screen page, while it's shaking, hold it down with your finger and slowly drag it to the extreme right or left, off of the screen, so that it bounces onto another of the Home Screen's pages.

Although you can customize which app icons will appear on which Home Screen page, the row of up to four app icons displayed at the very bottom of the iPhone's screen (or up to six app icons on the iPad's screen) will remain constant. Place your most frequently used apps in one of these positions so that they're always visible from the Home Screen.

As the app icons are shaking on the Home Screen, you can delete the icons that display a black-and-white "X" in the upper-left corner from your iPhone or iPad by pressing that "X" icon. The preinstalled (core) apps related to iOS 5 cannot be deleted. They can only be moved.

ADD FREQUENTLY USED WEB PAGE ICONS TO YOUR HOME SCREEN

Many people constantly return to their favorite websites for updates throughout the day or week. Instead of first accessing the Safari browser on your iPhone or iPad, and then choosing your favorite sites from your Bookmarks list, you can create individual icons for your favorite web pages, and display them on your Home Screen. This allows you to access that web page with a single tap of the finger from the Home Screen.

To create a Web Page icon (as shown in Figure 2.15) on your Home Screen, access Safari and visit your favorite web page. Next, tap the Share icon that's located next to the URL field (shown in Figure 2.16), and tap the Add to Home Screen option that appears.

FIGURE 2.15

A web page icon on your Home Screen looks similar to an app icon; however, when you tap it, Safari is launched and the web page that the icon is associated with is loaded automatically.

The menu that appears when you tap on the Share icon contains several features that are new to iOS 5, including the capability to Tweet the URL for the web page you're currently viewing, and the capability to add the web page to your Reading List.

When you return to your Home Screen, the icon for that web page will now be displayed, and will look very much like an app icon. To access that web page in the future, simply tap the appropriate icon on the Home Screen.

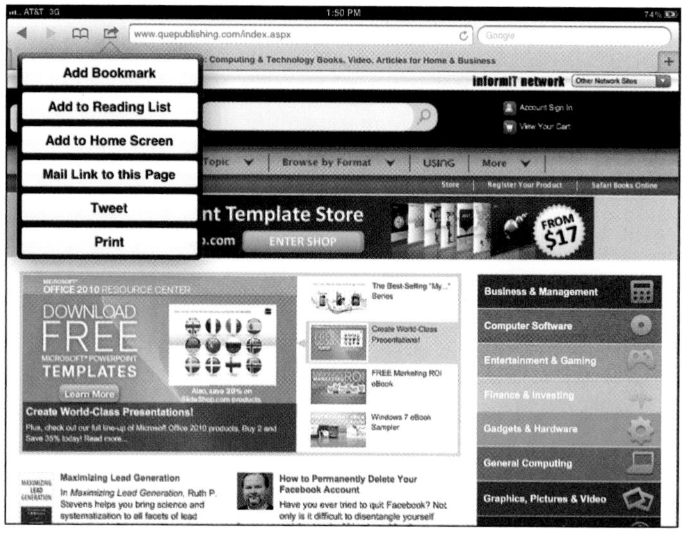

FIGURE 2.16

To create a web page icon that appears on your Home Screen, use the Add to Home Screen command displayed when you tap the Share icon.

HOW TO WORK IN MULTITASKING MODE

Your iPhone or iPad has the capability to run multiple apps simultaneously. From the Multitasking toolbar, you can quickly switch between apps without first closing one app and launching another.

To access Multitasking mode, quickly press the Home button on your iPhone or iPad twice. At the very bottom of the screen, a horizontal line of app icons that are currently running on your device is displayed. Using your finger, you can scroll left or right to view all the apps. Anytime the Multitasking icon bar is showing, you can also tap on any app to instantly switch to that app.

To exit out of Multitasking mode, either tap on an app icon that's displayed on the Multitasking bar or press the Home button again once.

> iOS 5 **WHAT'S NEW** On the iPad, one new finger motion introduced with iOS 5 involves holding three or four fingers together and dragging them from the very bottom of the iPad's screen toward the top to make the Multitasking bar appear (instead of pressing the Home button twice quickly).

Also, while in Multitasking mode (and while the Multitasking bar is visible), you can swipe your finger from left to right on the bar and scroll to the Music control panel that is part of iOS 5. This allows you to manage and play music in the background while you're using your iPhone or iPad for other purposes. Figure 2.17 shows the Music control panel that is accessible in Multitasking mode, without your having to launch the Music app separately. The icon displayed on the extreme left of the Music controls enables you to lock (or unlock) your iOS device's screen rotation.

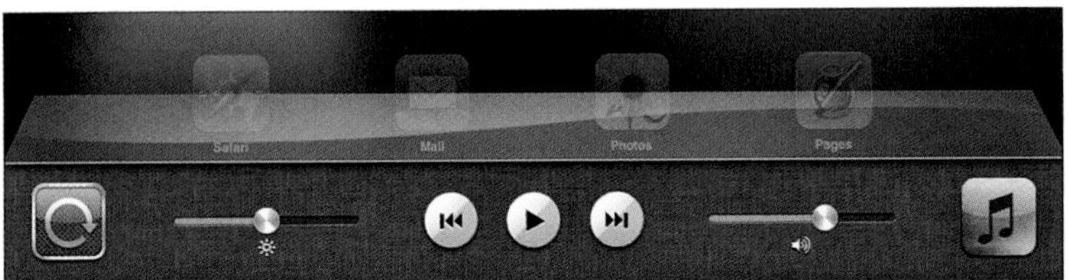

FIGURE 2.17

In Multitasking mode, you can access the Music control panel and play music in the background while you're using your iPhone or iPad for other tasks.

> **TIP** Multitasking mode is useful for a variety of things. For example, you can quickly use iOS 5's Select, Select All, Cut, Copy, and Paste commands to move text from one app to another.

IN THIS CHAPTER

- How to discover the difference between free, paid, subscription-based, advertiser supported, and in-app purchase apps
- How to find, purchase, and download different types of content for your iPhone or iPad

3

STRATEGIES FOR FINDING, BUYING, AND USING THIRD-PARTY APPS

In the process of improving its iOS 5 operating system, Apple has once again tinkered with the collection of preinstalled apps that you'll discover on your Home Screen. This collection of apps enables you to begin utilizing your iPhone or iPad for a wide range of popular tasks without first having to find and install additional apps.

However, one of the things that has set the iPhone and iPad apart from its competition, and has made these devices among the most sought after and popular throughout much of the world, is the library of optional apps available for them. Whereas other smartphones or tablets might offer a collection of a few hundred or even a few thousand optional apps, third-party developers have created an ever-growing collection of iPhone and iPad apps that's now in the hundreds of thousands of choices.

Thus, just as those Apple ads proclaim—"There's an app for that"—you can bet there probably is one. All the apps currently available for your iOS device can be found, purchased (if applicable), downloaded, and installed from Apple's online-based App Store.

APP STORE BASICS

There are two ways to access the App Store: directly from your iPhone or iPad (using the App Store app that comes preinstalled on your device), or using iTunes on your primary computer. The App Store app is used exclusively for finding, purchasing (if applicable), downloading, and installing apps directly on your device from the App Store; iTunes on your primary computer is used to access the App Store, but, among many other things, can also be used to access the iTunes Store and Apple's iBookstore to find, purchase (if applicable), download, and install many other types of content.

HOW NEW APPS INSTALL THEMSELVES

If you're shopping for apps directly from your iPhone or iPad, when you purchase a paid app or download a free app, after you confirm your decision, the app will automatically download and install itself on your device. After it's installed, its app icon appears on your iPhone or iPad's Home Screen and is ready to use.

However, if you're shopping for apps using iTunes on your primary computer, after you've confirmed your purchase or download decision (for a free app), the app will download to your computer, and will also automatically be saved in your iCloud account, but then must be transferred to your iPhone, iPad, or iPod touch.

Or, if you purchased an app on your iPhone, for example, and you also want to use it on your iPad or iPod touch, it can also be downloaded, for free, to that other device.

This transfer process can now be done via the iTunes sync process, or the app can be downloaded directly from your iCloud account using the App Store app on your device because as soon as you download any app once, it is saved online in your iCloud account, and ultimately becomes accessible from all your iOS devices that are connected to the Internet.

RESTORING OR REINSTALLING APPS YOU'VE ALREADY DOWNLOADED

To download an app that's already been purchased or downloaded onto another computer or device, in the App Store app on the iPad you're using, tap on the Purchased icon that's displayed at the bottom of the screen. (On the iPhone, tap on the Updates icon, and then tap on the Purchased icon that's displayed at the top of the Updates screen.) All your app purchases to date are displayed. However, instead of a Free or Price icon being associated with each app description, you see an iCloud icon. Tap on that iCloud icon to download the app (without having to pay for it again) to the iOS device you're currently using. You can only install previously purchased apps that are compatible with that iOS device. For example, you can't install an iPad-specific app onto an iPhone or iPod touch.

TIP From the Settings app, you have the option to have your iOS device automatically download and install any new (and compatible) music, apps, or books purchased using your Apple ID on any other computer or device. To set this up, launch Settings, select the Store option from the main Settings menu, and then adjust the Automatic Downloads options, which include Music, Apps, and Books. You can also decide whether this feature will work with a cellular data Web connection or just when a Wi-Fi Internet connection exists.

COMPATIBILITY: DOES THE APP RUN ON MULTIPLE DEVICES?

In terms of compatibility, all iOS apps fall into one of three categories:

- **iPhone-Specific**—These are apps designed exclusively for the various iPhone models that might not function properly on the iPad. Most iPhone-specific apps will run on an iPad, but will not take advantage of the tablet's larger screen.

  Figure 3.1 shows what an iPhone-specific app, in this case Skype for iPhone, that's running on an iPad looks like. The app functions fine but does not take full advantage of the tablet's larger screen. A useful trick is to tap on the 2x icon in the lower-right corner of the iPad's screen to double the size of what the iPhone app is displaying on the screen (as shown in Figure 3.2). However, in some cases, this causes text and graphics to become slightly distorted.

- **iPad-Specific**—These are apps designed exclusively for the iPad. They fully utilize the tablet's larger, high-definition screen. They will *not* function on the iPhone or on other iOS devices.
- **Hybrid**—These are apps designed to work on all iOS devices, including the iPhone and iPad. These apps detect which device they're running on and adapt. When you're reading an app's listing or description, and look at its Price icon, if that icon has a small plus sign in the upper-left corner (as shown in Figure 3.3), this indicates that it is a hybrid app, and will function properly on any iOS device, including any model of iPhone or iPad.

FIGURE 3.1

An iPhone-specific app running on an iPad will utilize only a small portion of the tablet's screen that's equivalent to the screen size of an iPhone.

FIGURE 3.2

Tapping the 2x icon doubles the size of the app on the tablet's screen.

FIGURE 3.3

You can pick out hybrid apps by looking at an app listing or the description's Price icon. If you see a plus sign in the upper-left corner of a Price icon, this indicates it's a hybrid app and will function on any iOS device.

TIP If you own two or more iOS devices, such as an iPhone and an iPad (or an iPod touch), and all the devices are registered using the same Apple ID account, you can purchase a hybrid (or iPhone-specific) app once but install it on all of your iOS devices. This can be done through iTunes sync or via iCloud after an app is initially purchased or downloaded.

When you're browsing the App Store from your iPhone, by default it displays all iPhone-specific apps, followed by hybrid apps, but the App Store will not display iPad apps. When you're browsing the App Store from your iPad, both iPad-specific and hybrid iPhone/iPad apps are listed.

TIP Because some app developers release the same app in both an iPhone-specific and an iPad-specific format, many iPad-specific apps have "HD" for High-Definition in their title, to help differentiate them from iPhone or Hybrid apps. For example, the popular game Angry Birds is for the iPhone, whereas Angry Birds HD is for the iPad.

Some iPad-specific apps include the words "for iPad" in their titles, such as GoodReader for iPad, FileMaker Go for iPad, PDF Reader Pro Edition for iPad, or Sid Meier's Pirates! for iPad.

QUICK GUIDE TO APP PRICING

Regardless of whether you use the App Store app from your iPhone or iPad, or visit the App Store through iTunes on your primary computer, you will need to set up an Apple ID account and have a major credit card or debit card linked to the account to make purchases.

If you don't have a major credit card or debit card that you want to link with your Apple ID account so that you can purchase apps from the App Store, you can purchase prepaid iTunes gift cards from Apple, or most places that sell prepaid gift cards, such as convenience stores, supermarkets, and pharmacies.

iTunes gift cards can be used to make app and other content purchases. iTunes gift cards (which are different from Apple gift cards, which are redeemable at Apple Stores or Apple.com) are available in $15, $25, and $50 denominations.

The first time you access the App Store and attempt to make a purchase, you are prompted to enter your Apple ID account username and password or set up a new Apple ID account, which requires you to supply your name, address, email, and credit card information. For all subsequent online app purchases, you'll simply need to enter your Apple ID password to confirm the purchase, and your credit card or debit card will automatically be billed (or the purchase amount will be deducted from your iTunes gift card balance).

The following sections summarize the different types of apps from a pricing standpoint.

FREE APPS

Free apps cost nothing to download and install on your phone or tablet. Some programmers and developers release apps for free out of pure kindness to share their creations with the iPhone- and/or iPad-using public. These are fully functional apps.

There are also free apps that serve as demo versions of paid apps. These are scaled-down versions of apps, or they have some type of limitation in terms of how long they can be used (usually 7, 14, or 30 days).

> **TIP** In some cases, basic features or functions of the app are locked in the free version, but are later made available if you upgrade to the paid or premium version of the app.

A third category of free apps comprises fully functional apps that display ads as part of their content. In exchange for using the app, you'll need to view ads, which offer the option to click on offers from within the app to learn more about the product or service being advertised.

A fourth category of free apps serves as a shell for premium (paid) content that must be loaded into the app to make it fully functional. For example, many newspaper and magazine publishers now offer free apps related to their specific publications, but require users to pay for the actual content of the newspaper or magazine, which later gets downloaded into the app.

The final type of free app is fully functional but allows the user to make in-app purchases to add features or functionality to the app, or unlock premium content. The core app, without the extra content, is free, however.

TIP Some fully functional apps are free because they're designed to promote a specific company or work with a specific service. For example, to use the free TiVo app, you must have a compatible TiVo DVR connected to your television set or home entertainment center. Likewise, to use the free Netflix app, you must be a paid subscriber to this movie service.

When you're looking at an app listing or description in the App Store, instead of having a Price icon associated with it, you'll see a Free icon (as shown in Figure 3.4). Tap on this icon, and then confirm your download decision by tapping on the Install icon that replaces it, to download and install a free app onto your iPhone or iPad.

FIGURE 3.4

A free app will have a Free icon displayed in its App Store listing or description.

PAID APPS

After you purchase an app, you own it and can use it as often as you'd like, without incurring additional fees. You simply pay a fee for the app upfront, which is typically between $.99 and $9.99. All future upgrades or new versions of the app are free of charge. In some cases, paid apps also offer in-app purchase options to access premium content.

In the app listing and description for a paid app, you will see a Price icon displayed for that app, which lists how much the app costs. To purchase the app, tap on this Price icon. It is replaced by a Purchase icon, which needs to be tapped, allowing you to confirm your purchase decision. It is then necessary to enter the password associated with your Apple ID account. The cost of the app is charged to the major credit card associated with your Apple ID account or deducted from the balance of your iTunes gift card.

SUBSCRIPTION-BASED APPS

These apps are typically free, and then you pay a recurring subscription fee for content, which automatically gets downloaded into the app. Many digital editions of newspapers, such as the *New York Times* and the *Wall Street Journal*, utilize a subscription app model, as do hundreds of different magazines.

Typically, the main content of the digital and printed version of a publication are identical. However, you can view the digital edition on your iPhone or iPad, and take advantage of added interactive elements built in to the app. If you're already a subscriber to the printed version of a newspaper or magazine, some publishers offer the digital edition free, while others charge an extra fee to subscribe to the digital edition as well. Or you can subscribe to just the digital edition of a publication.

With some magazines, you can download the free app for a specific publication and then, in the app, purchase one issue at a time, such as the current issue or a single past issue. There is no long-term subscription commitment, but individual issues of the publication still need to be purchased and downloaded. Or you can purchase an ongoing (recurring) subscription and new issues of that publication will automatically be downloaded to your iPhone or iPad as they become available.

MORE INFO Apps that offer subscription-based content always allow you to easily subscribe from within the app, usually with the single touch of an icon. However, if you want to cancel or change your recurring (paid) subscription, you'll need to access the Manage App Subscriptions section of iTunes on your primary computer, do this in the Newsstand app, or access your Apple ID Account Page from within the App Store app. The link to manage your Apple ID account (and also manage recurring subscriptions) is found near the very bottom of most pages in the App Store app.

The Daily, which is a digital newspaper published by News Corp., is created and published exclusively for use on the iPad. The app and a two-week trial subscription to *The Daily* are free, but after that, you'll need to pay for an ongoing subscription to have the daily publication automatically sent wirelessly to your tablet each day.

Digital editions of magazines and newspapers can be purchased from the App Store or the new Newsstand app. These publications each require their own proprietary app to access and read the publication's content. You will discover digital editions of many popular publications available from the App Store or Newsstand app.

iOS 5 WHAT'S NEW You can browse available digital publications and then manage your subscriptions using the new Newsstand app that comes preinstalled on your iPhone or iPad.

IN-APP PURCHASES

This type of app might be free, or it might be a paid app. However, as you're actually using the app, you can purchase additional content or add new features and functionality to the app by making in-app purchases. The capability to make in-app purchases has become very popular, and is being used by app developers in a variety of ways.

As you read an app's description in the App Store, if an app requires in-app purchases, it is revealed in the text included in the app description screen.

! CAUTION The price you pay for an app does not translate directly to the quality or usefulness of that app. There are some free or very inexpensive apps that are extremely useful and packed with features, and that can really enhance your experience using your iPhone or iPad. However, there are costly apps (priced at $4.99 or more) that are poorly designed or filled with bugs, or that don't live up to expectations or to the description of the app offered by the app's developer or publisher.

The price of each app is set by the developer or programmer that created or is selling the app. Instead of using the price as the only determining factor if you're evaluating several apps that appear to offer similar functionality, be sure to read the app's customer reviews carefully, and pay attention to the star-based rating the app has received. These user reviews and ratings are a much better indicator of the app's quality and usefulness than the price of the app.

HOW TO SHOP WITH THE APP STORE APP

From your iPhone or iPad's Home Screen, to access the App Store, tap on the blue-and-white App Store app icon. Your device must have access to the Internet via a 3G or Wi-Fi connection.

When you access the App Store via the App Store app (shown in Figure 3.5), you'll discover a handful of command icons at the top and bottom of the screen that are used to navigate your way around the online-based store.

FIGURE 3.5

The main App Store app screen on the iPad 2. Find, purchase, download, and install apps directly from your tablet.

If you already know the name of the app you want to find, purchase, download, and install, tap on the Search field, which is located in the upper-right corner of the screen in the iPad version. On the iPhone, tap on the Search option displayed at the bottom of the App Store app's screen.

Using the virtual keyboard, enter the name of the app. Tap the Search key on the virtual keyboard to begin the search. You can also perform a search based on a keyword or phrase, such as "word processing," "to-do lists," "time management," or "photo editing."

In a few seconds, matching results are displayed on the App Store screen. When you access the App Store from your iPhone using the App Store app, iPhone-specific and hybrid apps are displayed.

Likewise, if you're shopping for apps from your iPad, as you browse the App Store using the App Store app, iPad-specific apps will always be listed prominently. Hybrid apps will display a plus sign in the upper-left corner their Price icon.

TIP In general, when you're choosing apps for your iPad 2, for example, look for iPad-specific apps first, then apps that are designed for both iPad and iPhone. Most apps that are iPhone-specific will run fine on an iPad 2 but the app's graphics and user interface will be formatted for the iPhone's smaller screen. However, if you own both an iPhone and an iPad, look for hybrid apps first so you can purchase that app once but use it on both iOS devices.

At the bottom center of the main App Store screen (when using the App Store app) are several command icons, labeled Featured, Genius, Top Charts, Categories, and Updates on the iPad; and Features, Categories, Top 25, Search, and Updates on the iPhone. If you don't know the exact name of an app you're looking for, these command icons will help you browse the App Store and discover apps that might be of interest to you.

THE FEATURED COMMAND ICON

Tap on the Featured command icon that is displayed near the bottom of the App Store screen to see a listing of what Apple considers "Featured" apps. These are divided into a handful of categories, including New and Noteworthy and Staff Favorites.

MORE INFO Apps that are categorized as "App of the Week," "Featured," "New and Noteworthy," or "Staff Favorite" are selected by the experts at Apple who are in charge of testing and reviewing all third-party apps. These categorizations are supposed to be impartial, and help alert iOS device users of the best apps currently available.

Near the top of the screen are large graphic banners that constantly change. These banner graphics promote what Apple considers the "App of the Week," as well as other noteworthy apps the company wants to promote.

On the iPad, for example, under the New and Noteworthy section of the Featured screen, you'll see six app listings. On the right and left side of the New and Noteworthy pages are white arrow icons that point left and right. Tap on any of these arrow icons to scroll between the five New and Noteworthy sections. Or tap on the See All command that's displayed next to the New and Noteworthy heading.

When you tap on the See All command, the entire screen is replaced by app listings (as shown in Figure 3.6). On the iPhone, simply scroll down on the screen.

FIGURE 3.6

See all the apps that Apple deems as New and Noteworthy as you browse the App Store.

SPECIAL CATEGORIES: NEW, WHAT'S HOT, AND RELEASE DATE COMMAND ICONS

As you're looking at the Featured page of the App Store (using the App Store app), you will see three command tabs displayed at the top center of the screen. On the iPad, they're labeled New, What's Hot, and Release Date. On the iPhone, the tabs at the top of the screen are labeled New, What's Hot, and Genius. These are used to sort the app listings you see when you first tap on the Featured command icon.

Instead of showcasing New and Noteworthy apps when the New icon is selected, when you tap on the What's Hot icon, a different collection of Apple-recommended apps is displayed, this time under the What's Hot heading. On the iPad, toward the bottom of the screen are also recommended apps that fall into a very specific area of interest, which changes regularly.

At the very bottom of this screen on the iPad is a subsection labeled Quick Links. It offers six options for finding apps relating to a particular area of interest. Your options here include iPad Apps Starter Kit, iPad Games Starter Kit, iPad Hall of Fame, Previous Apps of the Week, Previous Games of the Week, and iWork. Tap on any of these options to see a collection of apps you might be interested in. On the iPhone, these options are displayed as graphic banners that you can tap on.

For example, if you're accessing the App Store from your iPad, tap on the iPad Apps Starter Kit option (shown in Figure 3.7), and you'll see a collection of apps that Apple recommends for beginner iPad 2 users, including iBooks, Pages, Twitter, CNN App for iPad, and Evernote.

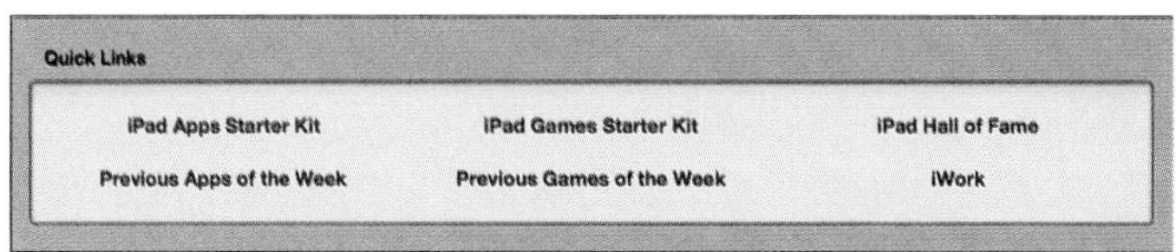

FIGURE 3.7

From the Quick Links section of the App Store, you can access apps that Apple included in the iPad App Starter Kit listing of recommended apps for new iPad 2 users.

THE GENIUS APP ICON

The App Store keeps track of all apps you purchase. When you tap on the Genius command icon that's displayed near the bottom center of the App Store screen on the iPad, or near the upper right on the iPhone screen, the App Store will analyze your past app purchases and offer suggestions for other apps you might be interested in.

THE TOP CHARTS ICON

When you tap on the Top Charts command icon, also located near the bottom center of the App Store app's screen, a listing of Top Paid Apps are displayed in order based on their popularity. This is a general listing of all currently popular apps, and it constantly changes.

On an iPhone, tap on the Top 25 icon at the bottom of the screen, followed by the Paid tab displayed near the top of the screen, to view a listing of Top 25 Paid iPhone apps. Or on an iPad, you will see the Top Paid iPad Apps listing on the left side of the screen.

Meanwhile, on the iPhone, tap on the Top 25 icon at the bottom of the App Store screen, followed by the Top Free tab displayed near the top of the screen, to view the listing of Top Free apps currently available from the App Store. On an iPad, tap on the Top Charts icon at the bottom of the App Store screen. The Top Free iPad Apps listing are displayed on the right side of the screen (as shown in Figure 3.8).

At the bottom of these charts is a Show More option. Tap on this to see additional apps listed in the chart. You also can view lists of Top Grossing apps.

By default, when you tap on the Top Charts icon, the Top Charts lists that are displayed are composed of apps from all categories. However, if your primary interest is apps that fall within a specific category, on the iPhone, tap on the Categories icon at the bottom of the App Store screen, and then at the top of the screen tap on the Top Paid or Top Free tabs.

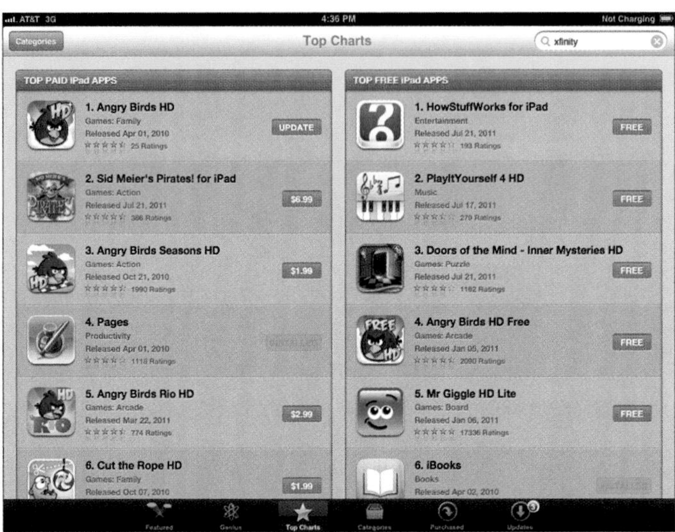

FIGURE 3.8

From the App Store app on the iPad, tap on the Top Charts icon at the bottom of the screen to view a list of Top Paid iPad apps (on the left) and Top Free iPad apps (on the right).

Or, on the iPad, tap on the top Charts icon displayed at the bottom of the App Store app, and then tap on the Categories icon that's displayed in the upper-left corner of this screen. A listing of various app categories are displayed (as shown in Figure 3.9). Choose one of the categories by tapping on it. When you tap on a specific category, such as Business, you can view the Top Paid Business Apps, Top Free Business Apps, or Top Grossing Business Apps charts.

THE CATEGORIES ICON

On an iPhone, when you tap the Categories icon displayed at the bottom of the App Store screen, you'll see three tabs displayed at the top of the screen that sort the app listings: Top Paid, Top Free, and Release Date. If you choose Release Date, you'll see a comprehensive listing of apps, starting with those that were released most recently.

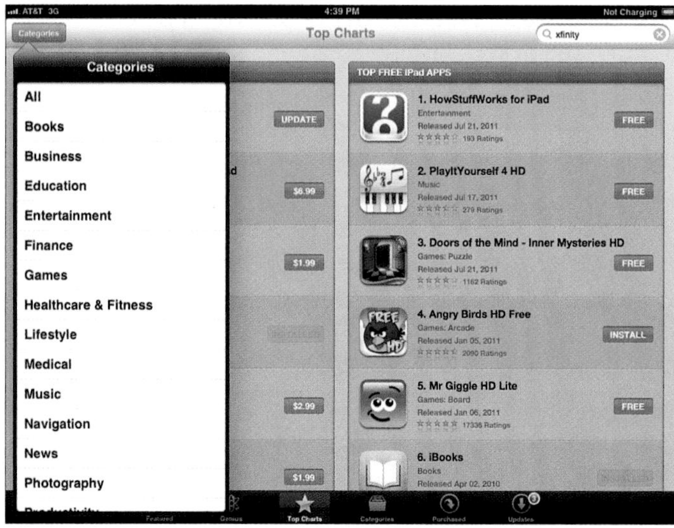

FIGURE 3.9

You can view Top Charts lists that showcase apps in various categories, such as Business, Finance, News, or Reference.

As you're browsing for apps using the iPad version of the App Store app, tapping on the Top Charts command icon reveals a listing of the top-selling apps in a specific category, or you can tap on the Categories command icon that's displayed near the bottom center of the App Store app screen to access all the apps that fall into any one of the App Store's main categories.

When you tap on the Categories icon, a list of all app categories is displayed. The app listed to represent each category is the currently most popular paid app in that category.

Tap on the category that most interests you, and you'll be able to browse through listings of all apps that fall into that category. Keep in mind that there might be thousands of apps in any given category, so you could wind up spending hours looking at app listings as you discover the vast selection of apps available.

After choosing an app category, on the iPhone, tap on the Twenty-Five More option to view additional apps. Or, on the iPad, use the right- or left-pointing arrow icons displayed on either side of the screen to scroll through app listings, which are displayed 12 to a page.

On the iPad, by default, the apps are displayed in order based on release date (with the most recently released apps displayed first). However, you can change the sort order by tapping on the Sort By command that's displayed in the upper-right corner of the screen. Your options include Name (for an alphabetical listing), Most Popular (starting with the best-selling apps), and Release Date.

As you're looking at the app listings, you can learn more about a particular app by tapping on its graphic icon or title. Or you can purchase, download, and install the app by tapping on its Price icon. (For free apps, when you tap on the Free icon, the app will automatically download and install, after you enter your Apple ID password.)

MANAGE ACCOUNT, REDEEM, AND SUPPORT

When you scroll down to the very bottom of the Featured, Genius, Top Charts (Top 25), or Categories sections of the App Store, you'll see three command icons: Account [Your Apple ID Username], Redeem, and Support.

Tap on the Account icon to manage your Apple ID account and update your credit card information, for example. Or tap on the Redeem icon to redeem a prepaid iTunes gift card. If you experience problems using the App Store, or have questions, tap on the Support icon.

To manage your recurring paid subscriptions, tap on the Apple ID account icon displayed at the bottom of the various App Store pages. When the Apple ID window appears (shown in Figure 3.10), tap on the View Account option. Then, when the Account window is displayed in a new window, scroll down to the Subscriptions heading and tap Manage. You'll then be able to modify or cancel your paid recurring subscriptions to digital newspapers or magazines, for example.

FIGURE 3.10

From the View Account option, you can change or cancel your recurring paid subscriptions for digital editions of newspapers and magazines.

FEATURES OF AN APP LISTING

As you browse the app store, each screen is composed of many app listings. Each listing promotes a specific app. Each app listing contains the app's name and price, the category the app falls into (such as Business, Reference, News, Lifestyle, or Games), the app's original release date, the average star rating the app has received from users, and a graphic icon that features the app's logo. A sample app listing from the iPad version of the App Store is shown in Figure 3.11.

FIGURE 3.11

A sample listing contains important details about that app, including its title and price.

To purchase an app (or download and install a free app), tap on its Price icon. The Price icon will change from gray and white to green and white. If it's a free app, this new icon is labeled Install App. If it's a paid app, the green-and-white icon will say Buy App. Tap on this icon to confirm your purchase decision.

Following this, an Apple ID Password window will appear on the screen. Your Apple ID username will already be displayed, but you will need to enter your Apple ID password in the password field. Using the virtual keyboard, type your Apple ID password, and then tap the OK icon that's displayed in this window. The app will automatically download and install itself on your iOS device, and in 15 seconds to several minutes, the app icon for the new app will appear on your iPhone or iPad's Home Screen and be ready to use. At the same time, the app is stored online in your iCloud account.

Keep in mind that it is necessary to enter your Apple ID Password whenever you attempt to download and install any app, even if it's a free app.

LEARN BEFORE YOU BUY: ACCESSING THE APP'S DESCRIPTION PAGE

Before committing to a purchase, as you're looking at an app's listing in the App Store, you can tap on its title or graphic icon. When you do this, the App Store screen is replaced with a detailed description of the app.

An app description screen (like the one shown in Figure 3.12) displays the app's title and logo near the top of the screen, along with a detailed description of the app under the Description heading.

Below the Description is information about what new features have been added to the app in the most recent version. As you scroll downward on this screen, you'll see one or more actual screenshots from the app. Use your finger to flick from right to left over the screenshots to scroll through multiple images, if applicable.

FIGURE 3.12

From an app's description screen, you can learn all about a specific app. This information can help you decide whether it's of interest to you, or relevant to your needs.

Displayed under the app's screenshots are the Customer Ratings for that app. You can sort these ratings by tapping on the Current Version or All Versions command tabs displayed on the right side of the screen, next to the Customer Ratings heading.

These Customer Ratings are based on a five-star system. Anyone who purchases or downloads an app has the option to rate it. A top rating is five stars. From the Ratings Summary chart (shown in Figure 3.13), you can see how many people have rated an app, discover the app's average rating, and then see a breakdown of how many one-star, two-star, three-star, four-star, and five-star ratings the app has received.

Obviously, an app with a large number of five-star ratings is probably excellent, whereas an app that consistently earns three stars or less is probably not that great or is loaded with bugs.

As you review an app's description, keep scrolling downward, below the star ratings summary chart, and you'll be able to read full reviews that your fellow users have written about that app. These reviews often describe the best features of the app and/or its worst problems.

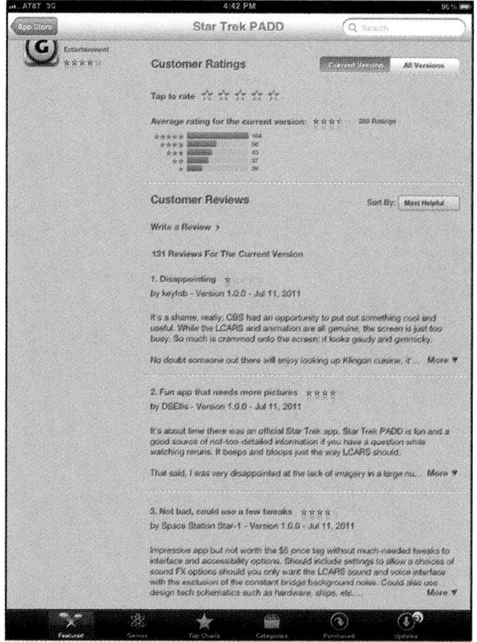

FIGURE 3.13

Every app description contains an average rating and a rating summary chart. Use it to quickly see what other users think about the app you're currently looking at.

At the bottom of the app description page on the iPad is a section labeled Customers Also Bought. These are listings for other apps, usually similar in functionality to the app you're looking at, which other customers have also purchased and downloaded.

Displayed near an app's graphic logo on the description page for each app, you'll see its Price icon, as well as specific information pertaining to that app, including its category, the date it was last updated, the current version of the app, the file size of the app, what language the app is in, and the seller/publisher of the app.

Included with this information is a summary of what age group the app is suitable for, as well as additional notes related to the app's content, including whether the app requires in-app purchases or a paid subscription to fully utilize it.

Also displayed on every app description page (when you're using the App Store app) are the system requirements for that app. This will tell you whether it's an iPad-specific app, for example, and which iOS operating system version it works with.

TIP Additional information about the app can also be obtained from the App Developer website or the App Support website, both of which are operated by the app developer. On the iPad, command icons that will launch Safari and take you directly to one of these websites are displayed along the left side of the app description page, as well as in the upper-right corner of an app description page. On the iPhone, information about the app developer is incorporated into the app description page and typically includes a link to the developer's website.

After reviewing the app's description page, if you want to be reminded of the app's existence (without downloading it) or you want to tell a friend about the app, tap on the Tell a Friend icon. When you do this, an email form will appear on the screen.

In the body of the email are details about the app. Using the iPhone or iPad's virtual keyboard, fill in the To field, to send the app-related information to yourself or someone else via email. Tap the Send icon to send the message.

TIP Using the Gift This App option that is displayed in an app's description page, you can purchase an app and send it to another iPad or iPhone user electronically.

To exit an app's description page and continue browsing the App Store, tap on the left-pointing arrow icon that's labeled App Store. It's displayed in the upper-left corner of the screen.

KEEP YOUR APPS CURRENT WITH THE UPDATES COMMAND ICON

One of the command icons that's constantly displayed at the bottom center of the App Store app's screen is the Updates icon. This is used to keep your currently installed apps up to date. More information about this feature is included later in this chapter, in the section "Keep Your Apps Up to Date with the Latest Versions."

QUICK TIPS FOR FINDING APPS RELEVANT TO YOU

As you explore the App Store, it's easy to get overwhelmed by the sheer number of apps that are available for your iOS device. If you're a new iPhone or iPad user, spending time browsing the App Store will introduce you to the many types of apps that are available, and will provide you with ideas about how your phone or tablet can be utilized in your personal or professional life.

However, you can save a lot of time searching for apps if you already know the app's exact title, or if you know what type of app you're looking for. In this case, you can enter either the app's exact title or a keyword description of the app in the App Store's Search field to see a list of relevant matches.

So if you're looking for a word processing app, you can either enter the search phrase "Pages" into the App Store's Search field, or enter the search phrase "word processor" to see a selection of word processing apps.

If you're looking for vertical market apps with specialized functionality that caters to your industry or profession, enter that industry or profession (or keywords associated with it) in the Search field. For example, enter keywords like "medical imaging," "radiology," "plumbing," "telemarketing," or "sales."

As you're evaluating an app before downloading it, use these tips to help you determine whether it's worth installing on your phone or tablet:

- Figure out what type of features or functionality you want to add to your iPhone or iPad.
- Using the Search field, find apps designed to handle the tasks you have in mind. Chances are, you'll easily be able to find a handful of apps created by different developers that are designed to perform the same basic functionality. You can then pick which is the best based on the description, screenshots, and list of features each app offers.

  Compare the various apps by reading their descriptions and viewing the screenshots. Figure out which app will work best for you, based on your unique needs.
- Check the customer reviews and ratings for the app. This is a useful tool to quickly determine whether the app actually works as described in its description. Keep in mind, an app's description in the App Store is written by the app's developer, and is designed to sell apps. The customer reviews and star-based ratings are created by fellow iPhone or iPad users who have tried out the app firsthand.

  If an app has only a few ratings or reviews, and they're mixed, you might need to try out the app for yourself to determine whether it will be useful to you. However, if an app has many reviews that are overwhelmingly negative (three stars or less), that's a strong indication that the app does not perform as described, or that it's loaded with bugs, for example.
- If an app offers a free (trial) version, download and test out that version of the app first, before purchasing the premium version. You can always delete any app that you try out but don't wind up liking or needing.

- Ideally, you want to install apps on your iPhone or iPad that were designed specifically for that device, if you have a choice. So if you're using an iPhone, choose the iPhone-specific version of an app, or if you're using an iPad, download the iPad-specific version of an app.

KEEP YOUR APPS UP TO DATE WITH THE LATEST VERSIONS

Periodically, app developers will release new versions of their apps. To make sure you have the most current version of all apps installed on your iPhone or iPad, while visiting the App Store using the App Store app on your phone or tablet, tap on the Updates command icon that's displayed at the bottom center of the screen.

If the Updates icon has a red-and-white circle in the upper-right corner of it (as shown in Figure 3.14), this is an indication that one or more of your apps has an update available. The number in the red circle icon relates to how many app updates are available, based on the apps currently installed on your device.

FIGURE 3.14

Keep your apps up to date with the latest versions. You can download updates directly from your iPhone or iPad if it's connected to the Internet.

Tap on the Updates icon to display a list of apps with updates available, and then tap on the Update All icon or an individual app icon that's displayed on the Updates screen to automatically download the new version of the app and install it. Doing this will replace the older version of the app.

Using the App Store app to check for updates will determine whether there are updated versions for apps currently installed on your device. However, if you check for app updates using iTunes on your primary computer, it will check for updates for all the apps you have ever downloaded using a specific Apple ID account (including backups of apps that are stored on your primary computer or iCloud, but that aren't currently installed on your iPhone or iPad).

TIP To ensure that you have the latest versions of your most commonly used apps installed on your iPhone or iPad, check for app updates once every week or two. Each time Apple releases an update to the iOS operating system, it's common for app developers to also release an updated version of their apps.

IN THIS CHAPTER

- How to set up Notification Center to manage alerts, alarms, messages, and notifications
- How to avoid becoming inundated by too many notifications
- How to stay informed about upcoming deadlines, appointments, and responsibilities

4

MAKE THE MOST OF NOTIFICATION CENTER

Many of the apps you'll probably be running on your iPhone or iPad are capable of generating messages, alarms, alerts, and/or notifications to inform you that some action needs to be taken.

Mail, for example, will alert you to new incoming emails. Phone (on the iPhone) or FaceTime will tell you if and when you've missed a call. Messages will get your attention when someone sends you a text message. Calendar can be set to remind you of your important upcoming appointments, and the new Reminders app will notify you whenever an item on one of your to-do lists requires your immediate attention.

If you play games or you're active on Twitter or Facebook, these apps also can notify you when actions need to be taken, or if someone is trying to get in touch with you.

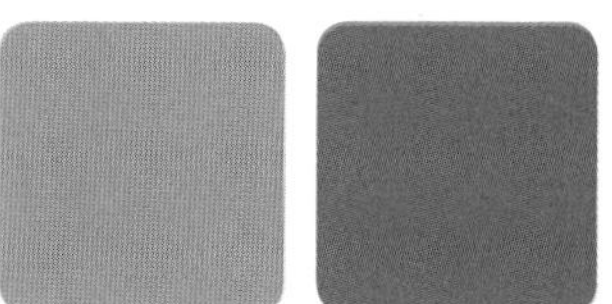

Many apps can also sound off audible alarms, whereas others display alert or notification windows. After you start relying on and using a handful of different apps, it's very easy to become inundated with messages, alerts, alarms, and notifications from them. Thanks to iOS 5, the solution to managing all of these items as they happen is a new app. It's called Notification Center.

> iOS 5 **WHAT'S NEW** Notification Center is a new, preinstalled app that's always running. It works with most other apps, serving as a central location to view messages, alert, alarms, and notifications—all of which get displayed in a single window (shown in Figure 4.1), which you can access on your iPhone or iPad screen when it's convenient for you.

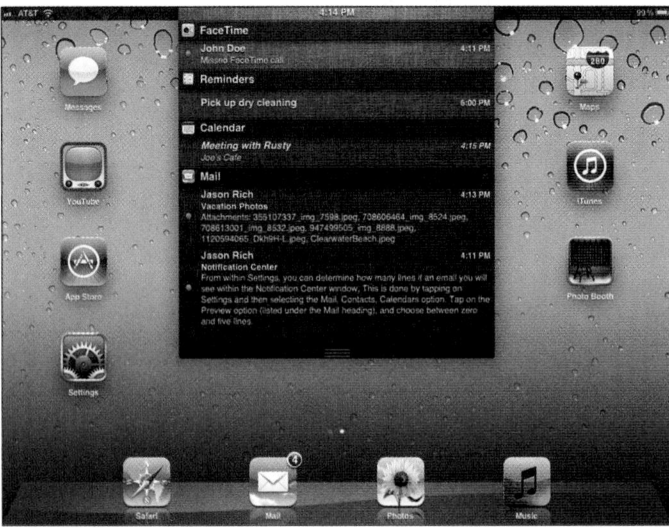

FIGURE 4.1

Notification Center is constantly running on your iPhone or iPad. In a single window that appears near the top of the screen, it lists all messages, alerts, alarms, and notifications from the various apps that it constantly monitors.

At any time, from the Notification Center window, you can tap on an individual item that's listed to instantly launch the relevant app, and have whatever it is that needs your attention quickly displayed on your iPhone or iPad's screen.

So if you're alerted to an upcoming appointment (as shown in Figure 4.2), simply tap on that alert, the Calendar app will launch, and then your pending appointment(s) are displayed.

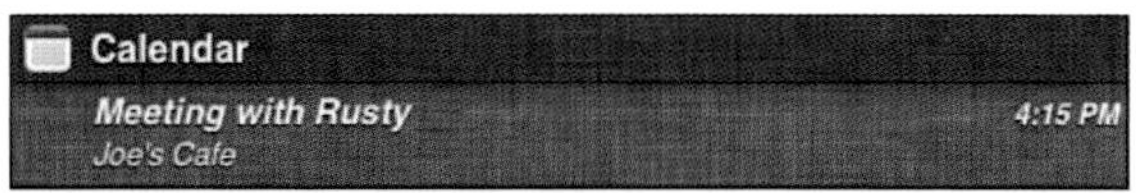

FIGURE 4.2

From the Notification Center window, tap on any alarm, alert, or notification listed to launch the relevant app and deal with whatever requires your attention.

You can access the Notification Center window anytime that your iPhone or iPad is turned on by swiping your finger from the very top of the device's screen in a downward direction.

A smaller version of the Notification Center window will also appear (and then automatically disappear) whenever a new alarm, alert, or notification (such as a missed call or incoming email) is triggered.

iOS 5 **WHAT'S NEW** If you're using an iPhone 4S it's easy to create reminders or alarms, which will ultimately be displayed in Notification Center. To create a reminder (to be stored and accessible from within the Reminders app), activate Siri, say, "Remind me to pick up my dry cleaning tomorrow at 2 PM," confirm your request, and the reminder (and a related alarm) will automatically be set up. When appropriate, the alarm relating to the Reminder listing will be displayed in the Notification Center window.

NOTIFICATION CENTER'S MAIN WINDOW

Based on how you personalize Notification Center, the app's main window will display 1, 5, 10, or 20 messages, alerts, alarms, or notifications from each app that it constantly monitors.

If you have Notification Center set to monitor the Mail app and display five alerts from the app at any given time, then when you view the Notification Center window, you will see a summary of the last five incoming emails you received. This is shown in Figure 4.3.

Having Notification Center display only one or five messages from each app will keep the Notification Center window less cluttered, making it easier to quickly determine what needs your attention. However, displaying more messages from each app will inform you about everything that currently requires your attention.

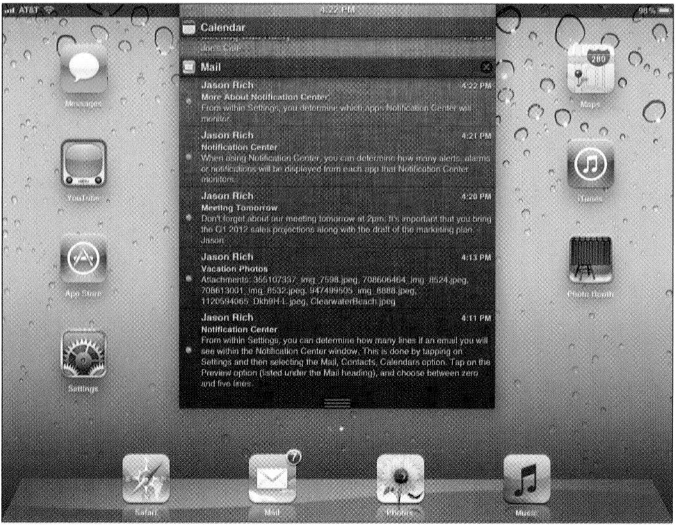

FIGURE 4.3

You decide exactly how many messages, alerts, alarms, or notifications are displayed in the Notification Center window pertaining to each app.

Keep in mind, if 10 apps are being monitored and each app generates 20 new alerts, your Notification Center window will display up to 200 individual listings. It will take you several minutes to review all this information, which isn't necessarily the most productive use of your time. All messages, alerts, alarms, and notifications are displayed in reverse chronological order by time (based on when each alert is generated), but also categorized by app for easy reference. When the Notification Center window is displayed, use your finger to scroll downward, as needed, to see the entire list.

When you view the Notification Center window, divider bars with the name of each app that is being monitored are displayed. Below each divider bar, shown in Figure 4.4, are the messages, alerts, alarms, or notifications generated by that particular app.

TIP To quickly clear the listings in the Notification Center window that relate to a particular app, tap on the circular "X" icon on the extreme right side of a divider bar, and then tap on the Clear icon that appears. Although Notification Center will continue monitoring that app, all older listings pertaining to messages, alerts, alarms, or notifications are removed.

At any time, tap on any listing in the Notification Center window to launch the relevant app and deal with what requires your attention, such as a missed call, a new incoming email, or an unread text message. Otherwise, to make the Notification Center window disappear, tap anywhere on the iPhone or iPad screen that is outside the window, or flick your finger in an upward direction, from the bottom of the notification center window toward the top.

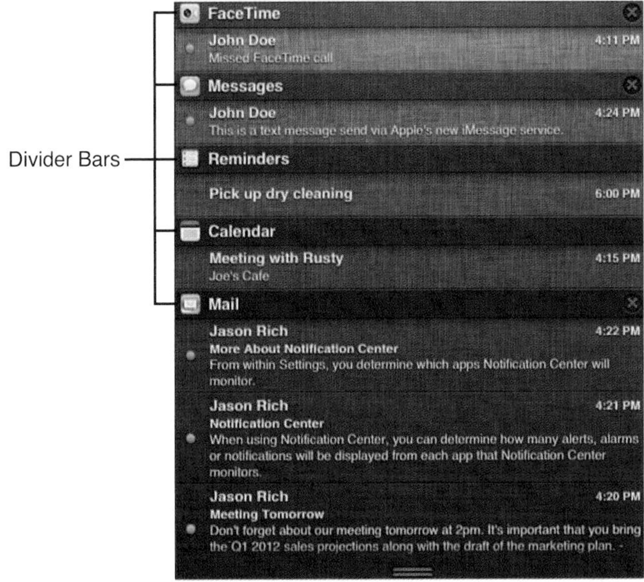

FIGURE 4.4

In the Notification Center window, divider bars are used to separate messages, alerts, alarms, and notifications generated from each app that the Notification Center app is constantly monitoring.

The current time is always displayed at the top center of the Notification Center window, and the time each message, alert, alarm, or notification was generated is displayed on the right side of each listing.

On the left side of each listing, when applicable, a blue dot (shown in Figure 4.5) will appear. This dot indicates that it's a new listing, and that you have not yet taken any action relating to it. After you tap on the listing to launch the relevant app, the blue dot will automatically disappear.

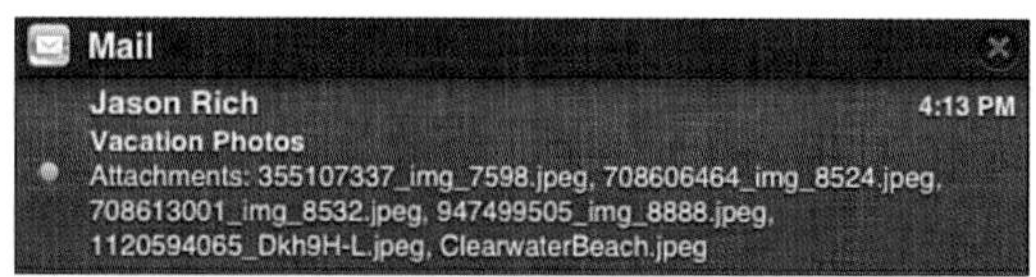

FIGURE 4.5

A blue dot is displayed on the left side of each listing in the Notification Center window if the listing is new and no action has yet been taken.

QUICK STRATEGIES FOR PERSONALIZING NOTIFICATION CENTER

By default, Notification Center works with many different apps simultaneously. So, unless you take charge and set preferences for how often these apps should alert you to various things, you could easily discover that Notification Center constantly becomes active and frequently tries to get your attention.

After all, you might put a very different priority on a missed call from your biggest client than you put on an alert notifying you that your virtual crops are about to wither as you're playing the popular game Farmville, or that construction of a new mushroom house has been completed as part of the game Smurfs' Village.

Notification Center can adapt to your personal needs and priorities, thus keeping you informed only about what you deem to be important.

Customize the settings related to Notification Center by accessing the Settings app. To do this, tap on the Settings app icon from the Home Screen. Then, tap on the Notifications option, shown in Figure 4.6. It's listed third in the main Settings menu (on the iPad, it is displayed on the left side of the screen).

FIGURE 4.6

After the Settings app is launched (shown here on the iPhone 4), tap on the Notifications option to customize the settings associated with Notification Center, and decide which apps will constantly be monitored.

After you've tapped on the Notifications option in Settings, a listing of apps currently being monitored by the Notification Center app is displayed under the In Notification Center heading (shown on the iPad 2 in Figure 4.7). Meanwhile, those apps that are compatible with Notification Center, but that are not currently being monitored, are displayed under the Not in Notification Center heading.

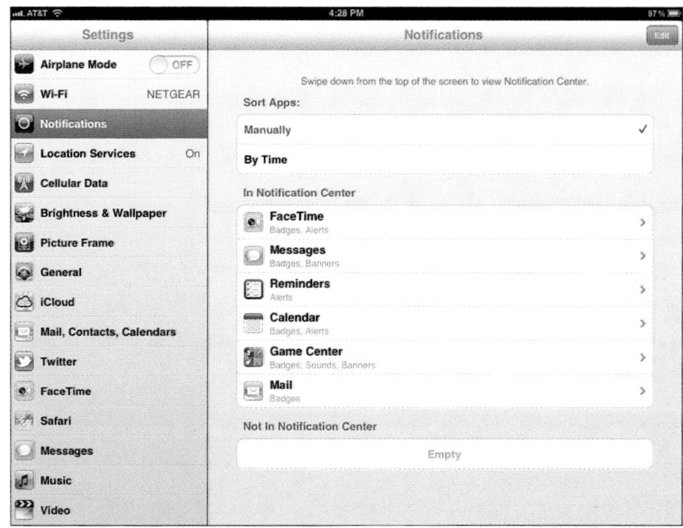

FIGURE 4.7

The apps that Notification Center is currently monitoring are displayed separately under the In Notification Center heading in the Settings app.

WHAT'S NEW Also from the Notifications screen of the Settings app, you can determine how you want alerts, alarms, and notifications to be displayed in your Notifications Center window in reverse chronological order. Your options include Manually or By Time. The By Time option lists each item displayed in the Notification Window in reverse chronological order. The Manually option lists items by App (which are displayed alphabetically).

One at a time, tap on any of the apps listed under the In Notification Center heading to customize the settings associated with how the Notification Center app handles that particular app.

The customizable options available to you in the submenu screen that appears will vary based on which app you're customizing.

STEP BY STEP: CUSTOMIZE HOW NOTIFICATION CENTER MONITORS APPS

To customize the Notification Center settings associated with FaceTime, for example, follow these steps:

1. From the Home Screen, tap on the Settings app icon to launch Settings.
2. Tap on the Notifications option.
3. Choose the FaceTime app from the listing of apps displayed under the In Notification Center heading.
4. The first option at the top of the submenu screen, which appears in Figure 4.8, is labeled Notification Center. The option is associated with a virtual on/off switch that is located to the right of the label. When this switch is turned on, Notification Center will monitor this app (in this example, FaceTime). If the virtual switch is turned off, Notification Center will no longer monitor this app, and messages, alerts, alarms, or notifications generated by this app will not appear in the Notification Center window.

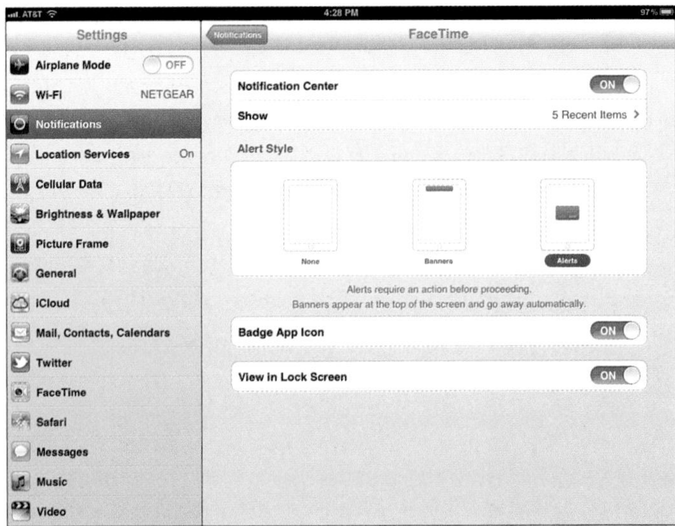

FIGURE 4.8

By turning the virtual switch associated with the Notification Center label to the on position, Notification Center will constantly monitor this app (in this case, FaceTime), and display related messages, alerts, alarms, and/or notifications in the Notification Center window.

5. If there's an app you don't deem important, turn the virtual switch associated with the Notification Center option to off. For example, if you're using your iPhone or iPad as a business tool, you might want to turn off this

setting for Games Center and any games listed (and that are installed on your iPhone or iPad) so that Notification Center does not monitor and display messages, alerts, alarms, or notifications associated with those particular (unimportant) game apps.

TIP You will need to turn on or off the Notification Center option for Game Center as well as any individual games installed on your device to eliminate all game-related content from being monitored by Notification Center.

6. Immediately below the Notification Center option that's associated with the virtual on/off switch is another option, labeled Show. Tap on this option to determine how many messages, alerts, alarms, or notifications relating to this particular app will display in the Notification Center window at any given time. When you tap on this option, a new submenu screen will appear, allowing you to choose between 1 and 20 recent items. Tap on the option of your choice.
7. To exit this submenu screen and return to the main Notifications screen in Settings (refer to Figure 4.7), tap on the left-pointing arrow icon appearing in the upper-left corner of the submenu screen. In this case, the icon says FaceTime. This will send you back to the previous submenu screen. Again, tap on the left-pointing icon that appears in the upper-left corner of this screen, which in this case is labeled Notifications, to return to the main Notifications screen in Settings.
8. Upon returning to the app listing displayed under the In Notification Center heading, tap on another app label to customize the settings associated with how the Notification Center app will handle that app. Repeat the steps outlined here for each app.

TIP If you turn the virtual switch associated with the Notification Center option for a particular app to the off position, this app will no longer be monitored by Notification Center. However, you can customize how messages, alerts, alarms, and/or notifications generated by this app will be displayed by adjusting the Alert Style, Badge App Icon, and/or View in Lock Screen settings, also displayed in this Settings submenu screen. Again, this is something you need to do with each app.

When you turn off the virtual switch associated with the Notification Center label, that app is removed from the In Notification Center listing, but will now be displayed in the Not in Notification Center list.

WHAT TO DO WHEN ALERTS, NOTIFICATIONS, AND ALARMS GET ANNOYING

If you allow all the compatible apps running on your iPad or iPhone to constantly notify you anytime one of the apps generates a message, an alert, an alarm, or a notification, not only will you discover that the Notification Center window quickly becomes cluttered, but you'll also be distracted by the constant flow of alerts.

To keep your Notification Center window organized, while customizing settings for your apps, follow these basic strategies:

- Turn off the Notification Center option if the app is not important to you.
- Limit the display of recent items that pertain to each app to either one or five.
- For apps like Mail, you can determine how many lines of content are displayed for each new message in the Notification Center window. Choose an option that gives you enough information but doesn't utilize too much onscreen space in the Notification Center window, thus causing clutter. This is a personal preference.

TIP For your most important apps (the ones that keep track of information that's essential to your daily life or work), from the Settings app, tap on the Notifications option, and then for those critical apps, turn on Notification Center. In addition, under the Alert Style option (refer to Figure 4.8), choose Alerts. Also, turn the virtual switches associated with Badge App Icon, Sounds (if applicable), and View in Lock Screen to the on position.

Doing this will allow those essential apps to use audible alerts, if applicable, plus display their own message windows (in addition to or instead of the Notification Center window). Displaying an Alert window requires you to take an action (such as tapping on a specific icon to acknowledge the message), even when the iPhone or iPad is in sleep mode.

STAY INFORMED OF YOUR APPOINTMENTS, DEADLINES, AND RESPONSIBILITIES

For Notification Center to do its job and keep you informed about important appointments, deadlines, and responsibilities, it's important that you fully utilize the Calendar and/or Reminders apps that come preinstalled with iOS 5 on your iPhone or iPad.

NOTE Calendars and Reminders are standalone apps. However, they can easily be integrated with Notification Center so that you are alerted of upcoming appointments, responsibilities, and deadlines.

When you maintain your scheduling and calendar information using the Calendar app (or sync data to this app from your primary computer or a compatible online-based scheduling app), and then set Notification Center to work with Calendar, you will easily be able to stay informed of your upcoming meetings, appointments, deadlines, and responsibilities.

HOW TO LIMIT THE CONTENT IN THE NOTIFICATION CENTER WINDOW

Certain apps, like Mail, allow you to choose how much content you get to view for each listing in the Notification Center window. For example, you can opt to view between zero and five lines of an incoming email's content (in addition to the name of the message's sender, its subject, and when it was received).

If specific adjustments relating to how much content for each listing can be viewed in the Notification Center window, this can be customized from within Settings. To choose how much of an incoming email's content you'll see, for example, follow these steps:

1. From the Home Screen, tap on the Settings app icon to launch Settings.
2. Tap on the Mail, Contacts, Calendars option that's listed under the main Settings menu.
3. In the Mail, Contacts, Calendars submenu, look for the Mail heading, and then tap on the Preview option.
4. From the Preview screen, tap on how many lines of the incoming email you want to preview. This decision impacts what you'll see both in the Mail app itself and in the Notification Center window. Your options include between zero and five lines. Figure 4.9 shows a sample incoming mail listing in which just one line of the message's body is displayed, and Figure 4.10 shows a sample incoming message listing in which five lines of a message's body are displayed.

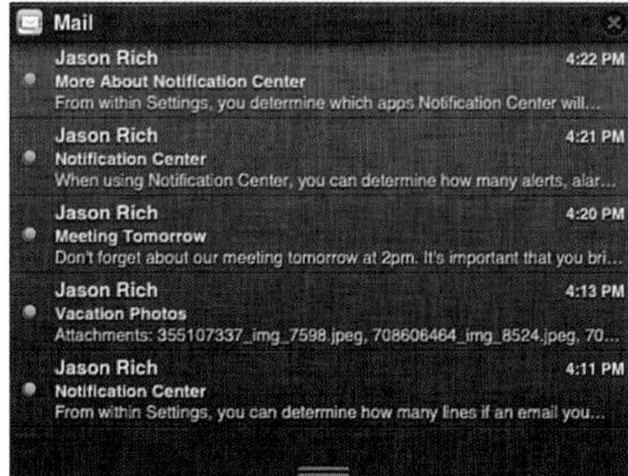

FIGURE 4.9

Here, the user selected to view just one line of each incoming email's body text in the Notification Center window.

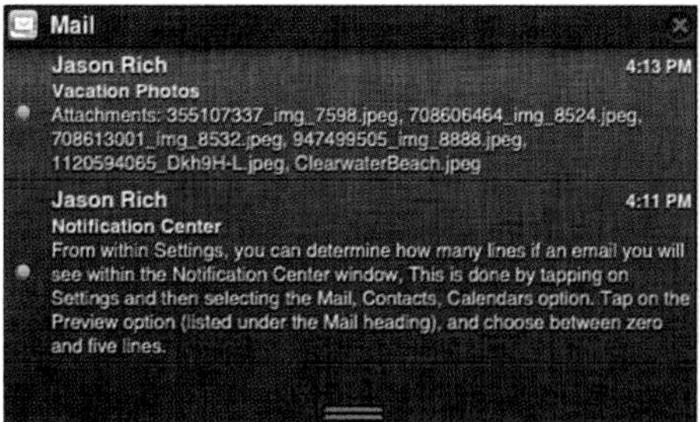

FIGURE 4.10

In this example, five lines of an incoming email message's body, as well as the sender, the email's subject, and the date it was received, can easily be seen in the Notification Center window.

INFORMATIVE NOTIFICATION CENTER WIDGETS YOU CAN ADD TO YOUR iPHONE

Available on the iPhone, Notification Center widgets are mini apps that appear at the top and/or bottom of the Notification Center window. They display very specific information.

A Weather Widget and Stock Widget come preinstalled in iOS 5 for the iPhone. When turned on and customized, the Weather Widget (which is automatically tied to the Weather app) shows the current weather forecast for your location (as shown in Figure 4.11), but in a concise way.

FIGURE 4.11

Quickly see the current weather forecast, which includes the current temperature, the day's high and low temperature, and a graphic that depicts the overall weather outlook for the day.

Meanwhile, the Stock Widget offers a scrolling ticker of the stocks and investments you have stored as part of a personal portfolio using the iPhone's Stocks app (which also comes preinstalled).

iOS 5 WHAT'S NEW From the Weather or Stocks app on your iPhone, customize the settings to determine what data is displayed in the Notification Center window. The Weather Widget or Stocks Widget, which is an optional feature of Notification Center, will then pull data from the respective app, such as your current city's weather forecast, or details about specific stocks or investments in your portfolio, and display that data in a separate section of the Notification Center window.

With the launch of iOS 5, the Weather Widget and Stock Widget are the only widgets that come preinstalled. In the future, Apple and/or third-party developers will most likely release additional widgets that can be used with Notification Center to display specific information in the Notification Center window.

TIP To turn off the Weather Widget or Stock Widget so that related data does not appear in your iPhone's Notification Center window, launch Settings, and then tap on the Notifications option. Under the In Notification Center heading, look for the Weather Widget or Stock Widget option and tap on it.

When the Weather Widget (or Stock Widget) submenu screen appears, turn the virtual switch that's associated with Notification Center to the off position. The Weather Widget or Stock Widget will then be listed under the Not in Notification Center heading, and when you access the Notification Center window, the widget(s) you turned off will no longer appear.

To customize the Weather Widget, from your iPhone's Home Screen, tap on the Weather icon. When the weather forecast screen appears, as shown in Figure 4.12, tap on the circular Info (i) icon.

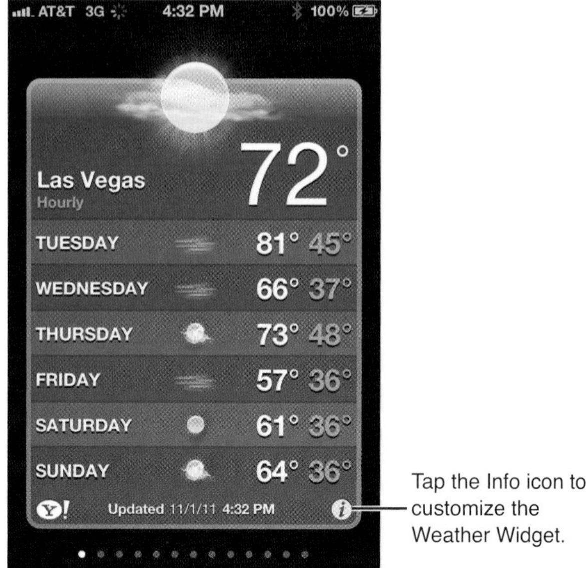

FIGURE 4.12

The main Weather app on the iPhone.

At the top of the Weather setup screen (shown in Figure 4.13), turn the virtual switch associated with the Local Weather option to the on position. This is data that will be displayed by the Weather Widget in Notification Center. If this option is turned off, the city that's currently active in the Weather app is displayed in the Weather Widget.

FIGURE 4.13

From the Weather app's setup screen, turn the virtual switch associated with the Local Weather option to the on position.

! CAUTION For the Weather Widget or Stock Widget to work and display current information, your iPhone must have access to the Internet. Otherwise, the most recent data stored on the iPhone (from when the app last had access to the Internet) is displayed. This information can be misleading or outdated.

To customize the Stock Widget, from the iPhone's Home Screen, launch the Stocks app. Next, tap the circular Info icon. To add stocks or investments, tap the plus-sign icon that appears in the upper-left corner of the screen. Or to delete a stock or an investment from the portfolio stored in the app, tap on the red-and-white icon containing the negative sign that's next to the investment you want to remove.

When you've customized your portfolio, tap on the blue-and-white Done icon displayed in the upper-right corner of the screen. This will return you to the main Stocks screen. This is the information that will now appear as part of the Stocks Widget in the Notification Center window (as shown in Figure 4.14).

FIGURE 4.14

The Stock Widget appears at the bottom of the Notification Center window. This is an iPhone-specific feature.

iOS 5 WHAT'S NEW If you're using an iPhone 4S, instead of relying on the Weather and Stock widget, for example, you can simply use Siri and ask your iPhone 4S for a weather forecast or an update on your investment portfolio.

To do this, activate Siri, and then when prompted, say something like, "What's today's weather forecast?" or "Do I need an umbrella?".

IN THIS CHAPTER

- How to use the Messages app on the iPhone or iPad
- How to send and receive text messages on your iPhone using your cellular service provider's text-messaging service, or use Apple's new iMessage service with your iPhone or iPad

COMMUNICATE EFFECTIVELY WITH iMESSAGE

Today's tweens and teens have a different way to communicate, and it's quickly spreading to adults as well. Most young people are equipped with a state-of-the-art cellphone these days. But instead of talking with their friends over the phone (and using up minutes of their airtime plan), or even conversing face to face, they often "talk" via text messaging.

Using short, text-based messages, and a newly evolved language composed of abbreviated terminology, such as "LOL" (meaning "laugh out loud") or "BRB" (meaning "be right back"), people of all ages have begun to rely on text messaging as a convenient way to communicate (as shown in Figure 5.1).

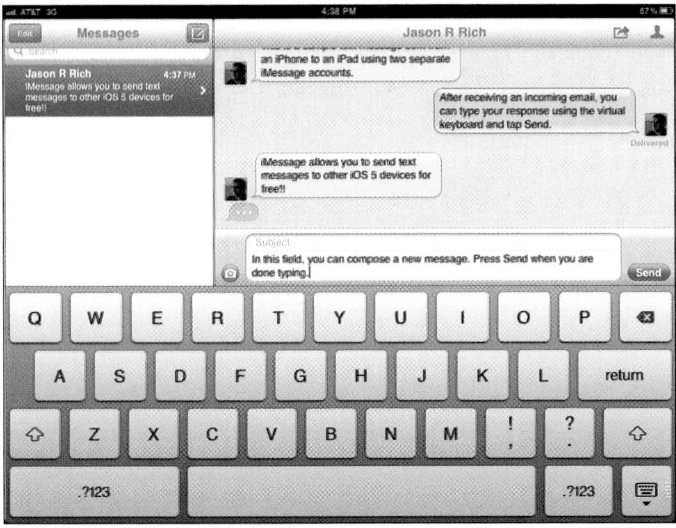

FIGURE 5.1

Text messaging is done using the Messages app. Text-based conversations are formatted to be easy to read and follow, and when users include a photo in their profiles on an iPad, a thumbnail-size image of them appears next to whatever text messages they send.

Every iPhone's cellular service plan through its wireless service provider has three components: voice, data, and text messaging. Upon subscribing to a plan, iPhone users choose a paid text-messaging plan that allows for the sending or receiving of a predetermined number of text messages per month, or you can pay extra for an unlimited text-messaging plan.

There are two types of text messaging:

- SMS stands for Short Message Service. It's the type of text messaging that's available through your cellular service provider. SMS messages have a 160-character limit.
- MMS stands for Multimedia Messaging Service. This is the type of text-messaging service that Apple utilizes for iMessage. It allows photos and video clips to be sent as part of messages, plus the text messages can be longer in length than 160 characters.

Text messaging using the service offered by your wireless service provider (such as AT&T Wireless, for example) allows iPhone users to send and receive messages and converse with any other cellphone user, regardless of which service provider their phone is registered with. So an iPhone user who uses AT&T Wireless can easily communicate with a cellphone user who uses Verizon Wireless or Sprint PCS as a cellular service provider.

On the iPhone, the process of composing, reading, sending, and receiving text messages is done using the Messages app. Because until now text messaging was done through a wireless cellular network (as opposed to via the Internet), this functionality was not available to iPad users.

However, with the release of iOS 5, not only was the Messages app enhanced with new features, it also was made compatible with Apple's new iMessage (MMS) service.

iOS 5 **WHAT'S NEW** iMessage is a free text-messaging service operated by Apple that utilizes the Web (as opposed to a cellular network), and allows iOS 5 device users to communicate, via unlimited text messages, with other iOS 5 device users, as long as the devices have access to the Web via a Wi-Fi or 3G connection.

If you're using an iPhone 4S, you can use Siri to dictate and send text messages using your voice. To do this, activate Siri and say something like, "Send text message to Jason Rich." When Siri says, "What would you like it to say?" Speak your message, and then confirm it. When prompted, tell Siri to send the text message you dictated. This feature works best if details about the person to which you're sending a text message are already stored in your Contacts database. Siri can also be used to read your newly received text messages, without having to look at or touch the iPhone's screen.

QUICK START: APPLE'S iMESSAGE SERVICE

Whether your iPhone or iPad is connected to the Internet via a Wi-Fi or 3G connection, using iMessage with the Messages app that comes preinstalled on your device, you now can communicate via text messages with other iOS 5 device users. Unlike the text-messaging services available through wireless service providers, Apple's iMessage service is free of charge, and it allows for an unlimited number of text messages to be sent and received.

The service also taps into your iPhone or iPad's other functions and allows for the easy sharing of photos, videos, locations, and contacts; plus, it works seamlessly with Notification Center.

iOS 5 **WHAT'S NEW** In addition to allowing you to communicate with individual people via text messaging, when the iMessage service is used with the Messages app, it enables you to send the same text message to multiple recipients. It uses a feature referred to as *group messaging* that enables everyone in that group to participate in the same text-message–based conversation.

The iMessage service is a hybrid between traditional text messaging that people have become accustomed to using on their cellphones, and instant messaging, which is something done on a computer that also involves communicating in real time by exchanging text-based messages (in addition to photos or web links, for example) with the person you're conversing with.

iMessage also enables you to participate in text-based but real-time conversations. You can see when someone is typing a message to you (as they're typing), and then you can view and respond to the message a fraction of a second after it is sent. (When someone is actively typing a message during a conversation on iMessage, a bubble with three periods in it appears. This is shown in Figure 5.1.)

NOTE To utilize iMessage with the Messages app, your iPhone or iPad must have access to the Internet. When you're using traditional text messaging (through your wireless service provider), your iPhone must have access to the service's cellular network.

SET UP A FREE iMESSAGE ACCOUNT

Because traditional text messaging is tied to a cellphone, which has a unique phone number, there is no need to have a separate username or account name when using the text-messaging feature through your cellular service provider. If you know someone's cellphone number, you can send a text message to that person from your cellphone (and vice versa). However, because iMessage is web-based, before using this service, you must set up a free iMessage account, which is tied to either your Apple ID or an existing email address.

The first time you launch the Messages app to use it with the iMessage service, you'll be instructed to set up a free account using your existing Apple ID (as shown in Figure 5.2). Or, instead of using your Apple ID, tap on the Create New Account option to create an account that's linked to another existing email address.

NOTE iPhone users can associate their cellphone number with their iMessage account to send and receive text messages using this service. However, an Apple ID or existing email address can be used as well.

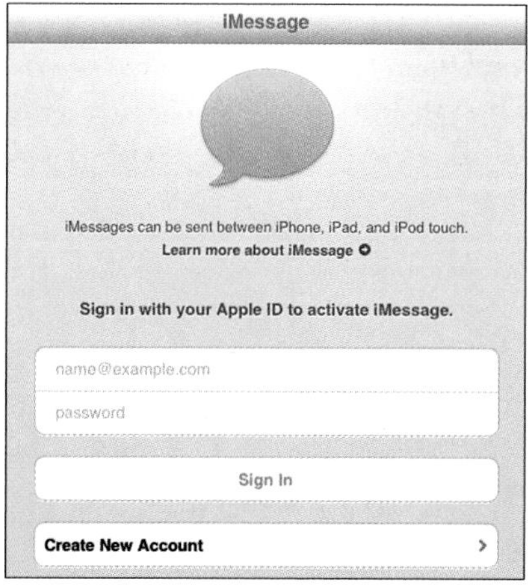

FIGURE 5.2

The first time you use the iMessage service, you'll need to set up a free account that can be linked to your Apple ID or any email address. (The same is true the first time you use FaceTime for videoconferencing.)

TIP If you've upgraded your iPhone to iOS 5, when you first launch Messages, you might discover the app automatically uses your existing Apple ID to establish your free iMessage account. You can modify this in the Settings app by selecting the Messages option from the main Settings menu.

To do this, you'll need to complete the information requested from the New Account screen (shown in Figure 5.3). This includes entering your first and last name and providing an email address. You also need to create and verify a password for the account, plus create a security question and provide an answer to that question. Finally, enter your birth month and day, and choose your country or region.

When the requested New Account information is entered, tap on the blue-and-white Done icon in the upper-right corner of the New Account window. Keep in mind that if you simply enter your existing Apple ID information to set up your iMessage account, and then tap on the Sign In icon (refer to Figure 5.2), the initial process for establishing an iMessage account is quick.

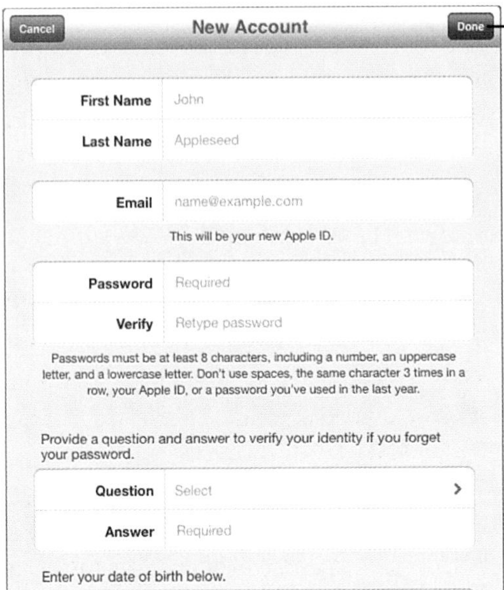

FIGURE 5.3

To begin using the Messages app and iMessage, provide the information requested on the New Account screen.

> **TIP** Just as when you're using FaceTime, the unique Apple ID, email address, or iPhone phone number you use to set up your iMessage account is how people will find you and be able to communicate with you via text messages. So if you want someone to be able to send you text messages via iMessage, that person will need to know the Apple ID or email address you used to set up the account. Likewise, to send someone a text message via iMessage, you'll need to know the Apple ID or email address the recipient used to set up his or her iMessage account.
>
> If you attempt to send a text message to someone's email address that is not registered with iMessage as an active account, the contents of your intended text message will be sent as a traditional email message and appear in the recipient's email inbox.

PROS AND CONS OF USING iMESSAGE

The biggest benefit to using iMessage over other text-messaging services is that it's free, and you can send/receive an unlimited number of messages. And because iMessage utilizes the Messages app, you'll discover that the app itself nicely integrates with other features, functions, and apps on your iPhone or iPad. Using the Camera app, for example, you can easily snap a photo or shoot a video clip using your iOS 5 device, and then use Messages to send that image or video clip to one or more friends via iMessage (without posting it in a public forum). Or if you're enjoying a cup of coffee at a local cafe, you can quickly share your exact location with a handful of friends and use iMessage to send out an invite for other people to join you.

If you're away from your iPhone or iPad when an incoming text message arrives, don't worry. The Notification Center app can continuously monitor the Messages app and will inform you of any missed messages in the Notification Center window.

Another convenient feature of iMessage is that you can begin a text-message–based conversation using your iPhone, for example, and then at any time switch to using your iPad and continue that conversation.

All text messages that are sent and received are saved, in reverse chronological order, and categorized by the person you communicated with. Until you manually delete the conversation, you always have a record of what was said, accompanied by the time and date messages were sent/received.

Currently, the biggest drawback to iMessage is that it's compatible only with iOS 5 devices, meaning you can send and receive text messages only with other iPhone, iPad, and iPod touch users who have upgraded to iOS 5 and who are active on the iMessage service. In the future, Apple might open up the service to all Mac users and/or all Internet users.

Another potential drawback to the iMessage service is that to find and communicate with someone, you must know the Apple ID or email address used to set up the person's iMessage account. However, after you know this, sending and receiving text messages with that person becomes a straightforward process. You can store the person's account information in your Contacts database (which links to the Messages app).

TIPS AND TRICKS FOR USING THE MESSAGES APP

The Messages app, which is used to access the iMessage service on the iPhone or iPad, or for iPhone users to send/receive text messages via their cellular service provider, can be launched from the device's Home Screen.

The Messages app on the iPhone has two main screens: a summary of text-message conversations that's labeled Messages, and an actual conversation screen that's labeled at the top of the screen using the name of the person's you're conversing with. Both of these screens have a handful of icon-based commands available that give you access to the app's features and functions.

On the iPad, the Messages screen is divided into two main sections (as shown in Figure 5.4). On the left is a listing of previous text-based conversations you've participated in. The heading at the top of this listing (displayed near the upper-left corner of the screen) is Messages, and below it, you'll see the names of the people you've previously conversed with using this app.

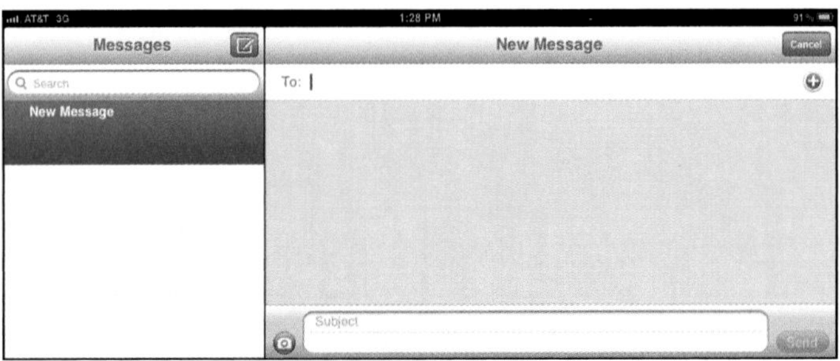

FIGURE 5.4

On the iPad, the Messages app's screen is split into two sections (shown here). On the iPhone, this information is divided into two separate screens.

When Messages is running, the right side of the iPad screen is the active conversation window. From here, you can initiate a new text-message–based conversation or respond to incoming text messages, one at a time.

> **NOTE** When you need to type text messages, the iPhone or iPad's virtual keyboard appears. To give you more onscreen real estate to reread a long conversation, tap on the Hide Keyboard key that always appears near the lower-right corner of the virtual keyboard when it's visible.

CREATE AND SEND A TEXT MESSAGE

The first time you launch Messages on the iPad, the New Message screen will be visible, the cursor will be flashing on the To field, and the virtual keyboard will be displayed (refer to Figure 5.4). If you have contact information stored in the Contacts app, as soon as you start typing in the To field, Messages will attempt to match up existing contacts with the name, cellphone number, or email address you're currently typing. When the intended recipient's name appears (because it's already stored in Contacts), tap on it.

To enter a recipient's name, cellphone number, Apple ID, or email address from scratch, simply type it using the iPhone or iPad's virtual keyboard.

Using an iPhone, from the Messages screen, tap in the New Message icon that's displayed in the upper-right corner to create a new outgoing text message and establish a new conversation.

TIP After you've sent and received text messages using the Messages app, to initiate a new text-message conversation with someone, tap on the New Message icon that appears in the upper-right corner of the Messages screen on the iPhone, or next to the Messages heading on the upper-left side of the iPad's screen.

To quickly search your Contacts database to find one or more recipients for your text messages, you can also tap on the blue-and-white plus icon in the To field as you're composing a new message. A scrollable list of all contacts stored in Contacts displays, along with a Search field you can use to search your contacts database from within the Messages app.

iOS 5 WHAT'S NEW If you're using an iPhone, to use your cellular service provider's text-messaging service to send a message to another cellphone user, enter the recipient's cellphone number in the To field of a new message.

If you're using an iPhone or iPad to send a text message to another iOS 5 device user via iMessage, in the To field, enter the recipient's Apple ID or the email address the user has linked with his iMessage account. (If the person is using an iPhone, his iMessage account might be associated with his iPhone's phone number, based on how he initially set up the account.)

In your Contacts database, you can create a separate field for someone's iMessage username, or when viewing the person's Contacts listing, simply tap on the appropriate contact information based on how you want to send the text message.

After filling in the To field with one or more recipients, tap on the optional Subject field (on the iPad only) to create a subject for your text message, and then tap on the blank field located to the left of the Send icon to begin typing your text message. On the iPhone, just a blank field for the body of your text message will be available, displayed to the left of the Send icon.

If you're only sending text within your message, enter the text and then tap on the blue-and-white Send icon. Or to attach a photo or video clip to your outgoing text message, tap on the camera icon that's displayed to the left of the field where you're typing the text message.

When you tap on the camera icon as you're composing a text message, two command options will be displayed (shown in Figure 5.5): Take Photo or Video and Choose Existing. Tap on the Take Photo or Video option to launch the Camera app from within Messages, and quickly snap a photo or shoot a video clip using your iPhone or iPad's built-in camera.

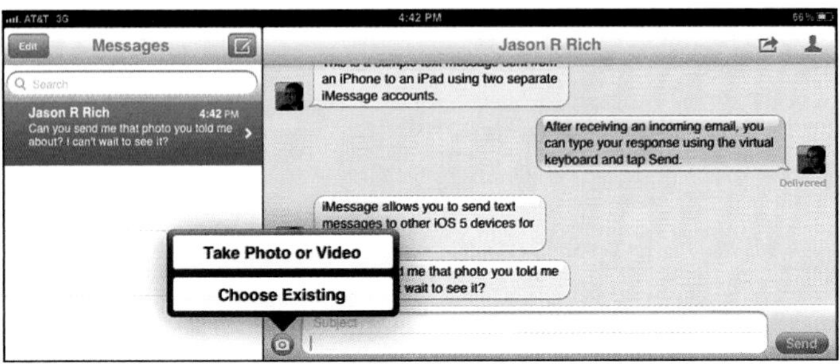

FIGURE 5.5

After tapping on the camera icon, choose to take a photo using your device's built-in camera, or select a photo or video clip that's already stored on your phone or tablet.

If you already have the photo or video clip stored on your phone or tablet that you want to share, tap on the Choose Existing option to launch the Photos app from within Messages, and then tap on the thumbnail for the photo or video clip you want to attach to the message.

When the photo or video clip has been attached to the outgoing text message, and you've typed any text that you want to accompany it, tap on the Send key to send the message.

! CAUTION Beware of the iPhone or iPad's auto-correction feature when texting. When turned on, your iOS device will automatically "fix" misspelled or incorrectly typed words. However, this auto-correction feature is not always accurate, especially if you're using abbreviations in your text messages, and could result in an embarrassing situation.

To turn on or off the Auto-Correction feature, launch the Settings app and select the General option from the main Settings menu. Scroll down to the Keyboard option, and tap on it. Tap on the virtual on/off switch associated with the Auto-Correction feature to turn it on or off.

As a general rule, whether you're composing text messages, email, or documents or using an instant messaging app on your iOS device, proofread everything carefully before tapping the Send icon.

PARTICIPATING IN A TEXT-MESSAGE CONVERSATION

As soon as you tap Send to initiate a new text-message conversation and send an initial message, the New Message window transforms into a conversation window, with the recipient's name displayed at the top center (as shown in Figure 5.6). On the left side of the conversation window will be the messages you've sent.

Displayed along the left margin of the conversation window will be the recipient's responses, shown within text bubbles. As the text-message–based conversation continues and eventually scrolls off the screen, use your finger to scroll upward or downward to view what's already been said.

FIGURE 5.6

The conversation window in the Messages app enables you to participate in a text-message–based conversation and easily determine who sent which message, based on which side of the screen it's displayed on.

> **TIP** Whenever there's a pause between the sending of a message and the receipt of a response, the Messages app automatically inserts the date and time in the center of the screen so that you can later easily track the time period during which each conversation took place. This is particularly helpful if there are long gaps and the conversation did not take place in real time.

On the iPhone, tap on the Edit icon in the upper-right corner of the screen to access command icons for deleting individual text messages, deleting entire text-message conversations, or forwarding a single message (or complete conversation) to someone else. On the iPad (shown in Figure 5.7), tap on the blue rectangle with an arrow at the bottom of the conversation screen to access similar command icons.

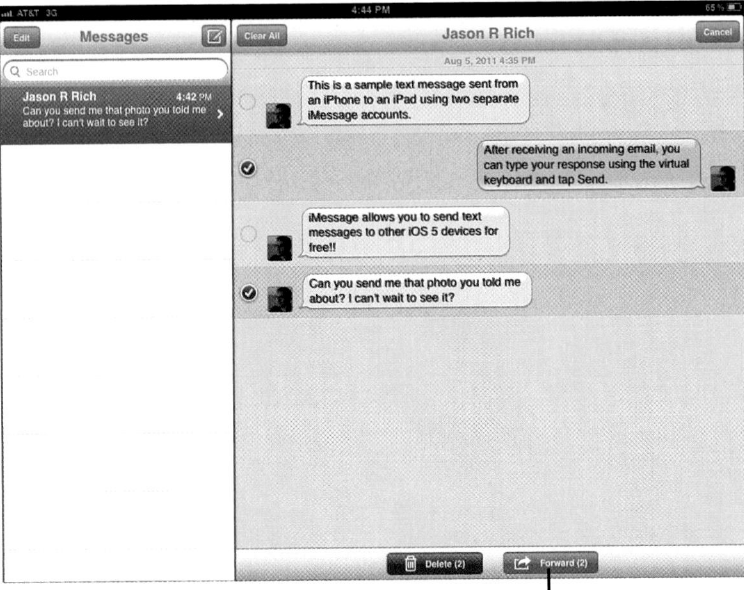

FIGURE 5.7

As you're conversing with someone via the Messages app, you can delete individual text messages or entire conversations, or forward them to other recipients.

> **TIP** From the Messages conversation screen on an iPad, tap on the person-shaped icon that's displayed in the upper-right corner of the conversation window to view the complete Contacts database entry for the person you're conversing with.

To delete entire conversations from within the Messages app, from the Messages screen on the iPhone (or the Messages listing on the left side of the iPad screen), swipe your finger from left to right along the listing for the conversation you want to delete. When the red-and-white Delete icon appears, tap on it to delete that entire conversation (as opposed to individual text messages within a conversation).

RESPONDING TO AN INCOMING TEXT MESSAGE

Depending on how you set up the Messages app from within Settings, you can be notified of an incoming text message in a number of ways. For example, notification of a new text message can be set to appear in the Notification Center window. Or if the Messages app is already running, a new message alert will be heard and a new message listing will appear on the Messages screen (iPhone) or under the Messages heading on the left side of the iPad screen.

TIP When a new message arrives, a blue dot appears to the left of the new message's listing (under the Messages heading on the iPad or on the Messages screen on the iPhone). The blue dot indicates it's a new, unread text message.

To read the incoming text message and enter into the conversation window and respond, tap on the incoming message listing. If you're looking at the listing in the Notification Center window, for example, and you tap on it, the Messages app will then launch, and the appropriate conversation window will automatically open.

After reading the incoming text message, use the virtual keyboard to type your response in the blank message field, and then tap the Send icon to send the response message.

CAUTION This should be common sense, but if you look around as you're out and about, you'll see it clearly isn't. Under no circumstances should you be attempting to drive and use text messaging on your iPhone or iPad at the same time. Likewise, as you're walking down the street or crossing a busy intersection, don't try multitasking by also sending or reading text messages. Every day, numerous accidents happen (some very serious) as a result of people just like yourself sending or reading text messages when they should be focused on something else.

RELAUNCH OR REVIEW PAST CONVERSATIONS

From the Messages screen on the iPhone, or from the left side of the screen on the iPad when the Messages app is running, you can view a listing of all saved text-message conversations. The Messages app automatically saves all text messages until you manually delete them.

Under the Messages heading on the iPad (or on the Messages screen on the iPhone), you'll see a listing, displayed in reverse chronological order, of all text-message conversations you've participated in to date. Each listing displays the person's name, the date and time of the last message sent or received, and a summary of the last message sent or received. Tap on any of the listings to relaunch that conversation in the Conversation window. Remember that a blue dot on the left side of the listing indicates an unread message. You can either reread the entire conversation or continue the conversation by responding to the last message that was sent or by sending a new message to that person.

By tapping on one conversation listing at a time, you can quickly switch between conversations and participate in multiple conversations at once.

On the iPhone, to exit the conversation screen you're currently viewing, tap on the left-pointing arrow icon that's displayed in the upper-left corner of the screen. It's labeled Messages (see Figure 5.8).

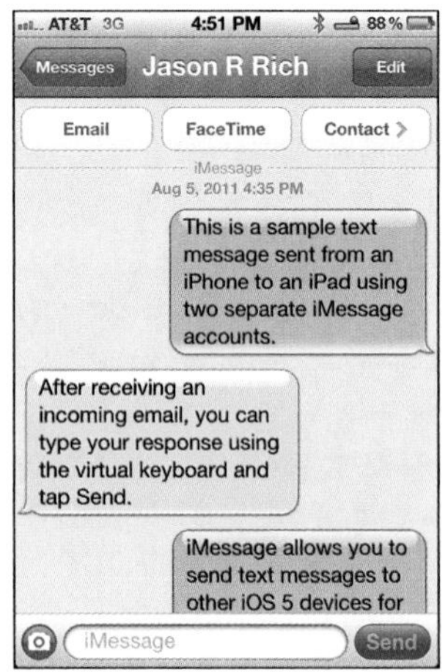

FIGURE 5.8

To exit a text-message conversation in Messages on the iPhone, tap on the left-pointing arrow icon displayed near the upper-left corner of the screen.

On the iPad, to exit a conversation, tap on one of the other listings under the Messages heading on the left side of the screen.

To exit the Messages app altogether, press the Home button.

From the Messages screen on the iPhone (or the Messages listing on the iPad that's displayed on the left side of the screen), tap on the Edit icon to quickly delete entire conversations with specific people. To do this, tap on the red-and-white icon that's displayed next to the listing under the Messages heading once you tap the Edit icon.

WHAT'S NEW You can set up Notification Center to alert you of new incoming text messages in the Notification Center window. This setup is done once from within the Settings app. You can also set it up so that your iPhone or iPad displays a banner or an alert on the screen, shows a Badge App Icon, and/or displays a message on the Lock Screen when a new incoming text message arrives.

To adjust these settings, launch the Settings app from the Home Screen, tap on the Notification option, and then adjust the Notification Center, Show, Alert Style, Badge App Icon, Show Preview, Repeat Alert, and View in Lock Screen options that are displayed under the Messages heading.

When you're using Messages on the iPhone, near the top of each conversation screen will be three command icons (refer to Figure 5.8), labeled Email, FaceTime, and Contact. Tap on Email to compose and send an email message to the person you're currently conversing with using the Messages app. The Mail app will automatically load, and the To field of the message will be filled in with the recipient's email address.

Tap on the FaceTime icon to initiate a FaceTime videoconference if both you and the person you're conversing with using Messages have access to a Wi-Fi Internet connection and an active FaceTime account.

Tap on the Contact icon to view the person's entry within your device's Contacts database, if the entry exists, or to create an entry for the person you're currently conversing with using Messages. While viewing a Contacts entry, you can tap on any phone number (when using an iPhone) to dial that number and initiate a call.

CAUTION Because they lack a front-facing camera, the iPhone 3G, iPhone 3Gs, and the original iPad are not compatible with FaceTime. Even if you upgrade to iOS 5, the FaceTime functionality won't work on these older iPhone and iPad models.

CUSTOMIZE THE MESSAGES APP

In Settings, you can customize several settings related to the Messages app. To do this, launch Settings from the Home Screen, and then tap on the Messages option that's displayed in the main Settings menu.

In the Messages setup window, you can turn on or off the iMessage service altogether, plus make adjustments that are relevant to sending and receiving text messages from your iOS 5 device. For example, by adjusting the virtual switch associated with the Send Read Receipts option to the on position, you will allow message senders to be notified as soon as you have read their text message(s). Thus, if you send someone important or timely information via text message, you will be notified when it's received, and don't have to worry about whether the intended recipient received your message.

On the iPhone (as shown in Figure 5.9), you can also set preferences for using SMS text messages versus iMessage.

FIGURE 5.9

In Settings, you can customize the Messages app to work with your cellular service provider's text-message service and/or Apple's iMessage service, plus you can personalize a handful of related options.

IN THIS CHAPTER

- How to find and subscribe to the digital edition of your favorite newspapers and magazines
- How to use the new Newsstand app
- How to reading digital publications on your iPhone or iPad
- How to managing your recurring paid subscriptions

STAY CURRENT USING NEWSSTAND

Not only is your iPhone or iPad capable of finding and downloading eBooks (using an online-based service like Apple's iBookstore), it's also a powerful, easy-to-use eBook reader. However, new to iOS 5, your iPhone or iPad also now has access to an ever-growing newsstand that's filled with digital newspaper and magazine selections that can be downloaded and managed using the Newsstand app or from the App Store.

When it has access to the Web via a Wi-Fi or 3G connection, your iOS device can access the App Store to find, subscribe to, and then download issues from hundreds of popular newspapers and full-color magazines, which you can then read on your device's screen using proprietary apps developed by each publication's publisher. (In some cases, a Wi-Fi connection is required to download a publication's content directly to your iOS device.)

The digital edition of most newspapers and magazines is identical to the printed edition in terms of appearance, content, and page layout; however, the digital publication is readable on your iPhone or iPad's screen.

Figure 6.1 shows a page of the *New York Daily News* newspaper. When you use the Daily News app to read the newspaper, the app also enables you to access the newspaper's website without first launching Safari.

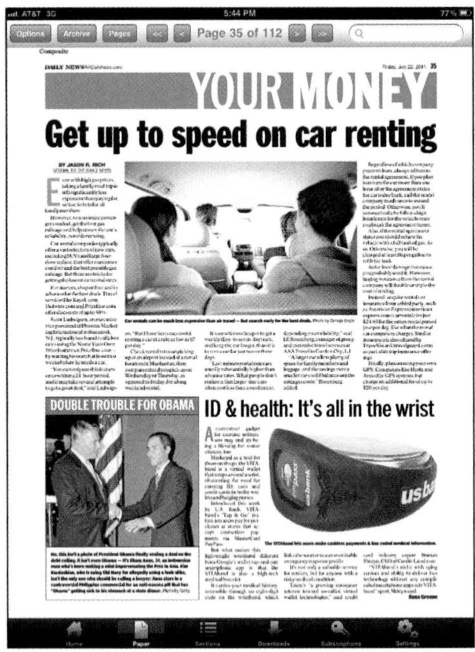

FIGURE 6.1

This sample page from the digital edition of the New York Daily News looks identical to the printed newspaper.

Some digital publications also offer bonus content that's not found in the printed publication, plus unique interactive elements, such as the capability to tap on a photo within a newspaper and stream a related video from the Internet.

There are several ways to find and access the digital editions of newspapers and magazines using your iOS 5 device. The easiest way, as you'll discover, is to use the new Newsstand app, which comes preinstalled on your iPhone or iPad. Newsstand is used to access the App Store but only to search for, subscribe to, and then manage digital publication apps and subscriptions.

WHY BUY DIGITAL PUBLICATIONS?

Reading your favorite newspaper and magazine in digital form has a few advantages. For example, you don't have to carry around the printed publication. In fact, you can store dozens or even hundreds of individual newspaper or magazine issues in your iOS device at any given time.

In addition, many digital editions of newspapers and magazines have interactive elements incorporated into them that is not available from the printed edition. For example, as you're reading the digital edition of *The New York Times*, you might discover a link to a video that's directly related to the article or news story you're reading. Or, instead of just one or two photos being displayed with an article, you might discover an onscreen link that opens an entire image gallery that showcases related photos.

Depending on the digital publication you're reading, you might discover the text in the publication is searchable by keyword, which makes finding exactly what you're looking for in an issue a much quicker process.

By working closely with the largest newspaper and magazine publishers in the U.S. and abroad, Apple now offers a vast selection of digital publications available through Newsstand and the App Store. Each publication requires its own proprietary app, which is free of charge, that you'll need to download and install on your device. This can be done from the App Store (on your primary computer, iPhone, or iPad) or using the Newsstand app (on your iOS 5 device).

After the app for a particular newspaper or magazine is downloaded and installed on your iPhone or iPad, you can pay for and download current (and sometimes past) issues of that publication, read the publication in its entirety, and access the bonus content or interactive elements associated with that publication.

Although the app associated with each digital publication is free, in most cases you'll need to pay for content. Just as you subscribe to traditionally printed newspapers and magazines or can purchase individual issues at a newsstand, the same is true with digital publications.

Some publications offered through Newsstand and the App Store come with a free sample issue, or a two-week or 30-day free trial subscription, after which you'll need to pay for content.

If you're already a paid subscriber to the printed edition of a publication, the publisher might offer you a free or discounted digital subscription, which you can read on your iOS device. However, if you want to subscribe to only the digital edition of a newspaper or magazine, the single-issue price will typically be between $.99 and $6.99, and a subscription will almost always cost a bit less than subscribing to the publication's printed counterpart.

In the *Popular Photography* magazine app, for example, you can either subscribe to and receive the current and future editions of the magazine or search through back issues (as shown in Figure 6.2) and purchase individual issues for $4.99 each.

FIGURE 6.2

After you've downloaded the proprietary app for a magazine, such as Popular Photography, *you can typically purchase back issues or the current issue without subscribing.*

> **! CAUTION** Although the Newsstand app is available on both the iPhone and the iPad, some of the proprietary apps developed by the newspaper and magazine publishers are iPad-specific and will not function on an iPhone. Or a scaled-down digital edition of the publication might be available for the iPhone that takes into account the smaller screen size.

SEARCH FOR YOUR FAVORITE PUBLICATIONS

There are several ways to discover whether digital editions of your favorite newspapers and magazines are available from the App Store and Newsstand. The easiest method is to use the App Store or Newsstand app on your iPhone or iPad and perform a search based on a publication name.

If a listing for the publication exists (as shown in Figure 6.3), this means there's a digital edition available. Next, determine whether the digital version is iPad-specific or whether it can be downloaded and read on an iPhone (or iPod touch) as well.

FIGURE 6.3

After you type "Sports Illustrated Magazine" in the Search field of the App Store, a listing for the iPad-specific app associated with this magazine is displayed. You can download it by tapping on the Free icon associated with the magazine's listing.

Download and launch the publication-specific app, and then follow the onscreen options within that app to take advantage of a free trial subscription, purchase a single issue of the publication, subscribe for a predetermined period, or sign up for a recurring (paid) subscription.

Figure 6.4 shows the subscription options displayed when the *Sports Illustrated* app is launched for the first time. From this screen, you can purchase the current issue or back issues. If you're already a paid subscriber to the magazine's print edition, you can sign in and receive the digital content of all available issues free.

TIP When a publisher offers print-edition subscribers free access to the digital edition of their publication(s), you will typically need to enter your subscription account number into the app. This number is usually displayed on the printed magazine's address label.

With the exception of taking advantage of a free issue or free trial subscription, purchasing single issues or a subscription will require an in-app purchase, which will be charged to the credit card associated with your Apple ID.

Instead of using the App Store to find, subscribe to, and manage subscriptions for digital publications, you also have the option of using the Newsstand app, which was designed exclusively for this purpose.

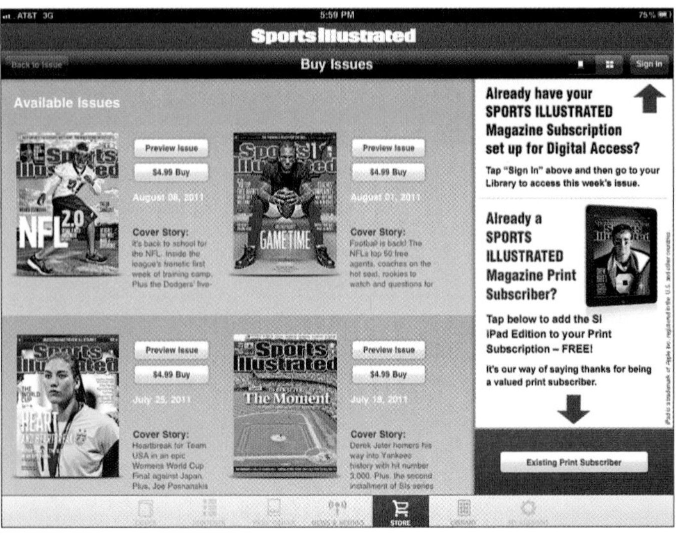

FIGURE 6.4

From the Sports Illustrated *app, you can purchase individual issues ($4.99 each) or get free access to the digital magazine if you're already a subscriber of the print edition.*

USE THE NEWSSTAND APP'S LATEST FEATURES

When it comes to acquiring content for your iPhone or iPad that's connected to the Internet, the iTunes app is used to find, purchase, and download music, TV shows, movies, and audiobooks, whereas iBooks is used to access iBookstore to find, purchase, download, and read eBooks. Newsstand, shown in Figure 6.5, is a digital newsstand app designed for finding and managing digital publications, along with their related apps and subscriptions (which can also be done from within the App Store).

All purchases made from Newsstand (or in-app purchases made using a publication's app) are charged to the credit card associated with your Apple ID account, just as if you were purchasing any other type of content from Apple, such as music from iTunes or an eBook from iBookstore.

The Newsstand app works very much like the App Store or iBooks when it comes to browsing online-based content (in this case, the digital editions of newspapers and magazines). To fully utilize this app, your iOS device will need access to the Internet.

FIGURE 6.5

You can launch Newsstand from the Home Screen and quickly access publications to which you subscribe.

To browse Apple's digital newsstand, tap on the Store icon that's displayed on the right side of the main Newsstand screen. You'll then be able to browse publications by title or subject, for example, plus determine the per-issue or subscription rates for the publications that are of interest. As you're browsing the newsstand, tap on a publication's cover graphic to learn more about it. If it's a publication you're interested in reading, opt to download the publication's free app.

The Newsstand shelf screen is used to manage all of your subscriptions and launch publication-specific apps. Or after it's loaded onto your iPhone or iPad, you can launch a specific publication's app from the Home Screen, just as you'd launch any app.

HOW TO CANCEL AUTOMATIC SUBSCRIPTION RENEWAL

If you purchase a single issue of a digital publication, this is considered a one-time purchase. In most cases (it depends on the publication), if you subscribe to a digital magazine or newspaper for a predetermined period, this too is considered a one-time purchase. However, in some cases, when your subscription to a digital publication expires, it will automatically be renewed unless you manually cancel the subscription. Or if you opt to purchase a recurring subscription for a publication, you will continuously be billed on a weekly, monthly, or annual basis, until you manually cancel the subscription.

A recurring subscription can be cancelled only from within the iTunes app, not from the publication's proprietary app that's used to read the publication. To manage your recurring subscriptions via the App Store on your iPhone or iPad (that's connected to the Internet), follow these steps:

1. From the Home Screen, launch the App Store app.
2. When the App Store launches, tap on the Featured or Top Charts icon that's displayed near the bottom of the screen.
3. When the Featured or Top Charts screen appears, scroll down to the very bottom of the screen (shown in Figure 6.6) by flicking your finger from the bottom of the screen toward the top.

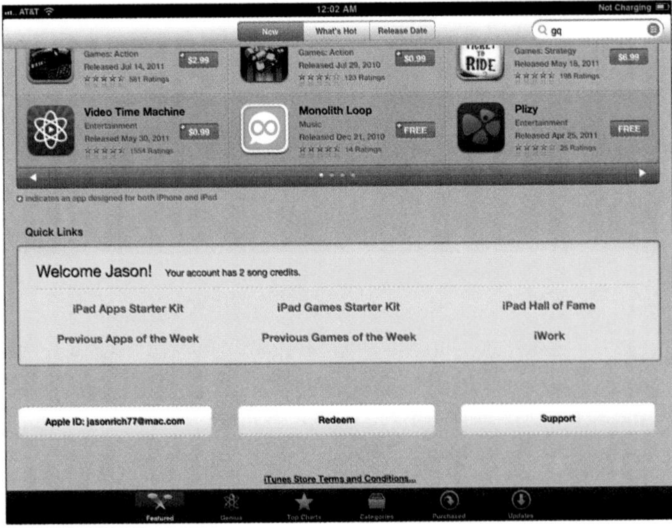

FIGURE 6.6

After App Store launches, tap on the Featured or Top Charts icon and scroll to the very bottom of the screen.

4. At the bottom of the screen are three icons, labeled Apple ID [Your Apple ID will be displayed], Redeem, and Support. Tap on the Apple ID icon.
5. An Apple ID window now appears on the screen. The three options available to you are View Account, Sign Out, and Cancel. Tap on the View Account option (shown in Figure 6.7).
6. When the Account screen appears, scroll downward until you see the Subscriptions heading. Tap on the Manage icon that's associated with it.

FIGURE 6.7

When the Apple ID window appears, tap on the View Account option to manage your recurring newspaper and magazine subscriptions.

7. A new window that lists each of your subscriptions will be displayed (as shown in Figure 6.8). Tap on any of the listings to manage that publication's recurring subscription. In Figure 6.8, the only active subscription is for the *Daily*.

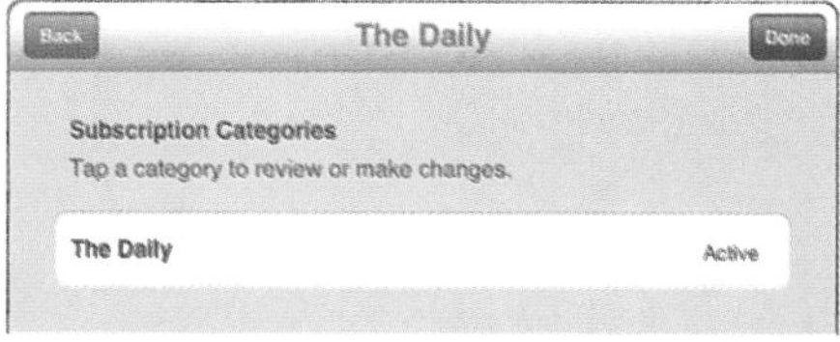

FIGURE 6.8

Choose an active subscription to manage from the displayed listing that appears. You can manage or change one subscription at a time.

8. For each publication, there's a separate subscription management screen that lists details about the duration of your current subscription. Under the Subscription Details heading will be options for renewing, changing, or cancelling your recurring subscription.
9. To turn off the Auto-Renewal feature of a subscription, turn the virtual switch associated with this option to off. If you do this, when the current subscription expires, it will not automatically renew and charge you. In Figure 6.9, under the Your Subscription heading, you can see that the purchased 7-day subscription expires on August 13, 2011 and the Auto-Renewal option is turned off. Thus, on August 14, before you can read the new issue of the *Daily*, a new subscription will be required. Under the Subscription Details heading, you can see there are 7-day and 1-year subscription options for this particular publication.

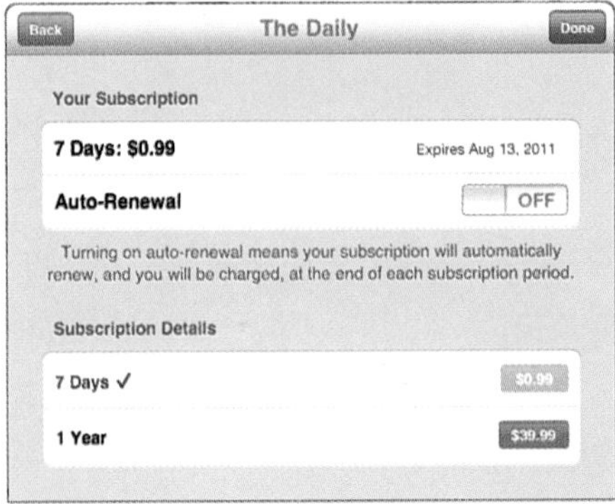

FIGURE 6.9

The subscription options for each subscription will be displayed. Shown here is the subscription page associated with the Daily *for the iPad.*

10. Each time you make a change to any of the options, they are saved automatically. To exit the subscription management section of the App Store, tap on the blue-and-white Done icon.

TAKE ADVANTAGE OF THE DIGITAL PUBLICATION READING EXPERIENCE

Unlike when visiting a website associated with a newspaper or magazine, a digital publication on your iPhone or iPad almost always has the same articles, photos, and ads as in the printed publication. Even the page layouts are often virtually identical (see Figure 6.10).

TIP When reading a digital publication, you'll typically use a right-to-left finger swipe to advance one page forward, or a left-to-right finger swipe to turn back one page. Most digital publications are designed to be read in portrait mode (vertically); some can also be read while you're holding your iPhone or iPad in landscape mode (horizontally). The direction is determined by the proprietary app associated with the publication.

When reading a digital publication on your iPhone or iPad, you can tap on embedded links to access related web-based multimedia content, tap on an interesting ad to access the advertiser's website (without manually launching Safari), or tap on an article title in the interactive table of contents to go directly to that page. In some digital publications, you can even zoom in on or out of specific articles, photos, or published content.

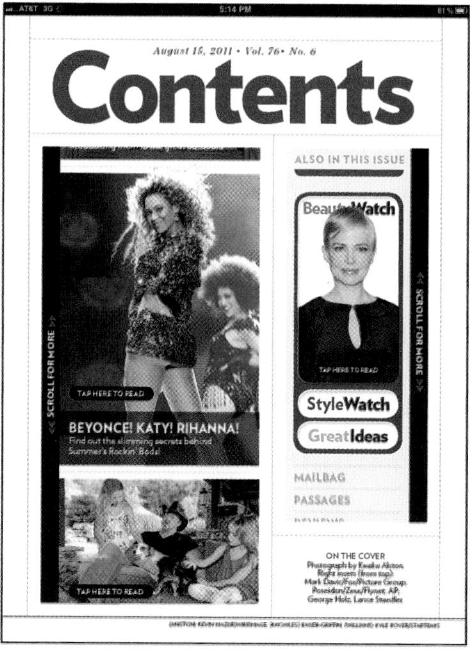

FIGURE 6.10

Unlike in the printed issue of People, *the Contents page of the digital edition is interactive and scrollable. You can tap on any article listed to jump to and read that article.*

Some publications let you bookmark interesting articles, print articles using your iPhone or iPad's AirPrint feature and a compatible printer, or share articles and/or photos from the publication via email or Twitter.

Some digital publications, such as *USA Today* and the *Daily*, feature interactive crossword puzzles or Sudoku puzzles that you can solve in the publication's app. As newspaper and magazine publishers create digital editions of their popular printed publications, they strive to offer value-added content or features that make the digital editions of their publications more interactive and interesting, as an incentive for subscribing to the digital edition.

For example, the digital edition of *USA Today*, which continues to offer a free subscription, uses the GPS feature built in to your iPhone or iPad to determine your location, and then displays the current weather forecast for that city on the main page. On the horoscope page, your daily horoscope is displayed, based on your birthday. Some apps also let you modify your location information manually; for example, so you can look up the weather forecast in another city.

When you subscribe to the digital edition of a publication through the App Store or Newsstand, new issues are downloaded to your iPhone or iPad automatically (your device must have Internet access). If you subscribe to the digital edition of a daily newspaper, such as the *New York Times* or the *Wall Street Journal*, you can set your device to download the latest issue every morning. You can manually download the current issue of your subscription by tapping on the refresh icon in the publication's app after you turn on Internet access by connecting to a Wi-Fi hotspot or by turning off Airplane mode.

IN THIS CHAPTER

- How to use iBooks to access iBookstore and shop for eBooks
- How to customize iBooks to transform your iPhone or iPad into the perfect eBook reader
- How to access and read PDF files on your iPhone or iPad using iBooks

7

CUSTOMIZE YOUR READING EXPERIENCE WITH iBOOKS

The Kindle eBook readers from Amazon.com and the Nook eBook readers from Barnes & Noble are inexpensive, lightweight, and ideal for doing one thing: reading eBooks. Your iPhone or iPad, on the other hand, is capable of doing many different tasks extremely well. Among your many options is to transform your iOS device into a powerful, yet easy-to-use eBook reader that has more functionality and customizable options than most Kindle or Nook models, not to mention a full-color touchscreen.

Anything having to do with shopping for, downloading, installing, and then reading eBooks on your iPhone or iPad is done using Apple's free iBooks app, which does not come preinstalled on your device. However, as soon as you begin using a new or newly upgraded iPhone or iPad, you'll be prompted to download and install the iBooks app.

iBooks has two main purposes. First, it's used to access Apple's online-based iBookstore. From iBookstore, you can browse an ever-growing collection of eBook titles (including traditional book titles from bestselling authors and major publishers that have been adapted into eBook form). Although some eBooks are free, most must be paid for.

TIP As with all purchases from iTunes, the App Store, or Newsstand, all online eBook purchases made from iBookstore get charged to the credit card associated with your Apple ID. Or these purchases can be paid for using a prepaid iTunes gift card.

After you've downloaded eBook titles to your iOS device (including your iPhone, iPad, or iPod touch), the iBooks app is used to transform your mobile device into an eBook reader, which accurately reproduces the appearance of each page of a printed book on your device's screen. So, reading an eBook is just like reading a traditional book in terms of the appearance of text, photos, or graphics on a page (or on the screen).

As you'll soon discover, as an eBook reader, iBooks allows you to customize the appearance of a book's pages. For example, you can select a font that is appealing to your eyes, choose a font size that's comfortable to read, and even turn on or off a sepia effect that adds a background color to the screen (which some people find less taxing on their eyes).

iBooks offers many features that make reading eBooks on your iOS device a pleasure, several of which will be explained shortly. For example, when you stop reading and exit the iBooks app (by pressing the Home button), the app automatically stores the page you're on using a virtual bookmark and reopens to that page when the iBooks app is restarted.

iOS 5 **WHAT'S NEW** iBooks allows you to store and manage a vast library of eBooks on your iOS device, the size of which is limited only by the storage capacity of the device itself. However, an iPhone 4, iPhone 4S, or iPad 2 with 16GB of storage can store hundreds of eBooks at once.

Thanks to iOS 5, however, all of your eBook purchases also automatically get saved to your iCloud account. Thus, you can easily download eBook titles you've previously purchased via iCloud when you want to access a particular eBook that is not currently saved on your device.

When used with iCloud, you can also begin reading a chapter of an eBook on your iPhone, for example, and then switch to reading that same book on your iPad, because even your virtual bookmarks get saved and synced.

DOWNLOAD AND INSTALL iBOOKS ON YOUR iOS DEVICE

iBooks is available free from the App Store. From your iPhone or iPad that's connected to the Internet, launch the App Store app. When you're connected to the App Store, use the Search feature in the app, and type "iBooks." Then, tap on the Search key to initiate your search.

NOTE Throughout this chapter, the term *purchased* eBooks refers to eBook titles you've already paid for, as well as free eBooks you've previously downloaded using iBookstore. In other words, it means all eBooks you've already acquired from iBookstore.

On the iPhone, access the Search feature by tapping on the Search icon displayed at the bottom of the screen. On the iPad, a Search field is constantly displayed in the upper-right corner of the App Store screen.

When the iBooks app listing appears in the App Store, tap on the Free icon to download and automatically install it.

TIP Your iPhone or iPad will need Internet access to download and install the iBooks app and browse or shop for eBooks via iBookstore. However, after one or more eBooks are loaded into your iOS device, the Internet is no longer required and can be turned off. Thus, you can read an eBook while on an airplane, for example, with your iPhone or iPad in Airplane Mode, as long as you preload the eBook(s) you want to read onto your device before your flight.

After the iBooks app is installed on your iPhone or iPad, launch the app from the device's Home Screen by tapping on the iBooks app icon.

THE iBOOKS MAIN LIBRARY SCREEN

When you launch iBooks for the first time, the app's main Library screen is displayed, which is also referred to as the Bookshelf screen. However, your virtual bookshelf will be empty (as shown in Figure 7.1). From this screen, tap on the Store icon to access Apple's iBookstore online service to browse and shop for eBooks. Your device must have access to the Internet to access iBookstore. On the iPhone, the Store icon is located in the upper-right corner of the Library (Bookshelf) screen. On the iPad, the Store icon can be found in the upper-left corner of the Library screen.

FIGURE 7.1

From the virtual Library (Bookshelf) screen, you can manage the eBook library stored on your iPhone or iPad. The iPhone version is shown here.

Typically, the Library screen displays all the eBook titles currently stored on your device (as shown in Figure 7.2). From this screen, you can manage your eBook library, access iBookstore, or access PDF files stored on your device.

FIGURE 7.2

Shown here is the Library screen on an iPad 2, with a collection of eBooks stored on the tablet.

After you've begun expanding your personal eBook library and have one or more eBook titles stored on your device, the cover art for each title gets displayed on the main Library (Bookshelf) screen. On the iPad, you can see an alternative view of this bookstore screen by tapping on one of the two formatting icons displayed in the upper-right corner of the screen, next to the Edit icon.

Figure 7.2 shows the default view. To see an alternative view, tap the icon that displays three horizontal lines (see Figure 7.3). To return to the default view, tap the icon showing four squares.

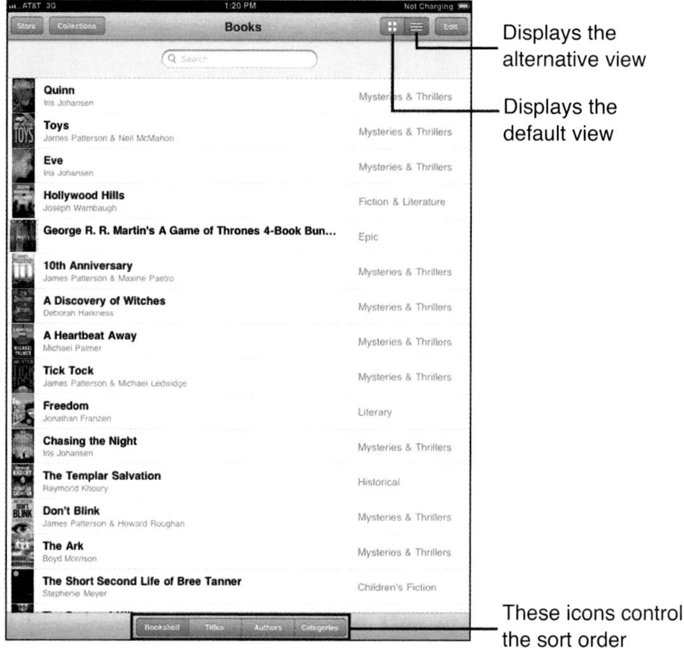

FIGURE 7.3

From this alternative Library screen, tap on any of the four icons at the bottom center of the screen to sort your eBook library.

While looking at this alternative view of the Library screen on your iPad, you can sort your eBook collection by tapping on any of the four icons that are displayed at the bottom center of the screen. They're labeled Bookshelf, Titles, Authors, and Categories.

You can change the order and sort your eBook collection based on which of the four icons displayed near the bottom center of the screen you select:

- Bookshelf displays your eBook titles in reverse chronological order, based on when each was downloaded to your device.
- Titles displays your eBook titles alphabetically by title.
- Authors displays the eBooks alphabetically, based on the author's name.
- Categories (shown in Figure 7.4) sorts your eBook collection by category, such as Historical, Literary, and Mysteries & Thrillers.

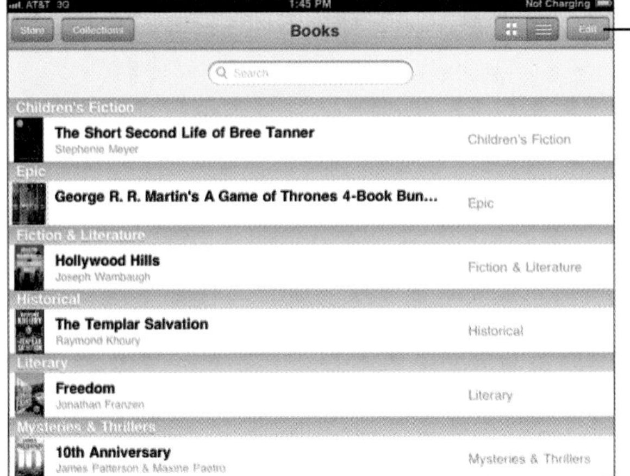

FIGURE 7.4

The Categories option allows you to sort your eBook collection based on the subject matter of each book and the category it falls into.

MANAGING YOUR EBOOK COLLECTION FROM THE LIBRARY SCREEN

As you're looking at the main Library (Bookshelf) screen with your collection of eBooks displayed, you can change the order in which the eBook titles are displayed, or delete eBook titles from your device, by tapping on the Edit icon. On the iPhone, the Edit icon is displayed in the upper-left corner of the screen. On the iPad, you'll find the Edit icon displayed in the upper-right corner of the screen. When you tap on Edit, new command icons, including Move and Delete, are displayed along the top of the screen.

ORGANIZE YOUR COLLECTION WITH THE MOVE COMMAND

After tapping on the Edit icon, tap on any eBook title(s) displayed on the Library screen (the virtual bookshelf). When you do this, both the Move and the Delete icons become active. On the iPad, the Select All icon (also displayed at the top of the screen) becomes active. The Select All icon enables you to quickly select all the eBook titles currently stored on your device instead of selecting one at a time.

When you tap on one or more eBook titles, a blue-and-white checkmark is displayed in the lower-right corner of the selected eBook's cover thumbnail (see Figure 7.5).

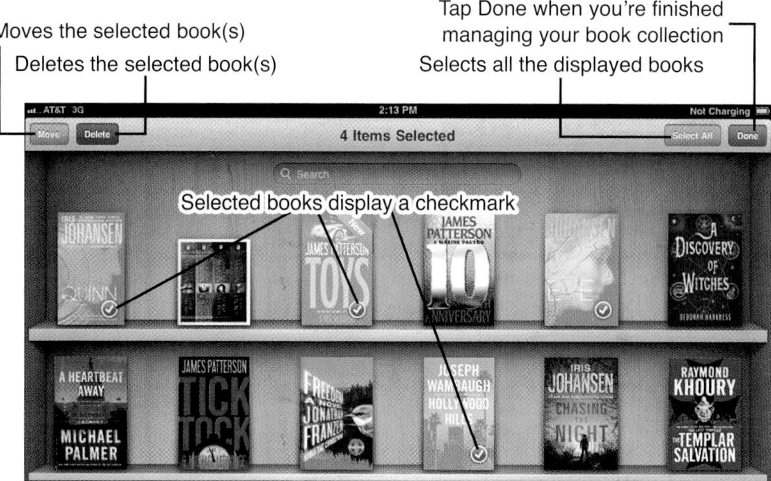

FIGURE 7.5

After tapping Edit, tap on one or more eBook titles displayed on the screen to select them.

After selecting the eBooks, tap on the Move icon to select from a list of choices, including the option to create your own folders for manually sorting and storing one or more eBook titles. Tap on the New icon, and then type a new folder name in which you want to store the preselected eBooks. In Figure 7.6, a folder called Favorites was created. Tap on the Done icon in the window to create the folder and move the selected eBooks into it.

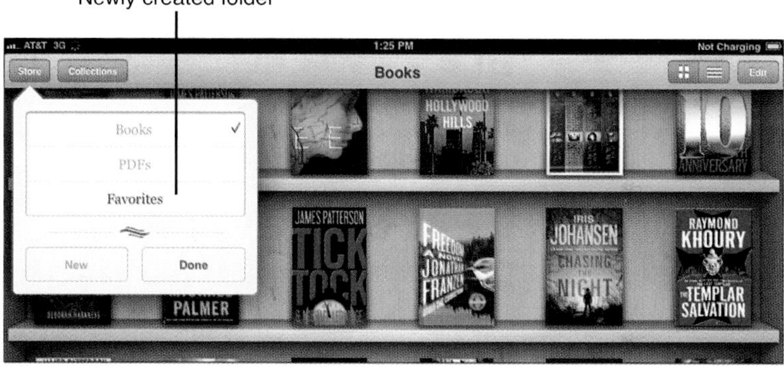

FIGURE 7.6

The selected eBooks will be moved into the new Favorites folder.

As you can see in Figure 7.7, a new bookshelf screen is displayed. The folder name Favorites is displayed at the top center, and the four preselected eBooks are displayed in the new folder. To return to the main Library (Bookshelf) screen, tap on the Collections icon, and then tap on the Books option.

FIGURE 7.7

Here, a new folder called Favorites has been created. Within it are the four eBook titles that were previously selected when the Move icon was first tapped.

REDUCE BOOKSHELF CLUTTER WITH THE DELETE COMMAND

At any time, you can delete one or more eBooks from your iOS device. However, those eBooks will remain available to you via iCloud and can be reloaded anytime.

> **NOTE** Although your iOS device will need to be connected to the Internet to access iCloud and reload a prepurchased eBook title, no Internet connection is required to delete eBooks, to manage your eBook collection from the Library screen, or to read them.

To delete an eBook from your iOS device, follow these steps:

1. From the main Library (Bookshelf) screen, tap on the Edit command icon.
2. Tap on one or more of the displayed eBook titles that you want to delete.
3. Tap on the red-and-white Delete icon that's displayed at the top of the screen.
4. When the Delete Book window appears (shown in Figure 7.8), tap on the Delete icon to confirm your decision. Or tap the Cancel icon to return to the Library screen without deleting the selected eBook title.
5. Tap on the blue-and-white Done icon to exit this option, and return to the main Library screen.

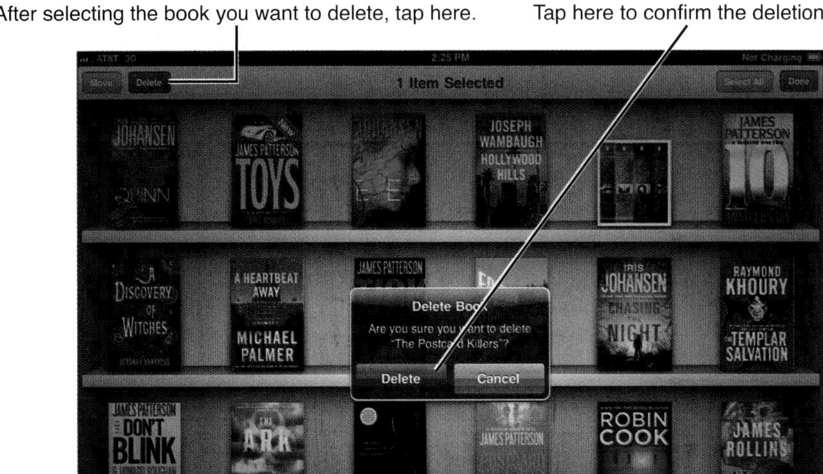
After selecting the book you want to delete, tap here.
Tap here to confirm the deletion.
1 Item Selected
Delete Book
Are you sure you want to delete "The Postcard Killers"?
Delete
Cancel

FIGURE 7.8

You must confirm your eBook deletion request by tapping on the Delete icon when the Delete Book window appears.

BROWSE AND SHOP FOR EBOOKS VIA iBOOKSTORE

When you're ready to begin browsing the eBook selection offered by iBookstore, make sure your iPhone or iPad is connected to the Web, and then tap on the Store icon that's displayed at the top of the Library (Bookshelf) screen. You'll discover that the interface and layout of iBookstore are similar to those of the App Store; however, what's offered here are exclusively eBooks.

> **TIP** You also have the option to shop for eBooks using iTunes on your primary computer. As soon as you make an eBook purchase, it will be added to your iCloud account, so you can then download it to your iOS device without having to perform an iTunes Sync. Remember, all purchases made from the App Store, iTunes Store, and iBookstore automatically get saved to your iCloud account and become accessible from any iOS device or computer that's also connected to your iCloud account.

Many of the eBooks offered from iBookstore are digital versions of traditionally printed books from bestselling authors and major publishers. However, as you browse iBookstore, you'll also find an ever-growing selection of self-published eBooks, which are written by up-and-coming or nonprofessional writers who are not affiliated with a major publishing house. Plus, you'll find self-published works by well-known authors, as well as books that were taken out of print but have been rereleased as eBooks.

> **! CAUTION** Without actually buying and reading some eBooks, it's very difficult to tell the difference between an eBook published by a well-known publishing house, such as Que, McGraw-Hill, or Random House, and a self-published book when you're browsing an online bookseller, such as iBookstore. As you read a book's description, pay attention to the publisher that's listed, and if you're not familiar with the author or publisher, pay extra attention to the book's description, as well as its ratings and reviews, before making a purchase.

iBookstore offers an ever-growing selection of eBooks, which you can browse by subject, title, author's name, or various other methods. When you access iBookstore, you'll see the main screen, which on the iPhone looks like what's shown in Figure 7.9. Figure 7.10 shows a sample of the main iBookstore screen on an iPad. Overall, the functionality is basically the same. The main command icons vary slightly between what you'll see when using iBooks on an iPhone versus an iPad.

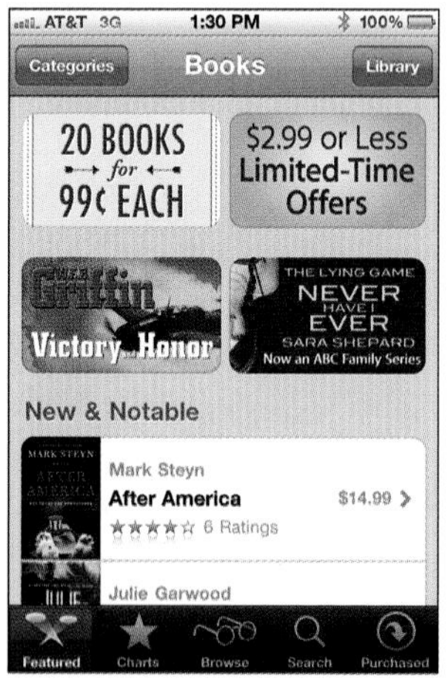

FIGURE 7.9

The iPhone version of the main iBookstore screen. From here, you can begin browsing for eBooks to purchase and download.

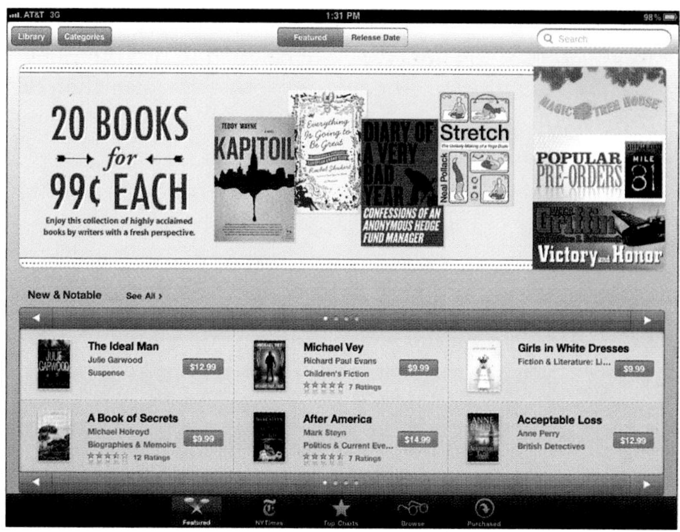

FIGURE 7.10

When you browse iBookstore using an iPad, more content can be displayed on the screen at once.

iBOOKSTORE COMMANDS ON THE iPHONE AND iPOD TOUCH

Displayed along the top of the main iBookstore screen when accessing this online bookseller from an iPhone, you'll see a Categories icon and a Library icon. Along the bottom of the screen are five additional command icons. Here's a summary of how these features work:

Categories—View eBooks by category, such as Arts & Entertainment, Business & Personal Finance, Classics, Fiction & Literature, Nonfiction, and Reference. There are 25 categories to choose from within iBookstore; they become accessible when you tap on the Categories icon.

Library—Tap this icon to exit iBookstore and return to the Library (Bookshelf) screen of iBooks.

Featured—View a selection of what Apple decides are "featured" eBook titles currently available from iBookstore.

Charts—View Top Charts or the *New York Times* Bestseller charts relating to paid and free eBooks available from iBookstore. The Top Charts lists are compiled based on sales from iBookstore. Both the Top Charts and the *New York Times* lists are updated regularly.

Browse—This option allows you to search for eBooks by author or category. Near the top of the screen, tap on the Top Paid or Top Free tabs to determine whether you want to view a selection of paid or free eBooks. When you first tap on the Browse option, an alphabetical listing of authors appears. Tap on any author's name to view a selection of their work that is available through iBookstore. Or tap on the Categories icon, choose a category, and then browse through the listed selections.

Search—When you tap on this command icon, a blank search field will be displayed. Enter the book title, author name, subject, or any keyword associated with an eBook title, subject, or description that you're looking for. Then, tap the Search key on the virtual keyboard to initiate the search and view the results.

Purchased—This command icon allows you to access your iCloud account and load any previously purchased (or downloaded) eBooks to your iOS device.

TIP Initially, 10 book listings are featured in each chart when viewed on an iPhone. Scroll down to the bottom of a chart and tap on the Ten More Books option to view additional eBook listings.

iBOOKSTORE COMMAND ICONS: iPAD

When you shop for eBooks through iBookstore from your iPad, much more information is displayed on the screen. Displayed along the top of the screen are the Library and Categories command icons, along with the Featured and Release Date tabs (if you have the default Features command selected from the bottom of the screen) and the Search field. Displayed along the bottom of the iBookstore screen are five command icons. Here's a summary of how these features work:

Library—Tap this icon to exit iBookstore and return to the Library (Bookshelf) screen of iBooks.

Categories—Tap on this command icon to reveal a list of 25 book categories, such as Business & Personal Finance, Computers & Internet, Humor, Parenting, Sci-Fi & Fantasy, and Travel & Adventure. Tap on the category of your choice to browse available eBooks relating to that subject matter.

Featured (Tab)/Release Date (Tab)—If you have the Featured command icon selected from the bottom of the screen, the Featured and Release Date tabs will be displayed at the top center of the screen. Tap on the Release Date tab to view Featured eBook titles based on the date they were released. The newest releases will be listed first.

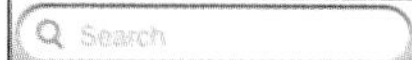

Search Field—Use this Search field to enter a book title, an author's name, a subject, or a keyword that is associated with a book's title or description that you'd like to find within iBookstore.

Featured—The leftmost command icon displayed at the bottom of the iBookstore screen allows you to search for books based on titles that Apple opts to feature. These tend to be new, noteworthy, or bestselling titles. Tap on either the Featured or the Release Date tab at the top center of the screen to determine how these eBook listings will be sorted.

NYTimes—Located to the right of the Featured icon, also near the bottom center of the screen, is the NYTimes icon. Tap on this to reveal two *New York Times* Bestsellers lists—one for Fiction (displayed on the left side of the screen) and one for Nonfiction (displayed on the right side of the screen), as shown in Figure 7.11.

FIGURE 7.11

Tap on the NYTimes command icon to reveal two separate New York Times Bestsellers lists.

Top Charts—Tap on this command icon to reveal two lists of the current most popular eBook titles among iBookstore customers. The Top Paid Books list is displayed on the left side of the screen, and the Top Free Books list is displayed on the right side of the screen.

Browse—When you tap on the Browse icon, a comprehensive list of authors is displayed on the left side of the screen. When you tap on an author's name, the books written by that author that are currently available from iBookstore display on the right side of the screen in the form of eBook listings. Next to the Top Authors heading (on the left side of the screen) are two tabs—one for Paid and one for Free. This enables you to search for paid eBooks versus eBooks you can download and read free.

As always, you can tap on any eBook listing to reveal a detailed description for that eBook title. In the upper-right corner of the screen, you can use the Search field to browse for books based on a title, a subject, an author name, or a keyword you enter.

When you tap on an author's name or view the search results after entering something into the Search field, you can sort the eBook listings you see by tapping on the Sort By tab that's displayed in the upper-right corner of the screen, just below the Search field. You can sort eBook listings by Most Popular, Name, or Release Date.

Purchased—This command icon enables you to access your iCloud account and load any previously purchased (or downloaded) eBooks to your iOS device.

TIP By default, the Top Charts lists you see are compiled from all eBooks offered by iBookstore. To view similar lists narrowed down by a specific subject category, tap on the Top Charts icon, and then tap on the Categories icon that's displayed in the upper-left corner of the screen. When the Categories listing appears, tap on your category selection. A Top Charts list will reload, this time focusing only on eBooks in a selected category (such as Classics, Humor, Mysteries & Thrillers, or Romance).

HOW TO FIND A SPECIFIC EBOOK—FAST!

Although you can use the various command icons and spend hours browsing through eBook titles, just as you can spend an equal amount of time perusing the shelves of a traditional bookstore, such as Barnes & Noble, here are some simple strategies for quickly finding a specific eBook title you're looking for.

As soon as iBookstore loads, use the Search field to enter the eBook title, author's name, subject, or keyword that's associated with what you're looking for. Entering a specific book title will reveal very specific search results. However, entering a keyword relating to a topic or subject matter will reveal a selection of eBook suggestions that somehow relate to that keyword.

If you're interested in reading eBooks about knitting, for example, but you don't know any specific book titles or authors who have written such books, simply enter the keyword "knitting" into the Search field. A series of individual eBook listings that relate to knitting displays in the main part of the iBookstore screen. Some of these are paid books, whereas others are free publications.

From a typical eBook listing, you can see a graphic thumbnail of a book's cover, plus view the eBook's title, its author, the category it falls into, its average star-based rating (which will be explained shortly), and its price. Tap on any listing to reveal a more detailed Description relating to a particular eBook. As you review a detailed description of an eBook, look carefully at its ratings and its written reviews, especially if it's a paid eBook.

> iOS 5 **WHAT'S NEW** Also available from iBookstore are a selection of enhanced, full-color, interactive eBooks. For example, some popular children's books fall into this category, as do some cookbooks. These enhanced eBooks include animations, interactive elements, "pop-up" graphics (which replace traditional pop-up book pages), and sound, and take full advantage of the iPhone or iPad's touchscreen. All of these enhanced books are available from iBookstore and the App Store.

LEARN ABOUT AN EBOOK FROM ITS LISTING AND DESCRIPTION

While browsing iBookstore, you will see individual eBook listings for titles that relate to what you are looking for. As you can see in Figure 7.12, a typical eBook listing includes a graphic of the eBook's title, author, category, star-based rating, and price icon.

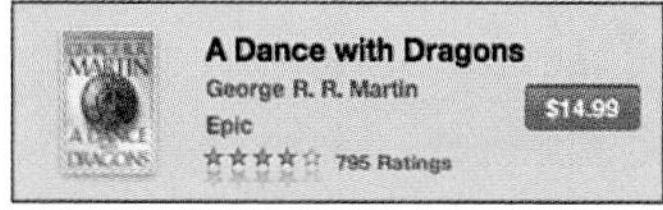

FIGURE 7.12

An eBook listing offers a quick summary of an eBook. As you're browsing iBookstore, many eBook listings can be viewed simultaneously.

While viewing a specific listing, tap on an eBook's title or cover artwork to access a more detailed description. For most eBook titles, this is also how you access the capability to download and read a free sample.

TIP To quickly purchase and download an eBook, tap on the price icon in its listing or description. When you tap on a price icon, it changes to a Purchase icon. Tap this new icon to confirm your purchase decision. You will then need to enter your Apple ID password to begin the download process.

If you're downloading a free eBook, tap on the Free icon that is displayed instead of a price icon. Then, instead of a Purchase icon, a Get Book icon will appear. Tap on this, enter your Apple ID, and download the free eBook. Even though you need to enter your Apple ID, you will not be charged to download a free eBook. However, at the same time it's downloaded to your device, it will also be saved to your iCloud account.

It takes between 5 and 20 seconds to download a full-length eBook to your iPhone or iPad. As soon as it's downloaded and ready to read, the book's front cover artwork will be displayed as part of the Library (Bookshelf) screen.

UNDERSTANDING THE BOOK'S DESCRIPTION

While you're looking at an eBook listing, if you tap on the book's title or cover thumbnail image, a detailed eBook Description will appear on the screen. It will be divided into several sections.

On both an iPhone and an iPad, displayed near the upper-left corner of a typical eBook Description, as shown in Figure 7.13, is the eBook's front cover artwork. To the right of this is a text-based summary of the book, including its title, author, the book's publication date and publisher, star-based rating, the language it's published in, its category, and the length.

From the iBookstore, to return to the main Library (Bookshelf) screen of iBooks, tap on the Library icon that's displayed near the upper-left corner of the screen.

If you look at the upper-right corner of an eBook Description window on an iPad, you'll see links for visiting the author's web page and sharing details about the eBook with someone else via email.

TIP You can preview an eBook before paying for it. In each book's description, you'll discover a Get Sample icon. Tap on it to download a free sample of that eBook. The length of the sample varies and is determined by the eBook's publisher. It will be between a few pages and a full chapter.

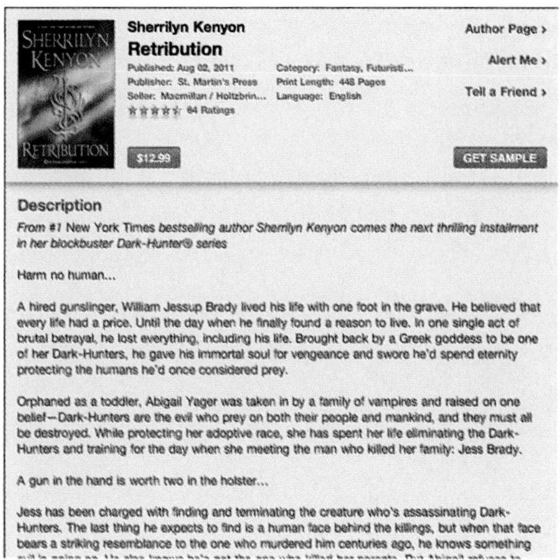

Sherrilyn Kenyon
Retribution
Published: Aug 02, 2011
Publisher: St. Martin's Press
Seller: Macmillan / Holtzbrin...
Category: Fantasy, Futuristi...
Print Length: 448 Pages
Language: English
64 Ratings
Author Page >
Alert Me >
Tell a Friend >
$12.99
GET SAMPLE
Description
From #1 New York Times bestselling author Sherrilyn Kenyon comes the next thrilling installment in her blockbuster Dark-Hunter® series
Harm no human...
A hired gunslinger, William Jessup Brady lived his life with one foot in the grave. He believed that every life had a price. Until the day when he finally found a reason to live. In one single act of brutal betrayal, he lost everything, including his life. Brought back by a Greek goddess to be one of her Dark-Hunters, he gave his immortal soul for vengeance and swore he'd spend eternity protecting the humans he'd once considered prey.
Orphaned as a toddler, Abigail Yager was taken in by a family of vampires and raised on one belief—Dark-Hunters are the evil who prey on both their people and mankind, and they must all be destroyed. While protecting her adoptive race, she has spent her life eliminating the Dark-Hunters and training for the day when she meeting the man who killed her family: Jess Brady.
A gun in the hand is worth two in the holster...
Jess has been charged with finding and terminating the creature who's assassinating Dark-Hunters. The last thing he expects to find is a human face behind the killings, but when that face bears a striking resemblance to the one who murdered him centuries ago, he knows something

FIGURE 7.13

Read a detailed description of an eBook before making your purchase and/or downloading it.

On an iPhone, links to the Author Page and the Get Sample icon are displayed below the price icon (as shown in Figure 7.14). Also on the iPhone (or iPod touch), instead of scrolling down to see details about the eBook's ratings and to read in-depth reviews, tap on the Reviews option, which displays the number of reviews for that eBook, as well as its average star-based rating.

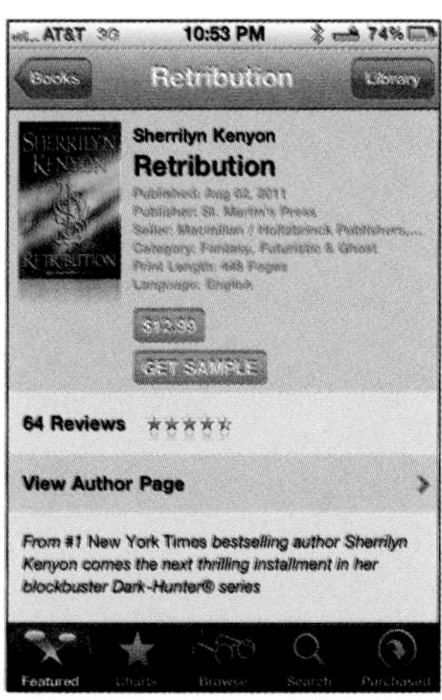

FIGURE 7.14

A book Description screen from iBookstore displayed on an iPhone shows the same basic information that you'd see on a comparable iPad screen, but the content is formatted differently.

In an eBook's description, the eBook's price icon appears near the book cover's graphic thumbnail. Tap on this icon to purchase the book and download it. Also part of a Description window is the eBook's star-based rating. Here, you can view an overall average rating for the eBook, which will be between one and five stars. Five stars is the highest rating possible. You'll also be able to determine how many ratings the book has received from other iBookstore customers and view a chart that depicts how many one-, two-, three-, four-, and five-star ratings the eBook has received (see Figure 7.15).

FIGURE 7.15

The ratings chart that accompanies each book description shows an overall average rating, the number of people who have rated the eBook, and exactly how many one-, two-, three-, four-, and five-star ratings it has received.

You can also read more detailed, text-based reviews written by others who have purchased, downloaded, and presumably read the eBook. To exit an eBook description, on the iPhone, tap on the left-pointing arrow icon that says Books. It's displayed in the upper-left corner of the screen. Or, on the iPad, tap anywhere on the tablet's screen that is outside the Description window.

Don't just pay attention to an eBook's average star-based rating. Also pay attention to how many people have rated that eBook. After all, it's harder to get a good idea of a book's true quality if it has a five-star rating but has been rated by only a small number of people, versus a book with dozens or hundreds of five-star ratings.

If the average star-based rating is inconclusive, take a look at the Customer Ratings chart that's displayed as part of the description. From this, you can see how many people have rated the eBook, as well as how many one-, two-, three-, four-, and five-star ratings it's received.

Still not sure whether an eBook is worth buying and/or downloading? Scroll down, below the customer ratings, and take a look at the more detailed text-based customer reviews. Here, people who have read the book have written their own (sometimes lengthy) reviews.

TIP After you discover an author you like, tap on the Alert Me feature, which is part of each eBook description. In the future, you'll be notified when that author releases a new book. Or as you're reading an eBook's description, tap on the Tell a Friend option to email someone else details about the eBook from within the iBooks app.

USING iCLOUD WITH iBOOKS

One new feature of iOS 5 is that all of your iBookstore purchases are automatically stored on iCloud and become accessible from all of your iOS devices that are linked to the same iCloud account. This means that you can purchase an eBook on your iPad, for example, but also download and read it on your iPhone, without having to repurchase that title.

If you have already purchased eBooks using your existing Apple ID, when you launch iBooks for the first time, a window appears asking whether you want to sync all of your eBooks and related bookmarks to that device. You also have the option of pulling just one eBook title at a time that you've previously purchased off of iCloud and loading it in your device.

iOS 5 WHAT'S NEW In addition to loading previously purchased eBook titles on multiple iOS devices via iCloud, all of your virtual bookmarks also get stored and synced. Thus, you can begin reading a particular eBook on one device but continue where you left off on another device that's linked to the same iCloud account.

HOW TO RELOAD A PREVIOUSLY PURCHASED EBOOK

To load a previously purchased or downloaded eBook from iCloud, follow these steps:

1. Launch iBooks from the Home Screen.
2. From the Library screen, tap on the Store icon.
3. Tap on the Purchased icon that is displayed at the bottom of the iBookstore screen.

4. When the Purchased screen appears, either use the Search field to type the title of the eBook you want to load or scroll through the list of prepurchased eBook titles that are not currently stored on your device.
5. When the listing for the prepurchased eBook you want to load is displayed, tap on the iCloud icon that's displayed to the right of that listing.
6. A detailed screen pertaining to that eBook title displays. Tap on the iCloud icon that appears as part of this description.
7. When prompted, enter the password that's associated with your Apple ID account. You will not, however, be charged again for this eBook.
8. The selected eBook title will be transferred from iCloud to your device. In a minute or so, it displays in iBook's Library (Bookshelf) screen. A blue-and-white New label, displayed across the book's cover, indicates that the eBook has just been added to your device and has not yet been accessed or read.
9. From the Library screen, tap on the eBook's cover to launch the eBook reader functionality of iBooks and begin reading your eBook.

CUSTOMIZE YOUR EBOOK READING EXPERIENCE USING iBOOKS

From the Library (Bookshelf) screen of iBooks, tap on a book cover thumbnail to open that eBook and start reading it. While reading eBooks, you can hold the iPhone or iPad in portrait or landscape mode, although if you're reading a digital edition of a traditional paperback or hardcover book, your reading experience will be more authentic if you hold the device in portrait mode (vertically).

As you're reading an eBook, tap anywhere near the top of the screen to make the various command icons and options appear.

> **TIP** Tap on the Library icon that's displayed near the upper-left corner of the screen to bookmark your location in that eBook and return to the iBooks Library (Bookshelf) screen.

On both the iPhone and the iPad, located to the right of the Library icon is the Table of Contents icon. Tap on it to display an interactive table of contents for the eBook you're reading (as shown in Figure 7.16).

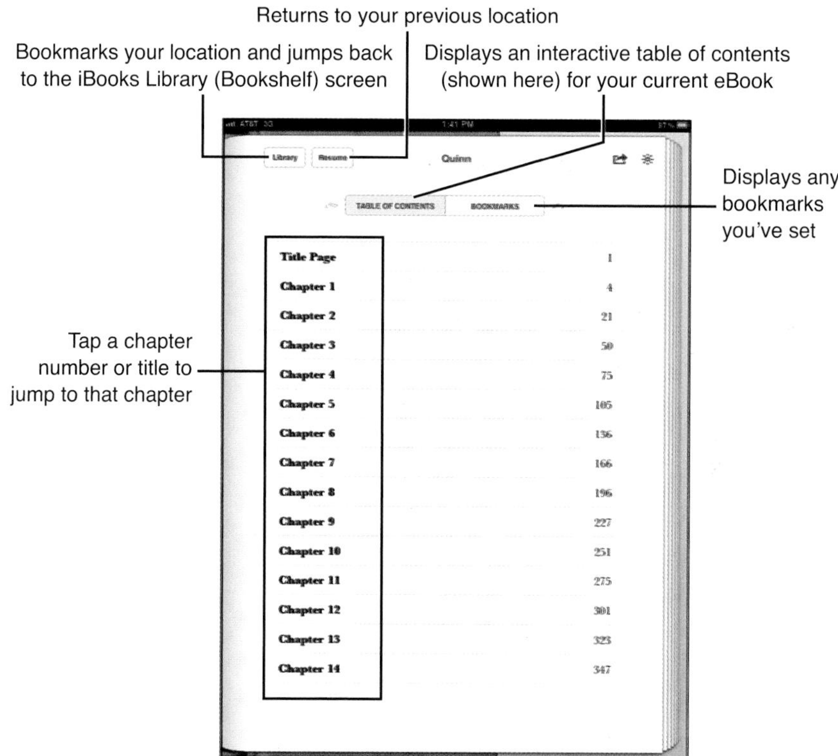

FIGURE 7.16

The Table of Contents screen for every eBook is interactive. Tap on the chapter number or chapter title to jump to the appropriate page.

As you're looking at a table of contents, tap on any chapter number or chapter title to immediately jump to that location in the book. Or near the top-center of the Table of Contents screen, tap on the Bookmarks icon to see a list of bookmarks you have previously set as you were reading that eBook (shown in Figure 7.17).

TIP Whenever you tap on the Library icon while reading an eBook, or press the Home button to return to the device's Home Screen, your current location in the book is automatically bookmarked and saved. At any time, you also have the option to add a virtual bookmark to as many pages in the eBook as you want. Then, by tapping on the Table of Contents icon, and then on the Bookmarks tab, you can see a complete listing of manually placed virtual bookmarks in that eBook.

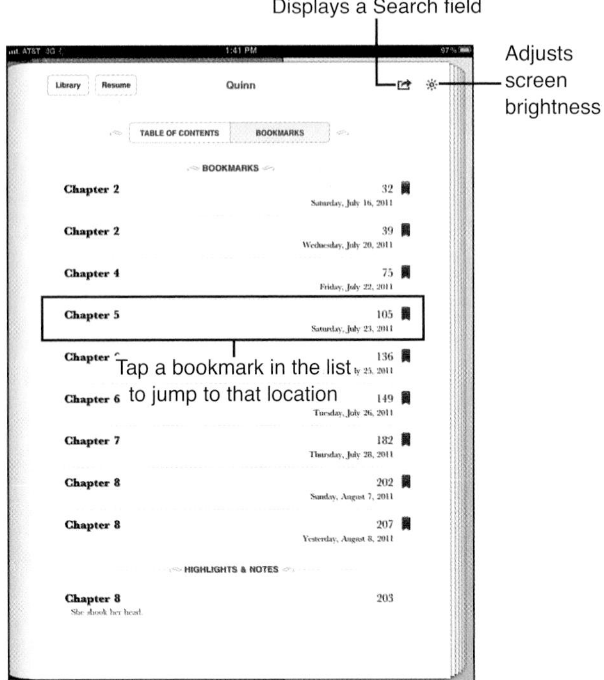

FIGURE 7.17

As you're reading, you can set bookmarks in an eBook and quickly return to those pages anytime later from the Bookmarks screen. Tap the bookmark you want, and the eBook jumps to that location.

To exit the Table of Contents screen and return to reading your eBook, tap on the Resume icon that is displayed near the upper-left corner of the screen.

As you're reading an eBook, if you look in the upper portion of the screen, you'll see additional command icons and options. The sun-shaped icon enables you to adjust the brightness of the screen as you're reading. Use your finger to adjust the slider to make the screen lighter or darker.

Tap the Search box (a rectangle with an arrow coming out of it) to display a Search field, which you can use to locate any keyword or search phrase that appears in the eBook you're currently reading.

> **TIP** Tap on the "aA" icon to change the font size of the text that's displayed as you're reading. You can also alter the font of the text and/or turn on or off the onscreen sepia effect, which some people prefer when reading text on their device's screen.

After tapping the "aA" icon to adjust the font size, tap on the small "a" icon to shrink the font size of the text in the eBook. Tap on the "A" icon to increase the font size of the text in the eBook. The changes appear immediately on the screen. Choose a font size and font that is the most visually appealing to you.

As you're reading, to turn the page, swipe your finger from right to left across the screen to move one page forward, or swipe your finger from left to right to back up one page at a time.

Displayed near the bottom center of the screen is the page number in the eBook you're currently reading, as well as the total number of pages in the eBook. The number of pages remaining in the current chapter is displayed to the right of the page number.

iOS 5 WHAT'S NEW As you're reading an eBook, hold your finger on a single word. A group of four command tabs appears above that word labeled Dictionary, Highlight, Note, and Search. Tap on the Dictionary tab to look up the definition of that word.

Tap on the Highlight tab to highlight the word in yellow. You can also highlight a full sentence or paragraph by moving the blue highlight dots to highlight additional text beyond a single word.

If you tap on the Note tab, a yellow virtual sticky note will appear on your device's screen, along with the virtual keyboard. Using the keyboard, type notes to yourself about what you're reading. When you're done typing, tap anywhere on the screen outside the yellow sticky note box. In the margin of the eBook, a sticky note icon will appear. You can later tap on this icon to read your notes or annotations.

Tap on the Search tab to enter any word or phrase and find it in the eBook. A search window will appear below the Search field. References to each occurrence of your keyword or search phrase will be displayed by chapter and page number. Tap on a reference to jump to that point in the book.

READ PDF FILES WITH iBOOKS, TOO

The iBooks app can also be used to read PDF files you download or transfer to your iPhone or iPad. This can include a wide range of business-related documents, ranging in length from a single page to a book-length manuscript.

CAUTION If you try to load an extremely long, graphic-intensive PDF file and read it on your iPhone or iPad's screen, it might not load properly due to the large file size. For these large PDF files, you might need to view them on your primary computer or convert them into a Pages (or Microsoft Word) document, for example, before loading them onto your iOS device.

When you receive an email with a PDF file as an attachment, tap on the PDF thumbnail in that email so the file downloads to your iPhone or iPad. Next, tap and hold your finger on that same PDF thumbnail for a few seconds, until a menu window appears. The options in this window (as shown in Figure 7.18) are Quick Look, Open in iBooks, and, if applicable, Open In.

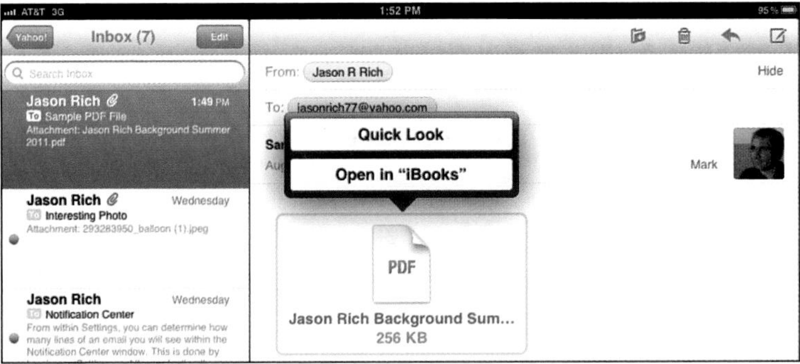

FIGURE 7.18

You can open and read a PDF file that is an attachment in an incoming email using the iBooks app.

The Open in iBooks command automatically launches the iBooks app and allows you to read the PDF document as if you're reading an eBook you downloaded from iBookstore.

NOTE If applicable, the Open In command enables you to open a PDF file using another third-party app. When you tap on this menu option, a list of compatible apps for viewing, printing, sharing, and/or annotating PDF files that are currently installed on your iPhone or iPad will be displayed. These apps might include PDF Reader, GoodReader, or UPAD, for example.

When a PDF file opens in iBooks, you'll see command icons displayed along the top of the screen, as well as small thumbnails of the PDF document's pages displayed along the bottom of the screen.

Tap on the Library command icon that is displayed near the upper-left corner of the screen to return to iBook's main Library (Bookshelf) screen. You'll notice when you do this, however, that the Bookshelf displays all the PDF files stored on your device—not eBooks downloaded from iBookstore.

To once again access your eBooks, tap on the PDFs icon on the iPhone, or the Collections command icon on the iPad, and then select the Books option.

> **TIP** As you're viewing a PDF file from within iBooks, next to the Library icon is the Table of Contents icon. Tap on it to display larger thumbnails of each page in your PDF document, and then tap on any of the thumbnails to jump to that page. Or tap on the Resume icon to return to the main view of your PDF file.

To the immediate right of the Table of Contents icon (near the upper-left corner of the iBooks screen as you're reading a PDF file) is a command icon that enables you to email or print the PDF document you're currently viewing. Near the upper-right corner of this screen are three additional command icons. The sun-shaped icon enables you to adjust the brightness of the screen. The magnifying glass–shaped icon enables you to search a PDF file for specific text in the document, and the Bookmark icon enables you to bookmark specific pages in the PDF file for later reference.

> **TIP** As you're viewing a PDF file using iBooks, you can zoom in on or out of the page using a reverse pinch or pinch finger motion on the touchscreen display, or by double-tapping on the area you want to zoom in or out on.

Also, as you're reading a PDF file, you can hold the device in either a vertical or a horizontal position. If you tap anywhere on the screen (except on a command icon or page thumbnail), the icons and thumbnails on the top and bottom of the screen disappear, giving you more onscreen real estate to view your PDF document. Tap near the top or bottom of the screen to make these icons and thumbnails reappear at any time.

IN THIS CHAPTER

- How to use the official Twitter app
- How Twitter now integrates with iOS 5 and your iPhone or iPad
- How to use the official Facebook app
- How to use other apps for online social networking

8

MAKE THE MOST OF SOCIAL NETWORKING APPS

There are more than 500 million active users worldwide on Facebook, several hundred million Twitter users, and a fast-growing following for the new Google+ online social networking service. In recent years, these services have redefined how people communicate, and the evolution is rapidly continuing. New features for sharing news, information, gossip, ideas, photos, videos, web URLs, and other content are continuously getting introduced and incorporated into these services.

One reason services like Twitter and Facebook have become so popular is that people are able to manage their accounts and become active within these massive online communities from virtually anywhere and at any time (24/7), using their computer, cellphone, or tablet.

For iPhone, iPod touch, or iPad users, staying active on Facebook, Twitter, Google+, LinkedIn, and other online social networking services is easy, thanks to a collection of apps currently available from the App Store.

WHAT'S NEW In addition to official Twitter, Facebook, Google+, and LinkedIn apps available for the iPhone and/or iPad, several of iOS 5's core apps, including Photos, Safari, Camera, maps, and YouTube, now have Twitter integration built in, so you can send tweets from within these apps without first launching the official Twitter app.

Although the official Twitter app does not come preinstalled on iOS 5 devices, it can be downloaded, installed, and set up from within the Settings app, as well as downloaded free from the App Store.

In Settings, you can add one or more existing Twitter accounts, plus update your Contacts database so that it automatically includes the Twitter usernames and photos of active Twitter users who are also in your Contacts database.

If you're already active on Twitter, Facebook, Google+, LinkedIn, or another popular online social networking site, start by downloading the free "official" app for any or all of these services:

- The official Twitter app (free) is available as a hybrid app that works with the iPhone and iPad. The official Facebook app, however, is available as an iPhone- or iPad-specific app.
- The official Google+ and LinkedIn apps are both free iPhone apps that work flawlessly on the iPad, but they don't take advantage of the iPad's larger screen beyond allowing you to tap on the 2x icon to double the size of the iPhone-formatted screens.

MORE INFO LinkedIn is a popular online social networking site that caters specifically to business professionals, entrepreneurs, consultants, freelancers, and small-business operators. The primary focus of this service is on professional networking.

Setting up a LinkedIn account is free, as is downloading and using the official LinkedIn hybrid iPhone/iPad app (which is available from the App Store). However, from the App Store, you'll also find third-party apps like the iPad-specific Link-Pad Pro ($4.99), which also allows you to manage your LinkedIn account from an iOS device.

Beyond the "official" apps for the popular online social networking services, there is a vast selection of third-party (free and paid) apps that also allow you to manage your Twitter, Facebook, Google+, LinkedIn, or other online social networking accounts. These apps all offer slightly different features and functions. Some are iPhone-specific, whereas others are iPad-specific or hybrid apps that work on all iOS devices.

TIP As long as your iOS device is connected to the Internet, you can use a specialized app to manage any of your online social networking accounts from virtually anywhere. For example, if you're out and about with your iPhone, you can snap and edit a photo, and then immediately tweet that photo to your followers or upload it to Facebook, all in a matter of seconds, while also updating your status.

TIPS FOR USING THE OFFICIAL TWITTER APP

When you first upgrade to iOS 5 or begin using a new iOS device, you'll need to install the official Twitter app on your device, plus add your existing Twitter account information to the Settings app, so that you can begin sending tweets from within other iOS 5 apps, such as Photos, Safari, Maps, or YouTube. If you don't yet have a free Twitter account, you can set one up in just minutes from within the official Twitter app or in the Settings app (by selecting the Twitter option from the main Settings menu).

The fastest way to accomplish both of these tasks is to launch the Settings app on your iPhone, iPod touch, or iPad from the Home Screen, and from the main Settings menu, tap on the Twitter option.

In Settings, from the Twitter menu screen (shown in Figure 8.1), start by tapping on the Install icon displayed next to the Twitter app icon that's found near the top of the screen. This installs the official Twitter app onto your iOS device without having to access the App Store. (A 3G or Wi-Fi Internet connection is required.)

FIGURE 8.1

You can download and install the official Twitter app for your iPhone or iPad from within the Settings app. Accessing the App Store is not necessary.

SETTING UP YOUR TWITTER ACCOUNT

If you already have a Twitter account and want to be able to send tweets from several popular iOS 5 apps, you'll need to enter your existing Twitter account username and password once into the Settings app.

From the Twitter menu screen in Settings, tap on the Add Account option. This will allow you to activate the Twitter integration built in to several iOS 5 apps, and at the same time link your existing Twitter account(s).

After tapping on Add Account, from the Add Account screen (shown in Figure 8.2), enter your username in the first field. Be sure to use the @ symbol in front of your username—for example, @JasonRich7. Next, enter the password associated with that Twitter account in the Password field, and then tap on the Sign In icon.

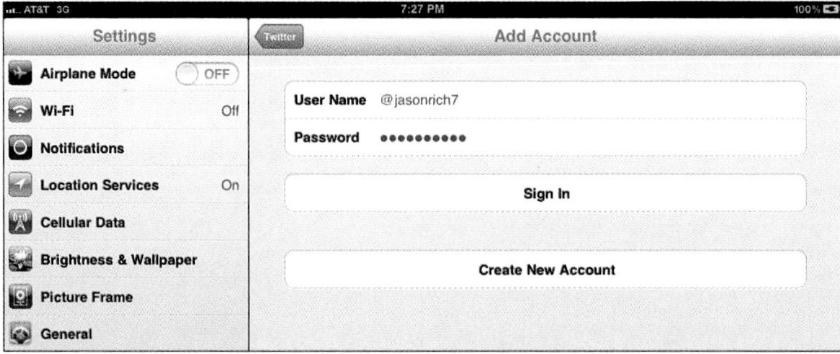

FIGURE 8.2

To take advantage of the integration between iOS 5 apps and Twitter, you'll need to enter and save your Twitter account information in the Settings app. This is separate from configuring and logging in to Twitter using the official Twitter app.

In Settings, you can also adjust two important settings associated with your Twitter account that directly impact your online privacy. The Find Me by Email option, when turned on, allows people to easily find you on Twitter via your email address. When the virtual switch associated with this feature is turned off, someone searching for you will need to know your unique Twitter username, as opposed to your email address.

You can also turn off the Tweet Location option. When it's turned on, whenever you send a tweet from your iPhone or iPad, for example, your exact location will be included with that outgoing message and broadcast to the public. When it's turned off, your outgoing tweets will not automatically include your geographic location.

When you see your existing Twitter account listed on the Twitter menu screen in Settings, you can either tap on the Add Account option again to add additional Twitter accounts, or tap on the Update Contacts option, which automatically compares your personal Contacts database with the Twitter user database and then adds the appropriate Twitter usernames and profile photos to your Contacts database for those contacts who are active on Twitter.

To exit this Settings menu, press the Home button on your iOS device. Or, on the iPhone, tap on the left-pointing arrow icon containing the word Settings that's displayed in the upper-left corner of the screen. On your iPad, tap on any other option under the Settings heading that's displayed on the left side of the screen.

To create a free Twitter account, launch the Settings app and select the Twitter option from the main settings menu. From the Twitter screen in Settings, tap on Add Account, then tap on the Create New Account icon and fill in the fields displayed in the New Account window that appears (shown in Figure 8.3).

FIGURE 8.3

You can create a new Twitter account in seconds from within the Settings app on your iPhone or iPad. Access Twitter's New Account screen and fill in the blank fields.

> **TIP** To create a Twitter account using Safari on your iOS device, visit http://mobile.twitter.com/signup. When the Sign Up screen is displayed, use the virtual keyboard to enter your full name, create a unique Twitter username, share your email address, and create a password for your new Twitter account.

When all the fields in the Sign Up screen have been filled in, tap on the Create My Account option. When the welcome screen appears, you're ready to begin tweeting and following other Twitter users. This can be done using the official Twitter app or another third-party app designed for use with Twitter on your iPhone, iPod touch, or iPad.

! CAUTION If you're concerned about privacy, be sure to turn off the Tweet Location option when you initially create a Twitter account using your iOS device. Or after adding your existing Twitter account information to the Settings app, tap on the listing for that account from the Twitter screen in Settings, and turn the virtual switch associated with Tweet Location to off. Otherwise, whenever you send a tweet from your iOS device, your exact current location will be included with that message and broadcast to the public.

CUSTOMIZING THE OFFICIAL TWITTER APP

In addition to adding your existing Twitter account information to the Settings app to take advantage of Twitter's integration within iOS 5, if you plan to use the official Twitter app to send and receive tweets and manage your account(s), you'll need to configure the app as well.

After downloading and installing the official Twitter app on your iOS device, launch the app from the Home Screen. Near the top center of the screen are two blue-and-white icons, labeled Sign In and Sign Up.

If you already have one or more active Twitter accounts, tap on the Sign In icon. When the Add Account screen appears, enter your Twitter username and password using the device's virtual keyword. When you're done, tap on the Save icon. After your account is authorized, the main Twitter screen will appear. You can manage multiple Twitter accounts using the official Twitter app.

On the iPad, running down the center of the screen is your main Twitter feed (also referred to as your Timeline). Along the left side of the screen (shown in Figure 8.4) is your account name and photo in the upper-left corner, with the following command options listed below it: Timeline, Mentions, Messages, Lists, Profile, and Search.

In the lower-left corner of the main Twitter screen (on the iPad) is the Create Tweet icon. Tap on this to compose a new tweet using the tablet's virtual keyboard (as shown in Figure 8.5). After the tweet (which can be up to 140 characters in length) is created, tap on the Send icon to publish it.

To the right of the Create Tweet icon (near the bottom of the screen) is the gear-shaped Set-Up icon. Tap on it to add or edit your Twitter account information, including the Notification options associated with the app. From this Settings screen, you can also tap on the Advanced option to control specific features in the app, such as the Image and Video Service you'll use when attaching photos or video clips to your outgoing tweets, the image quality of the photos you'll send, and whether you want to turn on or off the sound effects associated with this app.

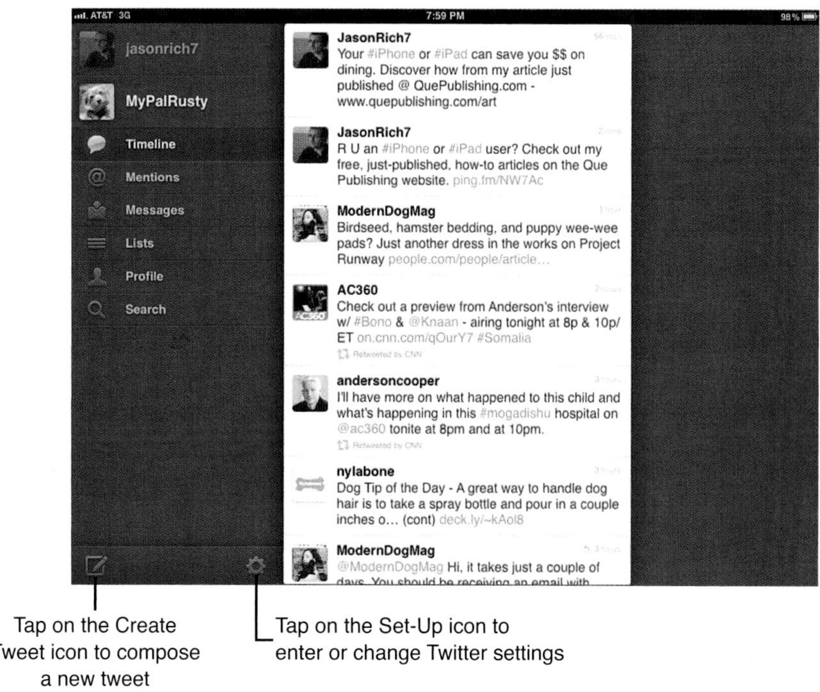

FIGURE 8.4

The official Twitter app on the iPad. You can view your Timeline, plus access most of the app's main commands and features, from this screen.

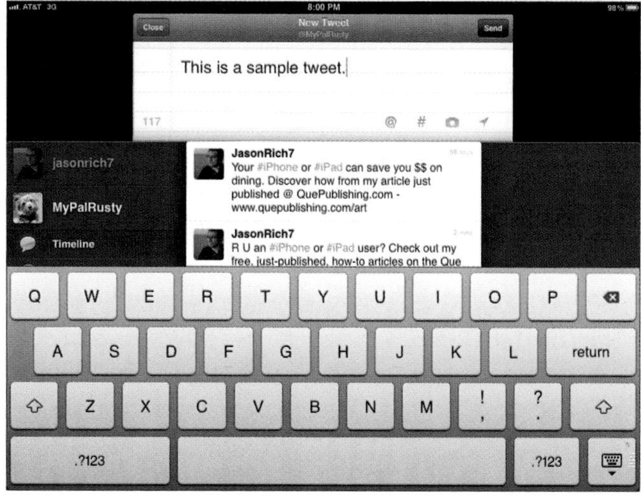

FIGURE 8.5

In this New Tweet window, you can compose and send a tweet from within the official Twitter app.

TIP On the iPhone 3Gs, iPhone 4, or iPhone 4S, the official Twitter app offers the same functionality as the iPad version; however, the screen layout and the position of various command icons will be slightly different. On the iPhone 4S, Siri works with the Twitter app.

USING THE OFFICIAL TWITTER APP

After it's configured to work with your Twitter account, you can manage one or more Twitter accounts using the official Twitter app. On the iPad (refer to Figure 8.4), the commands for doing this are displayed on the left side of the screen and include Timeline, Mentions, Messages, Lists, Profile, and Search.

On the iPhone, the main commands for using Twitter are displayed as icons at the bottom of the official Twitter app screen (as shown in Figure 8.6). At the upper-left corner of the screen, you'll see a left-pointing arrow icon labeled Accounts, which leads to the Account Management screen of the app. At the upper-right corner of the screen is the Create Tweet icon used for composing new outgoing tweets.

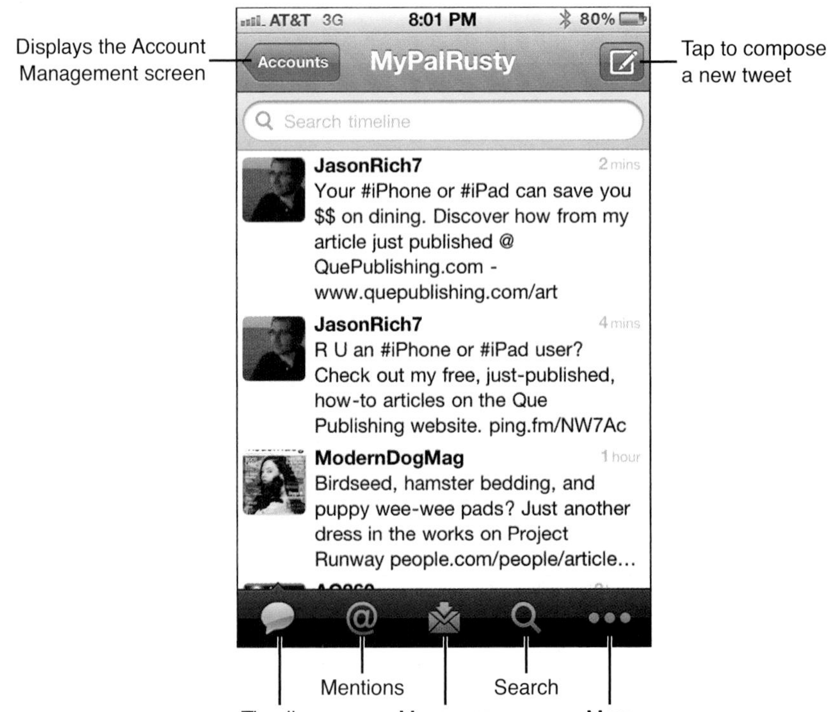

FIGURE 8.6

The main screen of the official Twitter app on an iPhone 4.

The main screen area is where your Twitter feed (or Timeline) is displayed. Along the bottom of the screen, from left to right, you'll see the Timeline, Mentions, Messages, and Search icons, along with an icon composed of three dots. This icon is used to access additional commands for managing your Twitter account, such as accessing the My Profile menu, viewing a listing of tweets marked as Favorites, and accessing functions associated with creating and managing lists.

Here's a quick summary of how these features are used:

Timeline—View a timeline of all incoming tweets on the app's main Twitter feed. The tweets are displayed with the newest ones on top from the various people, businesses, or organizations you're following.

Mentions—View all recent tweets in which your Twitter username (@username) is mentioned in other people's tweets. This will include public tweets addressed to you or tweets that mention your username in the body of the tweet. For example: "@jasonrich7 I am enjoying your *iPad and iPhone Tips and Tricks* book" or "The book *iPad and iPhone Tips and Tricks* written by @JasonRich7 is extremely informative." If these tweets were sent by others, they are displayed when the @jasonrich7 account is active in the official Twitter app and the @Mentions option is selected.

Messages—Read any direct (private) messages sent via Twitter from other users who follow you and whom you currently follow.

Lists—View and manage the lists associated with your Twitter account.

Profile—View or edit your Twitter profile. This includes being able to add or change your profile picture, bio, location, and website. You can also see how many followers you have and how many other people you're following from the active account. Tap on the Tweets icon after tapping on Profile to view a complete list of tweets you've composed and sent from the account, which are displayed in reverse chronological order. Tap the @Mentions icon to see recent mentions from other users, or tap on the Favorites icon to see any tweets you've marked as favorites from your main Twitter feed (Timeline).

Search—Tap on this option to search for people or topics others are tweeting about by entering information into the blank Search field that appears at the top of the screen. Plus, view a list of Trending Now topics (which is a summary of the most popular topics people are currently tweeting about).

COMPOSE AN OUTGOING TWEET

Using the official Twitter app, to compose an outgoing tweet, tap on the Create Tweet icon. When the New Tweet screen with the virtual keyboard appears, begin composing your tweet. Remember, you have up to 140 characters per tweet.

TIP At the top center of the New Tweet window, under the New Tweet heading is the Twitter account from which you'll be sending the outgoing tweet. If you are managing multiple Twitter accounts using the app, tap on this heading to select which account the tweet should be sent from. A Select Account window with each account username displays.

iOS 5 WHAT'S NEW Although you cannot verbally command Siri to compose a new tweet if you're using an iPhone 4S, from the New Tweet screen, when the virtual keyboard appears, tap the microphone key (shown in Figure 8.7) and dictate your outgoing tweet message instead of typing it on the virtual keyboard.

Whenever you see the microphone key (displayed to the left of the spacebar on the virtual keyboard), you can tap it to activate Siri and then dictate text instead of typing it. This works in a wide range of apps.

At the bottom of the New Tweet window are four icons. The @ symbol is used to address your tweet to a specific person or to mention specific Twitter users in a tweet. The # symbol is used to identify a topic or subject within a tweet. Tap on the camera-shaped icon to either take a photo using your iOS device's built-in camera or attach a photo to your tweet that's already store on your device. Tap on the diagonal-pointing arrow icon to manually attach your exact location to the tweet using your device's GPS capabilities.

TIP In the lower-left corner of the New Tweet window (displayed as you're composing an outgoing tweet) is a counter that shows the number of characters remaining. The counter starts at 140 and counts downward with each new character you type as part of your tweet.

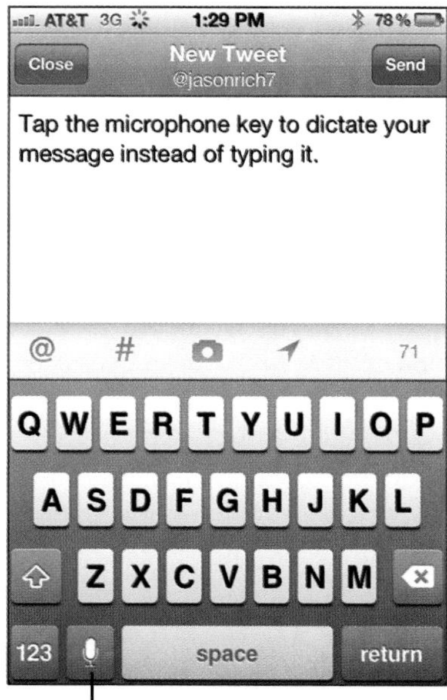

FIGURE 8.7

When using an iPhone 4S, whenever you see a microphone key displayed on the virtual keyboard, you can tap it and dictate text instead of typing it.

TIP If there are phrases or long words you use often, instead of having to constantly type them using the virtual keyboard built in to your iOS device, you can use the iOS 5 keyboard shortcuts feature. To set up this feature, launch the Settings app. Tap on the General option found under the main Settings menu. From the General screen, scroll down to the Keyboard option.

Under the Shortcuts heading, you can add your own shortcuts. For example, you can create an RL shortcut for the phrase, "I am running late." After you create the shortcut, you simply need to type RL and your iOS device will expand this to "I am running late" in compatible apps, including Twitter.

Using keyboard shortcuts enables you to save time when entering commonly used words, phrases, or sentences.

REPLYING TO TWEETS AND OTHER TWITTER FEATURES

As you're viewing your Timeline, if there's a tweet you want to reply to, tap on that tweet listing. On the iPhone, a separate Reply screen appears. On the iPad, the Reply window is displayed on the right side of the screen. The command icons associated with the Reply window include a left-pointing arrow icon that you can tap on to type your reply message. This will cause a New Tweet window to appear, but at the start of the message, the @Username will already be filled in with the username of the person you're replying to.

The star-shaped icon is used to tag a tweet as a Favorite and include it in your Favorites list. The square-shaped icon composed of two arrows is for re-tweeting a message.

On the iPhone, the paper clip–shaped icon will reveal a submenu (shown in Figure 8.8) with the following options: Mail Link, Repost Link, Read Later, and Cancel. The Mail Link option allows you to send an email to someone that includes the tweet message you've selected. The Repost Link option is the same as Re-tweet (which is described in the next section), and the Read Later option allows you to use the Instapaper feature to store the message on your device for later (offline) viewing.

FIGURE 8.8

You can share tweets via email from within the official Twitter app, without having to launch the Mail app.

On both the iPhone and the iPad, the Share icon (which is a square-shaped icon with an arrow coming out of it), which is displayed to the right of the other command icons, will reveal three additional command options, including Translate, Mail Tweet, and Copy Link to Tweet.

TIP If you're viewing a tweet in a foreign language, you can instantly translate it to the native language of your iOS device by tapping on the Translate option. A window with the translation of the selected message will be displayed.

Tap on the Mail Tweet option to email the contents of the selected message to someone from within the Twitter app without first having to launch the Mail app. When you use this command, the selected tweet will automatically be embedded in the body of the outgoing email message. You just need to fill in the To field and tap Send.

The Copy Link to Tweet option allows you to save the URL for that particular tweet in your iOS device's virtual clipboard. You can then use the Paste command to insert that information into another app.

HOW TO RE-TWEET MESSAGES

As you're reviewing your Timeline, which includes tweets composed by the various people you're following, if you stumble upon a particular tweet that you'd like to share with your own Twitter followers, instead of retyping the message from scratch, select it and then tap on the Re-Tweet option to copy that tweet and allow you to send it to your followers from your Twitter account. (Credit is automatically given to the original author of the tweet when you re-tweet a message.)

TIP In addition to communicating with your followers and the people you're following on Twitter, you can join in on virtual conversations happening between strangers. There are several ways to join in on a conversation about a specific topic.

First, use the Search option to find a specific topic based on a keyword or phrase. When using Twitter, topics or subjects are highlighted by a number sign (#) in front of the topic. For example, if you want to find a Twitter conversation relating to the iPad 2, you'd do a search for #iPad2. (Some people refer to the number sign as a pound sign or hashtag.)

Another way to find Twitter-based conversations to join in on is to view the ever-changing list of Trending Topics, tap on a topic that's of interest, and then respond to particular tweets from strangers that are displayed.

To view a list of Trending Now topics, on the iPhone, tap on the magnifying glass–shaped icon at the bottom of the official Twitter app's screen, and scroll down to the Trending Now heading. On the iPad, tap on the Search feature displayed on the left side of the screen, and then look under the Trending Now heading.

The Trending Now topics list updates constantly, as the most current topics people are discussing and tweeting about on Twitter change. Often, trending topics relate to late-breaking news stories or celebrity gossip, but they're always based on the most-tweeted-about subjects or topics.

! CAUTION Although virtually every celebrity, politician, professional athlete, author, or public figure has a presence on Twitter, there are also many impersonators and impostors out there.

To make sure you're following the actual celebrity or public figure that you intend, look for a blue-and-white check mark icon next to that person's username. This indicates that their identity has been verified by Twitter.

HOW TWITTER INTEGRATES WITH POPULAR iOS 5 APPS

As the iOS 5 operating system was being developed by Apple, the programmers included one new feature across a handful of apps that active Twitter users will appreciate. It's the capability to compose and send tweets from certain core apps without first having to launch the official Twitter app (or a third-party Twitter app).

Initially, Safari, Photos, Camera, Maps, and YouTube were among the iOS 5 apps to offer true Twitter integration. However, many third-party app developers are also starting to include this functionality in their own apps.

TIP Many apps that have a Share icon, which allows you to send content in that app to someone else via email or SMS/MMS message, also now offer a Tweet option that enables you to compose and share a tweet from within that app. More and more apps are starting to take advantage of this Twitter integration.

TWEETING FROM SAFARI

As you're surfing the Web using Safari, if you come across an interesting website that you'd like to share with your Twitter followers, simply tap on the Share icon (the square-shaped icon with the arrow coming out of it) that's displayed to the left of the URL field. A menu with six options appears: Add Bookmark, Add to Reading List, Add to Home Screen, Mail Link to This Page, Tweet, and Print.

Tap on the Tweet option. A Tweet window appears in Safari (shown in Figure 8.9) that will allow you to compose and send a tweet. Already attached to the tweet will be the URL for the website you want to share. You'll notice that some of the 140 characters available for the tweet are taken up by the length of the website address (URL). A character counter is displayed in the lower-right corner of the window.

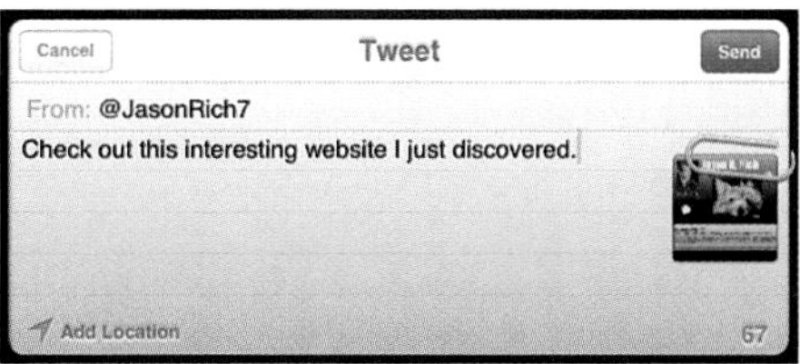

FIGURE 8.9

In specific iOS 5 core apps, including Safari, you can send an outgoing tweet without first launching the official Twitter app.

After composing your outgoing tweet, tap the Send icon (displayed in the upper-right corner of the window) to publish it as part of your Twitter feed. Your iOS device must have access to the Internet (via a Wi-Fi or 3G connection) to use the Tweet function of an app or to access Twitter in general.

TIP If you manage multiple Twitter accounts from your iPhone or iPad, when the Tweet window appears, the From field will automatically be filled in with one of your Twitter accounts. To change which account the tweet will be sent from, tap anywhere in the From field, and then tap on the Twitter account of your choice (as shown in Figure 8.10).

To include your current location as part of the tweet, tap on the Add Location option that's displayed in the lower-left corner of the Tweet window. A new window will appear that says, "Twitter would like to use your current location." Tap on the OK icon to continue. The small arrow icon next to the Add Location option will turn purple, indicating that your location will be shared as part of the outgoing tweet.

FIGURE 8.10

When managing multiple Twitter accounts, choose which account each outgoing tweet should be sent from by tapping on the From field.

TWEETING FROM THE PHOTOS AND CAMERA APPS

As you use the Photos app to browse through digital images stored on your iPhone or iPad (including images or video clips you've shot using your iOS device and images transferred and stored in the Photos app), you can share any image via Twitter from directly within the Photos app. To do this from the iPhone or iPad, as you're viewing an image in full-screen mode, follow these steps:

1. Launch the Photos app.
2. Select and view (in full-screen mode) the image you want to share via Twitter.
3. Tap on that image so that the various photo-related icons are displayed at the top and/or bottom of the screen.
4. Tap on the Share icon. On the iPhone, it's displayed in the lower-left corner of the screen as you're viewing a single image. On the iPad, the Share icon is displayed in the upper-right corner of the screen.
5. From the Share menu that appears, tap on the Tweet icon option (shown in Figure 8.11).

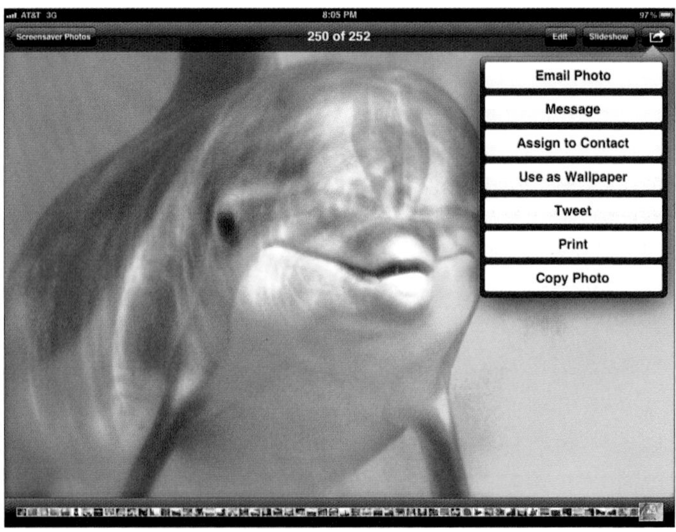

FIGURE 8.11

Tap on the Share icon in the app, tap the Tweet option, and then compose and send your tweet from the window that appears.

6. A Tweet window appears, along with the virtual keyboard. The selected photo will already be attached to the outgoing tweet.
7. From this point, follow the steps outlined in the preceding section to finish composing and then send your outgoing tweet with your attached photo.

TIP As you're looking at an album of digital images in thumbnail form on your iPhone or iPad (as opposed to a single image in full-screen mode), tap on the Share icon. Then, tap on any of the images in that album or folder. Next, tap on the other Share icon (this one actually displays the word "Share" in it), and select the Tweet option. The Tweet window will appear, and you can begin composing your outgoing tweet that will automatically have the selected photo attached to it.

Although you can attach, embed, and send up to five separate photos in an email message, you can attach only one photo or image to each outgoing tweet.

In the Camera app, after you shoot a photo (or video clip), a thumbnail for that file displays in the lower-left corner of the screen. Tap on that thumbnail. When the Share icon appears on the screen, tap on it. Next, choose the Tweet option from the menu. A Tweet window appears, allowing you to compose and send an outgoing tweet with the selected (just taken) photo or video clip already attached.

TWEETING FROM THE YOUTUBE APP

The YouTube online service is chock-full of free videos that are funny, entertaining, informative, and, in some cases, just plain bizarre. It's common for people to spend hours at a time watching various videos they come across using the YouTube app.

While viewing a video, to share it with your Twitter followers (and send a tweet about it), follow these steps:

1. Launch the YouTube app on your iPhone, iPod touch, or iPad from the Home Screen.
2. If you haven't ready done so, sign in to YouTube using your existing username and password.
3. Browse the various online-based videos you can stream from the Web using the YouTube app.
4. When you come across a video you want to tweet about, pause the video and wait for the various command icons to appear around it (as shown in Figure 8.12).

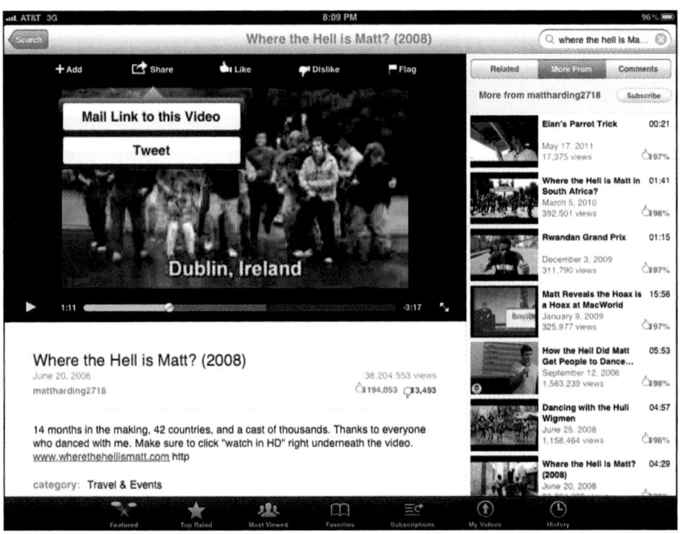

FIGURE 8.12

You can tweet a link to any YouTube video to share it with your Twitter followers.

5. Tap on the Share icon (the square-shaped icon with an arrow coming out of it), and select the Tweet option.
6. A Tweet window or screen will appear, allowing you to compose a new outgoing tweet. The video clip from YouTube will already be attached. Compose your tweet, and tap on the Send icon to share it with your Twitter followers.

MANAGE YOUR FACEBOOK ACCOUNT WITH THE OFFICIAL FACEBOOK APP

When it comes to online social networking, Facebook is by far the most popular service of its type in cyberspace. Its functionality goes well beyond what Twitter (which is basically a microblogging service) offers.

> **NOTE** Creating and managing a Facebook account is free, and it can be done from virtually any device that connects to the Internet, including an iPhone or iPad. To create a new Facebook account, using Safari, visit www.Facebook.com and complete the Sign Up form (shown in Figure 8.13). You can also create an account from within the official Facebook app. After your account is set up, complete your online profile and then invite people you already know to become your friends on Facebook.

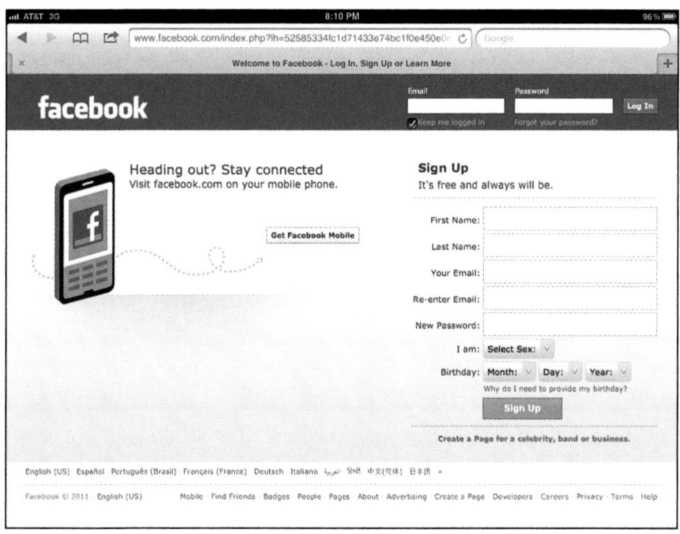

FIGURE 8.13

To set up a free Facebook account in just minutes, visit www.Facebook.com and fill in the Sign Up form.

In addition to sending updates to your Facebook friends, which can include short tidbits about what you're up to or what's on your mind, Facebook enables you to share photos (or video clips) and multi-image photo albums, send/receive email, participate in real-time chats with your friends, participate in online special-interest groups, play multiplayer games (like Words with Friends), and interact with people in a wide range of ways.

Much of Facebook's functionality is offered to iPhone and iPad users via the official Facebook apps, which are also among the all-time-most-popular apps offered from the App Store, according to Apple.

> **iOS 5 WHAT'S NEW** Facebook has released an iPad-specific app, as well as a separate iPhone app (that was revamped after the release of iOS 5). The iPad-specific app fully utilizes iOS 5 features, as well as the large-size, full-color touch-screen of the iPad. Both the iPhone and iPad versions of the official Facebook app are available, for free, from the App Store.

The official Facebook apps for iPhone and iPad are available, for free, from the App Store. Although there are also many third-party apps designed to be used with Facebook (some of which cost money), the official Facebook apps are the only ones designed and endorsed by Facebook.

While browsing the App Store, use the Search tool and enter the keyword "Facebook." Make sure, however, that you download and install the official Facebook app for whichever iOS device you're using. Choose the app that's published by Facebook, Inc. (as shown in Figure 8.14). Also, don't confuse the official Facebook app with the Facebook Messenger app, which has a different purpose.

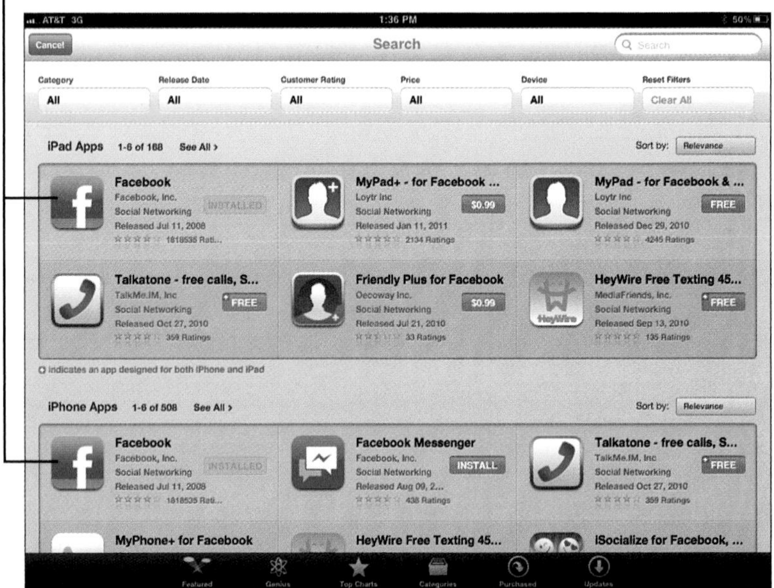

FIGURE 8.14

Only the official Facebook apps are designed and endorsed by Facebook, although many third-party apps enable you to manage your Facebook account and share photos, for example, from your iPhone or iPad.

> **TIP** After you download and install the official Facebook app on your iPhone or iPad, launch the Settings app, and then tap on the Facebook option displayed under the main Settings menu to customize some of the app's features. In Settings, also tap on the Notifications menu option, and then select Facebook from the In Notification Center menu to customize how your iPhone or iPad will display alerts, alarms, and notifications generated by the Facebook app.

When using the official Facebook app on your iPhone or iPad, the screen is divided into columns. To access the main menu, which enables you to access your profile and News Feed and access Facebook features such as Messages, Nearby, Events, Friends, Photos, and Chat, tap on the Menu icon that's displayed in the upper-left corner of the screen. It looks like three horizontal lines.

Located next to the Menu icon are icons that enable you to manage your friend requests, messages, and notifications.

Everything you're able to do using the Facebook app is done by accessing the main menu or through command icons that are displayed along the top or bottom of the screen.

On the iPad, a separate column displayed on the left side of the screen enables you to see which of your Facebook friends are currently online. By tapping on any friend listing, you can initiate a real-time text-based chat. On the iPhone, access the Chat feature from the main menu. It then opens a separate screen.

Also on the iPad, when either the Menu column (on the right side of the screen) or Chat column (on the left side of the screen) are visible, you can make them disappear by swiping your finger sideways in the direction that will close that feature.

TIP As you're looking at someone's contact information on their Profile page (or any other screens within the Facebook app), if you tap on an email address, the Mail app launches and you'll be able to send an email to that person. The To field is filled in automatically with the recipient's email address. Likewise, if you tap a website URL, Safari launches and automatically loads that website. Or, if you're using an iPhone and you tap on a phone number, your iPhone initiates a call to that number.

IN THIS CHAPTER

- How to use new features iOS 5 brings to the Camera and Photos apps
- How to use tips and tricks for shooting, editing, and sharing photos and videos
- How to use third-party photography apps that offer professional-quality editing features

SHOOT, EDIT, AND SHARE PHOTOS AND VIDEOS

People love taking photos, and thanks to the two digital cameras built in to the latest iPhones (the iPhone 4 and the iPhone 4S) and iPad 2, plus the major improvements made to the Camera and Photos apps with iOS 5, it's never been easier or more fun to shoot, edit, view, print, and share your digital images or video clips.

The iPhone 4S offers an improved 8MP rear-facing camera, along with the enhanced Camera and Photos apps that come preinstalled with iOS 5. Thus, it's possible to take crystal-clear photos and create up to 8″ × 10″ prints from the digital files. The trick to taking crystal clear images, however, is to hold the iPhone as steady as possible when shooting an image.

WHAT'S NEW The iOS 5 version of Photos app that comes preinstalled on your iPhone or iPad now enables you to edit and/or digitally enhance your photos after they're shot, as opposed to just viewing, printing, and sharing them. Now, if a photo you shoot appears slightly too light (overexposed) or too dark (underexposed), you can often fix it with a tap of the finger. You can also correct red-eye or crop and rotate images stored on the phone or tablet.

By tapping on the Share icon (a square icon with an arrow coming out of it) in the Photo app, you can now share your images in several ways. For example, you can attach up to five photos to an outgoing email message from within Photos, attach a photo to a text message, or tweet a photo to your Twitter followers. You also can sync your images with your primary computer or share your digital images with all your computers and iOS devices by setting up a Photo Stream via iCloud.

Using your digital images with other apps is also easier than ever, thanks to iOS 5. For example, you can assign a photo to a contact in the Contacts app, use a photo as your Lock Screen or Home Screen wallpaper, or easily copy a photo into another app, such as Pages or Keynote.

METHODS FOR LOADING DIGITAL IMAGES INTO YOUR iPHONE OR iPAD

Before you can view, edit, print, and share your favorite digital images, you'll first need to shoot them using the Camera or Photo Booth app that comes preinstalled on your iPhone or iPad, or transfer images into your iOS device.

Aside from shooting images using one of your iOS device's built-in cameras, there are several ways to import photos into your iOS device, and then store them in the Photos app:

- Use the iTunes sync process to transfer photos to your device. Set up iTunes to sync the image folders or albums you want, and then initiate an iTunes sync or wireless iTunes sync from your primary computer.
- Load photos from a Photo Stream (via iCloud). Later in this chapter, how to work with Photo Stream is explained.
- Receive and save photos sent via email. When a photo is embedded in an email, hold your finger on it for a second or two until a menu appears, giving you the option to save or copy the image to your device's virtual clipboard (after which you can paste it into another app). This feature is shown using the Mail app on an iPad 2 in Figure 9.1.

FIGURE 9.1

If you receive a digital photo attached to an incoming email, you can save the image in the Photos app by holding your finger on the image thumbnail (within the email), and then tapping on the Save Image option when it appears.

- Receive and save photos sent via text message or Twitter. Tap on the image you receive using the Messages app, and then tap on the Copy command to copy the image to your device's virtual clipboard (after which you can paste it into another app).
- Save images directly from a website as you're surfing the Web. Hold your finger on the image you're viewing in a website. If it's not copy-protected, after a second or two a menu appears, enabling you to save the image or copy it to your device's virtual clipboard (after which you can paste it into another app).
- Use the optional Camera Connection Kit ($29, available from Apple Stores or Apple.com) to load images from your digital camera's memory card directly into your iPhone or iPad.

NOTE When you use the Save Image command, the image will be stored in the Camera Roll album of Photos. You can then view, edit, enhance, print, or share it.

THE NEW AND IMPROVED CAMERA APP

The Camera app that comes preinstalled with iOS 5 has been given an overhaul, yet it still remains very easy to use if you want to snap a photo or shoot a video clip. To begin using the Camera app, launch it from your device's Home Screen.

The main camera viewfinder screen (shown in Figure 9.2) appears as soon as you launch the Camera app on an iPhone, iPod touch, or iPad. The main area of the screen serves as your camera's viewfinder. In other words, what you see on the screen is what you'll photograph or capture on video.

Use the camera selection icon to switch between front and back cameras
Options
The thumbnail shows the previous photo or video.
Tap the shutter button when you're ready to capture the photo or video.
The Camera/Video virtual switch toggles between camera and video modes.

FIGURE 9.2

From the Camera app's main screen, you can snap digital photos or shoot video. The app looks similar on the iPhone and iPad and works pretty much the same way.

Along the bottom of the screen are three icons. In the lower-left corner, you'll see a thumbnail image of the last photo or video clip you shot. Tap on it to view that image or video clip by automatically launching the Photos app.

At the bottom center of the screen is the camera's shutter button. Tap on this to snap a photo or to start and stop the video camera. In Camera mode, tap on this camera-shaped shutter button to snap a photo. You'll hear a sound effect, and a single photo will be saved. In Video mode, the camera-shaped icon transforms into an oval with a dim red dot inside it. The dot gets brighter when you tap on it to begin shooting a video clip.

In the lower-right corner of the Camera screen is the Camera/Video virtual switch. Tap on it to move the switch to the left and place the Camera app into Camera mode for shooting digital photos. Or move the virtual switch to the right to shoot video.

As you know, the iPhone 4, iPhone 4S, and iPad 2 each have two built-in cameras—one in the front, and one on the back of the device. The front-facing camera makes it easier to snap photos of yourself or participate in videoconferences, for example. The rear-facing camera allows you to photograph whatever you're looking at that's facing forward. Tap on the icon located in the upper-right corner of the screen to switch between cameras.

NOTE The older iPhone 3Gs lacks a front-facing camera. It offers a 3MP rear-facing camera, however, which can be used for taking photos or shooting video. If you're interested in taking the highest quality photos possible from an iPhone, consider upgrading to the iPhone 4S. It features a vastly improved 8MP-resolution camera and a better image sensor, which translates into superior digital photos.

On the iPad, displayed at the top center of the main Camera screen is the Options icon. Tap on it to reveal the Grid option. When it's turned on, a "Rule of Thirds" grid gets displayed on the main screen (your viewfinder when in Camera mode). How to use the Rule of Thirds while shooting to better compose and frame your shots is explained later in this chapter.

On the iPhone, the Options icon enables you to turn on/off the Rule of Thirds grid, as well as the HDR mode that's built in to the Camera app. Also on the iPhone, in the upper-left corner of the main Camera screen, you'll see an icon labeled Auto. You can turn this feature on or off. It controls whether the iPhone will automatically use the built-in flash when needed as you're shooting photos or video.

MORE INFO The HDR mode in the Camera app stands for High Dynamic Range. It can be used with the rear-facing camera only. When turned on, this feature captures the available light differently and can help you compensate for a photo that would otherwise be over- or underexposed.

When HDR mode is turned on, your iPhone will save two images each time you tap the shutter button to snap a photo. One will utilize HDR mode and the other will not. You can later view the images, choose which you like best, and discard the other one. The drawback to using HDR mode is that it takes several extra seconds to store both images each time you snap a photo, and this slows down the Camera app. Turn this feature on or off from the Photos menu in the Settings app on the iPhone.

HOW TO SNAP A PHOTO

Snapping a single digital photo using the Camera app is simple. Follow these steps:

1. Launch the Camera app from the Home Screen.
2. Make sure the virtual switch is set to Camera mode or the shutter button icon looks like a camera.
3. Tap on Options to turn on or off the Grid feature as you see fit, as well as the HDR feature on the iPhone.
4. Choose which of your device's two built-in cameras you want to use by tapping on the camera selection icon.
5. Compose or frame your image by holding up your iPhone or iPad and pointing it at your subject.
6. Select what the main subject of your photo will be, such as a person or an object. Tap your finger on the screen where your subject appears in the viewfinder. An autofocus sensor box appears on the screen at the location you tap. Where this box is positioned is what the camera focuses on (as opposed to something in the foreground, in the background, or next to your intended subject).

TIP As you're holding your iPhone or iPad to snap a photo or shoot video, be sure your fingers don't accidentally block the camera lens that's being utilized. On the iPhone 4 and iPhone 4S, next to the camera lens is a tiny flash. Keep your fingers clear of this as well.

7. If you want to use the Camera app's zoom feature, use a pinch motion on the screen. A zoom slider (shown in Figure 9.3) appears near the bottom of the screen. Use your finger to move the dot within the slider to the right to zoom in, or to the left to zoom out on your subject.

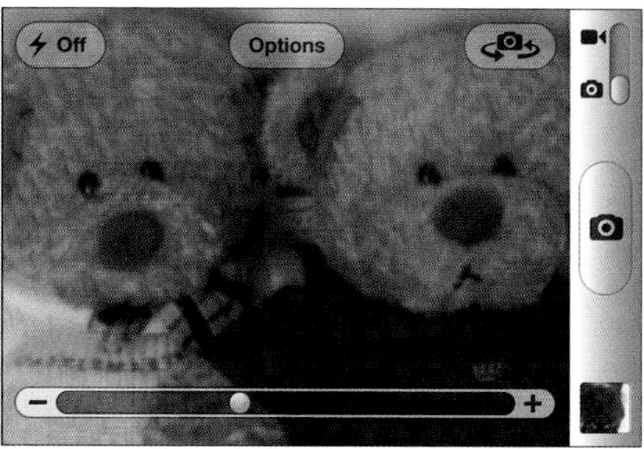

FIGURE 9.3

As you're framing an image, you can zoom in (or out) on your subject using the onscreen zoom slider. Use a pinch finger gesture on the screen to make this slider appear, and then move the slider to the right or left to increase or decrease the zoom level.

8. When you have your image framed within the viewfinder, tap on the shutter button to snap the photo. Or tap the Volume Up (+) button on the side of your iPhone. You'll see an animation of a virtual shutter closing and then reopening on the screen, indicating that the photo is being taken. At the same time, you'll hear an audio effect.
9. Within 1 and 5 seconds, the photo will be saved on your device in the Camera Roll album of Photos. You can now shoot another photo or view the photo using the Photos app.

> **TIP** In addition to the Camera icon that's displayed at the bottom-center of the Camera app that is used as the shutter button to snap a photo, you can press the Volume Up (+) icon that's located on the side of the iPhone to snap a photo when the Camera app is running.

HOW TO SHOOT VIDEO

Also from the Camera app, you can easily shoot video. Follow these basic steps for shooting video on your iPhone or iPad:

1. Launch the Camera app from the Home Screen.
2. Set the Camera app to Video mode with the Camera/Video virtual switch, or make sure the shutter button icon shows a dim red dot.

3. Choose which camera you want to use. You can switch between the front- and the rear-facing camera at any time.
4. Hold your iPhone or iPad up to the subject you want to capture on video. You can set up your shot by looking at what's displayed on the screen.
5. When you're ready to start shooting video, tap on the shutter button. The red dot will get brighter. This indicates you're now filming. Your iPhone or iPad will capture whatever images you see on the screen, as well as any sound in the area.
6. As you're filming video, you'll notice a timer displayed in the upper-right corner of the screen. Your only limit to how much video you can shoot is based on the amount of available memory in your iOS device and how long the battery lasts. However, this app is designed more for shooting short video clips, not full-length home movies.
7. Also as you're filming, tap anywhere on the screen to focus in on your subject using the app's built-in autofocus sensor. On the iPhone, you can also turn on or off the Auto Flash icon, which when needed can shed light on your subject as you're shooting.
8. To stop filming, tap again on the red dot shutter button. Your video footage will be saved. You can now view, edit, and share it from within the Photos app.

iOS 5 **WHAT'S NEW** Although the Photos app enables you to trim your video clips as well as view and share the videos, if you want to edit your videos, plus add titles and special effects, you'll definitely want to purchase and use Apple's feature-packed iMovie app, which is available from the App Store ($4.99). For more information about iMovie, visit www.apple.com/ipad/from-the-app-store/imovie.html.

USE PHOTO BOOTH TO SNAP WHIMSICAL PHOTOS

In addition to the Camera app, the Photo Booth app that comes preinstalled with iOS 5 enables you to shoot photos and immediately incorporate one of eight special effects, which are displayed on the main viewfinder screen as you're shooting. When an image is shot using Photo Booth, it's saved in the Camera Roll folder of Photos and can easily be viewed, edited, enhanced, printed, or shared.

The special effects available from within Photo Booth (shown in Figure 9.4) include X-Ray, Light Tunnel, Stretch, Mirror, Twirl, Thermal Camera, Kaleidoscope, and Squeeze. Photo Booth offers a more whimsical option for snapping photos using the front- or rear-facing camera of your iPhone or iPad.

FIGURE 9.4

The Photo Booth app enables you to snap photos on your iOS device and add whimsical effects to those images as they're shot.

USING THE PHOTOS APP TO VIEW, EDIT, ENHANCE, PRINT, AND SHARE PHOTOS AND VIDEOS

You can launch the Photos app from your iOS device's Home Screen or from within the Camera app by tapping on the image thumbnail icon displayed in the lower-left corner of the main Camera app screen.

First and foremost, you'll want to use the Photos app to view images stored on your iOS device. On the iPhone, the functionality of the Photos app is almost identical to the iPad version; however, the appearance of some of the screens and the position of certain command icons and menus will be different (due to the smaller size of the iPhone's screen). On the iPhone, for example, instead of a single Video Images screen, you'll see a separate Albums screen, followed by a Photos screen.

VIEWING PHOTOS AND VIDEOS

The View Images screen on the iPad (shown in Figure 9.5) can have up to three viewing tabs displayed at the top center of the screen labeled Photos, Albums, and Places.

FIGURE 9.5

From the View Images screen, tap on the Photos tab to view thumbnails of all images stored on your tablet in the Photos app.

TIP The Places tab appears only when photos are stored that include geo-tagging information.

On the iPad, tap on the Photos tab to see thumbnails of all images stored on your tablet (shown in Figure 9.5), regardless of which album they're stored in. Use your finger to move upward or downward and scroll through your images. When the Photos tab is active, the Slideshow and Share icons will be displayed in the upper-right corner of the screen. Tap Slideshow to create a slideshow of your images and adjust specific settings, such as transition effects and what music will be played.

On the iPad, when viewing your image thumbnails by tapping on the Photos tab (refer to Figure 9.5), tap on the Share icon in the upper-right corner of the screen to share, copy, move, or delete any of the images being displayed.

When you tap the Share icon, the Select Items screen will be displayed, again showing thumbnails of all images stored on your iOS device. At this point, tap on one or more image thumbnails to select them. When selected, a thumbnail will display a check mark icon in the lower-right corner.

In the upper-left corner of this screen, the other Share icon (this one displays the word "Share"), along with a Copy and Delete icon, will be visible. In the upper-right corner of the screen, an Add To and Cancel icon will be seen.

Tap on the Share icon to email or print the selected photo(s). Tap on the Copy icon to move the selected image(s) to another album. Or tap on the Delete icon to erase the selected images from your iOS device altogether.

Tap on the Add To icon to copy the selected images into a New Album that you can create when prompted. Tapping on the Cancel icon will exit this screen.

From the main View Images screen, tap on the Albums tab (displayed at the top center of the screen) to view thumbnails representing the individual albums that contain your photos. By default, all photos and videos shot using the Camera app will be saved in the Camera Roll album. From this screen, tap on any album thumbnail to reveal thumbnails of the images stored within that album.

TIP When you're viewing Album thumbnails on the iPad (or Album listings on the iPhone), by accessing the View Images screen of the Photos app, and then tapping on Albums, you can tap on the Edit icon (displayed in the upper-right corner of the screen) to create new albums. A New Album icon will appear in the upper-left corner of the screen. Tap on it, and then enter the album name when the New Album window appears. You can then copy or move photos into that new album using the Copy or Add To commands.

From the main View Images screen, tap on the Places icon to see a map showcasing where images were shot. This geo-tagging feature works with all photos shot using your iPhone or iPad, or with images shot with a digital camera that has a geo-tagging feature. If none of the images stored on your iOS device have geo-tagging associated with them, this Places feature will not be displayed.

In the Photos app, the thumbnails for video clips shot using the Camera app will also be displayed. However, in the lower-left corner of a video clip's thumbnail will be a movie-camera icon, and in the lower-right corner, the length of the video will be displayed (as shown in Figure 9.6).

FIGURE 9.6

The thumbnails for video clips stored in the Photos app look a bit different than those for photos. Video clips have a video-camera icon in the lower-left corner and the length of the video displayed in the lower-right corner of its thumbnail.

VIEW AN IMAGE IN FULL-SCREEN MODE

When viewing thumbnails of your images from the main View Images screen, tap on any single image thumbnail to view a full-screen version of that image. As you're then viewing an image, tap on it to make the various command icons for editing and sharing the image appear on the screen (as shown in Figure 9.7).

To exit the single-image view and return to the multi-image thumbnail view offered by the main View Images screen, tap anywhere on the screen to make the command icons appear, and then tap on the left-pointing arrow-shaped icon displayed in the upper-left corner of the screen. The word displayed in this icon will be the Album name the photo is stored in, such as Camera Roll. If you were previously looking at the main View Images' Albums screen (on the iPad) with the Albums tab selected, this icon will have the word Albums displayed in it.

As you're viewing a single image in full-screen mode, on the iPad along the bottom of the screen will be a filmstrip depiction of all images stored in the current album, or all images stored on your iOS device if you were previously in Photos viewing mode.

Also on the iPad, in the upper-right corner are three command icons used for editing, viewing slideshows, and sharing images. On the iPhone, the Edit command is displayed in the upper-right corner of the screen, and the Share command icon is displayed in the lower-left corner of the screen (as shown in Figure 9.8).

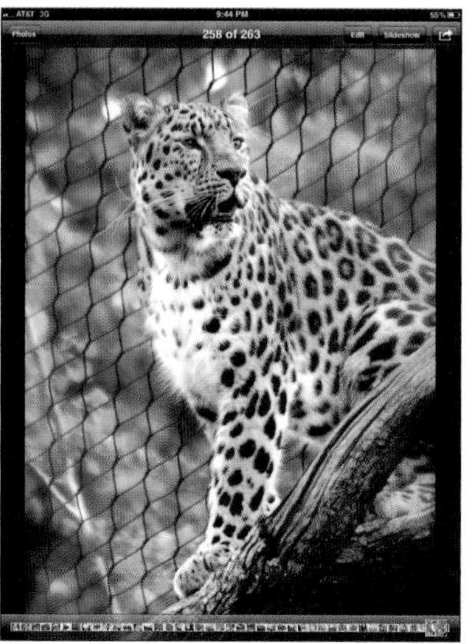

FIGURE 9.7

When viewing an image in full-screen mode, tap anywhere on that image to reveal the command icons you'll use to edit, enhance, and share that image.

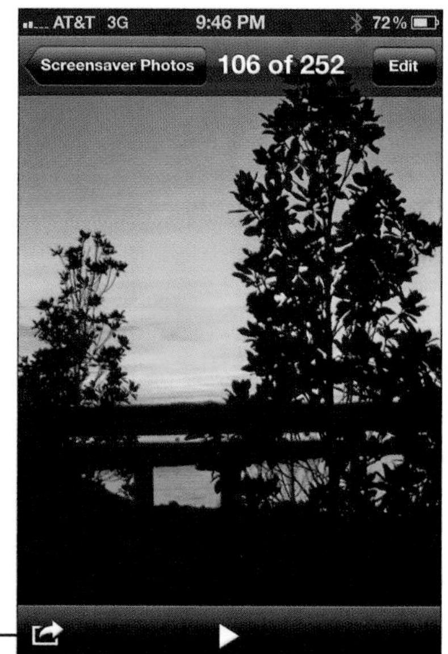

FIGURE 9.8

On the iPhone, the positions of the Edit and Share commands are different than on the iPad, but the functionality is the same.

EDITING PHOTOS AND VIDEOS

After selecting a single image to view in full-screen mode, tap on the Edit icon (displayed in the upper-right corner of the screen) to access the Edit commands for photos.

TIP When you tap on the thumbnail for a video clip, you'll have the option to play that clip in the Photos app. Or you can tap anywhere on the screen (except for the Play icon in the center of the screen) to access the video trimming (editing) feature, as well as the Share icon and the trash can icon (used to delete the video clip from your iOS device).

To trim a video clip, look at the filmstrip display of the clip located at the top of the screen, and move the left or right editing tabs accordingly to define the portion of the clip you want to edit. The box around the filmstrip display turns yellow, and the Trim command icon appears on the right side of the screen. Before tapping on Trim, tap on the Play icon to preview your newly edited video clip. If it's okay, tap on the Trim icon to save your changes. Two additional command icons will appear, labeled Trim Original and Save As New Clip. Trim Original alters the original video clip and replaces the file, whereas the Save As New Clip option creates a separate file and keeps a copy of the original clip.

COMMANDS FOR EDITING PHOTOS

When you tap on the Edit command icon while viewing a single image in full-screen mode, the following command icons are displayed on the screen. These icons provide the tools for quickly editing and enhancing your image. On the iPhone, these command options are displayed as graphic icons, whereas on the iPad, their purpose is spelled out. The commands available include the following:

- **Rotate**—Tap on this icon once to rotate the image counterclockwise by 90 degrees. You can tap the Rotate icon up to three times before the image will return to its original orientation.
- **Enhance**—Tap on the Auto-Enhance feature to instantly sharpen the photo and make the colors in it more vibrant. You should notice a dramatic improvement in the visual quality, lighting, detail, and sharpness of your image. Once you tap the Auto-Enhance feature, it works automatically.
- **Red-Eye**—If any human subject in your photo is exhibiting signs of red-eye as a result of your using a flash, tap on the Red-Eye icon to digitally remove this unwanted discoloration in your subject's pupils.

- **Crop**—Tap on this icon to crop the image and reposition your subject in the frame. If you forgot to incorporate the Rule of Thirds while shooting a photo, you can sometimes compensate by cropping a photo. You also can cut away unwanted background or zoom in on your subject, based on how you crop it. When the crop grid appears, position your finger in any corner or side of the grid to determine how you'll crop the image. When you're done, tap on the Crop icon to confirm your changes.

> **TIP** If you're cropping an image by moving around the cropping grid using your finger, if you first tap on the Constrain icon, this will force the basic dimensions of your image to stay intact. This will allow you to make perfectly sized prints later, without throwing off the image dimensions.

- **Revert to Original**—Tapping on this icon instantly removes all your edits and returns the photo to its original appearance.
- **Undo**—If you tap Undo, the last edit you made to the image is undone but any other edits remain intact.
- **Save**—After you've used the various editing commands to edit or enhance your image, tap on the Save command to save your changes.
- **Cancel**—Tap on this icon to exit the photo-editing mode of the Photos app without making any changes to the photo you're viewing.

PRINTING PHOTOS

iOS 5 is fully compatible with Apple's AirPrint feature, so if you have a photo printer set up to work wirelessly with your iOS device, you can create photo prints from your digital images using the Print command in the Photos app. Follow these steps to print an image:

1. Launch the Photos app from the Home Screen or by tapping on the photo thumbnail in the Camera app.
2. From the main View Images screen, tap on any thumbnail to view an image in full-screen mode. (You might need to open an album first by tapping on the Album's thumbnail, if you have the Albums viewing option selected.)
3. Tap on the full-screen version of the image to make the various command icons appear.
4. Tap on the Share icon that's displayed in the upper-right corner of the screen on the iPad or the lower-left corner of the screen on the iPhone.

5. From the Share menu, select the Print option.
6. When the Printer Options submenu appears, select your printer, determine how many copies of the print you'd like to create, and then tap on the Print icon.

MORE INFO To print wirelessly from your iOS device using the Air-Print feature, you must have a compatible printer. Hewlett-Packard currently offers a comprehensive line of printers, including several home photo printers and laser printers that are compatible with your iOS device. To learn more about AirPrint, and to configure your printer for wireless printing from your iPhone or iPad, visit http://support.apple.com/kb/HT4356.

SHARING PHOTOS AND VIDEOS

The Photos app offers several new ways to show off and share your favorite digital images. As you're looking at a photo in full-screen mode on the iPad, tap on the Slideshow icon to create a slideshow of your images and view it on your iPad screen. (You can also connect your tablet to an HD television or monitor to display your slideshow, or connect it to your home theater system via Apple TV.)

On the iPhone, iPod touch, or iPad, to access some of the other ways you can showcase and share your favorite images using the Photos app, tap on the Share icon, and then tap on one of the menu options.

HOW TO EMAIL A PHOTO

Tap on the Email Photo option to send one to five images to one or more recipients via email from within the Photos app. When viewing a single image, tap the Share button, followed by the Email Photo option. A compose email screen will appear with that photo already attached to the body of the email. Use the virtual keyboard to fill in the To field and Subject field (as shown in Figure 9.9), and then tap the Send icon.

To send between one and five photos within a single email message, follow these steps:

1. Launch the Photos app from the Home Screen or by tapping on the photo thumbnail in the Camera app.

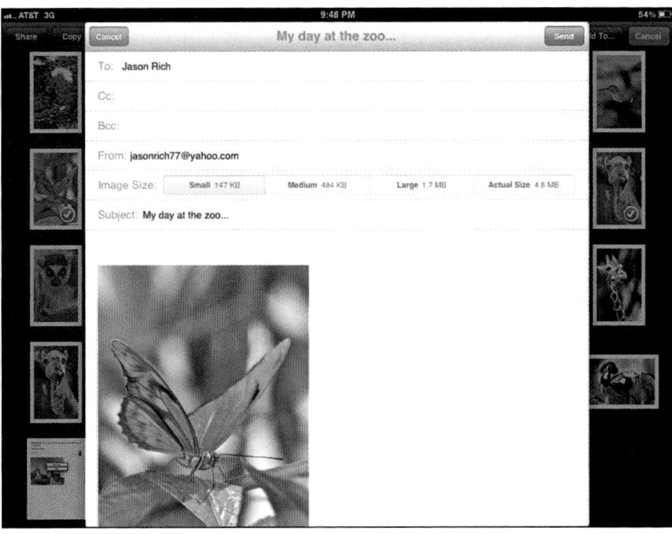

FIGURE 9.9

You can send an email with one to five photos attached to it from within the Photos app.

2. From the main View Images screen on the iPad, tap on the Photos tab. On the iPhone, tap on an album listing from the Albums screen.
3. Tap on the Share icon that's displayed in the upper-right corner of the screen on the iPad or the lower-left corner of the screen on the iPhone.
4. Using your finger, tap on one to five image thumbnails to select the images you want to include in an email. As you select each image from the Select Items screen, a checkmark icon will appear in the lower-right corner of each thumbnail.
5. After you've selected the images, tap on the other Share icon. It displays the word "Share" in it.
6. Tap on the Email option that appears.
7. When the compose email screen is displayed, your selected photos will already be attached to (embedded within) the outgoing email message. Simply fill in the To field with the email addresses for your intended recipients, and then fill in the Subject field using the virtual keyboard.
8. Tap the Send icon to send the email containing your images.

ASSIGN A PHOTO TO A CONTACT

To link an image stored in the Photos app to a specific contact in the Contacts app, follow these steps:

1. From within the Photos app, select a single photo and view it in full-screen mode.
2. Tap on the image while in full-screen mode to make the various command icons appear.
3. Tap on the Share icon.
4. Tap on the Assign to Contact option.
5. An All Contacts window, displaying the names associated with all your contacts, will be displayed. Scroll through the listing, or use the Search field to find the specific entry with which you want to associate the photo.
6. Tap on that person's or company's name from the All Contacts listing.
7. When the Choose Photo window opens, use your finger to move or scale the image. What you see in the box is what will be saved.
8. Tap on the Use icon in the upper-right corner of the Choose Photo window to save the photo and link it to the selected contact.
9. When you launch Contacts and access that person's entry (as shown in Figure 9.10), you will now see the photo you selected appear in that entry.

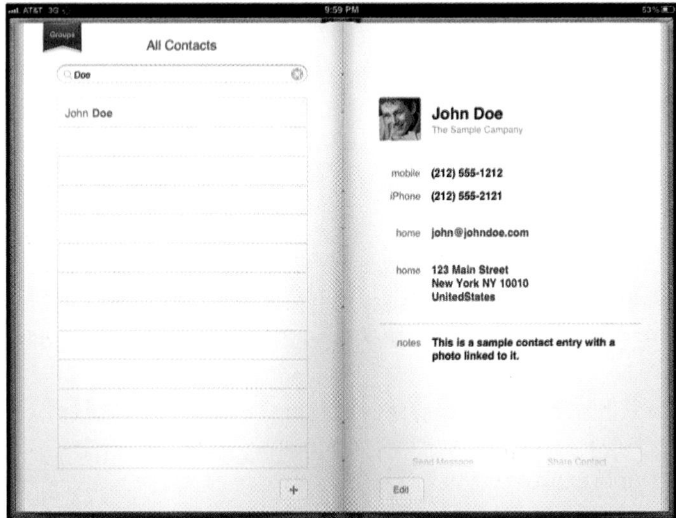

FIGURE 9.10

If you use the Contacts app to manage your contacts database, you can link a photo to each contact entry.

TWEET A PHOTO

Twitter functionality has been integrated into several iOS 5 apps, allowing you to compose and send tweets from within those apps. Photos is one of the apps that integrates with Twitter, allowing you to select a photo and tweet it to your followers, along with an accompanying text-based message.

Basically, after tapping the Share icon while viewing a single photo in full-screen mode, select the Tweet option. Compose your tweet message (which will already have the selected image attached), and then tap the Send icon.

COPYING A PHOTO

From within the Photos app, you can store a photo in your iOS device's virtual clipboard, and then paste that photo into another compatible app. To copy a photo into your device's virtual clipboard, follow these steps:

1. From within the Photos app, select a single photo and view it in full-screen mode.
2. Tap on the image while in full-screen mode to make the various command icons appear.
3. Tap on the Share icon.
4. Tap on the Copy Photo option. The photo will now be stored in the virtual clipboard.
5. Launch a compatible app and hold your finger down on the screen to use the Paste option and paste your photo from the clipboard into the active app.

DELETING PHOTOS STORED ON YOUR iOS DEVICE

To delete photos stored in the Photos app on the iPad, access the main View Images screen and tap on the Photos tab. Next, tap on the Share icon. On the iPhone, from the Albums screen, tap on any of the album listings. When the album opens and reveals the thumbnails for the images stored in that album, tap on the Share icon.

When you see the Select Items screen (shown in Figure 9.11), which is the same as the Select Photos screen on the iPhone (shown in Figure 9.12), use your finger to select one or more images. After the images are selected, tap on the red-and-white Delete icon that's displayed in the upper-left corner of the Select Items screen.

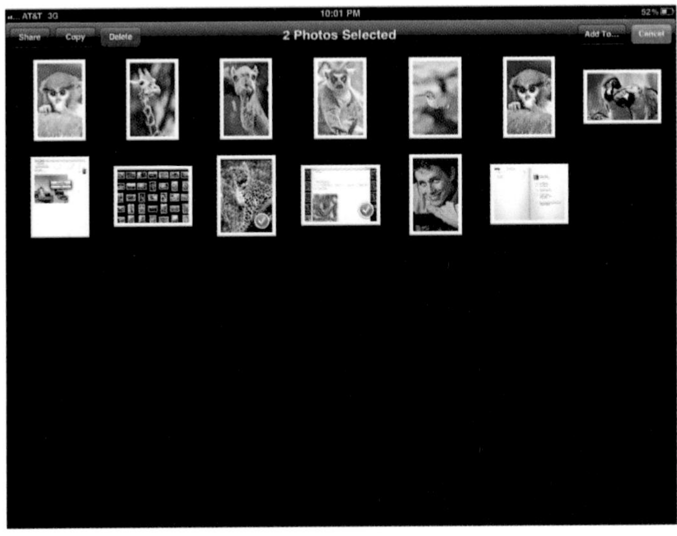

FIGURE 9.11

On the iPad, from the Select Items screen, you can select image thumbnails and then tap on the Delete icon to erase those images from your iOS device.

FIGURE 9.12

The Select Photos screen on the iPhone 4. Select the images you want to delete, and then tap on the Delete icon.

CREATE AND MANAGE A PHOTO STREAM VIA iCLOUD

You already know that you can easily transfer images into your iOS device and export them from your device using various methods. One new feature of iOS 5 is the capability to create and manage a Photo Stream via iCloud.

A Photo Stream enables you to store a collection of up to 1,000 of your digital images on iCloud, and automatically sync those images with your primary computer and all your iOS devices, including Apple TV. Thus, your most recent images are always readily available to you, and you never have to worry about backing them up or manually transferring them to a specific computer or device.

NOTE A Photo Stream can include up to 1,000 images. By default, this will be the most recent 1,000 you shoot or transfer to your Photo Stream. Beyond the 1,000 images stored on iCloud, all your digital images are automatically backed up and stored on your primary computer's hard drive (or on a hard drive connected to your primary computer).

To create and use the Photo Stream feature of iCloud, you'll need to set up a free iCloud account, plus have the latest version of OS X Lion installed on your Mac, as well as the most current version of iTunes. In addition, you'll need to update your iPhoto '11 software on your Mac with the latest version (iPhoto '11 version 9.2 or later).

To utilize iCloud's Photo Stream feature, from the Settings app on your iOS device, tap on the Photos option listed under the main Settings menu. Then, turn on the Photo Stream option from the Photos menu screen. To utilize this feature and be able to upload and download photos to and from your iOS device, a Wi-Fi Internet connection is required.

TIP You can store any image from your Photo Stream on your iOS device indefinitely. As you're viewing an image from your Photo Stream, tap on the Share icon and select the Save To Camera Roll option.

Your Photo Stream will be connected to the email address you linked with your iCloud account.

IN THIS CHAPTER

- How to use the calling features you'll find useful
- How to manage Favorites, Recents, Contacts, and Voicemail
- How to participating in Conference Calls
- How to using a wireless Bluetooth headset

10

MAKING AND RECEIVING CALLS WITH AN iPHONE

Although your iPhone is capable of surfing the Web, sending and receiving emails, accessing online social networking services, taking and sharing photos, managing your contacts database, helping you manage your schedule and to-do lists, and enabling you to listen to your favorite music, the fundamental purpose of Apple's iPhone is for it to serve as a feature-packed cellphone.

Your iPhone is capable of making and receiving voice calls using a wireless service provider that you selected when the phone was acquired. The Phone app that comes preinstalled on your iPhone offers a vast selection of calling features that make it easy to stay in touch with people.

TIP If you're an iPad user, you can make and receive Voice over IP (Internet-based) phone calls using the Skype app. These calls can be made to (or received from) any landline or cell phone. You also can participate in Skype-to-Skype calls for free. In summer 2011, Skype released an iPad-specific version of its app that can also be used for free videoconferencing.

The iPhone or iPad version of Skype is ideal for saving money when you're making international calls from the U.S., or to avoid hefty international roaming charges when you're calling home to the U.S. when traveling overseas.

After you set up and activate your new iPhone with a wireless service provider and choose a calling plan, it's capable of receiving incoming calls and enables you to make outgoing calls using the Phone app.

In the United States, several wireless service providers now offer the iPhone. When you purchase an iPhone 3G or iPhone 4, you must decide, in advance, which wireless service provider you'll sign up with (a two-year service agreement with a hefty early termination fee is involved).

The iPhone 4S is a global phone, meaning it will work with any compatible service provider, anywhere in the world. However, unless you purchase an unlocked and contract-free iPhone 4S, you still will need to activate it with a participating wireless service provider and sign a two-year service agreement.

Choose a wireless service provider that offers the best coverage area where you'll be using it, the most competitively priced calling plan based on your needs, and the extra features you want or need.

TIP From Apple's website, you can compare iPhone rate plans for wireless service providers that support the iPhone. In the U.S., visit https://static.ips.apple.com.edgekey.net/ipa_preauth/content/catalog/en_US/index.html.

For example, not all wireless service providers enable iPhone users to talk and surf the Web at the same time. Likewise, some offer better international roaming coverage than others, while some are more generous when it comes to monthly wireless data allocation. When it comes to the iPhone 3G and iPhone 4, the iPhone hardware is slightly different based on which wireless service provider you choose, so you can't switch after you've acquired the iPhone.

TIP For your iPhone to make or receive calls, it must be turned on and *not* in Airplane mode. A decent cellular service signal, which is displayed in the upper-left corner of the screen in the form of bars, is also a necessity. The more bars you see (up to five), the stronger the cellular signal (which is based on your proximity to the closest cell towers).

ANSWERING AN INCOMING CALL

Regardless of what you're doing on your iPhone, when an incoming call is received, everything else is put on hold and the Phone app launches, unless the iPhone is turned off or in Airplane mode, in which case calls automatically go to voicemail.

To control the volume of the ringer, press the Volume Up or Volume Down buttons on the side of your iPhone.

TIP While your iPhone is still ringing, to send an incoming call to voicemail (without answering it), press the Power button on the top of the phone once, or tap the Decline icon displayed on the screen.

There are several ways to answer an incoming call. If you're doing something else on your iPhone and it starts to ring, the caller ID for the incoming caller will be displayed, along with a green-and-white Answer icon and a red-and-white Decline icon (as shown in Figure 10.1). Tap the Answer icon to answer the call. If you tap Decline or wait too long to answer the call, it will automatically go to voicemail.

FIGURE 10.1
Your iPhone will notify you when an incoming call is received. You can then answer or decline that call.

If the iPhone is in Sleep mode when an incoming call is received, you'll need to unlock the phone by swiping your finger from left to right on the Slide to Answer slider, which automatically takes the phone out of Sleep mode, unlocks it, and answers the incoming call (as shown in Figure 10.2). Again, if you ignore the incoming call, it will be sent to voicemail after several rings.

FIGURE 10.2

If your iPhone is in Sleep mode when a call is received, you will need to slide your finger along the Slide to Answer slider to unlock the phone and answer the call.

> **TIP** If you're too busy to answer an incoming call on your iPhone, you can let the call go to voicemail (so that the caller can leave you a message), or you can set up call forwarding so that the incoming call automatically gets rerouted to another phone number, such as your home or office number. To set up call forwarding, and turn this function on or off as needed, launch the Settings app, and then tap on the Phone option under the main Settings menu.
>
> From the Phone menu in Settings, you can view your iPhone's phone number, set up and turn on call forwarding, turn on or off call waiting, and decide whether you want your iPhone's number to be displayed on someone's caller ID when you initiate a call.
>
> Also from Settings, you have the option to turn on or off the International Assist feature, which makes initiating international calls much less confusing.

After you answer an incoming call, again you have a few options. You can hold the iPhone up to your ear and start talking, or you can tap the Speaker icon and use your iPhone as a speakerphone (assuming you're not in a public area where doing this will annoy the people around you). You also can use the phone with a wired or wireless headset, which offers hands-free operation. The headset option is ideal when you're driving, plus it offers privacy and better sound quality (versus using the iPhone's speaker phone option).

! CAUTION If you're driving, choose a headset that covers only one ear, or use the Speaker option for hands-free operation. Refrain from holding the phone up to your ear or covering both ears with a headset. (See the section "A Few Thoughts About Wireless Headsets" for headset considerations.) Make sure you're familiar with state and local laws in your area related to the use of cellphones while driving. Some jurisdictions limit or prohibit using a cellphone while driving, even if the phone is a hands-free model, and many other areas across the country are considering similar legislation. If you're on the road a lot and need to use your iPhone or iPad to make calls while driving, check with AAA (www.aaa.com) or the Insurance Institute for Highway Safety (www.iihs.org/laws/cellphonelaws.aspx) for information about the laws in other localities where you might be driving.

Many people find it very convenient to use a wireless Bluetooth headset with their iPhone. You'll learn more about headsets later in this chapter. When using a Bluetooth headset, you don't need to hold the phone up to your ear to carry on a conversation. If you're using a headset, tap on the headset's answer button when you receive an incoming call to answer it. There's no need to do anything on your iPhone.

As soon as you answer an incoming call, the Phone apps screen will change, giving you access to the Call Menu screen (shown in Figure 10.3). This screen contains seven command icons: Mute, Keypad, Speaker, Add Call, FaceTime, Contacts, and End. At the top of the screen, the caller's information (or Caller ID) and a call timer are displayed.

FIGURE 10.3

The main Call Menu screen on the iPhone appears when you're participating in an incoming or outgoing call.

NOTE When you receive an incoming call, if the caller ID for that caller matches up with a contact stored in your Contacts database (in the Contacts app), that person's name, which number the call is from (Home, Work, Mobile, etc.), and the caller's photo (if you have a photo of that person linked to the contact) are displayed (refer to Figure 10.1 or Figure 10.2).

If there's no match in your Contacts database, the regular caller ID data will be displayed, which might include the person's name, phone number, and the city and state the call is originating from. However, not all incoming calls will display all this information.

You could receive calls labeled Private or Unknown; or just the phone number, along with the city and state from which the call is originating, might be listed.

Here's a summary of the command icons available to you from the Call Menu screen during a phone conversation (after you answer a call or after your outgoing call connects):

- **Mute/Hold**—Tap on this icon to turn off your iPhone's microphone. You will still be able to hear what's being said to you, but the person you're speaking with will not hear you. (When you're ready to be heard again, make sure you turn off the Mute feature by tapping on this icon again.) To place a call on hold, press and hold down the Mute button during a call. It turns blue. Tap the button again to take the person off hold and begin speaking to the person again.
- **Keypad**—Replace the current menu screen with the numeric telephone keypad. This is necessary for navigating your way through voicemail trees (for example, when you're told to press 1 for English, press 2 to speak with an operator, press 3 to connect to a call center in India, and so on).
- **Speaker (or Audio Source)**—Tap the Speaker icon to switch from Handset mode (in which you hold the iPhone up to your ear to have a phone conversation) to Speaker mode, which turns your iPhone into a speakerphone. If you're using your iPhone with a headset, a third Headset option will be listed, and this menu feature will be labeled Audio Source as opposed to Speaker.
- **Add Call (+)**—During a conversation with someone, you can initiate a conference call and bring a third party into the conversation by tapping on Add Call. How to do this is described later in this chapter.
- **FaceTime**—If the person you're talking to on your iPhone is also calling from an iPhone, and both devices have access to a Wi-Fi Internet connection, tap on the FaceTime icon to switch from a traditional phone call to a real-time videoconference using the FaceTime app. You also can initiate a FaceTime call and launch the FaceTime app by tapping on this icon.

- **Contacts**—While you're conversing on the phone, you can access your Contacts database and look up someone's information by tapping on this icon.
- **End**—At any time during a phone conversation, tap on the large red-and-white End icon to terminate the call. Or tap the end call button on your headset, if applicable. Unlike when you use a landline phone, you will need to tap the End icon to end a call after you say goodbye (as opposed to hanging up the receiver on a traditional phone), unless the person you're speaking with disconnects first.

iOS 5 WHAT'S NEW Depending on your wireless service provider, you might be able to participate in a phone conversation and surf the Web at the same time by taking advantage of iOS 5's multitasking capabilities. To do this, double-tap on the Home button to enter multitasking mode, and then tap on any app icon that appears in the multitasking bar. Or press the Home button once to access your iPhone's Home Screen, and then launch and use any app.

When you view the Home Screen while still on the phone, near the top of the Home Screen will be a green-and-white banner that shows, "Touch to return to call," along with a call timer. Tap on this green bar to return to the Phone app.

Keep in mind that your phone conversation can continue while you're using other apps. While some wireless service providers enable you to talk and web surf at the same time, others don't. Even if this is the case, you can still access and use other iPhone apps during a phone conversation.

RESPOND TO A CALL WAITING SIGNAL WHILE ON THE PHONE

As you're chatting it up with the person you're speaking with on the phone, if you have the Call Waiting feature turned on (it's controllable from the Settings app), and if someone else tries to call you, you will hear a call waiting tone, and a related message will appear on your iPhone's screen (as shown in Figure 10.4).

TIP When you accept a second incoming call via Call Waiting, the command icons on your iPhone change. You'll now be able to merge the two calls by tapping on the Merge Calls icon (creating a three-way conference call) or using the Swap icon to switch between calls (always keeping one party on hold). This is much easier to do when you're using a wireless Bluetooth headset or a hands-free car kit, so you can talk while looking at the iPhone's screen.

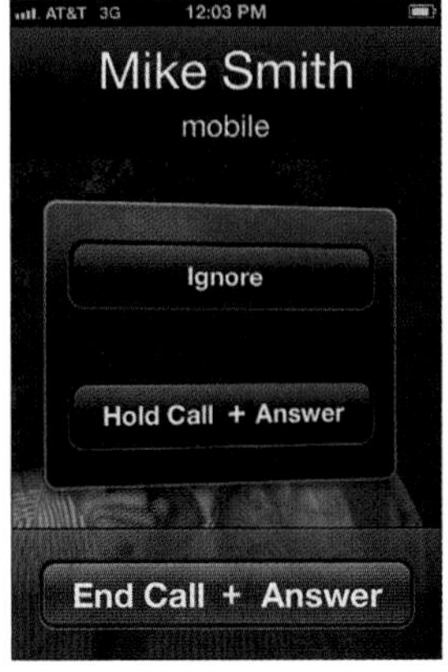

FIGURE 10.4

When the call waiting signal is heard, you can ignore the new call, put the current caller on hold and answer the new call, or disconnect the current caller and answer the new call.

The second caller's caller ID information will be displayed on the screen, along with three command icons, labeled Ignore, Hold Call + Answer, and End Call + Answer. Here's what each of these commands is used for:

- **Ignore**—Disregard the incoming call (send it to voicemail) and continue speaking with the person you're already on the phone with.
- **Hold Call + Answer**—Place the person you're speaking with on hold and answer the new, incoming call. You can then switch back to the original conversation, or merge the two calls and create a conference call.
- **End Call + Answer**—Disconnect from the person you're speaking with and answer the new, incoming call.

> **TIP** When the call waiting signal goes off on your iPhone, typically only you will hear it. Thus, the person you're speaking with on the other end of the line will not know you've received another call. So before tapping Hold Call + Answer or End Call + Answer, be sure to tell the person you were originally speaking with what's going on.

While engaged in a conference call on your iPhone, the names of the parties you're speaking with (or their caller ID phone numbers) scroll across the top of the screen. The title Conference is displayed near the top center of the screen (shown in Figure 10.5). Tap on the > icon to the right of the Conference title to reveal a new screen that enables you to place either party in the conference call on hold. To reestablish the conference call, tap on the Merge Calls icon again.

While you're engaged in a three-way call (with two other parties), you can tap on the Add Call option again to add more parties to the conference call.

FIGURE 10.5

When you're engaged in a conference call, you can place one party on hold and continue speaking with the other parties by tapping on the > icon displayed next to the Conference title.

MAKING CALLS FROM YOUR iPHONE

There are several ways to initiate a phone call from your iPhone; however, you must first launch the Phone app. Then, you can do the following:

- Dial a number manually using the keypad.
- Access a listing from your Contacts database (from within the Phone app), choose a number, and dial it.
- Use your iPhone's Voice Dialing feature. Or, if you're using an iPhone 4S, use Siri.
- Redial a number from your Recents call log.
- Select and dial a phone number from the Phone app's Favorites list.
- Redial a number used by someone who left you a voicemail message
- Dial a number displayed in another compatible app, such as Maps, Safari, or Contacts. When you tap on the phone number, it dials that number and initiates a call.

MANUAL DIALING

To initiate a call by manually dialing a phone number, follow these steps:

1. Launch the Phone app from the Home Screen.
2. Tap on the Keypad icon displayed at the bottom of the screen (as shown in Figure 10.6).

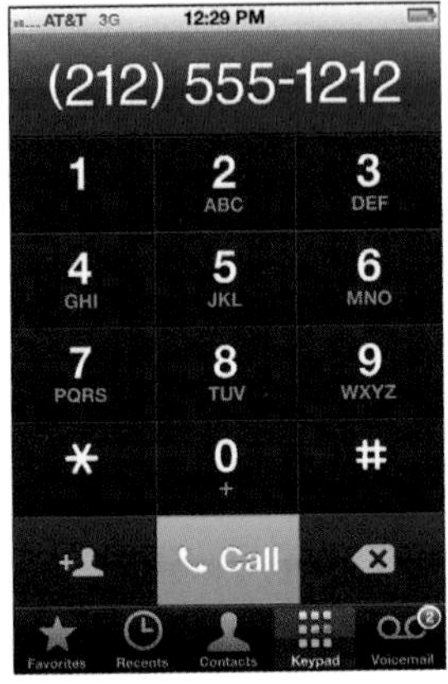

FIGURE 10.6

A telephone numeric keypad appears when you tap on the Keypad option (displayed at the bottom of the screen) within the Phone app.

3. Using the numeric phone keypad, dial the number you want to reach, including the area code. (If you're making an international call, include the country code as well.)
4. If you make a mistake when entering a digit, tap the Backspace key displayed to the right of the Call button.
5. When the 10-digit phone number is entered and displayed at the top of the screen, tap the green-and-white Call button to initiate the call. If you're making an international call, entering additional digits will be required.
6. The display on the iPhone will change. A "Calling" message is displayed until the call connects, at which time the Call Menu screen is displayed (refer to Figure 10.3).

iOS 5 **WHAT'S NEW** As you enter a phone number using the keypad, if that number is already stored in your Contacts database (within the Contacts app), the person's name will automatically be displayed at the top of the screen, just below the phone number you entered.

TIP You can use the Cut, Copy, and Paste features of iOS 5 to copy a phone number displayed in another app, and then paste it into the phone number field on the Keypad screen.

DIALING FROM A CONTACTS ENTRY IN THE PHONE APP

From within the Phone app, you can look up any phone number stored in your personal Contacts database that's associated with the Contacts app. The Phone and Contacts apps work nicely together on your iPhone. To use this feature, follow these steps:

1. Launch the Phone app from the Home Screen.
2. Tap on the Contacts icon displayed at the bottom of the screen.
3. An alphabetized listing of the contacts stored in the Contacts app will be displayed (as shown in Figure 10.7). At the top of the screen is a blank Search field. Using your finger, either scroll through the alphabetized list of contacts or use the iPhone's virtual keyboard to find a stored listing.

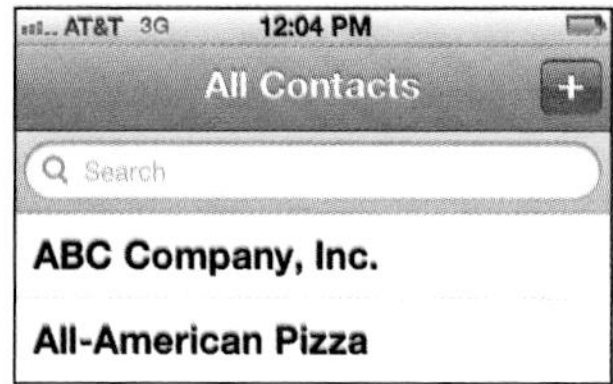

FIGURE 10.7

From the All Contacts screen, select the contact you want to call, or use the Search field to find a specific contact.

4. Tap on any listing to view its complete Contacts entry. This might include multiple phone numbers, such as Home, Work, and Mobile. From a contact's entry screen, tap on the phone number you want to dial.
5. The display on the iPhone will change. A "Calling" message is displayed until the call connects, at which time the Call Menu screen is displayed (refer to Figure 10.3).

VOICE DIALING

After you have made entries into your Contacts database using the Contacts app, you can use the Phone app's Voice Control feature to dial someone's phone number by speaking into the iPhone. Voice Control works with the iPhone 3Gs and iPhone 4. If you're using an iPhone 4S, you can use Siri to initiate calls using your voice.

The Siri voice control feature of the iPhone 4S is fully compatible with the Phone app. To use Siri to initiate a call, activate the Siri feature, and when you hear the audio prompt, say, "Call [insert name] at [insert location, such as home or work]," or "Call mom on her cell."

The first time you refer to your mom, dad, or grandma, for example, Siri will ask you who that person is, so that person can be matched up with their Contacts entry. Siri then remembers this information, so when you say, "Call dad at work," Siri knows exactly who you're talking about.

Using Siri, you can also say, "Dial," and then speak the digits of a phone number to initiate a call.

TIP The Voice Command feature (on the iPhone 3Gs and iPhone 4) also works with the Music app to control the music you're listening to. Or, you can ask the iPhone, "What time is it?" and it will respond by speaking the current time. However, this feature is most useful for making hands-free calls from your iPhone, without having to look at the screen.

To use Voice Dialing on the iPhone 3Gs or iPhone 4, follow these steps:

1. While using any iPhone app (or viewing the Home Screen), press and hold down the Home button on your iPhone for a few seconds. The Voice Control screen appears (shown in Figure 10.8), replacing the Phone app screen.

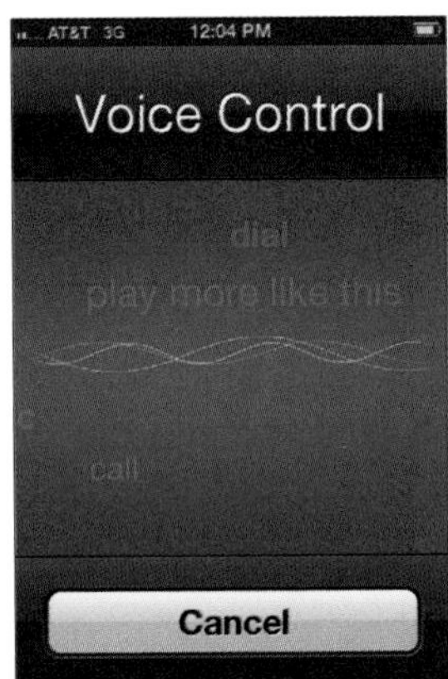

FIGURE 10.8

The Voice Control screen on your iPhone. When it appears, start talking directly into your phone and tell it what to do.

2. When you hear a beep that's associated with the Voice Control screen, speak into your iPhone, and use a command such as "Call" or "Dial," followed by the person's name. For example, say, "Call Jason Rich," or "Dial Jason Rich." As you're speaking a contact's name into your iPhone, say both first and last names.
3. If the entry in your Contacts database has more than one phone number listed, you'll need to be more specific with your voice command and say something like, "Call Jason Rich at Home," "Call Jason Rich at Work," or "Call Jason Rich, Mobile."
4. Assuming that your iPhone understands you (you must speak slowly and clearly), the Phone app dials the number you requested.

TIP To use the Voice Control feature to dial a phone number that is not already stored in your Contacts database, follow steps 1, 2, and 3 above, but then speak each digit of the 10-digit phone number. For example, you'd say, "Dial 2-1-2-5-5-5-1-2-1-2." Be sure to speak each digit separately. However, when dialing a toll-free 800 number, you can say, "eight hundred" instead of "eight-zero-zero." This also works when making international calls. Simply speak each digit of the phone number, including the country code, for example.

INITIATING A CONFERENCE CALL

During a typical phone conversation with one other person, you can initiate a conference call and bring a third party into the call. To do this, from the Call Menu screen (refer to Figure 10.3), tap on the Add Call (+) icon. The Call Menu screen will be replaced by the All Contacts screen (which includes a listing of all contacts stored in your Contacts database), as well as a blank Search field.

You can either look up the phone number you want to add to your conference call or tap on the Keypad icon (displayed at the bottom of the screen) to manually enter the phone number. When you do this, the Call Menu screen will change slightly. The Add Call and FaceTime command icons are replaced by Merge Calls and Swap icons. During this process, the person you were speaking with will be placed on hold. Tap Merge Calls to make both calls active and initiate the conference call. Or tap Swap to switch between calls, one at a time.

TIP If you're already on a call and you hear the call waiting tone, you will have the option to place the current caller on hold and answer the new incoming call by tapping on the Hold Call + Answer icon. At this point, you can swap back and forth between the calls, or merge the two calls to initiate a conference call.

MANAGING YOUR VOICEMAIL

Your unique iPhone phone number, provided by your wireless service provider, comes with voicemail, which allows people to leave you messages if you're not able to speak with them when they call.

Just as with any voicemail service, you can record your outgoing message, play back missed messages from your iPhone, or call your iPhone's voicemail service and listen to your calls from another phone.

> **TIP** To set or change your voicemail password, launch the Settings app and tap on the Phone option. From the Phone menu in Settings, scroll down to the Change Voicemail Password option and tap on it. When the Password screen appears, use the keypad to create and enter a password. To change a password, first enter your current password, tap Done, and then enter a new voicemail password.

RECORD YOUR OUTGOING MESSAGE

To record your outgoing voicemail message, which is what people will hear when they call your iPhone and you don't answer, follow these steps. Or you can have a computer-generated voice instruct callers to leave a message.

1. Launch the Phone app from the Home Screen.
2. Tap on the Voicemail icon, displayed in the lower-right corner of the screen.
3. In the upper-left corner of the Voicemail screen (shown in Figure 10.9), tap on the Greeting icon.

FIGURE 10.9

The Voicemail screen on the iPhone. From here, you can listen to your messages or choose to record an outgoing greeting.

4. From the Greeting screen, tap on the Default option to skip recording a message and have a computer voice use a generic message. Or tap on the Custom option to record your own outgoing voicemail message.
5. After you tap the Custom option, it will be highlighted in blue. Tap on the Record icon that's displayed in the lower-right corner of the Greeting screen. Hold the phone up to your mouth and begin recording your message.
6. A sample message might say, "Hello, you've reached the cellular voicemail for [insert your name]. I am not available right now, but please leave your name and phone number, and I will return your call as soon as possible. Thank you for calling."
7. When you're done recording, tap on the Record button again. You can now play back your message by tapping on the Play icon, or tap on the Save icon (displayed in the upper-right corner of the screen) to save your message and activate it.

HOW TO PLAY AND DELETE VOICEMAIL MESSAGES

If you receive an incoming call that you either missed or opted to avoid answering (such as that dreaded call from your mother-in-law or a bill collector), you can listen to the voicemail message the caller left, either from your iPhone or by calling your iPhone's voicemail from another phone.

LISTEN TO VOICEMAIL FROM YOUR iPHONE

From your iPhone, to listen to and then save or delete an incoming voicemail message, follow these steps:

1. Launch the Phone app from the Home Screen.
2. Tap on the Voicemail icon that's displayed in the bottom-right corner of the screen.
3. Under the Voicemail heading seen at the top of the screen will be a listing of missed voicemail messages (refer to Figure 10.9). Tap on any of the messages to highlight it.

NOTE When you see a blue dot to the left of a voicemail message listing, this indicates it's a new, unheard message. After you listen to the message, the blue dot will disappear. When you tap on the message to listen to it, the blue dot will transform into a Pause/Play icon.

4. Near the bottom of the screen, you will see a slider that depicts the length of the message, along with Call Back and Delete icons.
5. After a message is highlighted, tap on the small play/pause icon that appears to the left of the message listing. The message will begin playing. It might, however, take a few seconds for the message to load. A brief pause should be expected.
6. As your message plays, the dot on the timer slider near the bottom of the screen moves to the right. You can listen to parts of the message again by moving this slider around with your finger.
7. When you're done listening to the message, you can leave the listing alone (which keeps the message saved on your phone), or you can tap the Delete icon to erase it. You also have the option to call back the person who left the message by tapping on the Call Back icon.
8. To exit the voicemail options, tap on any of the other command icons displayed at the bottom of the Phone app's screen, or press the Home button on your iPhone.

TIP You might find it easier to listen to your voicemail messages via speaker phone, by first tapping on the Speaker icon in the upper-right corner of the voicemail screen.

TIP If you accidentally delete an important voicemail, don't panic. From the voicemail screen, scroll to the very bottom of your voicemail message list and tap on the Deleted Messages icon. Tap on the message you want to undelete to highlight it, and then tap on the Undelete icon.

LISTEN TO YOUR iPHONE'S VOICEMAIL FROM ANOTHER PHONE

You also have the option to use another phone to call your iPhone's voicemail service and listen to the messages that were left. Follow these steps:

1. From any other phone besides your iPhone (including a landline or another cellphone), dial your iPhone's phone number.
2. When your iPhone's voicemail picks up, press the * key on the phone you're calling from.
3. When prompted by the computer voice, enter the numeric password that's associated with your voicemail.

4. Follow the voice prompts to listen to or delete your messages.
5. As you're listening to your messages:
   - Press 1 to play back your messages.
   - Press 5 to hear details about a message, including the incoming phone number and the time/date it was recorded, as well as the message length.
   - Press 7 to delete the current message.
   - Press 9 to save the message.
   - Press # to skip the current message.
   - Press 0 for more options.
6. Hang up when you're finished listening to your voicemail messages.

CREATE AND USE A FAVORITES LIST

From within the Phone app, you can create a Favorites list, which is a customized list of your most frequently dialed contacts. To access this list, launch the Phone app, and then tap on the Favorites icon that's displayed near the bottom-left corner of the screen.

To add a contact to the Favorites list (shown in Figure 10.10), tap on the plus-sign (+) icon that you see in the upper-right corner of the screen. Select any listing from your Contacts database and tap on it. When the complete listing for that entry appears, tap on the specific phone number you want listed in your Favorites list. The newly created Favorites listing will automatically appear at the end of your Favorites list.

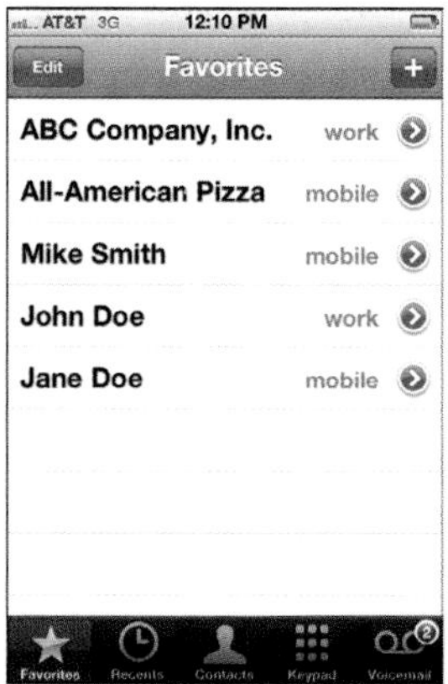

FIGURE 10.10

The Favorites list on your iPhone displays your most frequently called contacts, allowing for one-tap dialing.

TIP Each favorites entry can have one name and one phone number associated with it. So, if a Contact entry has multiple phone numbers listed, choose one. Or, if you want quick access to someone's home, work, and mobile number from your Favorites list, create three separate entries for that person. When you create the entry in Favorites, the type of phone number it is (Home, Work, Mobile, iPhone, and so on) is displayed to the right of the person's name.

To edit the contacts already listed in your Favorites list, tap on the Edit icon in the upper-left corner of the screen. After tapping Edit, you can change the order of your Favorites list by holding your finger on the rightmost icon next to a listing, and then dragging it upward or downward to the desired location. Or you can delete a listing by tapping on the red-and-white negative-sign icon displayed to the left of a listing. When you're finished making changes, tap on the Done icon that's displayed in the upper-left corner of the screen.

To dial a phone number listed in your Favorites list, simply tap on its listing. The Phone app automatically dials the number and initiates a call.

ACCESSING YOUR RECENTS CALL LOG

The Phone app on your iPhone automatically keeps track of all incoming and outgoing calls. To access this detailed call log, launch the Phone app from the Home Screen, and then tap on the Recents command icon displayed at the bottom of the screen.

At the top of the Recents screen (shown in Figure 10.11) are two command tabs, labeled All and Missed, along with an Edit command icon. Tap on the All tab to view a detailed listing of all incoming and outgoing calls, displayed in reverse-chronological order. Missed incoming calls are displayed in red. Tap on the Missed tab to see a listing of calls you didn't answer. Tap on the Edit icon to delete specific calls from this listing.

TIP Missed calls will also be displayed in the Notification Center window on your iPhone or as an icon badge or alert on your Home Screen, depending on how you set up Notifications for the Phone app within the Settings app. To customize the Notifications options for the Phone app, launch Settings from the Home Screen and tap on the Notifications option. From the Notifications screen in Settings, tap on the Phone option. You can adjust how your iPhone will alert you to missed calls by personalizing the options on this Phone screen.

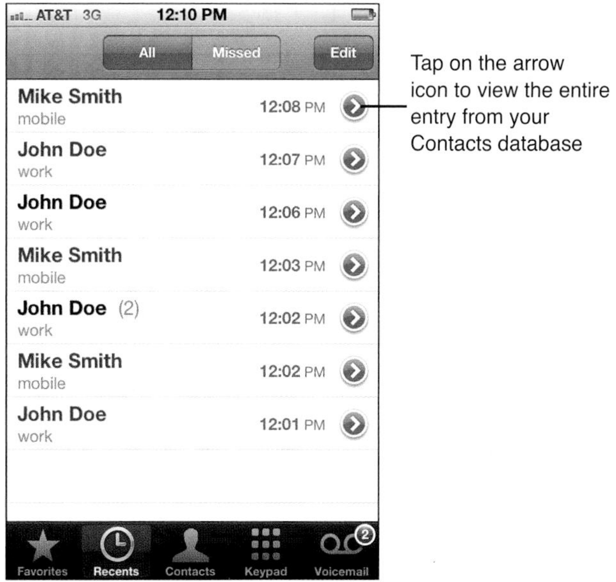

FIGURE 10.11

Your iPhone maintains a detailed log of all incoming and outgoing calls, which you can access from the Recents screen in the Phone app.

Each listing in the Recents call log will display the name of the person you spoke with (based on data from your Contacts database or the Caller ID feature) or their phone number. If it's someone from your Contacts database, below the name will be information about which phone number (home, work, mobile, or such) the caller used.

If the same person called you, or you called that person, multiple times in a row, a number in parentheses will indicate how many calls were made to or from that person. This is displayed to the right of the name or phone number.

On the right side of the screen, with each Recents listing, is the time the call was made or received. To view the Contacts entry related to that person, tap on the right-pointing blue-and-white arrow icon that's associated with the listing. At the top of a contact's entry screen are details about the call itself, including its time and date, whether it was an incoming or outgoing call, and its duration.

To call someone back who is listed in the Recents list, tap anywhere on that listing, except for on the blue-and-white arrow icon.

DO YOU TALK TOO MUCH? KEEPING TRACK OF USAGE

Every iPhone voice plan come with a predetermined number of talk minutes per month. Some plans offer unlimited night and weekend calling, but calls made or received during the day count against your monthly minute allocation.

> **! CAUTION** Contact your wireless service provider (or read your service agreement carefully) to determine the time period that's considered prime daytime, versus night or weekend, as it varies greatly. Unlimited night and weekend calling does not start until 9:00 p.m. with some wireless service providers. If you have a truly unlimited calling plan, however, this is not a concern.

To keep track of your monthly usage, launch the Settings app and tap on the General option. From the General screen within Settings, scroll down to the Usage option and tap on it. Scroll to the bottom of the Usage screen, and tap on the Cellular Usage option.

Or for the exact number of minutes used thus far during the current billing period, contact your wireless service provider by phone or via the company's website. If you go over your monthly minute allocation, you will be charged a hefty surcharge for each additional minute used.

> **TIP** All the wireless service providers that support the iPhone offer a free app for managing your wireless service account. It's available from the App Store. Use it to manage all aspects of your account, pay your monthly bill, and view your voice, data, and text-messaging use at any time. You can also set the alert option in the app to remind you each month when the bill is due for payment.

CUSTOMIZING RINGTONES

Thanks to iTunes, you can purchase and download custom ringtones for your iPhone. You can use one ringtone as your generic ringtone for all incoming calls, or you can assign specific ringtones to individual people.

> **TIP** To shop for ringtones, launch the iTunes app from your iPhone. At the bottom of the iTunes screen, tap on the More (...) icon. When the More screen appears, tap on the Ringtones option and start shopping.

When you purchase and download a new ringtone, it will become available on your iPhone's internal ringtones list. Most ringtones from the iTunes Store cost $1.29 each. However, it is possible to create your own ringtones on a computer and then send them to your iPhone using the iTunes Sync process.

To choose a default ringtone that you'll hear for all your incoming calls, launch the Settings app and select the Sounds option. From the Sounds screen within Settings, scroll down to the Ringtone option and tap on it. A complete listing of ringtones stored on your iPhone is displayed. iOS 5 comes with 25 ringtones pre-installed that you can choose from. From the Ringtones screen in Settings, tap on a ringtone to listen to it and select it as your new default. Or, at the top of this screen, tap on the Buy More Tones option to shop for more via iTunes.

CUSTOM RINGTONES FOR SPECIFIC CONTACTS

To assign a custom ringtone to a specific person so that you hear it when that person calls your iPhone, follow these steps:

1. Launch the Contacts app from the iPhone's Home Screen.
2. From the All Contacts screen, find the specific contact with whom you want to link a custom ringtone. You can scroll through the listing or use the Search field to find a contact.
3. When the contact is selected and you're looking at that Contacts entry, tap the Edit icon that's displayed in the upper-right corner of the screen.
4. From the Info screen that displays that contact entry's data, scroll down to the Ringtone field and tap on it. It will show that the ringtone assigned to the contact is the iPhone's default ringtone.
5. When the Ringtone screen appears, select a specific ringtone from the list that you want to assign to the contact and tap on it. You can choose a specific song (purchased from iTunes) or ringer sound that reminds you of that person.
6. Tap on the Save icon to save your selection and return to the contact's Info screen. Tap on the Done icon to save your changes.
7. When that contact calls you, the ringtone you'll now hear will be the one you just linked to that contact (as opposed to the default ringtone).

A FEW THOUGHTS ABOUT WIRELESS HEADSETS

Many states have outlawed using a cellphone while driving unless you have a wireless headset or hands-free feature on your phone. Although the speakerphone feature of your iPhone counts as a hands-free feature, to ensure the best possible call quality while you're driving, invest in a wireless Bluetooth headset.

Not only can you use a wireless Bluetooth headset while driving, but you can keep it on your person throughout the day and use it whenever you make or receive calls using your iPhone. This allows you to keep your hands free while you're talking, or to easily access other apps or iPhone features during a phone conversation. If you invest in only one accessory for your iPhone, and you plan to use the iPhone to make and receive phone calls, a wireless Bluetooth headset is a worthwhile investment (although a good-quality iPhone case is also highly recommended).

Bluetooth wireless headsets are priced as low as $20 but can cost as much as $200. If you want to ensure the highest-quality phone conversations possible, so that people can hear you and you can hear them, even if there's background noise present, invest in a good-quality Bluetooth wireless headset that includes a noise-canceling microphone and a good-quality speaker. Plus, choose a headset that's comfortable to wear and that has a long battery life.

Although you have literally hundreds of wireless Bluetooth headsets to choose from, some of the best ones on the market, that work perfectly with an iPhone, are available from a company called Jawbone (www.Jawbone.com). Jawbone has several wireless Bluetooth headset models available, including the Jawbone Era ($129.99) and Jawbone Icon ($99.99). Both models are available online, at stores like Best Buy, or wherever cellphone accessories are sold.

TIP The first time you use a wireless Bluetooth headset (or any Bluetooth device) with your iPhone, you must turn on the Bluetooth feature on your phone and then "pair" the device with your iPhone. To prepare your iPhone for this, launch the Settings app, tap on the General menu option, and from the General menu screen, tap on the Bluetooth option.

Turn on the virtual switch associated with the Bluetooth option, and then follow the "pairing" directions that came with your headset to finish the process. Your headset then appears under the Devices heading on the Bluetooth screen within Settings, and the Bluetooth icon is displayed in the upper-right corner of the screen, next to the battery life indicator.

IN THIS CHAPTER

- How to use new features in the iOS 5 version of Safari
- How to use "tabbed browsing" when surfing the Web
- How to create and use Reading Lists
- How to use Safari Reader

11

USE NEW SAFARI FEATURES TO SURF MORE EFFICIENTLY

Chances are, if you know how to use a Mac or PC, you already know how to surf the Web using Safari, Microsoft Internet Explorer, Foxfire, or Google Chrome, for example, on your computer.

Well, the Safari web browser on your iPhone (shown in Figure 11.1) or iPad (shown in Figure 11.2) offers the same basic functionality as the web browser for your desktop or laptop computer, but it's designed to maximize the iPhone or iPad's touchscreen and screen size.

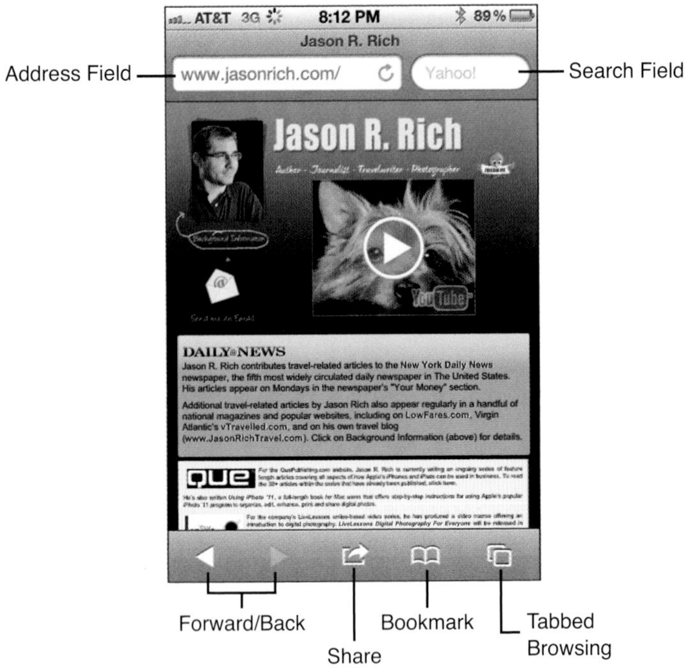

FIGURE 11.1
The main screen of the Safari web browser on the iPhone 4.

With the release of iOS 5, Apple redesigned the Safari app, giving it a handful of new features that will make web surfing a more enjoyable, secure, and streamlined experience.

> **iOS 5 WHAT'S NEW** Three of the many new features added to the iOS version of Safari are tabbed web browsing; the capability to create, manage, and access a Reading List; and the capability to send tweets directly from Safari. Plus, the new iOS 5 version of Safari fully integrates with iCloud, so all of your saved bookmarks can automatically be synced with the web browser on your primary computer, as well as with your other iOS devices.

As you'd expect from your iPhone or iPad, surfing the Web using the Safari app is a highly customizable experience. For example, you can hold your device in Portrait or Landscape mode while surfing.

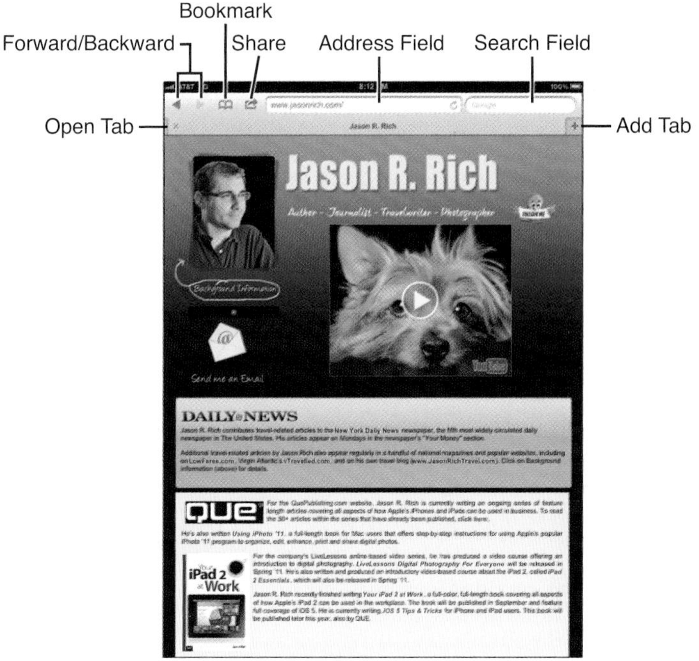

FIGURE 11.2

The main screen of the Safari web browser on the iPad 2.

On most websites, you can also zoom in on or zoom out of specific areas or elements, such as a paragraph of text or a photo, using the reverse-pinch finger gesture (to zoom in) or the pinch gesture (to zoom out), or by double-tapping on a specific area of the screen to zoom in or out.

Although many improvements have been made to the web-surfing capabilities of Safari on the iPhone and iPad, what's still missing is Adobe Flash compatibility. Adobe Flash is a website programming language used to generate many of the slick animations you see on websites. Unfortunately, these animations won't be visible when you access a Flash-based website using the iOS version of Safari.

If you want limited Flash compatibility on your iPhone or iPad, try using a third-party web browser app, such as Photon Flash Web Browser for iPhone ($3.99) or Photon Flash Web Browser for iPad ($4.99). Both versions are available from the App Store and offer compatibility with some (but not all) Flash-based content you'll encounter on the Web.

WHAT'S NEW If you're using an iPhone 4S, you can instruct Siri to find information for you on the Web using your voice. For example, after activating Siri, you can say, "Find me information about [insert topic]." Siri will respond, "If you'd like, I can search the web for [insert topic]." Respond "yes" to initiate an online search.

Or you can instruct Siri to "Find [insert topic] on the web," and Siri automatically launches Safari and initiate a search. The relevant search engine listings are displayed on your iPhone's screen. When speaking with Siri, you're also able to mention a website by name. For example, you can say, "Find www dot Jason Rich dot com" to find search engine listings for my website.

CUSTOMIZE YOUR WEB SURFING EXPERIENCE

As soon as you upgrade your iPhone or iPad to iOS 5, the new version of Safari will be available to you from the Home Screen. However, you can customize your web surfing experience at any time from the Settings app.

To do this, launch the Settings app from the Home Screen, and then tap on the Safari option that's displayed under the main Settings menu (as shown in Figure 11.3). When the Safari screen appears, you'll see a handful of customizable menu options. Here's a summary of what each is used for:

- **Search Engine**—As you use Safari, in the upper-right corner of the screen is a blank Search field, which is used to find what you're looking for on the Web via a search engine, such as Google, Yahoo!, or Bing. This option enables you to select your default (favorite) Internet search engine. So if you select Google as your default, whenever you perform a search using Safari's Search field, the browser automatically accesses Google to obtain your search results.

TIP Regardless of which Internet search engine (Google, Yahoo!, or Bing) you select to be your default from within the Settings app, you can always add the other two (or any other search engine) to your Bookmarks or Bookmarks bar, so that you can access the other search engines directly, by pointing Safari to www.Google.com, www.Yahoo.com, www.Bing.com, and so on.

FIGURE 11.3

Customize your web surfing experience when using Safari from the Settings app on your iOS device.

- **AutoFill**—One of the more tedious aspects of surfing the Web is constantly having to fill in certain types of data fields, such as your name, address, phone number, and email address.

  This feature, when turned on, remembers your responses, and automatically inserts the data into the appropriate fields. It also pulls information from your own contacts entry in the Contacts app. To customize this option and link your personal contact entry to Safari, tap on the AutoFill icon, turn on the Use Contact Info option (as shown in Figure 11.4), and then tap on My Info to select your contact entry in Contacts. You can also set whether Safari will remember usernames and passwords for specific websites you visit.

- **Open Links (iPhone only)**—Instead of using onscreen tabs, Safari on the iPhone creates separate windows for each web page that's open. You can quickly switch between viewing open web pages by tapping on the Open Links icon that's displayed in the lower-right corner of the Safari screen.

- **Open New Tabs in Background (iPad only)**—When turned on, this feature enables you to open up new web pages in separate tabs while remaining on the web page you're currently viewing. Then, when you're ready, you can tap on the other tab(s) to view the additional websites.

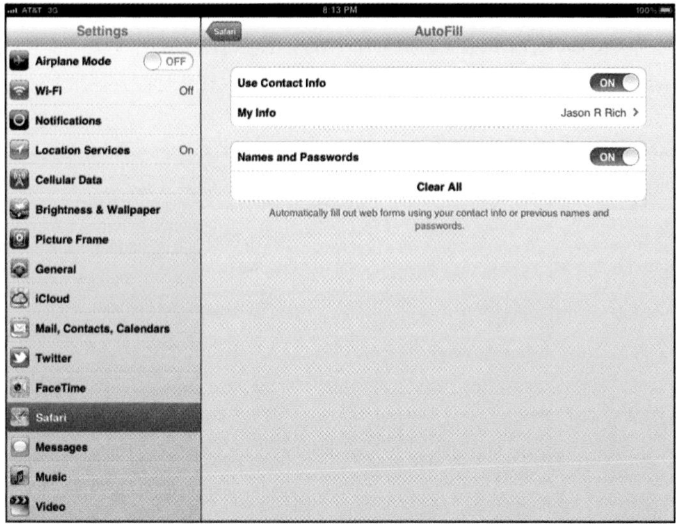

FIGURE 11.4

To avoid constantly having to enter your personal info when you visit various websites, link your own contact entry in Contacts to Safari from within the Settings app.

- **Always Show Bookmarks Bar (iPad only)**—This feature enables you to constantly display your Bookmarks bar as you use Safari so that your favorite websites are literally only one tap away. Although this feature adds convenience and speed to your web browsing experience, it also takes up one line of valuable onscreen real estate. When it's turned off, the Bookmarks bar is displayed automatically anytime you manually enter a website URL into the Address field, or when you use the Search field. It then disappears from the screen.
- **Private Browsing**—By default, Safari automatically keeps track of every website you visit in the History folder (which is accessible from the Bookmarks icon). It also remembers data you type into certain data fields on websites when you use AutoFill. If you turn on Private Browsing, however, none of this information gets saved on your iPhone or iPad. Thus, it becomes much more difficult (although not impossible) for someone to track what you've been doing on the Web. So if you're concerned about privacy, consider turning on this feature.
- **Accept Cookies**—Many websites use cookies to remember who you are and your personalized preferences when you're visiting that site. This is actually data that gets saved on your iPhone or iPad but that's accessible by the

websites you revisit. When this option is turned on, Safari will accept cookies from websites you visit, or whenever a cookie is supplied (based on the option you select). When it's turned off, this information will not be saved. Thus, you will need to reenter specific information, such as your username and password or particular preferences, each time you visit that site.

- **Clear History**—Using this feature, you can delete the contents of Safari's History folder that stores details about all the websites you have visited.
- **Clear Cookies and Data**—Use this command to delete all cookies related to websites you've visited that Safari has stored on your iOS device.
- **Fraud Warning**—This feature will help prevent you from visiting impostor websites designed to look like real ones, which have been created for the purpose of committing fraud or identity theft, for example. It's not foolproof, but keeping this feature turned on gives you an added level of protection, especially if you use your iOS device for online banking and other financial transactions.
- **JavaScript**—Some website designers use a programming language called JavaScript to control the functionality of a website. You can turn off this feature, which in turn will limit what some websites you visit will do. However, for the ordinary person, leaving the JavaScript feature turned on is fine.
- **Block Pop-ups**—When turned on, this feature prevents a website you're visiting from creating and displaying extra windows or opening a bunch of unwanted browser pages. The default for this option is turned on. You will probably enjoy your web surfing experience more if you leave it that way.
- **Advanced**—In addition to the History folder and cookies, Safari maintains information about sites you've visited in a Website Data folder, which you can delete manually by tapping on the Advanced option, followed by the Website Data option. At the bottom of the Website Data screen, tap on the red-and-white Remove All Website Data icon to delete this content. (Or access this file to determine which websites someone else has visited while using your device.)

TIP As you make changes in the Settings app relating to Safari, they are automatically saved, and those changes take effect the next time you launch the Safari app. When you're finished customizing the Safari app in Settings, press the Home button to exit Settings and return to the Home Screen.

HOW TO USE TABBED BROWSING WITH SAFARI

Safari's Title bar contains the various command icons used to navigate the Web. On the iPhone, it's divided into two sections that are constantly displayed along the top and bottom of the Safari screen. At the top of the Safari screen on the iPhone, you'll see the Address bar and the Search field. Along the bottom of the screen, the Left and Right navigation icons, along with the Share, Bookmarks, and Open Links icons, are displayed.

If you're using Safari on an iPad, the Title bar displays all of Safari's command icons along the top of the screen. Immediately below the Title bar, if you have the option turned on, your personalized Bookmarks bar will be displayed. Below the Bookmarks bar, the Tabs bar becomes visible if you have more than one web page loaded in Safari at any given time.

TIP Depending on the model of your iPhone and/or iPad, you have the option to surf the Web using a 3G Internet connection or an often much-faster Wi-Fi connection. When you sign up with a wireless service provider for a data plan, it typically includes a predetermined monthly data allocation, such as 2GB. When you go beyond it, you wind up paying a hefty surcharge. If you find yourself surfing the Web often, streaming content from the Web, or sending/receiving many large files, try to utilize a Wi-Fi Internet connection.

To access a Wi-Fi Internet connection, you must be within a Wi-Fi hotspot, which typically has a radius of less than 150 feet from the wireless Internet router. If you stray too far, the Wi-Fi web connection will drop. (When connected to the Web via 3G, you can travel anywhere there's a 3G signal.) However, there are no limits put on sending, receiving, or streaming data via a Wi-Fi connection.

If you're tapping in to a Wi-Fi hotspot at an airport, hotel, or Internet café, you might be charged a per-minute, hourly, or daily fee to use that Wi-Fi connection. There are no additional charges if you use a free Wi-Fi hotspot or a wireless home network.

SWITCHING BETWEEN WEB PAGES ON AN iPHONE

The iPhone version of "tabbed browsing" involves Safari opening separate browser windows for each active web page. By tapping on the Open Links icon that's constantly displayed near the bottom-right corner of the Safari screen, you can quickly switch between browser windows (shown in Figure 11.5) by flicking your finger on the screen from right to left or left to right.

FIGURE 11.5

On the iPhone, after tapping the Open Links icon, swipe your finger left to right or right to left to switch between multiple web browser windows that can simultaneously be loaded in Safari.

When you're viewing the Open Links screen, tap on the New Page icon (displayed in the lower-left corner of the screen) to create a new (empty) browser window and then manually surf to a new website (by typing a URL into the Address bar, using the Search field, or selecting a saved bookmark). On an iPhone, up to eight browser windows can be open simultaneously. On an iPad, you can create up to nine browser window tabs.

Tap the Done icon (displayed in the lower-right corner of the screen) to exit the Open Links screen and return to the main Safari web browser screen. Or tap on one of the web page thumbnails as you scroll through them on the Open Links screen.

TABBED BROWSING ON THE iPAD

When you tap on a link in a web page that causes a new web page to automatically open, a new tab in Safari is created and displayed (shown in Figure 11.6).

As you're viewing a web page, you can simultaneously open another web page by tapping on the plus icon that is displayed to the extreme right of the Tab bar. When you do this, a new tab is created, and you can visit a new web page without closing the previous page.

Along the Tab bar on the iPad, you can have multiple web pages accessible at once. Simply by tapping on a tab, you can instantly switch between web pages.

To close a tab, tap on the small "x" that appears on the left side of that tab.

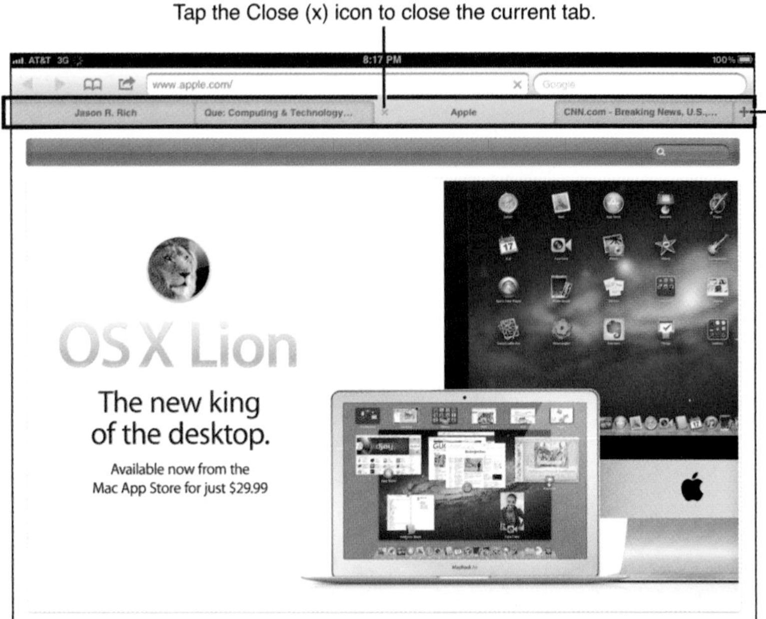

FIGURE 11.6

Instead of separate windows, Safari on the iPad uses onscreen tabs that enable you to instantly switch between web pages that are simultaneously open.

REMOVE SCREEN CLUTTER WITH SAFARI READER

Another new feature iOS 5 brings to the Safari web browser is Safari Reader. This feature works on the iPhone and iPad and enables you to select a compatible website page; strip out graphic icons, ads, and other unwanted elements that cause onscreen clutter; and then read just the text (and view related photos) from that web page on your iOS device's screen.

The Safari Reader works only with compatible websites, including those published by major daily newspapers and other news organizations. If the feature is available while you're viewing a web page, a Reader icon (as shown in Figure 11.7) is displayed next to that web page's URL in the Address field of Safari.

When you see the Reader icon displayed, tap on it. A new, uncluttered window that contains just the article or text from that web page, along with related photos, is displayed. Use your finger to scroll up or down.

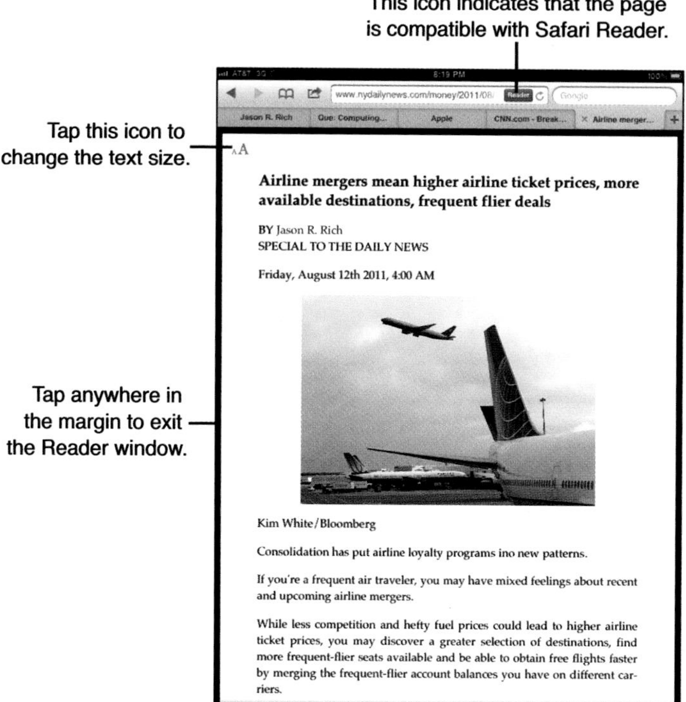

FIGURE 11.7

When you see a Reader icon appear in the Address bar of Safari, you can open that content in the Reader window and view it clutter free.

In the upper-left corner of the Reader window, tap on the aA icon to increase or decrease the size of the onscreen text. To exit the Reader window and return to the main web page, tap anywhere in the margins of the screen, outside the Reader window.

> **TIP** Tap on the Share icon in the Reader window (or Safari's Title bar) to add the article to your Reading List, or share it using one of the other methods offered from the Share menu.

CREATE AND MANAGE READING LISTS

As you're surfing the Web, you'll often come across specific web pages, articles, or other information that you know you'll want to refer to later. From within Safari, you can always create a bookmark for that website URL and have it displayed in your Bookmarks list or on your Bookmarks bar, or you can add it to your Reading List, which is another way to store web page links and content that's of interest to you.

As you're reading a website or web-based article, for example, to add it to your personalized Reading List for later review, tap on the Share icon and select the Add to Reading List option. Figure 11.8 shows an example of a Reading List.

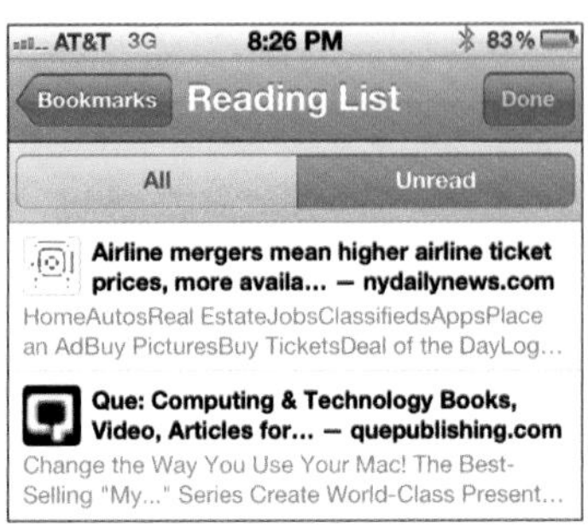

FIGURE 11.8

Creating a Reading List is another way to store links related to specific content on the Web that you want to easily be able to find again and access later.

When you want to refer to items stored in your Reading List, from Safari, tap on the Bookmarks icon, and then tap on the Reading List option. A listing of your saved web pages or articles previously saved to your Reading List is displayed.

> **TIP** Like your Bookmarks list and Bookmarks bar, the items stored in your Reading List can automatically be saved to iCloud, and almost instantly made available on any other computer or iOS device that's linked to your iCloud account. See the section "Create, Manage, and Sync Safari Bookmarks" for details on setting up these features for backup to iCloud.

NEW OPTIONS FOR SHARING WEB CONTENT IN SAFARI

There will probably be times when you're surfing the Web and come across something funny, informative, educational, or just plain bizarre that you want to share with other people, add to your Bookmarks list, or print, for example. The iOS 5 version of Safari makes sharing web links extremely easy, plus it now gives you a handful of other options.

Anytime you're visiting a web page that you want to share with others, tap on the Share icon to reveal a menu that's chock-full of new features (as shown in Figure 11.9).

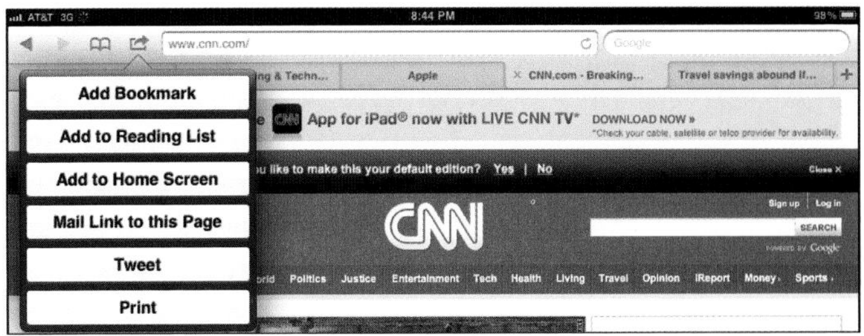

FIGURE 11.9

The Share icon in Safari offers a handful of new options, like the capability to send a tweet (via Twitter) from within the web browser.

On the iPhone, the Share icon is displayed near the bottom center of the Safari screen. On the iPad, the Share icon can be found to the immediate left of the Address bar.

The following options are available from the Share icon:

- **Add Bookmark**—Tap on this option to add a bookmark to your personal Bookmarks list or Bookmarks bar that's stored in Safari. You can later access your bookmarks by tapping on the Bookmark icon.

  When you opt to save a bookmark, an Add Bookmark window appears. Here, you can enter a title for the bookmark and decide whether you want to save it as part of your Bookmarks list or in your Bookmarks bar.

> **TIP** To access your Bookmarks list, tap on the Bookmarks icon that's displayed next to the Share icon in Safari, and tap on the Bookmarks icon to view your personalized list of saved website bookmarks.

- **Add to Reading List**—Instead of adding a web page URL to your Bookmarks list or Bookmarks bar, you can save it in your Reading List for later reference. To access your Reading List, tap on the Bookmarks icon, and then tap on the Reading List option.
- **Add to Home Screen**—In addition to saving a website URL in the form of a bookmark or within your Reading List, another option is to save it as a Home Screen icon.

- **Mail Link to This Page**—To share a website URL with someone else via email, as you're looking at the web page or website you want to share, tap on the Share icon and select the Mail Link to this Page option. In Safari, an outgoing email window will appear.

  Simply fill in the To field with the recipient's email address, and tap the Send icon (as shown in Figure 11.10). The website URL automatically is embedded within the body of the email, with the website's heading used as the email's subject. Before sending the email, you can add to the email's message or change the Subject.

FIGURE 11.10

In Safari, you can email information about a website to one or more recipients without exiting Safari and opening the Mail app.

- **Tweet**—If you have an active Twitter account that's set up for use with iOS 5, tap on the Tweet icon from the Share menu to create an outgoing tweet that automatically has the website URL attached.

  When the Tweet window appears (shown in Figure 11.11), enter your tweet message (up to 140 characters, minus the length of the website URL). Tap the Send icon when the tweet message is composed and ready to share with your Twitter followers.

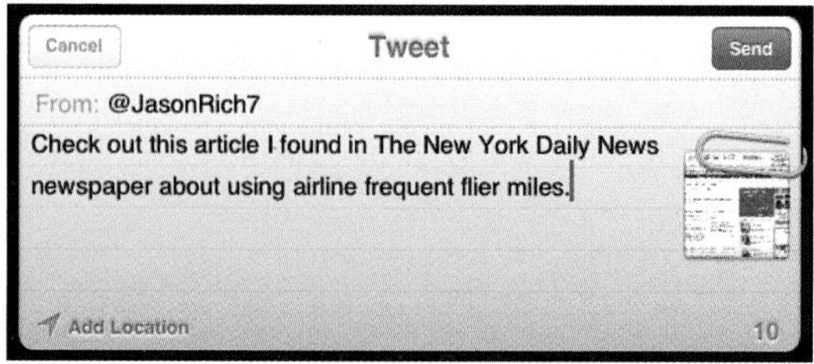

FIGURE 11.11

Send out a tweet to your Twitter followers from within Safari, and automatically include a link to the web page you're viewing.

TIP If you're managing multiple Twitter accounts from your iOS device, within the outgoing tweet window, tap on the From field, and then select from which of your Twitter accounts you want to send the tweet you're composing.

- **Print**—In Safari, you can wirelessly print a website to any AirPrint-compatible printer that's set up to work with your iOS device. To print a web page, tap on the Print command. From the Printer Options screen, select the printer you want to use, and then choose the number of copies you want printed. Tap the Print icon at the bottom of the Print Options window to send the web page document to your printer.

NOTE When using Safari on the iPhone, you can maintain a Bookmarks bar (if you sync this data from a computer or other iOS device); however, to conserve onscreen space, the Bookmarks bar is not displayed across the top of the Safari screen like it is on an iPad. Instead, on an iPhone, the Bookmarks bar is displayed as an additional Bookmark folder when you tap on the Bookmarks icon.

CREATE, MANAGE, AND SYNC SAFARI BOOKMARKS

Thanks to the fact that Safari is now fully integrated with iCloud, if you have an active iCloud account, your iOS device will automatically sync your Bookmarks and related Safari data with your other iOS devices, as well as the compatible web browsers on your primary computer(s).

To activate this iCloud sync feature, access the Settings app from the Home Screen, and then tap on the iCloud option that's displayed in the main Settings menu. When the iCloud screen appears, make sure your iCloud account is listed at the top of the screen, and then tap on the Bookmarks option to make sure the virtual on/off switch associated with Bookmarks is turned on.

Your Bookmarks list, Bookmarks bar, and Safari Reading List will now automatically be continuously synced with your iCloud account. Thus, when you add a new bookmark while surfing the Web on your iPad, within seconds that same bookmark will appear in your Bookmarks list on your iPhone and on Safari that's running on your Mac, for example.

> **! CAUTION** If you have an active iCloud account and an active MobileMe account (which will remain functioning until June 30, 2012), you must use the free iCloud Migration tool offered by Apple to switch over from using MobileMe to iCloud. Do this as soon as possible, or at least turn off the MobileMe sync feature. Otherwise, both MobileMe and iCloud will attempt to sync your Safari Bookmarks, and you'll wind up with multiple copies of each bookmark stored in the web browser on each of your computers and iOS devices.

LAUNCH YOUR FAVORITE WEBSITES FAST WITH HOME SCREEN ICONS

If you regularly visit certain websites, you can create individual bookmarks for them. However, to access those sites, you'll still need to launch Safari from your iPhone or iPad's Home Screen, tap on the Bookmarks icon, and then tap on a specific bookmark listing to access the related site.

An alternative that will save you time is to create a Home Screen icon for each of your favorite websites (as shown in Figure 11.12). To create a Home Screen icon, surf to one of your favorite websites. After it loads, tap on the Share icon, and choose the Add to Home Screen option.

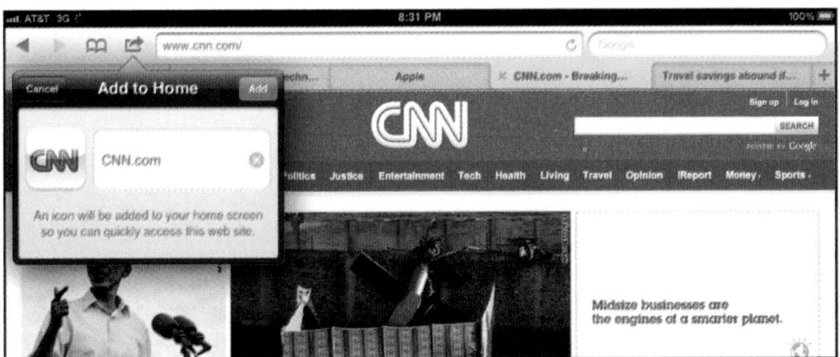

FIGURE 11.12

Create a Home Screen icon for your favorite websites so that you can launch them directly from your iOS device's Home Screen with a single tap.

A new Add to Home window appears. It displays a thumbnail image of the website you're visiting and enables you to enter the title for the website (which will be displayed below the icon on your device's Home Screen). Keep the title you choose short. When you've created the title (or if you decide to keep the default title that Safari creates), tap on the Add icon that's displayed in the upper-right corner of the window.

NOTE When you use the Add to Home feature in Safari, if you're creating a shortcut for a website designed to be compatible with an iPhone or iPad, a special website-related icon (as opposed to a thumbnail) is displayed.

Safari closes, and you are returned to your device's Home Screen. Displayed on the Home Screen will be what looks like a new app icon; however, it's really a link to your favorite website. Tap on this icon to automatically launch Safari from the Home Screen and load your web page.

TIP After a Home Screen icon is created for a web page, it can be treated like any other app icon. You can move it around on the Home Screen, add the icon to a folder, or delete the icon from the Home Screen.

IN THIS CHAPTER

- How to get started using Apple's iCloud service
- How to synch files, documents, and data via iCloud
- How to download your iTunes purchases from iCloud

12

SYNC AND SHARE FILES USING iCLOUD

iOS 5 includes full integration with Apple's iCloud online-based file-sharing service, which was launched with this version of the operating system. Initially, you might think that iCloud is just another cloud-based file-sharing service. However, for iOS 5 users, it does much more than simply allow you to store content on a remote server that's located somewhere in cyberspace. In fact, iCloud introduces a handful of new features and functions to your iPhone or iPad that you'll soon be wondering how you ever lived without. There are several compelling reasons to begin using iCloud with your iOS device (and primary computer).

First, an iCloud account is free. When created, your iCloud account includes 5GB of online storage space for your personal data and files, plus an unlimited amount of additional online storage space for all your iTunes, App Store, and iBookstore (and Newsstand) purchases, including apps, music, TV shows, movies, eBooks, audiobooks, ringtones, and so on.

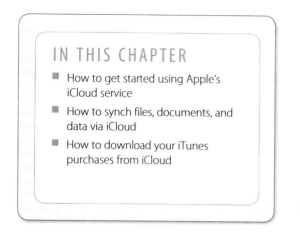

An iCloud account also includes a free [Username]@me.com email address, which you can use to send and receive email from all your devices that are linked to your iCloud account. And iCloud will automatically keep your email account synchronized on all devices.

If you need to upgrade your iCloud account to utilize additional online storage space, it can be purchased directly from your iOS device for an annual fee (as shown in Figure 12.1).

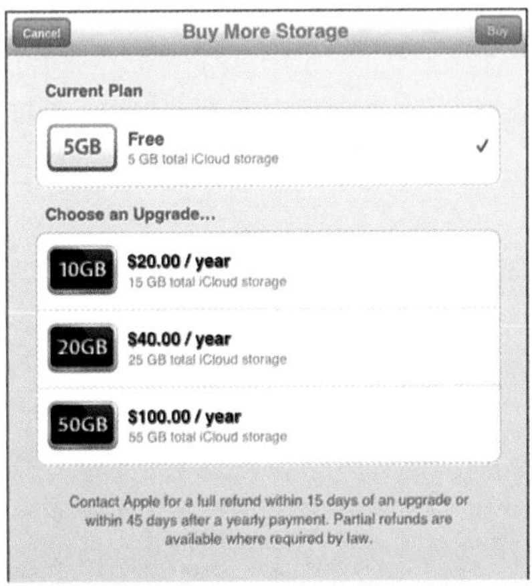

FIGURE 12.1

From the Buy More Storage window, accessible from several iCloud-related screens in the Settings app, you can buy additional online storage, beyond your free 5GB of allocated storage space.

WHAT'S NEW To purchase additional online storage space for use with iCloud, tap on the Buy More Storage icon that appears in several of the iCloud-related screens accessible through the Settings app.

An additional 10GB of online storage is priced at $20 per year (which gives you a total of 15GB, including the 5GB of free online storage). An additional 20GB is priced at $40 per year, and 50GB is priced at $100 per year.

CONTENT SAVED TO iCLOUD IS AVAILABLE ANYWHERE

By default, as soon as you establish a free iCloud account, anytime you acquire and download content from iTunes, a copy of that content automatically gets saved in your iCloud account and immediately becomes available on all your compatible computers and iOS devices (including Apple TV) that are linked to that iCloud account. This includes all past iTunes purchases and downloads as well.

So if you hear an awesome new song on the radio while you're out and about, you can immediately purchase and download it from iTunes using your iPhone, and then you can access that same song from your primary computer, iPad, iPod touch, and/or Apple TV device, without having to ever repurchase it. This feature also works with TV shows and movies purchased from iTunes, as well as with hybrid apps you want to install on both your iPhone and your iPad, for example, without having to purchase that same app twice.

If you ever opt to delete any iTunes purchase from your iOS device, for whatever reason, you always have the option of downloading and installing it again, free, from iCloud.

> **iOS 5 WHAT'S NEW** Although your iTunes music purchases might represent a portion of your overall personal digital music library, chances are, that library also includes CDs (which you have ripped into digital format), as well as online music purchases and downloads from other sources (such as Amazon.com).
>
> For an additional fee of $24.99 per year, you can upgrade your iCloud account by adding the iTunes Match services. This will grant you full access to your entire personal digital music library (including non-iTunes purchases) from all of your computers and devices that are linked to your iCloud account.

Because Apple has maintained detailed records of your iTunes, App Store, and iBookstore purchases to date, all content from past purchases also immediately becomes accessible to computers or devices linked to your iCloud account.

Let's look at an example. While using iTunes on your primary computer, suppose you purchase and download the *Never Over* EP released by *American Idol* Season 4 top-4 finalist Anthony Fedorov. The six songs on that EP get immediately downloaded to your computer's hard drive.

Now, thanks to iCloud, those six songs are also instantly made available via your iCloud account to your iPhone, iPad, iPod touch, and/or Apple TV device. So after purchasing Anthony Fedorov's EP, for example, on your primary computer via iTunes, follow these steps to load that same music into your iPad 2 (or another iOS device) via iCloud:

1. Make sure that your iOS device is connected to the Web via a 3G or Wi-Fi connection.
2. Launch the iTunes app on your device. If prompted, when the Apple ID Password window pops up on your screen, use the virtual keyboard to enter your Apple ID password.

3. When iTunes launches on your device, because this is a new purchase, tap on the Downloads icon. You'll discover that the songs you just purchased on iTunes (via your primary computer) will also be listed on the iTunes Downloads screen on your iPad. Tap on the right-pointing, arrow-shaped Purchased icon that is displayed in the upper-right corner of the screen to download these songs to your iPad, without having to repurchase them from iTunes.
4. You'll also discover that all songs you just purchased or have previously purchased from iTunes are listed when you tap on the Purchased icon in iTunes on your iOS device (as shown in Figure 12.2). Next to each listing, instead of a Price icon or a Free icon, there's a cloud-shaped icon. Tap on this icon to download the selected, already purchased, content to the device you're currently using.

> **TIP** After tapping on the Purchased icon in iTunes on your iPad, tap on the View icon to switch between a listing of music, TV shows, and movies you've purchased. (The View icon is displayed in the upper-left corner of the iTunes Purchased screen.) On the iPhone or iPod touch, separate listings for each type of content can be accessed from the main Purchased screen of iTunes.

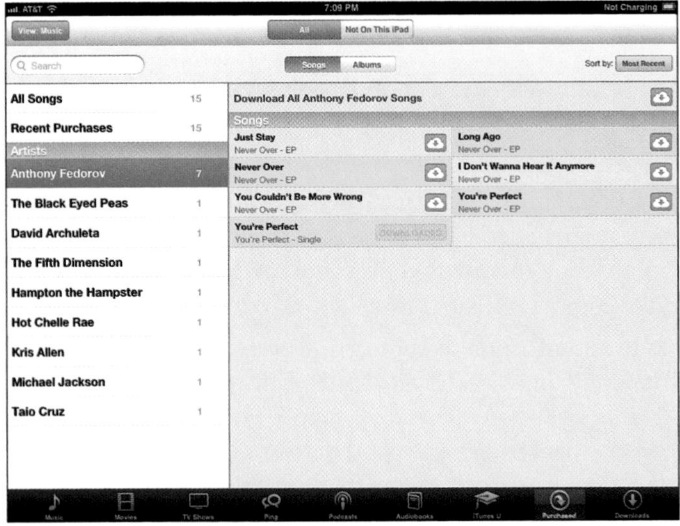

FIGURE 12.2

From any device that runs iTunes, you can access and download your previous purchases by tapping on the Purchased icon.

5. Within two minutes or so, the new music from Anthony Fedorov's EP, or whatever music you purchased and downloaded, will be available to listen to on the iOS 5 device you're currently using.
6. Exit iTunes by pressing the Home button.
7. Launch the Music app on your iOS device.
8. When the Music app launches, tap on the Albums tab. Anthony Fedorov's EP, titled *Never Over*, will be displayed. Tap on the album-cover artwork to choose which song from the EP to play, or tap on the Play icon to begin listening to the entire EP (as shown in Figure 12.3).

> **TIP** If your iTunes purchase was a TV show episode or movie, for example, after downloading that file from iCloud (tap on the Purchased icon in iTunes, and then the cloud icon associated with the video-based content), launch the Videos app to watch the video-based content.
>
> When you need to download large files from iCloud, such as TV show episodes or movies, a Wi-Fi Internet connection is needed. However, for music, ringtones, and audiobooks, for example, a 3G connection will work from your iOS device.

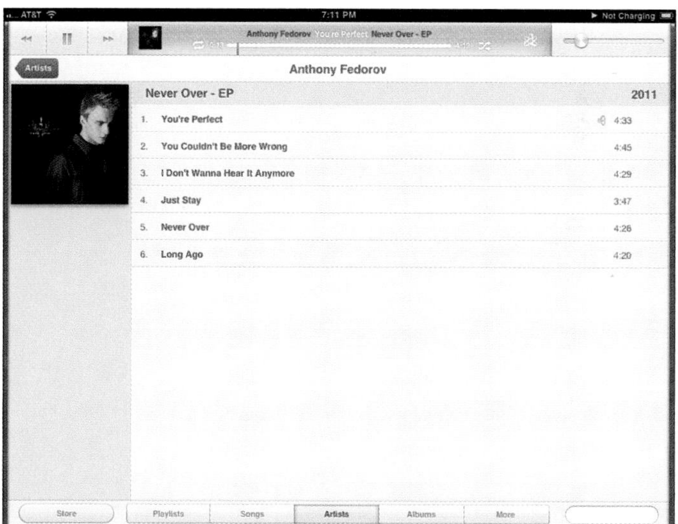

FIGURE 12.3

This music was initially purchased from iTunes on a Mac, but also downloaded (at no additional cost) to an iPad 2 that is connected to the same iCloud account.

! CAUTION When you access your music from iCloud from your iPhone or iPad, you have the option to stream that music or download it to your device. When you stream the music, it is sent to your iOS device to be heard but not saved. To stream content, you always need to have an Internet connection established (and unless you're using Wi-Fi, this will quickly use up your monthly wireless data allocation from your service provider). You can download the music to your iOS device from iCloud and then listen to it anytime later, whether or not an Internet connection is present.

USE iCLOUD TO SYNC YOUR APPS, DATA, DOCUMENTS, AND FILES

Most cloud-based file-sharing services serve mainly as a place in cyberspace to remotely store files. However, you manually have to transfer those files to and from the "cloud." Thanks to iCloud's integration with iOS 5, many of the core apps that come with iOS 5, as well as a growing number of third-party apps, will automatically keep data and files created or managed using those apps synchronized with other devices and/or your primary computer that's also linked to the same iCloud account.

Using your iOS device's Settings app, you can turn on or off iCloud support for all compatible apps on your device, which include Contacts, Calendars, Reminders, Safari (Bookmarks), Notes, Photos, iBooks, and Mail (relating to your free me.com email account that comes with iCloud).

MORE INFO iCloud is also fully compatible with Apple's iWork apps for the iPhone and iPad, which include Pages (word processing), Numbers (spreadsheet management), and Keynote (for digital slide presentations).

When you turn on the iCloud functionality with the Contacts app, for example, your iOS device will automatically sync your contacts database with iCloud, and all your computers and/or other iOS devices linked to your iCloud account. Thus, if you add or update a contact entry on your iPhone, that addition or change will automatically synchronize and become available on the Contacts app running on your other iOS devices, as well as within the compatible contact management software that's running on your primary computer (such as Address Book on a Mac).

This same functionality also works with the Calendar and Reminders apps, for example. If you add or modify an appointment using iCal on your Mac, or Calendar on your iPad, that new information will immediately and automatically synchronize to all your linked devices.

As you surf the Web using Safari, if you add a bookmark or web page to your Reading List, that information will also automatically synchronize via iCloud and then with your other devices, as will notes created using the Notes app and eBook purchases acquired from iBookstore (for use with iBooks).

To share your photos between iOS devices, your primary computer, and/or an Apple TV device, you'll need to set up a Photo Stream using iCloud.

> **TIP** The Documents & Data setting enables you to set up your iOS device to automatically sync (share) documents related to specific apps using iCloud, making them almost instantly and automatically available on your computer(s) and other iOS devices. This feature works with all iWork for iOS apps (Pages, Numbers, and Keynote), for example.

CUSTOMIZING iCLOUD TO WORK WITH YOUR APPS

It's important to understand that the app-related synchronization feature offered by iCloud is different from iCloud Backup (which creates a complete backup of your entire iOS device that gets stored online as part of your iCloud account). The app-related synchronization feature replaces (but also enhances) the synchronization functionality formerly offered by Apple's MobileMe service.

When you set up iCloud to work with a specific compatible app, that app will automatically access the Web, connect to iCloud, and then upload or download app-related files, documents, or data as needed.

To customize which of your compatible iCloud apps will utilize iCloud functionality, follow these steps:

1. Launch the Settings app from your iPhone or iPad's Home Screen.
2. Select the iCloud option from the main Settings menu.
3. When the iCloud window appears (shown in Figure 12.4), at the top of the screen, make sure the Apple ID–linked email address that's also associated with your iCloud account is displayed next to the Account option. If it's not, you'll need to use your existing Apple ID to create or access an iCloud account by tapping on the Account option.
4. Below the Account option is a list of all preinstalled iCloud-compatible apps on your iOS device. To the right of each listing is a virtual on/off switch. To turn on the iCloud functionality associated with a specific app, set its related virtual switch to the on position.

5. When you have turned on the iCloud functionality for all the apps that you want to be able to synchronize via iCloud, exit the Settings app to save your changes. (Press the Home button to do this.)
6. Repeat this process on each of your iOS devices. So if you have an iPhone and an iPad, you'll need to turn on the iCloud functionality for Contacts, for example, on both devices to keep Contacts data synchronized via iCloud on both devices.

FIGURE 12.4

Turn on or off iCloud functionality for specific apps that come preinstalled with iOS 5 from this main iCloud screen in the Settings app.

TIP After you've turned on the iCloud functionality for specific apps and created your iCloud account, for the various apps on your iOS devices (and your primary computer) to stay synchronized, each computer or device must have access to the Internet. For this use of iCloud on your iPhone or iPad, either a 3G or a Wi-Fi Internet connection works fine. For certain other iCloud features, such as Photo Stream and iCloud Backup, your iOS device will require a Wi-Fi Internet connection.

CREATE A PHOTO STREAM USING iCLOUD

iCloud also offers an innovative and easy way to share up to 1,000 of your most recently shot or imported digital photos between your primary computer (such as a Mac that runs iPhoto '11), your iOS device(s), and/or your Apple TV device. To share photos and keep them synchronized and accessible, turn on the Photo Stream feature offered by iCloud.

> **TIP** Photo Stream requires that each of your iOS devices has access to a Wi-Fi Internet connection. It does not work with a 3G connection from your iPhone, iPad, or iPod touch. This feature also works with both Macs and PCs.

The concept behind Photo Stream is pretty simple. When you snap (or import) a photo using your iPhone or iPad, for example, it automatically gets uploaded to iCloud's Photo Stream and becomes accessible from any other device that's linked to your iCloud account. There's no need to manually sync or send the photo. The digital images are available when and where you want or need them.

The Photo Stream album that's created when you turn on this feature will hold a maximum of 1,000 of your most recently shot or imported digital images for up to 30 days. By default, all your digital images from your Photo Stream automatically get stored on your primary computer's hard drive, which is where you'll find images left in your Photo Stream beyond 30 days. From this centralized database of your images, you can move photos in or out of your active Photo Stream to make them available on other devices via iCloud.

The Photo Stream feature is also compatible with Apple TV, so you can view your favorite digital images on your HDTV at home or at work, as standalone images or as part of an animated slideshow.

> **TIP** After a digital image appears as part of your Photo Stream, you can manually save it to the Camera Roll album (or any other album you select) on any of your iOS devices, where it will remain indefinitely until you manually delete it.

To set up Photo Stream, make sure that your iOS device has access to the Web via a Wi-Fi connection, and follow these steps:

1. Launch the Settings app from your iOS device's Home Screen.
2. Tap on the iCloud option, which is found under the main Settings menu.
3. From the iCloud screen within Settings, turn the virtual switch associated with the Photo Stream option to the on position.
4. Exit Settings. From this point forward, Photo Stream will automatically synchronize with iCloud when your iOS device has Internet access. Photo Stream is integrated with the Camera and Photos apps, so newly shot or imported pictures automatically get added to your Photo Stream.

NOTE An imported photo might be saved from a website you visit using Safari, saved on your iOS device from an incoming email or text message, or loaded into your device using Apple's optional Camera Connection kit, for example.

5. Repeat this process for each of your iOS devices from which you want to access your Photo Stream.

To use the Photo Stream feature on your Mac, you must upgrade to the latest version of the OS X Lion operating system, as well as the most recent version of iPhoto '11 or Aperture 3. You also need to turn on this feature in iPhoto '11.

TIP Although you can add or view photos in your Photo Stream from any computer or iOS device linked to your iCloud account, you cannot delete photos from your Photo Stream manually. However, if you're looking at an image or thumbnail from your Photo Stream that isn't saved on your iPhone or iPad, you can transfer the image to a specific album on that device.

To reset your Photo Stream (and delete its contents) from your primary computer or iOS device, go to www.iCloud.com and click on your username. When the Account window appears, click on the Advanced option. In the Advanced window, click on the Reset Photo Stream option to clear the images from iCloud's Photo Stream. The images will still be stored on the original device(s) or computer(s) on which they were downloaded. To delete the files from each iOS device, turn off the Photo Stream feature from the Settings app, and select the Delete Photos option when prompted.

AUTOMATICALLY TRANSFER DOCUMENTS USING iCLOUD

In addition to the iCloud compatibility built in to many of the core (preinstalled) apps that are included with iOS 5, a growing number of other apps also offer iCloud compatibility and allow you to easily (and automatically) transfer or synchronize app-related documents and files.

This functionality is built in to Apple's iWork apps for the iPhone and iPad, which include Pages (word processing), Numbers (spreadsheet management), and Keynote (for digital slide presentations). Be sure to upgrade your iWork for iOS apps for the iPhone to the latest versions for this functionality to work.

If you turn on iCloud functionality with Pages, Numbers, Keynote, or other compatible third-party apps, when you create or revise a document, that revision is stored on your iOS device and on iCloud. From iCloud, that same app running on another iOS device (or compatible software running on your primary computer) can access that most recent version of the file within seconds.

So if you're working with the Pages word processor on your iPhone, your iPad, or the Mac, you always know that when you access a Pages document from any compatible device, you're working with the most up-to-date version of that document. The synchronization process happens automatically and behind the scenes, assuming that your iOS devices and primary computer are connected to the Internet.

NOTE To use iCloud's "Documents in the Cloud" feature, your iOS device can utilize a 3G or Wi-Fi Internet connection.

The processes for turning on iCloud functionality within compatible apps on your iPhone, iPad, and iPod touch are almost identical. To turn on the iCloud functionality in Pages on an iPad 2, for example, follow these steps:

1. From your iOS device, launch the Settings app from the Home Screen.
2. Scroll down on the main menu of Settings until you find the Apps heading. Below this heading will be a listing of apps you have installed on your iOS device that can somehow be customized from within Settings (shown in Figure 12.5).

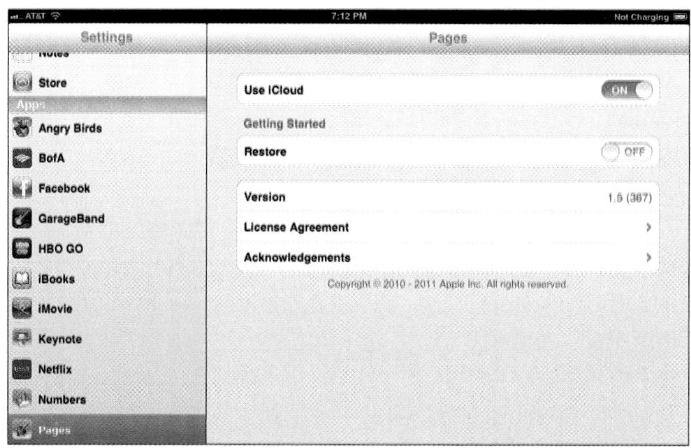

FIGURE 12.5

To control iCloud functionality for apps that don't come preinstalled with iOS 5, scroll down to the specific app listings on the main Settings menu, and tap on the app of your choice, such as Pages (if applicable).

3. Locate the listing for Pages (or the app of your choice) from within the main Settings menu.
4. When the Pages screen appears in Settings, tap on the virtual switch that's associated with the Use iCloud option, and switch it to the on position. If you turn this feature to the off position, your documents will be stored only on your iPad 2 (in this example), and will not be synchronized with other devices via iCloud, because the selected app will not access iCloud via the Internet.
5. Exit Settings. From this point forward, your Pages documents will automatically synchronize with iCloud when your iPad 2 (in this example) has Internet access.
6. Repeat this process for each iCloud-compatible app, on each of your iOS devices.

WHO NEEDS iTUNES SYNC? USE iCLOUD BACKUP INSTEAD

Until Apple launched iOS 5 and the iCloud service, creating and maintaining a complete backup of your iOS device on your primary computer required you to use the iTunes Sync process. This option (which is still available) meant that you needed to manually connect your iOS device to your primary computer via the supplied USB cable, and then run iTunes on your primary computer.

iOS 5 OFFERS WIRELESS iTUNES SYNC

With the release of iOS 5, two additional options for maintaining a backup of your iOS device became available. The first is Wireless iTunes Sync. If your primary computer and iOS device can connect to the same Wi-Fi network, you can manually sync your iPhone, iPad, or iPod touch wirelessly. The USB cable connection between your computer and your iOS device is not needed.

Using the Wireless iTunes Sync feature, your wireless iOS device must be plugged in to power. After the wireless connection is initiated, you can begin the wireless backup process from within the Settings app on your iOS device. However, iTunes must be running on your primary computer, and the iTunes Sync over Wi-Fi Connection option must be selected.

iOS 5 WHAT'S NEW The Wireless iTunes Sync feature enables you to create a full backup of your iOS device. The related backup files get stored on your primary computer's hard drive, just as they would if you used the traditional iTunes sync process. This new iOS 5 feature does not, however, utilize iCloud.

To create a backup of your iOS device using the new Wireless iTunes Sync feature, follow these steps:

1. On your primary computer, launch iTunes.
2. Before you can use the Wireless iTunes Sync process for the first time, connect your iOS device to your primary computer via the supplied USB cable. When the connection between your device and computer is established, on the left side of the iTunes screen, under the Devices heading, click on your iOS device's name.
3. Near the top center of the main iTunes screen, click on the Summary tab to see details pertaining to your iOS device.
4. On the Summary screen, use the mouse to add a check mark to the Sync over Wi-Fi Connection option that's displayed under the Options heading (as shown in Figure 12.6).

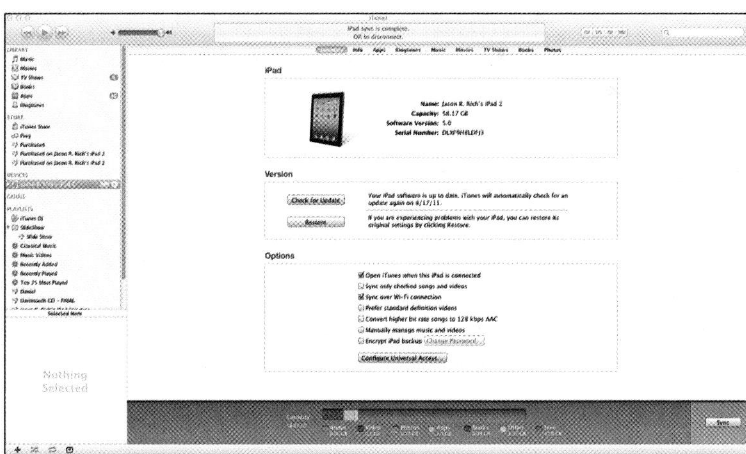

FIGURE 12.6

To use the Wireless iTunes Sync feature, it must be turned on from within iTunes on your primary computer and on your iOS device. On your primary computer, click on the Sync over Wi-Fi Connection option.

5. You can now disconnect your iOS device from your primary computer. The USB cable is no longer needed.
6. Make sure that your primary computer and your iOS device are connected to the same Wi-Fi network.
7. From your iOS device, launch the Settings app.
8. Tap on the General option, listed under the main Settings menu on your iOS device.
9. When the General screen appears, scroll down to the iTunes Wi-Fi Sync option, and tap on it.
10. If you haven't already done so, plug in your iOS device to an electrical outlet.
11. On your iOS device, tap the Sync Now option that appears on the iTunes Wi-Fi Sync screen (as shown in Figure 12.7). The Wireless iTunes Sync process will begin. The end result is a backup of your iOS device that's stored on your primary computer's hard drive (just as if you had used the traditional iTunes Sync process by connecting the devices via the supplied USB cable).

TIP After a backup of your iOS device has been created using the iTunes Sync or Wireless iTunes Sync process, you can restore your iOS device (or a new iOS device of the same type) from that backup. For example, you can restore an iPhone from an iPhone backup or an iPad from an iPad backup, but you cannot restore an iPhone from an iPad backup (or vice versa).

When you're reinstalling your iOS device, when prompted, select the Restore from iTunes option, and follow the onscreen prompts.

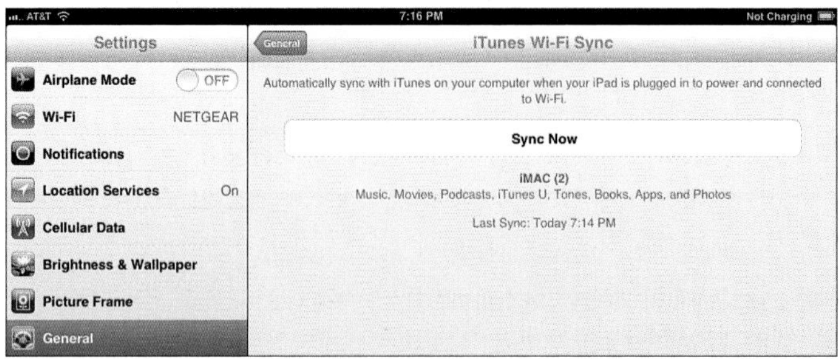

FIGURE 12.7

Initiate the Wireless iTunes Sync process from within the Settings app on your iOS device, whether it's an iPhone, iPad, or iPod touch.

iCLOUD BACKUP: NO CABLE NEEDED

One new feature of iOS 5 is the capability to create a complete backup of your iOS device wirelessly, and have the related backup files stored on iCloud. Using this feature, your iOS device can be connected to any Wi-Fi Internet connection. Your primary computer is not needed. Thus, the backup can be created from anywhere, and you can later restore your device from anywhere a Wi-Fi Internet connection is present.

TIP When you activate the iCloud Backup feature, if you later connect your iOS device to your primary computer, the iTunes Sync process will not work. If you wanted to create a backup of your device using iTunes Sync and have the backup files stored on your primary computer's hard drive (instead of on iCloud), you'd need to first turn off the iCloud Backup feature from within the Settings app.

When activated, your iOS device will automatically create a backup to iCloud once per day (when the device is connected to the Internet via a Wi-Fi connection but isn't otherwise in use). However, at any time, you can manually create a backup of your device to iCloud from within the Settings app.

To activate and use the iCloud Backup feature, the process is the same as when you're using an iPhone or iPad. However, although the commands and steps are the same, the location of various menu screens and menu options are slightly different, due to the size of each device's screen.

Follow these steps to activate and use the iCloud Backup feature on an iPad 2:

1. Make sure that your iOS device is connected to the Internet via a Wi-Fi connection and plugged in to an external power source.
2. From the Home Screen, launch the Settings app.
3. Tap on the iCloud option from within the main Settings menu.
4. Tap on the Storage & Backup option that's located near the bottom of the iCloud screen in Settings.
5. About halfway down on the Storage & Backup screen, tap on the virtual switch that's associated with the iCloud Backup option. Turn the virtual switch to the on position.
6. A new Back Up Now option appears near the bottom of the Storage & Backup screen (as shown in Figure 12.8). Tap on it to begin creating a backup of your iOS device. The backup file will be stored on iCloud.

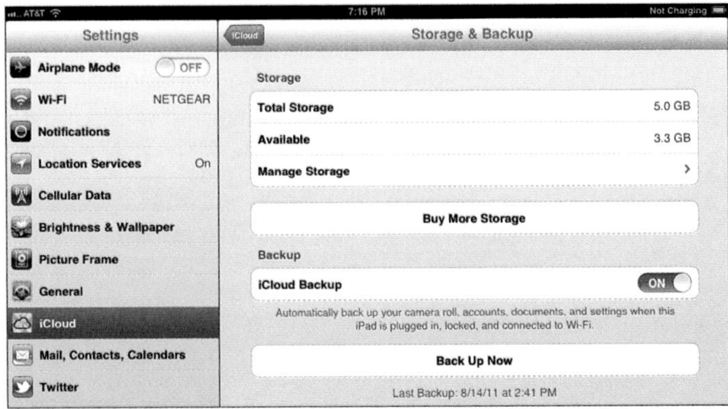

FIGURE 12.8

Manage and launch the iCloud Backup feature from the Storage & Backup screen, accessible from within the Settings app.

iOS 5 **WHAT'S NEW** The first time you use the iCloud Backup feature to create a wireless backup of your iOS device, the process could take up to an hour (or longer), depending on how much data you have stored on your device.

After the backup process begins, a progress meter will be displayed at the bottom of the Storage & Backup screen within Settings. While the backup is being created this first time, refrain from using your iOS device. Just kick back and allow the iPhone or iPad, for example, to connect with iCloud and create the initial backup.

In the future, the iCloud Backup process will take place once per day, automatically, when your iOS device is not otherwise in use. These backups will save all newly created or revised files and data only, so subsequent iCloud Backup procedures will be much quicker.

At the bottom of the Storage & Backup screen within Settings, the time and date of the last backup is displayed. If, for some reason, the backup process could not be completed because the device could not connect to the Internet, for example, an error message displays, and you can manually create an updated backup by tapping on the Back Up Now icon that's displayed on the Storage & Backup screen.

The purpose of creating and maintaining a backup of your device is so that you have a copy of all your apps, data, files, content, and personalized settings stored, if something goes wrong with your device. If and when you need to access the backup to restore your device using iCloud, when prompted, choose the Restore from iCloud option.

IN THIS CHAPTER

- How to use the new features added to the iOS 5 version of the Mail app
- How to add your existing email accounts to the Mail app
- How to compose, send, and manage emails on your iPhone or iPad

13

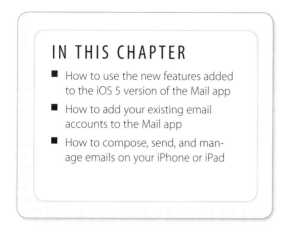

MANAGE YOUR EMAIL EFFECTIVELY

If you're someone who's constantly on the go, being able to send and receive emails from virtually anywhere there's a 3G or Wi-Fi Internet connection enables you to stay in touch, stay informed, and be productive from wherever you happen to be. Managing one or more email accounts from an iPhone or iPad has just gotten a bit easier, thanks to the improvements made to the Mail app that comes preinstalled with iOS 5.

iOS 5 WHAT'S NEW The ability to compose and send email messages from within apps has been improved in iOS 5. For example, by tapping on the Share icon in preinstalled apps such as Photos, Contacts, YouTube, or Safari, you can choose the Email option to quickly send app-specific content without launching the Mail app. This feature also works in many other iPhone and iPad apps, including Pages, Keynote, and Numbers.

The Mail app offers a comprehensive set of tools, features, and functions to help you compose, send, and receive emails from one or more existing accounts. So, from your iPhone or iPad, you can simultaneously manage your personal and work-related email accounts, as well as the free email account that's provided to you when you set up an iCloud account.

Before you can begin using the Mail app, it's necessary to set up your existing email accounts within the Settings app. This process takes just a few minutes.

If you don't yet have an email account, there are several ways to get one. You can sign up for a free Apple iCloud account, which includes an email account. In addition, Google offers free Gmail email accounts (http://mail.google.com), and Yahoo! offers free Yahoo! Mail accounts (http://features.mail.yahoo.com), both of which are fully compatible with your iOS device's Mail app.

HOW TO ADD EMAIL ACCOUNTS TO THE MAIL APP

To initially set up your iOS device to work with your existing email account(s), use the Settings app that's accessible from the Home Screen. This process works with virtually all email accounts, including Yahoo! Mail, Google Gmail, AOL Mail, iCloud/MobileMe Mail, Microsoft Exchange, and other email accounts established using industry-standard POP3 and IMAP email services.

If you have an email account through your employer that doesn't initially work using the setup procedure outlined in this chapter, contact your company's IT department or Apple's technical support for assistance.

NOTE The process for setting up an existing email account to use with your iPhone or iPad and the Mail app needs to be done only once per account.

Follow these steps to set up your iOS device to work with each of your existing email accounts:

1. From the Home Screen, tap on the Settings app icon.
2. From the main Settings menu, tap on the Mail, Contacts, Calendars option.
3. When the Mail, Contacts, Calendars screen appears, tap on the Add Account option that's displayed near the top of the screen, below the Accounts heading.
4. From the Add Account screen, select the type of email account you have. Your options include iCloud, Microsoft Exchange, Gmail, Yahoo! Mail, AOL Mail, Windows Live Hotmail, MobileMe, and Other (shown in Figure 13.1).

Tap on the appropriate option. If you have a POP3 or IMAP-compatible email account that doesn't otherwise fall into one of the provided email types, tap on the Other option, and follow the onscreen prompts.

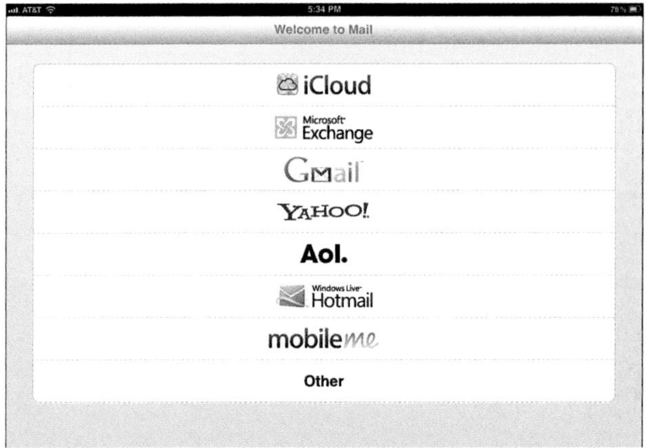

FIGURE 13.1

Choose the type of email account you'd like to add by tapping on the appropriate menu option.

If you have an existing Yahoo Email account, for example, tap on the Yahoo icon. When the Yahoo! screen appears (shown in Figure 13.2), use the iPhone or iPad's virtual keyboard to enter your account name, email address, password, and a description for the account.

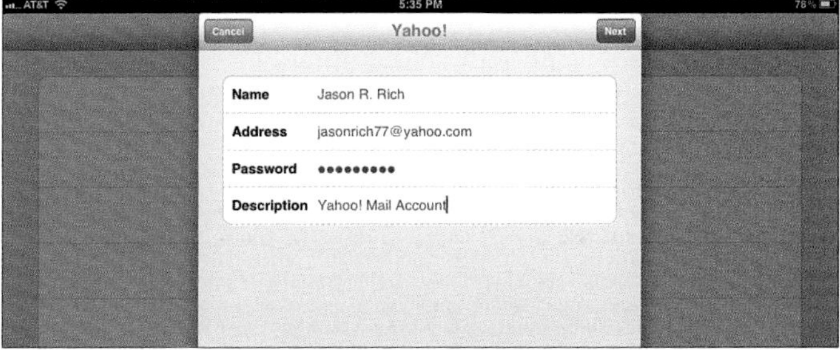

FIGURE 13.2

If you're setting up a Yahoo! Mail account, tap on the Yahoo! option, and then fill in the email account–related fields that appear on the screen using your existing email account details, such as your email address and password.

TIP As you're adding an email account from the Settings app, the account name should be your full name because this is what will automatically appear in your outgoing email messages in the From field (alongside your email address). You can, however, opt to use just your first name or a nickname, based on what you want to share with the recipients of your emails. The description can be anything that will help you personally differentiate that account from your other accounts, such as Home Email, Work Email, or Yahoo! Email.

5. Tap on the Next icon that's located in the upper-right corner of the window.
6. Your iOS device will connect to the email account's server and confirm the account details you've entered. The word Verifying will appear on the screen.
7. After the account has been verified, a new window with four options is displayed. They're labeled Mail, Contacts, Calendars, and Notes. Each will have a virtual on/off switch associated with it. The default for the last three options is On. They're used to determine which additional data can be linked with the Mail account.
8. Tap on the Save icon that's located in the upper-right corner of this window. An "Adding Account" message will briefly be displayed.
9. Details about the email account you just set up will now be added to your iOS device and will become immediately accessible via the Mail app.
10. If you have another existing email account to set up, from the Mail, Contacts, Calendars screen in the Settings app, tap on the Add Account option again, and repeat the preceding procedure. Otherwise, exit the Settings app and launch the Mail app from the Home Screen.

Depending on the type of email account you're setting up for use with your iPhone or iPad, the information you'll be prompted for will vary slightly. For example, to set up an existing Microsoft Exchange email account, the prompts you'll need to fill in during the email setup procedure include Email Address, Domain, Username, Password, and a Description for the account.

To set up an existing iCloud or MobileMe email account, you'll need to enter your existing Apple ID and password. To set up a Gmail or AOL Mail account, you'll need to enter your name, email address, and password, as well as an account description.

After the account is set up, it will be listed in the Settings app when you tap on the Mail, Contacts, Calendars option.

> **TIP** When you purchase a new iOS device, it comes with free technical support from AppleCare for 90 days. If you purchased AppleCare (or AppleCare+) with your iOS device, you have access to free technical support from Apple for two years. This includes the ability to make an in-person appointment with an Apple Genius at any Apple Store and have them set up your email accounts on your iPhone or iPad.
>
> To schedule a free appointment, visit www.apple.com/retail/geniusbar. Or call Apple's toll-free technical support phone number and have someone talk you through the email setup process. Call 800-APL-CARE (275-2273).

HOW TO CUSTOMIZE MAIL OPTIONS FROM SETTINGS

From the Settings app, select Mail, Contacts, Calendars from the main Settings menu. Then, on the Mail, Contacts, Calendars screen (shown in Figure 13.3), you will see a handful of customizable features pertaining to how your iOS device will handle your email accounts.

At the top of the Mail, Contacts, Calendars screen is a listing of the individual email accounts you have already linked with the Mail app.

FIGURE 13.3

From Settings, you can customize a handful of settings relating to the Mail app.

Below the Accounts heading on the Mail, Contacts, Calendars screen in the Settings app is the Fetch New Data option. Use this to determine how often your iOS device will automatically access the Web to check for and download new incoming email messages. (You can set this option for Manual as well.)

By scrolling down on this screen, you'll see the Mail heading. Below this heading are a handful of customizable options relating to how the Mail app will manage your email accounts and email messages:

- **Show**—This feature determines how many messages within a particular email account the Mail app will download from the server and display at any given time. Your options include 50, 100, 200, 500, and 1,000 Recent Messages.
- **Preview**—As you look at your Inbox using the Mail app, you can determine how much of each email message's body text will be visible from the Inbox summary screen, in addition to the From, Date/Time, and Subject. You can choose None, or between one and five lines of the email message.

> **TIP** The Preview option also impacts the email-related notifications that will appear within Notification Center if you assign the Notification Center app to continuously monitor the Mail app. You can also do this in Settings by tapping on the Notifications option under the main Settings menu.

- **Minimum Font Size**—Regardless of the font size used by the sender, your iPhone or iPad can automatically adjust the font size so that messages are more easily readable on the device's display. You can change the default font size for emails to be Small, Medium, Large, Extra Large, or Giant. The default option is Medium, which is acceptable to most people.
- **Show To/Cc Label**—To save space on your screen as you're reading emails, you can decide to turn off the To and Cc label within each email message by tapping the virtual switch associated with this option and switching it to the off position.
- **Ask Before Deleting**—This option serves as a safety net to ensure that you don't accidentally delete an important email message from your iOS device. When this feature is turned on, you will be asked to confirm your message deletion request before an email message is actually deleted. At least until you become comfortable using the Mail app, it's a good idea to leave this feature turned on. Keep in mind that, by default, you cannot delete email messages stored on your email account's server. When you delete a message

from the Mail app, it is deleted from only your iPhone or iPad but will still be accessible from other devices. On your iOS device, it might also appear in the Trash folder that's related to that email account, depending on how it is set up.

- **Load Remote Images**—When an email message has a photo or graphic embedded in it, this option determines whether that photo or graphic will automatically be downloaded and displayed with the email message. You can opt to have your iOS device refrain from automatically loading graphics with email messages. This will reduce the amount of data transferred to your iPhone or iPad (which is a consideration if you're connected to the Web via 3G). You always have the option to tap on the placeholder icon in the email message to manually download the graphic content in a specific message, including photos.
- **Organize by Thread**—This feature enables you to review messages in reverse chronological order if a single message turns into a back-and-forth email conversation, in which multiple parties keep hitting Reply to respond to messages with the same Subject. When turned on, this makes keeping track of email conversations much easier, especially if you're managing several email accounts on your iPhone or iPad. If it's turned off, messages in your Inbox are displayed in reverse chronological order, as they're received, and are not also grouped together by subject or sender.
- **Always Bcc Myself**—To ensure that you keep a copy of every outgoing email you send, turn on this feature. A copy of every outgoing email will also be sent to your Inbox if this feature is turned on. Typically, all outgoing messages automatically get saved in a Sent folder that's related to that account.
- **Signature**—For every outgoing email that you compose, you can automatically add an email signature. The default signature is "Sent from my iPhone" or "Sent from my iPad." However, by tapping on this option in the Settings app, you can use the virtual keyboard to create a customized signature. A signature might include your name, mailing address, email address, phone number(s), and so forth.

After you make whatever adjustments you want to the Mail app-related options from the Settings app, exit the Settings app by pressing the Home button and return to the Home Screen. You're now ready to begin using the Mail app to access and manage your email account(s).

TIPS FOR VIEWING YOUR INCOMING EMAIL

The Mail app has three main purposes. It allows you to do the following:

- Compose and send new email messages or respond to email.
- Read incoming email messages.
- Manage one or more of your email accounts simultaneously, and keep your incoming and outgoing emails well organized.

When you launch the Mail app on your iPhone or iPad, the Inbox for your various email accounts is displayed. You can opt to display incoming messages for a single email account, or display the incoming messages (in reverse chronological order, based on when each was received) from all of your email accounts.

Even though Mail enables you to simultaneously view incoming emails from multiple accounts within a single listing, behind the scenes, the app automatically keeps your incoming and outgoing emails, and your various email accounts, separate. So if you opt to read and respond to an email from your work-related Inbox, for example, that response will automatically be sent out from your work-related email account and be saved in the Sent Folder for that account.

iOS 5 WHAT'S NEW The Mail app is fully compatible with Siri on the iPhone 4S. If you want to read your new (incoming) email messages, for example, activate Safari and say, "Read my new email." Siri displays a list of new email messages on the iPhone's screen.

Or if you want to compose an email, activate Siri, and then say, "Send an email to [insert name]." If multiple email addresses are stored in your Contacts database for that person, Siri will ask you which email address to use, based on the Home, Work, or Other label associated with each.

Siri then prompts you to dictate the subject of the email. Once you speak what the subject line of the email should say, Siri will then say, "What would you like the email to say?"

When you hear the prompt tone, start dictating the body of your email message. After you stop speaking, Siri displays the message on the iPhone's screen and ask whether you're ready to send it.

Viewing all the Inboxes for all of your accounts simultaneously makes it faster to review your incoming emails, without having to manually switch between email accounts.

If you have multiple email accounts being managed from your iOS device, to view all your Inboxes simultaneously, or to switch between Inboxes, follow these steps:

1. Launch the Mail app.
2. The Inbox you last looked at will be displayed.
3. Tap on the left-pointing, arrow-shaped Mailboxes icon that's displayed in the upper-left corner of the screen to select which Inbox you want to view.
4. From the menu that appears, the first option is All Inboxes. Tap on this to view a single listing of all incoming emails. Or tap on any single email account that's listed under the Inboxes heading.
5. When you tap on your option, the Inbox screen returns, and the incoming emails (from the account or accounts you selected) are displayed. You can modify this option at any time.

FETCH NEW DATA

You can set up your iOS device to automatically access the Internet and retrieve new email messages by tapping on the Fetch New Data option, and then adjusting its settings. Or simply make sure that the Push option, listed at the top of the Fetch New Data screen, is turned on.

To adjust these settings, launch the Settings app and select the Mail, Contacts, Calendars option from the main Settings menu. Then, scroll down to the Fetch New Data option and tap on it.

From the Fetch New Data screen, you can turn on the Push option, which means the iPhone or iPad will access new emails automatically. Or you can turn off the Push option but set the Fetch option to check for new emails every 15 minutes, every 30 minutes, hourly, or manually.

! CAUTION One reason you might consider turning off the Push feature and using Fetch to periodically check for emails (or do this manually) is to reduce your 3G wireless data usage. When you signed up for a 3G wireless data plan with your wireless service provider, you probably selected a plan with a predetermined wireless data allocation per month. Having your iPhone or iPad constantly check for new incoming emails will quickly use up this allocation. This is not a concern, however, if you're using a Wi-Fi Internet connection or have an unlimited 3G data plan.

COMPOSING AN EMAIL MESSAGE

In the Mail app, you can easily compose an email from scratch and send it to one or more recipients. To compose a new email, tap on the Compose icon. On an iPhone, the Compose icon can be found in the lower-right corner of the screen when you're viewing your Inbox(es). On an iPad, the Compose icon is displayed in the upper-right corner of the main Inbox screen. When you tap on the Compose icon, a blank email message template will appear on the iPhone or iPad's screen. Using the virtual keyboard, fill in the To, Cc, Bcc, and/or Subject fields (as shown in Figure 13.4). At the very least, you must fill in the To field with a valid email address for at least one recipient. The other fields are optional.

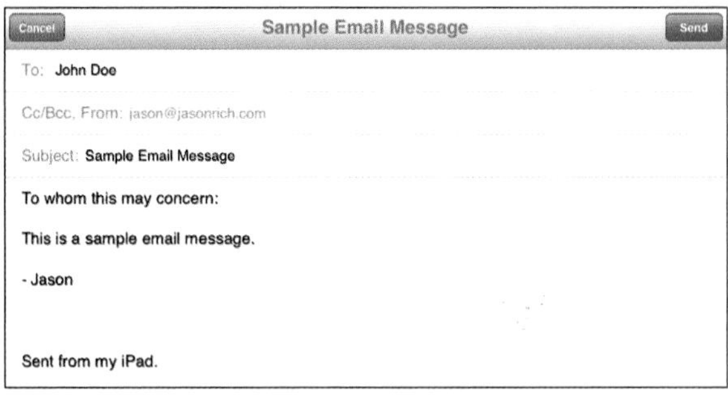

FIGURE 13.4

Tap on the Compose icon to create an email from scratch and send it from your iOS device.

You can send the same email to multiple recipients by either adding multiple email addresses to the To field or adding additional email addresses to the Cc and/or Bcc fields.

If you're managing one email address from your iOS device, the From field will automatically be filled in with your email address. However, if you're managing multiple email addresses from the iPhone or iPad, tap on the From field to select which email address you want to send the message from.

TIP As you fill in the To field when composing an email, the Mail app will automatically access your Contacts database and match up entries based on what you type in the To field. This can save you time because you don't have to manually enter email addresses. Plus, if you know that the person you're sending an email to already has an entry in your Contacts database, you can type the person's name, as opposed to email address, in the To field.

Next, tap on the Subject field and use the virtual keyboard to enter the subject for your message. As you do this, the subject will appear at the very top center of the Compose window.

> **TIP** In the Contacts app, to compose and send an email, without first launching the Mail app, select and view a specific contact entry in the Contacts app. When you tap on any email address listed, a New Message screen appears, with the To field for the outgoing email message already filled in. Use the virtual keyboard to compose your email, and then tap on the Send icon. The email message is sent and you are returned to the Contacts app.
>
> As you're viewing a Contacts entry, you can also tap on any phone number listed to initiate a phone call with that contact, without first launching the Phone app. To send a text message to that person from within the Contacts app, scroll down to the bottom of their Contacts entry and tap the Send Message icon.

To begin creating the main body of the outgoing email message, tap in the main body area of the message template on the screen, and begin using the virtual keyboard (or the external keyboard you're using with your iPhone or iPad) to compose your message.

> **! CAUTION** If you have the Auto-Correction and/or Spell Check feature turned on (which are adjustable from the Settings app), as you type, the iPhone or iPad will automatically correct anything that it perceives as a typo or misspelled word.
>
> Be very careful when using these features because they are notorious for plugging the wrong word into a sentence. Especially if you're creating important business documents and emails, make sure you proofread whatever you type on your iOS carefully before sending it. Typically, these features are helpful, but they do have quirks that can lead to embarrassing and unprofessional mistakes.

The signature you set up from within the Settings app will automatically be displayed at the bottom of the newly composed message. You can return to the Settings app to turn off the Signature feature, or change the signature that appears.

When your email is fully written and ready to be sent, tap on the blue-and-white Send icon that's displayed in the upper-right corner of the Compose window. In a few seconds, the message will be sent from your iOS device, assuming that it is connected to the Internet. A copy of the message will appear in your Sent or Outbox folder.

As a message is being sent, a "Sending" notification will appear near the bottom of the screen.

> **iOS 5 WHAT'S NEW** The iOS 5 version of the Mail app enables you to format your outgoing email messages and include **bold**, *italic*, and/or underlined text (as well as combinations, like ***bold-italic*** text).

To format text in an email message you're composing, type the text as you normally would using the virtual keyboard. After the text appears in your email, hold your finger on a word to make the Select, Select All, Paste, and Quote Level command tabs appear above that word.

Tap on Select, and then use your finger to move around the blue dots that appear to highlight the text you want to modify. Select the word, phrase, or sentence, for example, that you want to highlight using bold, italic, and/or underlined text.

When the appropriate text is highlighted in blue, tap the right-pointing arrow that appears above the text (next to the Cut, Copy, Paste, and Replacement commands), and then tap on the **B**/*I*U option. A new menu appears above the highlighted text with three options, labeled Bold, Italics, and Underline. Tap on one or more of these tabs to alter the highlighted text (as shown in Figure 13.5).

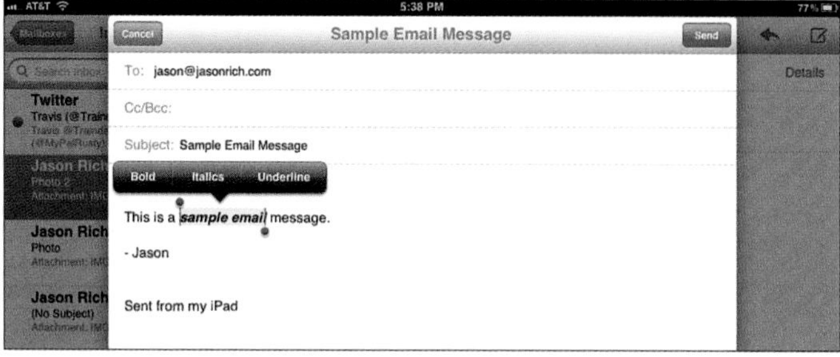

FIGURE 13.5

The iOS 5 version of Mail enables you to use bold, italic, and/or underlined text in the body of your outgoing email messages.

USING SELECT, SELECT ALL, CUT, COPY, AND PASTE

The iOS operating system offers Select, Select All, Cut, Copy, and Paste commands, which are accessible from many iPhone or iPad apps, including Mail. Using these commands, you can quickly copy and paste content from one portion of an app to another or from one app into another app, whether it's a paragraph of text, a phone number, or a photo.

To use these commands, use your finger to hold down on any word or graphic element on the screen for one or two seconds, until the Select and Select All tabs appear above that content. To select a single word or select what content you want to copy or cut, tap on the Select tab. Or to select all the content on the screen, tap the Select All tab.

After text (or a graphic element, such as a photo) is selected, tap on the Cut tab to delete that selected content from the screen (if this option is available in the app you're using), or tap the Copy tab to save the highlighted content in your iPhone or iPad's virtual clipboard.

Now, move to where you want to paste that saved content. This can be in the same email or document, for example, or in another app altogether. Choose the location on the screen where you want to paste the content, and hold your finger on that location for two or three seconds. When the Paste tab appears, tap on it. The content you just copied will be pasted into that location.

iOS 5 WHAT'S NEW In the Mail app, as you use the Select, Select All, Cut, Copy, and Paste commands, you'll also notice a Quote Level option that appears on the menu above the highlighted text or content that you select. Tap on this to increase or decrease the indent of that content, which impacts how it's formatted on the screen.

HOW TO SAVE AN UNSENT DRAFT OF AN EMAIL MESSAGE

If you want to save a draft of an email (in your Draft folder, for example), without sending it, as you're composing the email message, tap on the Cancel icon that appears in the upper-left corner of the Compose message window. Two command icons will appear, labeled Delete Draft and Save Draft. To save the unsent draft, tap on Save Draft.

If you have a saved but unsent draft of an email, you can return to it later to modify and/or send it. To do this, from the main Inbox screen within Mail, tap on the left-pointing Mailboxes icon that looks like an arrow (displayed near the upper-left corner of the screen). From the Mailboxes screen, scroll down to the Accounts heading, and tap on the listing for the email account from which the email draft was composed. When you see a list of folders related to that email account, tap on the Drafts folder (a number in a gray oval will appear to the right of the Drafts folder name, indicating there are draft email messages stored in it). When you see the listings for the saved draft emails, tap on the appropriate listing to open that email message. You can now edit the message or send it.

TIP To send an email message that contains an attachment, such as a Pages document or a photo, those attachments must be sent from within a specific app, not from the Mail app.

A Pages, Word, or PDF document can be sent from within Pages, a Numbers or Excel (spreadsheet) file can be sent from within Numbers, and a photo can be sent from within the Photos app, for example. In a compatible app, tap on the Share icon, and then select the Email option.

Currently, attachments cannot be added to outgoing messages composed using the Mail app, but this could change as new versions of the app are released.

TIPS FOR READING EMAIL

If you'll be managing multiple email accounts with your iPhone or iPad, it's important to understand that while the Mail app enables you to view email messages in all your accounts simultaneously (when you're looking at the All Inboxes view), the app actually keeps messages from your different accounts separate.

Also, as you view your incoming email messages, by default, the app groups emails together by message thread, allowing you to follow an email-based conversation that extends through multiple messages and replies. When turned on, this feature displays emails in the same thread in reverse chronological order, with the newest message first, and then displays all previous emails and your replies in sequence.

TIP To send and receive emails from your iPhone or iPad using the Mail app, your iOS device must be connected to the Internet via a Wi-Fi or 3G connection. Keep in mind that emails with large attachments, such as photos, Microsoft Office documents, or PDF files (sent from within specific apps) will deplete your monthly wireless data allocation from your wireless service provider much faster, as will having your iOS device automatically check for new incoming emails often.

After you launch the Mail app, you can access the Inbox for one or more of your existing email accounts, compose new emails, or manage your email accounts. Just like the Inbox on your main computer's email software, the Inbox of the Mail app (shown in Figure 13.6 on an iPhone, and Figure 13.7 on an iPad) displays your incoming emails.

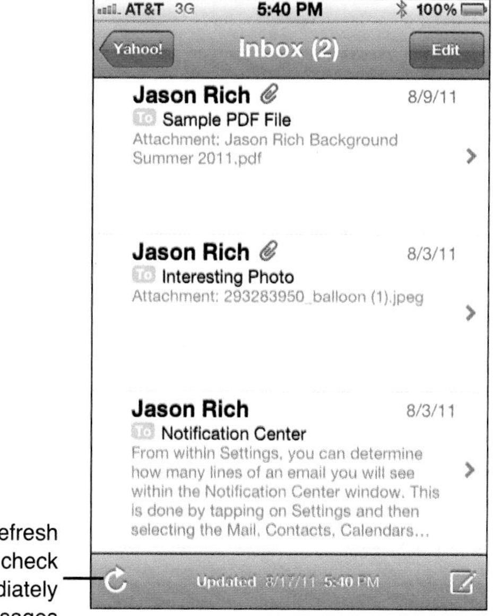

FIGURE 13.6

The Inbox screen of the Mail app displays a listing of your incoming emails on the iPhone.

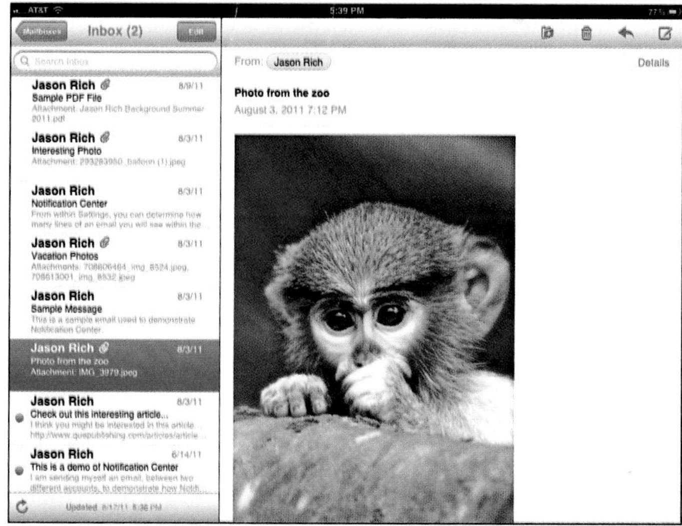

FIGURE 13.7

On the iPad, the Inbox, displayed on the left side of the Mail app's screen, provides a listing of your incoming emails.

THE MAIL APP'S INBOX

When you're viewing your Inbox(es), a list of the individual emails will be displayed. A blue dot to the left of an email message's details indicates that the message is new and has not yet been read.

Based on the customizations you make from the Settings app that pertain to the Mail app, the Sender, Subject, Date/Time, and up to five lines of the message's body text can be displayed for each incoming message listing.

On the iPhone, when viewing your Inbox and the listing of incoming (new) email messages, tap on any message listing to read that message in its entirety. When you do this, a new message screen appears. At the bottom of this screen will be a series of command icons for managing that email.

On the iPad, the email message that's highlighted in blue on the left side of the screen is the one that's currently being displayed, in its entirety, on the right side of the screen. Tap on any email listing on the left side of the screen to view the entire message on the right side of the screen. Icons at the top of the screen are used for managing that email.

> **TIP** Tap on the Refresh icon to manually refresh your Inbox and check for new incoming emails. The message "Updated," accompanied by the date and time, indicates the last time your Inbox was refreshed.
>
> Use this Refresh icon after you have linked a new email account to the Mail app from within Settings, and then return to the Mail app. This will immediately populate the Mail app with the new (incoming) messages associated with the newly added email account.

At the top of the Inbox message listing are two command icons, labeled Mailboxes and Edit. In between these two icons is the heading Inbox, along with a number that's displayed in parentheses. This number indicates how many new, unread messages are currently stored in your Inbox.

Just below this Inbox heading is a Search field. Tap on this Search field to make the iPhone or iPad's virtual keyboard appear, allowing you to enter a search phrase and quickly find a particular email message. You can search the content of the Mail app using any keyword, a sender's name, or an email subject, for example.

THE EDIT COMMAND ICON

Located on top of the Inbox message listing (to the right of the Inbox heading) is a command icon that's labeled Edit. When you tap on this icon, you can quickly select multiple messages from your Inbox to delete or move to another folder (as shown in Figure 13.8).

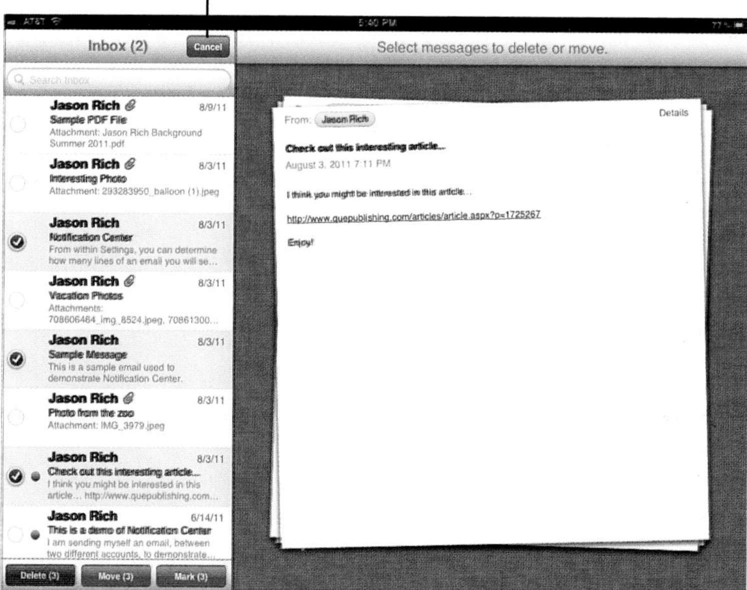

FIGURE 13.8

Tap the Edit icon to manage your incoming messages, delete them in quantity, or move them to other folders to keep them organized.

After you tap the Edit icon, an a empty circle icon appears to the left of each email message summary. To move or delete one or more messages from the Inbox listing, tap on the empty circle icon for that massage. A red-and-white check mark will fill the empty circle icon when you do this, and the Delete and Move command icons displayed at the bottom of the screen will become active.

After you've selected one or more messages, tap the Delete icon to quickly delete one or more messages simultaneously from your Inbox (which sends them to the Trash folder), or tap the Move icon, and then select which folder you want to move those email messages to.

In Edit mode while reviewing your Inbox, you can select one or more messages and move them from your Inbox to another folder by selecting the Move command.

On the iPhone, from the Inbox screen, tap on the Edit icon (that's displayed in the upper-right corner of the screen). Tap on one or more messages you want to select and then move. When the messages are selected and have a checkmark next to them, tap on the Move icon displayed at the bottom of the screen. A list of available folders relating to that email account is displayed. Tap on the folder in which you want to store that email. It will then be removed from your Inbox but appear in that folder.

Or as you're reading a single email on the iPhone, tap on the File icon that's displayed at the bottom of the screen, and then choose a folder that's associated with that email address to store the message in.

On the iPad, to use the Move command, as you're viewing the Inbox on the left side of the screen, tap the Edit icon that's displayed in the upper-right corner of the Inbox column. Tap on the email messages you want to select and then move. A checkmark appears next to each selected message.

Tap on the Move icon after you've selected one or more messages. A list of available folders is displayed on the left side of the iPad's screen. Tap on the folder to which you want to move the messages.

Or as you're reading an email message, tap on the File icon that's displayed near the upper-right corner of the screen, and then choose a folder that's associated with that email address to store the message in. The folder options are displayed on the left side of the screen.

To exit this option without doing anything, tap on the Cancel icon.

HOW TO DELETE INDIVIDUAL INCOMING MESSAGES

On your iPhone or iPad, as you're looking at the listing of messages in your Inbox, you can also delete individual messages, one at a time. Swipe your finger from left to right over a message listing. A red-and-white Delete icon will appear on the right side of that email message listing (shown in Figure 13.9 on an iPhone 4). Tap on this Delete icon to delete the message.

FIGURE 13.9

Swipe your finger from left to right over a single email message listing to make the Delete icon appear, allowing you to delete the message from your Inbox and send it to the Trash folder.

> **TIP** Another way to delete a message from your Inbox, or any folder, is to tap on a message listing to view that message. To then delete the message, tap on the Trash Can icon. On the iPhone, the Trash Can is displayed at the bottom center of the screen. On the iPad, it's displayed in the upper-right corner of the screen. Doing this will immediately send the message to the Trash folder and remove it from its current folder, such as your Inbox.

HOW TO VIEW YOUR EMAILS

When a single email message is selected from the Inbox listing, that message will be displayed, in its entirety. At the top of the message, you'll see the From, To, Cc (if applicable), Bcc (if applicable), Subject, and the Date/Time it was sent.

In the upper-right corner of the email message will be a blue Hide command. If you tap on this, some of the message header information will no longer be displayed. To make this information reappear, tap on the Details command that appears in the upper-right corner of the message.

Located to the right of the date and time the email was received is a blue Mark command. Use it to flag the message (meaning it's important), or tap the Mark As Unread option so that it remains in your Inbox as an unread message with a blue dot next to its listing.

TIP As you're reading email on the small screen of your iPhone (or even on the iPad screen), if the text is difficult to see, you can automatically increase the size of all text displayed in the Mail, Contacts, Calendar, Messages, and Notes apps by adjusting the Accessibility option in the Settings app.

To make this font size adjustment, launch Settings. From the main Settings menu, select the General option. Scroll down to the Accessibility option and tap on it. From the Accessibility menu screen in Settings, tap on the Large Text option. You can now select the font size you'd like your iOS device to use when displaying your emails and other content from the Contacts, Calendar, Messages, and Notes app.

You might want to mark a message as Unread, so when you refer to your emails later, you'll know you still need to respond to or reread that message.

iOS 5 WHAT'S NEW When you flag a message, a tiny flag-shaped icon is displayed next to the message's subject. This is a visual way to differentiate an email and mark it as urgent.

HOW TO DEAL WITH INCOMING EMAIL MESSAGE ATTACHMENTS

The Mail app enables you to access certain types of attachment files that accompany an incoming email message. Photos (in the .JPEG, .GIF, and .TIFF format), audio files (in the .MP3, .AAC, .WAV, and .AIFF format), video clips, and PDF files, as well as Pages, Keynote, Numbers, Microsoft Word, Microsoft Excel, and Microsoft PowerPoint files, can all be viewed or accessed from the iPhone or iPad using the Mail app.

If an incoming email message contains an attachment that is not compatible or accessible from your iOS device, you will see that an attachment is present but you won't be able to open or access it. In this case, you'll need to access this content from your primary computer.

To open an attached file using another app, in the incoming email message, tap and hold down the attachment icon for one to three seconds. If the attachment is compatible with an app that's installed on your iPhone or iPad, you'll be given the option to transfer the file to that app or directly open or access the file using that app.

ORGANIZE EMAIL MESSAGES IN FOLDERS

Email messages appearing in your Inbox, for example, can easily be moved into another folder, allowing you to better organize your emails. Here's how to do this:

1. From the Inbox listing, tap the Edit icon that's located above the Inbox listing. Or, if you're viewing an email message, tap on the file folder–shaped icon. On the iPhone, this file folder icon can be found at the bottom of the screen. On the iPad, it's located in the upper-right corner of the screen.
2. When you tap the file folder icon (as shown in Figure 13.10), the various folders available for that email account will be displayed.

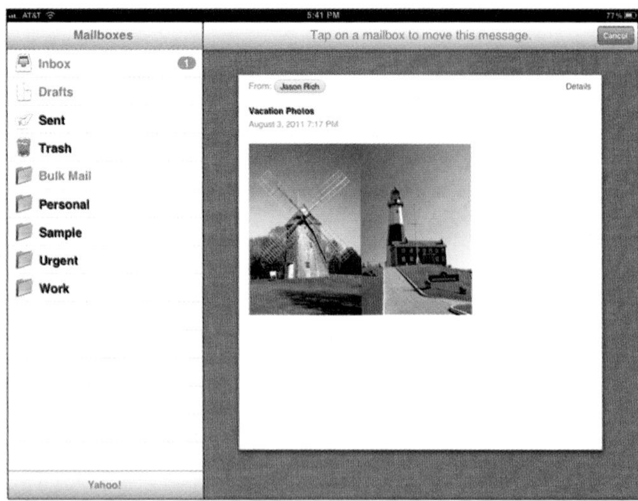

FIGURE 13.10

To move a file, tap on the file folder–shaped icon, and then tap on the name of the folder to which you want to move the message. The message will be transferred from your Inbox to that folder.

3. Tap on the folder to which you want to move the message. The folders available will vary for different types of email accounts, and might vary depending on whether you have created your own folders in the Mail app (which is a new iOS 5 feature). The email message will be moved to the folder you select.

iOS 5 **WHAT'S NEW** As you're managing incoming and outgoing emails, the Mail app will use the default folders that are already associated with that email account, such as Inbox, Drafts, Sent, Trash, and Junk. However, you can create your own folders as well, and then move individual messages into those folders, to customize the way you organize them.

To create a custom folder for use with an email account (assuming that your existing email account allows for this feature), from the Inbox, tap on the Mailboxes icon. When the Mailboxes screen appears, under the Accounts heading, choose one of your accounts for which you want to create a folder, and tap on its listing. A listing of the existing folders for that account will be displayed. Tap on the Edit icon that appears near the top of the screen. Then, tap on the New Mailbox icon that appears near the bottom of the screen. Enter the name of the folder you want to create, and then tap on the Save icon. Your new folder will now be displayed with that email account. The process works the same on the iPhone and iPad, but the position of the various icons varies slightly.

FORWARDING, PRINTING, AND REPLYING TO MESSAGES

From the Mail app, you can forward any incoming message to someone else, reply to the message, or print the email by tapping on the left-pointing, curved-arrow icon that's displayed when you're viewing an email. On an iPhone, the curved-arrow icon is displayed at the bottom of the screen. On an iPad, it can be found in the upper-right corner of the main Inbox screen (next to the Trash Can icon).

When you tap on this icon, as you're reading any email message, a menu will be displayed with the following three options: Reply, Forward, and Print.

To reply to the message you're reading (and respond to the sender), tap on the Reply icon. A blank email message template will appear on the screen.

To forward the email you're reading to another recipient, tap on the Forward icon. If there's an attachment associated with this email, you'll be asked, "Include attachments from original email?" and you'll see two options displayed on the screen, labeled "Include" and "Don't Include." Tap on the appropriate response.

When you opt to forward an email, a new message template will appear on the screen. However, in the body of the email message will be the contents of the message you're forwarding. Start the message-forwarding process by filling in the To field. You can also modify the Subject field (or leave the message's original Subject), and then add to the body of the email message with your own text. This text will appear above the forwarded message's content.

TIP To forward an email to multiple recipients, enter each person's email address in the To field of the outgoing message, but separate each address with a comma (,). Thus, you'd type **Jason@JasonRich.com, JasonRich77@yahoo.com** in the To field to forward or send the message to these two recipients simultaneously. Or tap on the plus icon (+) that appears to the right of the To field to add more recipients.

When you're ready to forward the message to one or more recipients, tap on the blue-and-white Send icon that appears. Or tap the Cancel icon to abort the message-forwarding process.

If you have a wireless printer set up to work with your iOS device (using the AirPrint feature built in to the iOS 5 operating system and some printers), you can tap the Print icon that appears when you tap the left-pointing curved-arrow icon as you're reading an email.

TIP As you're reading emails, you'll discover that all the touchscreen finger motions you've learned will work on the section of the iOS device's screen that's displaying the actual email messages. You can scroll up or down and/or zoom in or out. Plus, you can use the Select, Cut, Copy, and Paste features built in to the iOS operating system to manipulate the contents of an email message and utilize that content in other apps, for example. Or you can select, cut, and paste a portion of one email and insert it into another email message you're composing.

IN THIS CHAPTER

- How to use new features added to the iOS 5 editions of the Schedule and Contacts apps
- How to use the new Reminders app
- How to use strategies for staying organized, on time, and productive using your iPhone or iPad

14

STRATEGIES FOR MANAGING CALENDARS, CONTACTS, AND REMINDERS

If you have a busy life, and most of us do, your iPhone or iPad can be used to help you manage your schedule and day-to-day appointments, plus allow you to stay in contact with the people you know (and manage those contacts using the Contacts app), while also helping you maintain one or more detailed to-do lists.

Veteran iOS device users will immediately discover some nice improvements to the iOS 5 edition of the Calendar app, which now offers additional onscreen calendar views, plus the capability to view event-related attachments from directly within the app.

The majority of the Contact app's improvements related to iOS 5 come in the form of integration with other apps, which can now more readily access your personal contacts database. This enables you to utilize contact data from the Contacts app without actually launching Contacts. Yet the information you

need will be placed exactly where you need it, such as in the To field of an email, a tweet, or a text message you're composing.

Meanwhile, many people rely on scraps of paper to maintain their daily to-do lists. With the help of the new Reminders app, not only can you easily manage multiple to-do lists simultaneously, and add alarms and deadlines to individual to-do items, but you also can be reminded of responsibilities, tasks, or objectives exactly when you need this information, based on your geographic location or a predetermined time and date.

In keeping with iOS 5's theme of inter-app integration, the Calendars, Contacts, and Reminders apps are all fully compatible with iCloud, which makes synchronizing your app-related data a straightforward process.

Plus, both Calendars and Reminders can easily be set up to work with Notification Center, so all of your alerts, alarms, reminders, and notifications are consistently displayed in one place—the Notification Center window—that's constantly available to you on your iPhone or iPad.

Best of all, Calendars, Contacts, and Reminders, as well as Notification Center, are among the apps that come preinstalled with iOS 5, so they're immediately available to you, without your having to first visit the App Store.

NOTE The features and functions offered by the Calendars, Contacts, and Reminders apps are virtually identical on the iPhone, iPad, and iPod touch. However, due to varying screen sizes, the location of specific command icons, options, and menus will sometimes vary. However, after you get to know how the app functions in general, you'll easily be able to switch between using it on your iPhone or iPad, for example, without confusion.

On the iPad, all information relevant to a specific app or function is typically displayed on a single screen. On the iPhone, however, that same information is often split up and displayed on several separate screens.

TIP If you're an iPhone 4S user, you'll discover that Siri works seamlessly with the Calendar, Contacts, and Reminders apps and enables you to access and update information using voice commands.

GET ACQUAINTED WITH THE CALENDAR APP

With its multiple viewing options for keeping track of the scheduling information stored in it, the iOS 5 version of the Calendar app for the iPhone or iPad is a highly customizable scheduling tool that enables you to easily sync your scheduling data with your primary computer's scheduling software (such as Microsoft Outlook on a PC or iCal on a Mac). To sync your Calendar data with other apps, an additional third-party app or file conversion software on your computer might be needed. Like many other apps, Calendar works seamlessly with Notification Center, as well as Apple's iCloud service.

> **TIP** The Calendar app works with your iPhone or iPad held in either landscape or portrait mode, so which you choose is a matter of personal preference.

Plus, you can share some or all of your schedule information with colleagues and maintain several separate, color-coded calendars to keep personal and work-related responsibilities, as well as individual projects, listed separately, while still being able to view them on the same screen.

CONTROLLING THE VIEW

Launch Calendar from your iOS device's Home Screen, and then choose in which viewing perspective you'd like to view your schedule data. Your options include these:

- **Day**—This view displays your appointments and scheduled events individually, based on the time each item is scheduled for (as shown in Figure 14.1).

  On the iPhone, the Day view displays the date at the top of the screen, and then an item-by-item listing of your scheduled appointments and obligations, displayed in chronological order, based on the time each is scheduled for on that day.

  On the iPad, the Day display is split into two sections. You'll see the date, along with a small calendar for the month, and a summary listing of appointments and/or events displayed on the left side of the screen. On the right side of the screen is an item-by-item listing of your scheduled appointments and obligations, displayed in chronological order, based on the time each is scheduled for on that day.

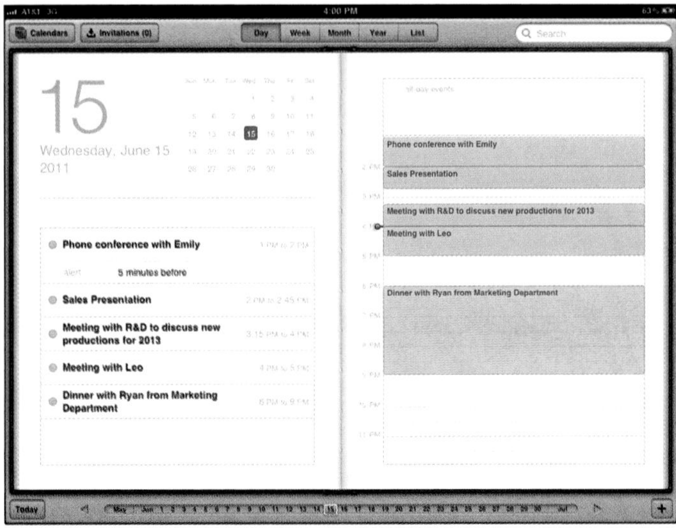

FIGURE 14.1

The Day view of the Calendar app lets you see your schedule broken down one day at a time, in one-hour increments.

> **TIP** Use the Day view of the Calendar app to see a detailed outline of scheduled appointments and events for a single day. Swipe your finger to scroll up or down to see an hour-by-hour summary of that day's schedule.

On the iPhone, tap on the left or right arrows displayed at the top of the screen, to the right and left of the date, to view another day's schedule.

On the iPad, tap the left or right arrows displayed at the bottom of the screen, or tap a particular month and day icon, also displayed at the bottom of the screen, to view another day's schedule.

- **Week**—This view uses a grid format to display the days of the week along the top of the screen and time intervals along the left side. With it, you have an overview of all appointments and events scheduled during a particular week (Sunday through Saturday).

  Use the small icons at the bottom of the screen to change the date range you want to view in the main portion of the screen.

iOS 5 WHAT'S NEW On the iPhone, to see the Week view, first tap the List, Day, or Month view tab at the bottom of the screen, and then rotate your iPhone from portrait mode to landscape mode to automatically switch to the new Week view. You can then swipe your finger from left to right, right to left, and/or up and down on the screen to scroll through your appointments in the Week view of the Calendar app.

- **Month**—This month-at-a-time view (shown in Figure 14.2) enables you to see a month's worth of appointments and events at a time. Tap any single day to immediately switch to the Day view to review a detailed summary of appointments or events slated for that day. On an iPad, this requires a double-tap on a specific day.

FIGURE 14.2

The Month view of Calendar, shown here on an iPhone 4, enables you to view one month at a time. Tap on any day to view that day's schedule in greater detail.

TIP On the iPhone, use the left and right arrows, displayed to the right and left of the Month and Year, to quickly jump between months as you view the calendar in Month view.

On the iPad, tap on the small year and month icons, displayed at the bottom of the screen, to quickly jump between months as you view the calendar in Month view.

- **Year** (iPad Only)—This Year view (new to iOS 5) in Calendar enables you to look at 12 minicalendars and see a color-coded preview of your schedule (with minimal detail displayed). For example, you can block out vacation days, travel days, and so on, and get a comprehensive view of your overall annual schedule.
- **List**—See a complete summary listing of all appointments and events stored in the Calendar app. You can tap on an individual listing to see its complete details. This is a fast and convenient way to see your upcoming appointments in chronological order. Using this view, you can scroll through upcoming events and appointments without knowing their exact date. It also enables you to more easily use the Calendar app as a to-do list manager (instead of the Reminders app).

TIP Regardless of which view you select, at any time, you can view the current day's schedule by tapping the Today button that's located in the lower-left corner of the screen. On the calendar itself, the current date is always highlighted in blue.

HOW TO ENTER A NEW APPOINTMENT

Regardless of which calendar view you're using, follow these steps to enter a new appointment:

1. Tap the plus icon that's displayed in the upper-right corner of the screen on the iPhone or the lower-right corner of the screen on the iPad. This causes an Add Event window to be displayed.

NOTE When you're using the Calendar app, the appointments, meetings, and other items you enter are referred to as "events."

2. The first field in the Add Event window is labeled Title. Using the virtual keyboard, enter a heading for the appointment or event, such as "Lunch with Rusty," "Ryan's Soccer Practice," "Call Email," or "Mandatory Sales Meeting at Work."
3. If there's a location associated with the event, tap the Location field that's located below the Title field, and then use the virtual keyboard to enter an address or a location. Entering information into the Location field is optional. You can be as detailed as you want when entering information into this field.

4. To set the time and date for the new appointment to begin and end, tap the Starts and Ends field. A new Start & End window is displayed, temporarily replacing the Add Event window.
5. When viewing the Start & End window, tap the Starts option so that it becomes highlighted in blue, and then use the scrolling Date, Hour, Minute, and AM/PM dials to select the start time for your appointment.
6. After entering the start time, tap on the Ends option, and again use the scrolling Date, Hour, Minute, and AM/PM dials to select the end time for your appointment. Or if the appointment lasts the entire day, tap the All-Day virtual switch, moving it from the off to the on position.

> **TIP** You can also adjust the Time Zone option if the meeting will be taking place in a different time zone than the one you're currently in. So if you're based in Los Angeles but the meeting or appointment will take place at 2:00 p.m. (EST) in New York, you can enter the correct time for the location of the meeting and the iPhone or iPad will adjust accordingly when you travel.

7. After you enter the start time and end time for the appointment, you must tap the blue-and-white Done button to save this information and return to the Add Event window.

   If the appointment you're entering repeats every day, every week, every two weeks, every month, or every year, tap the Repeat option, and choose the appropriate time interval. The default for this option is Never, meaning that it is a nonrepeating, one-time-only appointment.
8. To set an audible alarm for the event, tap the Alert option displayed below the Repeat option in the Add Event window. The Event Alert window temporarily replaces the Add Event window.
9. In the Event Alert window, tap to specify when you want the audible alarm to sound to remind you of the appointment. Your options are None (which is the default), 5 minutes before, 15 minutes before, 30 minutes before, one hour before, two hours before, one day before, two days before, or On Date of Event. When you tap your selection, a check mark that corresponds to that selection displays on the left side of the window.
10. Tap the blue-and-white Done button that's displayed in the upper-right corner of the Event Alert window to save the information and return to the Add Event screen.

TIP After you've added an alert, a Second Alert option displays in the Add Event window. If you want to add a secondary alarm to this appointment, tap the Second Alert option, and when the Event Alert window reappears, tap on the time when you want the second alarm to sound. Again, don't forget to tap on the Done button.

This is useful if you want to be reminded of an appointment or deadline several hours (or days) before it's scheduled to occur, and then again several minutes before, for example. You can pick the time periods between the two alarms.

11. When you return to the Add Event window, if you're maintaining several separate calendars in the Calendar app, you can choose in which calendar you want to list the appointment or event by tapping on the Calendar option and then selecting the appropriate calendar.

iOS 5 WHAT'S NEW One new feature of Calendar for iOS 5 is the capability to easily add invitees to appointments and events stored in the Calendar. As you're creating an event, meeting or appointment, from the Edit screen, tap on the Invitees icon and then add a list of invitees. You can manually type names or tap the plus-sign icon to add contacts from your Contacts database. The person you add as an invitee will be sent an email automatically, allowing them to respond to the invite.

It is essential that you tap the blue-and-white Done button to save the new appointment information and have it displayed in your calendar. The alternative is to tap the Cancel icon (displayed in the upper-left corner of the Add Event, Start & End, Repeat, or Event Alert window), which is used to exit that window without saving any new information.

TIP As you scroll down in the Calendar window, you will see an optional URL and Notes field. Using the virtual keyboard, you can manually enter a website URL that somehow corresponds to the event. Or, you can tap on the Notes field and manually type notes pertaining to the appointment (or paste data from other apps in this field).

The alternative to manually entering appointment information into the Calendar app on your iPhone or iPad is to enter your scheduling information in a scheduling program on your primary computer, such as Microsoft Outlook (PC), iCal (Mac), or Microsoft Entourage (Mac), and then sync this data with your iOS device using the iTunes sync process, the Wireless iTunes Sync process, or iCloud.

You can also sync scheduling data with other online or network-based scheduling applications offered by Yahoo! and Google, for example. This can be set up from within the Settings app. In Settings, select the Mail, Contacts, Calendars option from the main Settings menu, and then select your Yahoo! or Google email account, for example. From the Yahoo! or Google menu screen in Settings, turn on the virtual switch that's associated with the Calendars option by tapping on it.

VIEWING INDIVIDUAL APPOINTMENT DETAILS

From any Calendar view in the Calendar app, tap an individual event (appointment, meeting, and so on) to view all the details related to that item.

When you tap on a single event listing, a new window opens. In the upper-right corner of the window is an Edit icon. Tap it to modify any aspect of the event listing, such as the title, location, start time, end time, alert, or notes.

To delete an event entry entirely, tap the red-and-white Delete Event icon that's displayed at the bottom of the Edit window. Or, when you're done making changes to an Event entry, tap on the blue-and-white Done button that's displayed in the upper-right corner of the window.

TIP The Calendar app works with several other apps, including Contacts and Notification Center. For example, in Contacts, you can enter someone's birthday in a record, and that information can automatically be displayed in the Calendar app.

To display birthday listings, for example, from within Calendar, tap the Calendars button, which is displayed in the upper-left corner of the screen, and then tap on the Birthdays option to add a check mark to that selection. All recurring birthdays stored in your Contacts app will now appear in Calendar.

QUICKLY FIND APPOINTMENT OR EVENT DETAILS

In addition to viewing the various calendar views offered within the Calendar app, to find individual appointments, you can use the Search field. On the iPhone, the in-app Search field can be found at the top of the screen when you tap on the List option (displayed at the bottom of the screen for viewing events). On the iPad, the Search field can always be found in the upper-right corner of the Calendar app.

Tap the Search field, and then use the virtual keyboard to enter any keyword or phrase associated with the appointment you're looking for.

Or, from the iPhone or iPad's Home Screen, swipe your finger from left to right to access the Spotlight Search screen. In the Search field that appears, enter a keyword, search phrase, or date associated with an appointment. When a list of relevant items is displayed, tap the appointment you want to view. This launches the Calendar app and displays that specific appointment.

VIEWING ONE OR MORE COLOR-CODED CALENDARS

One of the handy features of the Calendar app is that you can view and manage multiple color-coded calendars at once on the same screen, or you can easily switch between calendars.

To decide which calendar information you want to view, tap the Calendars icon that is displayed in the upper-left corner of the screen. When the Show Calendars window appears, select which calendar or calendars you want to view on your device's screen by tapping on their listings.

You can view one or more calendars at a time, or you can select to view data from all your calendars on one screen simultaneously. Each calendar is color-coded, so you can tell entries apart when looking at multiple calendars on the screen at once. If you're using color-coding on your Mac with iCal, for example, this coding will transfer to your iOS device when you sync scheduling data. Otherwise, each time a new Calendar is created within the Calendar app, a color will be assigned to it by the app.

CUSTOMIZING THE CALENDAR APP

As you begin using the Calendar app, you'll discover that there are many ways to customize it beyond choosing between the various calendar views. For example, from the Calendar app, you can set audible alerts to remind you of appointments, meetings, and events.

TIP To customize the audio alert generated by the Calendar app, launch the Settings app, and then select the General option. Next, tap on the Sounds option.

Make sure the Calendar Alerts option, displayed in the Sounds screen of Settings, is turned on. If this option is turned off, a text-based message displays on the iPhone or iPad's screen as an event reminder instead of an audible alarm sounding.

If you are able to receive meeting or event invites from others, from the Settings app, tap on the Mail, Contacts and Calendars option. Then scroll down to the Calendars heading and make sure the New Invitations Alerts option is turned on. This enables you to hear an audible alarm when you receive a new invitation.

Also from this screen, under the Calendars heading, determine how far back in your schedule you want to sync appointment data between your primary computer and your iOS device. Your options include Events 2 Weeks Back, Events 1 Month Back, Events 3 Months Back, Events 6 Months Back, and All Events.

ADJUSTING TIME ZONE SUPPORT

When the Time Zone Support option is turned on and you've selected the major city that you're in or near, all alarms are activated based on that city's time zone. However, when you travel, turn off this option. With Time Zone Support turned off, the iPhone or iPad determines the current date and time based on the location and time zone you're in (when it's connected to cell network or Internet), and adjusts all your alarms to go off at the appropriate time for that time zone.

To access the Time Zone Support feature, follow these steps:

1. Launch the Settings app.
2. Select the Mail, Contacts, Calendars option.
3. Scroll down to the options listed under Calendars, and then tap on Time Zone Support.
4. When the Time Zone Support screen appears, you will see a virtual switch for turning this feature on or off. When it's turned on, below the switch is a Time Zone option. Tap it, and then choose your home city (or a city in the time zone you're in).

When turned off, Time Zone Support displays event times in your Calendar and activates alarms based on the time zone selected. So if New York City (Eastern Time Zone) is selected, for example, and you have an appointment set for 2:00 p.m. with an accompanying alarm, you see that appointment listed at 2:00 p.m. and hear the alarm at 2:00 p.m. Eastern Time, regardless of where, or in what time zone, you're actually physically located.

However, if you travel to Los Angeles (Pacific Coast Time), for example, and Time Zone Support is turned on, you'll hear the alarm go off at 11:00 a.m. local time, which is 2:00 p.m. EST. If you turn off this feature when you travel, however, the alarm sounds at 2:00 p.m. regardless of which time zone you're physically in.

USE CONTACTS TO KEEP IN TOUCH WITH PEOPLE YOU KNOW

The art of networking is all about meeting new people, staying in contact with them, making referrals and connections for others, and tapping the knowledge, experience, or expertise of the people you know to help you achieve your personal or career-related goals.

If you become good at networking, over time you will establish a contact list composed of hundreds, or even thousands, of individuals.

In addition to the contacts you establish and maintain within your network, your personal contacts database might also include people you work with, customers, clients, family members, people from your community whom you interact with (doctors, hair stylist, barber, dry cleaners, and so on), and friends.

NOTE Contacts is a powerful and customizable contact management database program that works with several other apps that also came preinstalled on your iPhone or iPad, including Mail, Calendar, Safari, FaceTime, and Maps.

THE CONTACTS APP IS HIGHLY CUSTOMIZABLE

Chances are, the same contacts database that you rely on at your office or on your personal computer at home can be synced with your iPhone or iPad and made available to you using the Contacts app.

Of course, Contacts can also be used as a standalone app, enabling you to enter new contact entries as you meet new people and need to keep track of details about them on your iOS device.

The information you maintain in your Contacts database is highly customizable, which means you can keep track of only the information you want or need. For example, within each contact entry, you can store a vast amount of information about a person, including the following:

- First and last name
- Name prefix (Mr., Mrs., Dr., and so on)
- Name suffix (Jr., Sr., Ph.D., Esq., and so on)
- Job title
- Company
- Multiple phone numbers (work, home, cell, and so on)
- Multiple email addresses
- Multiple mailing addresses (work, home, and so on)
- Multiple web page addresses
- Facebook, Twitter, Skype, Instant Messenger, or other online social networking site usernames

You can also customize your contacts database to include additional information, such as each contact's photo, nickname, spouse's and/or assistant's names, birthday, and Instant Messenger usernames, as well as detailed notes about the contact.

When you're using the Contacts app, your entire contacts database is instantly searchable using data from any field within the database, so even if you have a database containing thousands of entries, you can find the person or company you're looking for in a matter of seconds. And with the iOS 5 version of Contacts, you can now link contacts together.

THE CONTACTS APP WORKS SEAMLESSLY WITH OTHER APPS

After your contacts database has been populated with entries, you'll discover that the Contacts app works with other apps on your iPhone and/or iPad, such as Mail:

- When you compose a new email message from within Mail, in the To field you can begin typing someone's full name or email address. If that person's contact information is already stored within Contacts, the relevant email address automatically displays in the email's To field.
- If you're planning a trip to visit a contact, from the Maps app, you can pull up someone's address from your Contacts database and obtain driving directions to the person's home or work location.
- If you include each person's birthday in your Contacts database, that information can automatically be displayed in the Calendar app to remind you in advance to send a card.
- As you're creating each Contacts entry, you can include a photo of that person—by either activating the Camera app from the Contacts app to snap a photo or using a photo that's stored in the Photos app—and link it with the contact.
- From within FaceTime, you can create a Favorites list of people you videoconference with often. You will compile this list from entries in your Contacts database, but you can access it from FaceTime. On the iPhone, the Favorites list for the Phone app and FaceTime are the same. On the iPad, launch the FaceTime app, tap on the Favorites command icon, and then tap the plus-sign icon to add each new contact to the Favorites list.
- From the Messages app, you can access your Contacts database when filling out the To field as you compose new text messages to be sent via iMessage. As soon as you tap on the To field, an All Contacts window appears, allowing you to select contacts from your Contacts database (or you can manually enter the recipients' info).

- If you're active on Facebook, for example, you have the option to add each contact's Facebook profile page URL in the Contacts entry. When you do this, the app automatically downloads each entry's Facebook profile picture and inserts it into your Contacts database. (The easiest way to do this is to download and install the free, official iPhone- or iPad-specific Facebook app.)

When you first launch the Contacts app, its related database will be empty. However, you can create and build your database in two ways:

- You can sync the Contacts app with your primary contact management application on your computer, on your network, or on an online (cloud)-based service, such as iCloud.
- You can manually enter contact information directly into the app.

Ultimately, as you begin using this app and come to rely on it, you can enter new contact information or edit entries either on your iOS device or in your primary contact management application, and keep all the information synchronized, regardless of where the entry was created or modified.

WHO DO YOU KNOW? HOW TO VIEW YOUR CONTACTS

From the iPhone or iPad's Home Screen, tap the Contacts app to launch it.

On the iPhone, what you'll see when the Contacts app launches is the All Contacts screen, which displays an alphabetical listing of your contacts. Along the right side of the screen are alphabetic tabs, and a Search field is located near the top of the screen.

On the iPad, on the extreme left side of the screen are alphabetic tabs. Near the upper left of the screen, you'll see the All Contacts heading. Below it is a Search field. After you have added entries in your contacts database, they will all be listed alphabetically on the left side of the screen, below the Search field (as shown in Figure 14.3).

> **TIP** If you tap the Search field, you can quickly find a particular entry by entering any keyword associated with an entry, such as a first or last name, city, state, job title, or company name. Any content in your Contacts database is searchable from this Search field.
>
> You can also tap a letter tab on the screen to see all entries "filed" under that letter by a contact's last name, first name, or company name, depending on how you set up the Contacts app from within the Settings app's Mail, Contacts, Calendars option.

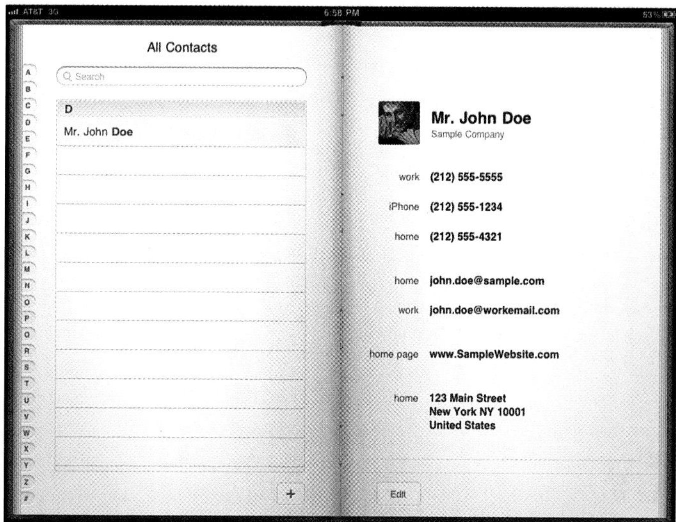

FIGURE 14.3

On the iPad, the All Contacts listing and individual listings are shown on the left and right side of the screen, respectively. On the iPhone, this information is divided into two separate screens.

On the iPhone, to see the complete listing for a particular entry, tap on its listing from the All Contacts screen. A new screen will be displayed containing the specific contact's information.

On the iPad, to see the complete listing for a particular entry, tap on its listing from the All Contacts display on the left side of the screen. That entry's complete contents will then be displayed on the right side of the screen.

TIP In addition to using the search field in the Contacts app, you can quickly find information from within this app by accessing the Spotlight Search screen from your iPhone or iPad's Home Screen.

To use the Spotlight Search screen, start on the first Home Screen page, and swipe your finger from left to right across the display. The Spotlight Search screen enables you to search for content within your entire iOS device (including the Contacts app).

If you're using Siri with an iPhone 4S, you can quickly find and display any contact within your Contacts database by activating Siri and saying, "Find [insert name] within Contacts." The appropriate info screen for that contact will be displayed.

MEET SOMEONE NEW? CREATE A NEW CONTACTS ENTRY

To create a new Contacts entry, tap the plus icon. On the iPhone, it's displayed in the upper-right corner of the All Contacts screen. On the iPad, the plus icon can be found near the bottom center of the Contacts screen. When you do this, the main Contacts screen is replaced by an Info screen, and the virtual keyboard appears.

NOTE As you're creating each Contacts entry, you can fill in whichever fields you want. You can always go back and edit a contact entry to include additional information later.

Within the Info window are a handful of empty fields related to a single Contacts entry, starting with the First Name field (shown in Figure 14.4). By default, the fields available in this app include First Name, Last Name, Company, Photo, [Mobile] Phone Number, Email Address, Ringtone, Text Tone, Home Page (Website) URL, Address, and Notes.

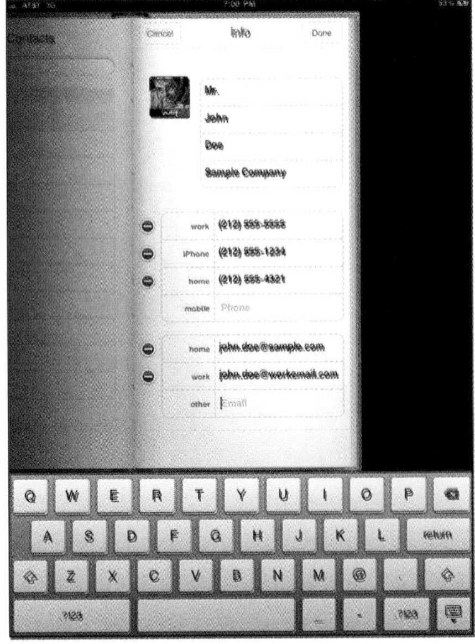

FIGURE 14.4

From this screen, you can create a new contact and include as much information pertaining to that person or company as you want.

> **TIP** When creating or editing contacts, it's extremely important to associate the correct labels with phone numbers, email address, and address data.
>
> For each phone number you add to a contact's entry, for example, it can include a Home, Work, Mobile, iPhone, or Other label (among others). For many of the features of iOS 5 that utilize data from your Contacts database to work correctly, it's important that you properly label content you add to each Contacts entry. This is particularly important if you'll be using Siri with an iPhone 4S.

However, some of these fields, including Phone, Email, and Mailing Address, allow you to input multiple listings, one at a time. So you can include someone's home phone, work phone, and mobile phone numbers within the entry. Likewise, you can include multiple email addresses, and/or a home address and work address for an individual.

Begin by filling in one field at a time. To jump to the next field, tap it. So after using the virtual keyboard to fill in the First Name field, tap on the Last Name field to fill it in, and then move on to the Company field, if applicable, by tapping it.

> **TIP** For each type of field, the virtual keyboard modifies itself accordingly, giving you access to specialized keys. You can change the label associated with certain fields (which are displayed in blue) by tapping the field label itself. This reveals a Label menu, offering selectable options for that field.
>
> For example, the Label options for the Phone Number field include Mobile, iPhone, Home, Work, Main, Home Fax, Work Fax, Pager, and Other. At the bottom of this Label window, you can tap the Add Custom Label option to create your own label if none of the listed options applies.
>
> Tap the label title of your choice. A check mark appears next to it, and you are returned to the Info window.

As you scroll down in the Info window and fill in each field, at the bottom of the window you'll discover an Add Field option. Tap this to reveal a menu containing 14 additional fields you can add to Contacts entries, such as a Middle name, Job Title, Nickname, Instant Message username, Twitter username, (Facebook) Profile, and Birthday (as shown in Figure 14.5). There's also a field to add Related People, such as the names of your contact's mother, father, parent, brother, sister, child, friend, spouse, partner, assistant, manager, or other. You can also add your own titles for the Related People field.

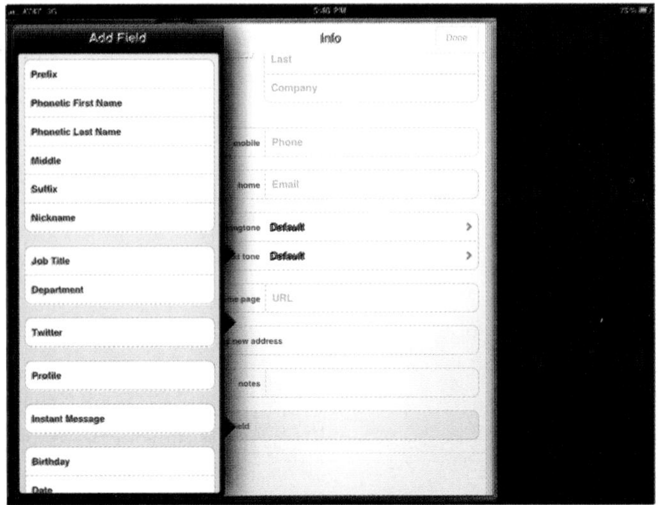

FIGURE 14.5

From the Add Field option, choose what additional information you want to include in a particular contact's entry, such as the person's birthday, spouse's name, Twitter username (@Username), or Instant Message username. This information can automatically be used by other apps.

TIP When you enter a contact's phone numbers, it's important to differentiate between a mobile phone number and an iPhone phone number. If you know that someone has an iPhone, use the iPhone label because the FaceTime app uses what's in this field to identify someone's FaceTime ID (which, if the contact is an iPhone user, is usually the person's iPhone's phone number).

A green-and-white plus icon that is displayed next to a field (on the left) means that you can have multiple entries for that field, such as several phone numbers, email addresses, or mailing addresses.

If there's a field displayed that you don't want to utilize or display, you can tap the red-and-white minus sign icon to delete the field from the Info window.

Each time you add a new mailing address to a contact's entry from within the Info screen, the Address field expands to include a Street, City, State, ZIP, and Country field.

TIP In the Notes field, you can enter as much information pertaining to that contact as you want. Or, you can paste content from another app into this field using the iOS's Select, Copy, and Paste commands, and using the multitasking capabilities of your iPhone or iPad to quickly switch between apps.

After you have filled in all the fields for a particular entry, tap the Done button, which is displayed in the upper-right corner of the Info window. Your new entry gets added to your contacts database.

HOW TO ADD A PHOTO TO A CONTACTS ENTRY

To the immediate left of the First Name field is a square box that says Add Photo. When you tap this field, a submenu with two options—Take Photo and Choose Photo—is displayed.

Tap Take Photo to launch the Camera app from within the Contacts app and snap a photo to be linked to the Contacts entry you're creating. Or tap on the Choose Photo option. In this case, the Photos app launches so that you can choose any digital image that's currently stored on your iOS device. When you tap the photo of your choice, a Choose a Photo window displays on the Contacts screen, enabling you to move and scale the image with your finger.

After cropping or adjusting the photo selected, tap the Use icon that's displayed in the upper-right corner of the Choose Photo window to link the photo with that contact's entry (as shown in Figure 14.6).

FIGURE 14.6

Linking a photo with someone's Contacts entry enables you to visually identify the person as you're reviewing your contacts.

TIP If you also use an iPhone or FaceTime on your iPad, from the Ringtone option in the Info window, you can select the specific ringtone you hear each time that particular contact calls you. Your iPhone or iPad has 25 preinstalled ringtones (with Marimba being the default). From iTunes, you can download thousands of additional ringtones, many of which are clips from popular songs.

EDITING OR DELETING AN ENTRY

As you're looking at the main Contacts screen, you can edit an entry by tapping on its listing from the All Contacts screen. This results in the complete entry being displayed for that contact. To edit the contact, tap on the Edit icon. The Edit icon is displayed in the upper-right corner of the screen on the iPhone, but near the bottom of the screen on the iPad.

When the Info window appears, tap any field to modify it using the virtual keyboard. Delete any field(s) altogether by tapping on the red-and-white minus sign icon associated with it.

You can also add new fields within an entry by tapping any of the green-and-white plus sign icons and then choosing the type of field you want to add.

When you're done editing a Contacts entry, again tap the Done button.

TIP To delete an entire entry from your Contacts database, as you're editing a contact entry and looking at the Info window for that entry, scroll down to the bottom of it and tap the Delete Contact option.

INTERACTIVE CONTACTS ENTRIES

Whenever you're viewing a Contacts entry, tapping a listed email address causes the iPhone or iPad 2 Mail app to launch, which enables you to compose an email message to that recipient. The To field of the outgoing email is automatically filled in with the email address you tapped on from within Contacts.

TIP On the iPhone, tap any phone number listed in a Contacts entry to dial that phone number and initiate a call. Or at the bottom of the contact entry's Info screen, tap on the Send Message or FaceTime icon to either send a text message to that person or initiate a FaceTime videoconference.

Likewise, from within an entry, tap any website URL that's listed, and the Safari web browser will launch and automatically display the appropriate web page.

This also works with the Twitter field (if you have the Twitter app installed). Tap on someone's Twitter username to send a tweet. The appropriate @Username will be displayed at the beginning of the tweet automatically.

> **TIP** If you tap on a street address, this will automatically launch the Maps app, which will display that address. (At this point, you can tap on the Directions icon to obtain directions to that contact's location.)

HOW TO LINK CONTACT ENTRIES TOGETHER

Depending on how you use the Contacts app, you might find it useful to group contacts based on relationships. For example, you might have separate listings for multiple people in the same family, or multiple employees who work for the same company. By linking these contacts, it makes it easier for you to organize people into groups, and then find them quickly in the Contacts app.

When you're in edit mode, modifying content in a contact's entry, scroll down to the very bottom of the window or screen to link contact entries together.

On the iPhone, tap on the Link Contact icon that's displayed under the Linked Contacts heading, and then choose one or more contact entries to link to the one you're editing.

On the iPad, you link contacts by scrolling down below the red-and-white Delete contact icon when editing an entry. Here, you will notice a small icon with a silhouette of a head with a plus sign next to it. Tap on this icon to link this contact with one or more other contacts already in your database.

SHARING CONTACT ENTRIES

From the main Contacts screen, tap a contact that you want to share details about. When the contact's entry is displayed, scroll down to the bottom of the entry until you see the Share Contact button displayed. Tap it.

An outgoing email message form displays on your iPhone or iPad's screen. Fill in the To field with the person or people you want to share the contact info with. The default subject of the email is Contact. However, you can tap this field and modify it using the virtual keyboard.

The Contacts entry you selected (stored in .vcf format) is already embedded in the email message. When you've filled in all the necessary fields in the outgoing email form, and added additional text to the body of the message (if you so desire), tap the blue-and-white Send icon that's located in the upper-right corner of the Contact window to send the email message to the intended recipient(s). Upon doing this, you are returned to the Contacts app.

Within a minute or two, the recipient should receive your email. When she clicks on the email's attachment (the contact entry you sent), she can automatically import that data into her contact management application as a new entry, such as in Address Book on her Mac or Contacts on her iPhone or iPad.

TIP If someone shares a Contacts entry with you via email, when you're viewing the incoming email on your iPhone or iPad, tap the email's attachment. The Contacts entry that was emailed is displayed in a window. At the bottom of this window, as the recipient of the contact's information, tap the Create New Contact or Add to Existing Contact option to incorporate this information into your Contacts database.

ADDITIONAL WAYS TO MAKE CONTACT FROM WITHIN CONTACTS

When you're viewing any single contact, in addition to the Share Contact button you see displayed, you'll notice three other command buttons, including Send Message, FaceTime, and Add to Favorites. Tap on the Send Message icon to send that person a text message via the Messages app. Or, tap on the FaceTime app to initiate a FaceTime videoconference with that person.

If you tap on the Add to Favorites button, that contact will appear in your Favorites list that's displayed in the Phone and FaceTime apps.

USE REMINDERS TO MANAGE YOUR TO-DO LISTS

If you've just acquired a new iPhone or iPad or recently upgraded to iOS 5, you'll discover an app that's preinstalled on your device, called Reminders. On the surface, this is a straightforward to-do list manager. However, after you start using this innovative but easy-to-use app, you'll discover that it offers a plethora of interesting and useful features.

NOTE Reminders is just one option for managing to-do lists on your iPhone or iPad. If you use the Search feature in the App Store (with the keyword "to-do list"), you'll find many more apps created by third parties that can be used for this purpose but that offer different features.

For starters, Reminders works seamlessly with Notification Center and iCloud and easily syncs with iCal and/or Outlook on your primary computer. Plus, you can create as many separate to-do lists as you need to properly manage your personal and professional life, or various projects you're responsible for.

iOS 5 WHAT'S NEW To make juggling a wide range of tasks, and keeping track of deadlines and your ongoing responsibilities, an easier process, every item on your to-do list can be given unique alarms, which can be associated with specific times and/or dates. However, each alert can also be location-based.

Because your iPhone has GPS capabilities, it always knows exactly where it is. Thus, you can create a to-do list or an item on a list that is associated with an alarm that will alert you when you arrive at or depart from a particular geographic location, such as your home, your office, or a particular store.

For example, you can have your morning to-do list or call list automatically display on your iPhone's screen when you arrive at work. Or, if you're maintaining a list of office supplies you need to purchase at Staples, you can have your shopping list that was created using Reminders pop up on the screen when you arrive at your local Staples office supply superstore.

In addition, you can have a reminder alarm set to warn you of an upcoming deadline, and then have a second alarm alert you when that deadline has actually arrived.

KEEP UP TO DATE WITH REMINDERS

When you launch Reminders for the first time, on the iPhone, a blank to-do notepad will be displayed. On the iPad, on the left side of the screen, you will see the control center for this app. On the right side of the screen will be a simulated sheet of lined paper, with the heading Reminders at the top. This serves as your blank to-do notepad (as shown in Figure 14.7).

To begin creating a single to-do list under this Reminders heading, tap on the top empty line of the simulated sheet of paper, or tap on the plus sign icon that's displayed near the upper-right corner of the screen. The virtual keyboard appears. Enter the first item to be added to your to-do list, and tap on the Return key on the keyboard.

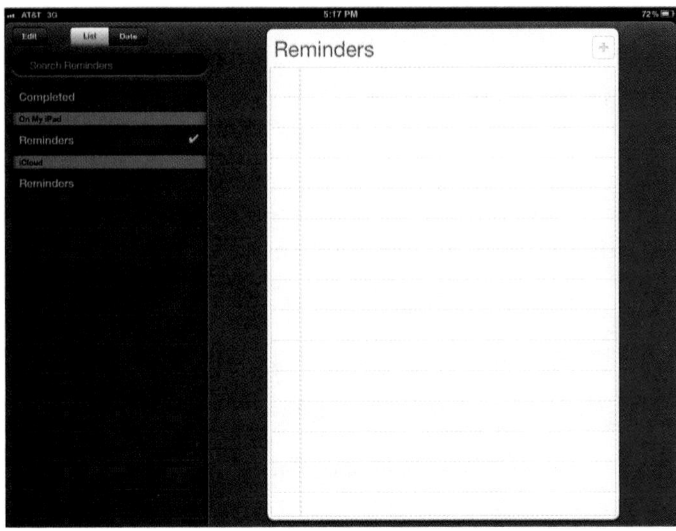

FIGURE 14.7

From this screen in Reminders, you can create and manage one or more to-do lists.

When you tap on the Return key, an empty check box will appear in the margin, to the left of the to-do list item you just entered. You can mark the completion of this task later by tapping on this check box to add a check mark to it. The item is then moved to the master Completed list. However, as soon as you're done entering the to-do list item, you can tap on it to make the app's Details window appear. From this window, you can set a Remind Me alarm by tapping on the Remind Me option. Or, you can tap on the Show More option to set a Due Date and Priority for the to-do item.

> **TIP** If you're managing multiple to-do lists, you can also assign the to-do item to a specific list. Under the List heading within the Details box, you will see iCloud listed. Select this option to send just this one to-do list option to your iCloud account and ultimately have it sync with your primary computer or other iOS devices.

When you scroll down to the bottom of the Details window, you'll see a Delete option. Tap on it to delete the item from your list.

On the iPhone only, if you tap on the Remind Me option in the Details box, you can choose between two options, which include On a Day or At a Location. To set a date-specific alarm, turn the virtual switch associated with On a Day to the on position, and then tap on the date and time line that appears below it to set the date and time for the alert.

TIP Prior to using a location-based alarm on your iPhone, if you'll be using this feature when running errands, one at a time, use the Maps app to find the locations of the businesses or stores you'll be visiting, and then save them as contacts in your Contacts database.

For example, if you'll be creating a grocery list using the Reminders app, from the Maps app, find the address of your supermarket using the Search feature of the Maps app. Enter "Shaw's Supermarket, Sharon, MA," for example. Include the business name, city and state in the Maps search.

When the location of the supermarket is displayed on a map, tap the blue-and-white > icon to reveal details about the supermarket's address and phone number.

Scroll down on the screen to the Add To Contacts icon, and tap on it. An entry for the supermarket (complete with its address) will be stored in your Contacts database and will now be accessible from the Reminders app, so you can use it with the location-based reminders feature.

To set an alarm based on a location, turn on the virtual switch associated with the At a Location option, choose the desired location you want the alert to be associated with, and then decide whether you want to be alerted when you arrive or when you leave that destination. On the iPad, you can only set an alarm based on a date and time.

iOS 5 WHAT'S NEW When you opt to associate an alert with a location, you can select your current location, select your Home address, or choose an address from your Contacts database. You also have the option to set a priority with each to-do list item. Your Priority options include None, Low, Medium, and High.

Again, these alarms can be associated with each item in each of your to-do lists. You also have the option to create a to-do list item but not associate any type of alert or alarm with it.

When any alarm goes off with a to-do list item, a notification will automatically appear in your iOS device's Notification Center window, assuming that you have this feature turned on.

TIP To ensure that Reminders will work with the Notification Center, launch the Settings app and tap on the Notifications option. When the Notifications screen appears on the right side of screen, tap on the Reminders option and make sure that the Notification Center option is turned on.

When it comes to managing your to-do list and accomplishing tasks listed in it, as you complete each listing, tap on the check box associated with that item. This causes a check mark to appear in the check box, and causes the to-do list item to be moved to the Completed section.

On the iPhone, to view the Completed listing, swipe your finger from left to right across the Reminders screen. Or tap on the icon in the upper-left corner of the main Reminders screen (it looks like three horizontal lines), and then tap on the Completed option.

On the iPad, the Completed section is displayed on the left side of the screen. At any time, you can view your list of completed items by tapping on the Completed heading.

MANAGE MULTIPLE TO-DO LISTS SIMULTANEOUSLY WITH REMINDERS

To create multiple to-do lists using Reminders on the iPhone, follow these steps:

1. From the main Reminders screen, tap on the List Management icon displayed in the upper-left corner of the screen with the three horizontal lines.
2. Tap on the Edit icon that's displayed in the upper-right corner of the screen.
3. From the Lists screen that appears, tap on the Create New List option.
4. Using the virtual keyboard, type a name or title for the new to-do list.
5. Tap on the Done icon.
6. Begin adding individual to-do items to the list.

To create multiple to-do lists using Reminders on the iPad, follow these steps:

1. From the main Reminders screen, tap on the Edit icon that's displayed in the upper-left corner.
2. On the left side of the screen, tap on the Create New List option, after deciding where you want the list to be stored.
3. Using the virtual keyboard, type a name or title for the new to-do list (as shown in Figure 14.8).
4. Tap on the Done icon.
5. Begin adding individual to-do items to the list.

TIP You can create a list to be stored on your iPhone or iPad, or one that will automatically be sent and stored on iCloud so that it will be accessible from all of your iCloud-linked iOS devices and computers.

FIGURE 14.8

Whenever you create a new to-do list, you can give it a unique title or name. Then, begin adding to-do items to that list, one at a time. Each individual to-do item can have a deadline and/or alarm associated with it.

HOW TO DELETE AN ENTIRE TO-DO LIST

In Edit mode, delete a list by tapping on the red-and-white circular icon with a negative sign displayed in it that is associated with the list you want to delete. Or to change the order of your lists, place your finger on the icon that looks like three horizontal lines that's associated with a list, and drag it upward or downward.

To exit Edit mode, tap on the Done icon.

HOW TO VIEW YOUR INDIVIDUAL LISTS

On the iPhone, from the main Reminders screen, tap on the List Management icon that's displayed in the upper-left corner of the screen (with the three horizontal lines) to view the Lists screen. It displays all the separate to-do lists currently stored on your device, along with the Completed listing. Tap on any list from the Lists screen to view that list.

On the iPad, tap the List button that is displayed near the upper-left corner of the screen. On the left side of the Reminders screen, you will then see a list of the various to-do lists stored on your tablet, allowing you to view any of them with a single tap.

However, on the iPad, when you tap on the Date button that's displayed to the immediate right of the List button, the left side of the Reminders screen is replaced by month-by-month calendars. You can tap on a specific date to view upcoming deadlines or due dates associated with specific to-do list items.

TIP To quickly find items in any of your to-do lists, tap on the Search Reminders field. On the iPhone, it's displayed at the top of the Lists screen. On the iPad, the Search field is displayed in the upper-left portion of the main Reminders screen. Use the virtual keyboard to enter any text that is associated with what you're looking for, and then tap the Search key on the keyboard.

After you get into the habit of entering all of your to-do list items, upcoming deadlines, or various other tidbits of information into the Reminders app, you'll quickly discover that it can be used to manage many types of information in your personal and professional life. Chances are, you'll quickly find that Reminders, when used with Notification Center, iCloud, and Calendar, for example, is a wonderfully powerful to-do list management tool that's extremely versatile and customizable to meet your unique needs.

IN THIS CHAPTER

- How to play games on your iPhone or iPad
- How to find games you'll love
- How to connect to Apple's Games Center

15

iOS 5 GAMING

The latest iPhone and iPad models are chock-full of ways to entertain yourself. Thanks to their crisp HD touchscreens and superior sound systems, not to mention the built-in three-axis gyro and accelerometer, your iOS device is able to offer truly immersive interactive gaming experiences.

Because your iPhone or iPad also connects directly to the wireless Web, it allows you to easily engage in multiplayer games in various ways, so you can challenge others in high-action or turn-based games whether your opponents are sitting next to you on a couch, are located across town, or are on the opposite side of the country.

Simply by visiting the App Store or becoming active on Apple's Games Center, you'll find literally thousands of fun, challenging, cutting-edge, and often addictive games, developed by some of the greatest video and computer game developers in the world.

So, whether you have five minutes in between meetings and want to experience some type of puzzle game, or you want to immerse yourself for hours at a time in an intricate computer-generated world, you'll find plenty of gaming experiences that cater to your wants, needs, time constraints, and skill level.

As you'll discover, some games are iPhone/iPod touch–specific or iPad-specific, meaning they're designed to work only on that device. However, others are hybrid apps, so they'll work on all iOS devices and can easily be shared between your devices via iCloud. For hybrid apps, you'll need to purchase each game only once, yet will be able to experience it on your iPhone, iPad, and iPod touch.

The advanced touchscreen built in to the iPhone 4S, combined with its ultra-fast dual-core A5 chip, makes this new iPhone ideal for playing graphics-intensive, high-action games that feature highly detailed graphics.

MANY DIFFERENT GAMING EXPERIENCES

The games available from the App Store are divided into different categories or genres. Some of the types of gaming experiences you can experience on your iPhone, iPad, or iPod touch include these:

- **Action/Adventure**—From character-based games to high-action shoot'em-ups, you'll discover iOS games that feature highly detailed graphics, realistic sound effects, and plenty of fast-paced challenges.
- **Action/Puzzle Challenges**—Games like Tetris (shown in Figure 15.1), the massively popular Angry Birds (shown in Figure 15.2), and Flight Control are among the many types of action-based puzzle games that will make you think and test your reflexes. The best puzzle games are easy to learn, difficult to master, and extremely addicting.
- **Casino and Card Games**—Some of these games faithfully re-create the casino experience (slot machines, roulette, craps, and so on), whereas others allow you to compete against real players or computer-controlled opponents as you play popular card games, like blackjack, many variations of poker, or solitaire. The Solitaire app from Mobility Ware is one of many solitaire games offered from the App Store. It's shown on the iPhone in Figure 15.3.

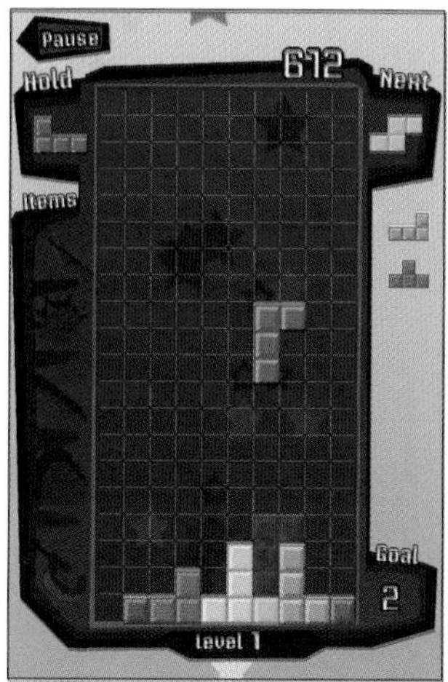

FIGURE 15.1

Tetris is one of the most popular puzzle games in video game history. It's available for both the iPhone (shown here) and the iPad.

FIGURE 15.2

Angry Birds and its sequels are among the most popular games of all time for the iPhone and iPad. They're suitable for people over the age of six and offer countless hours of whimsical challenges.

FIGURE 15.3

Card games and casino simulations of all kinds are available for the iPhone or iPad. Shown here is just one popular version of Solitaire.

- **Classic Arcade and Video Games**—Pac-Man (shown in Figure 15.4), Sonic the Hedgehog 2, Space Invaders, Asteroids, Centipede, and many others have been faithfully re-created for play on the iPhone and/or iPad, complete with their original graphics and sound effects.

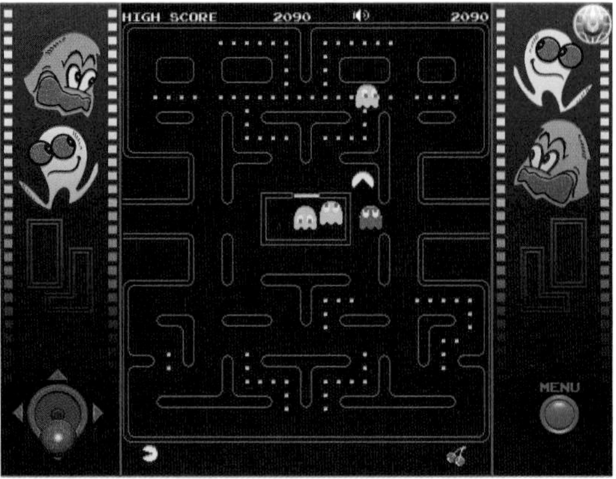

FIGURE 15.4

Pac-Man and dozens of other classic video games are now playable on your iPhone or iPad (shown here). These are authentic adaptations of the classic video and arcade games.

- **Classic Board Games**—Faithful adaptations of classic board games, such as Monopoly, chess, checkers, backgammon, Life, Dominoes, Boggle, Scrabble, Uno, Risk, and Yahtzee, are all available for the iPhone and iPad as single or multiplayer games.

iOS 5 **WHAT'S NEW** To make classic arcade games, as well as action/adventure games, more realistic, a company called ThinkGeek (www.thinkgeek.com) offers a removable joystick attachment that sticks onto your iPad's screen, giving you more arcadelike control over the onscreen action. It's priced at $24.99 for one or $39.99 for two.

The Fling for iPad, from Ten One Design ($17.96, http://tenonedesign.com/fling.php), offers similar game-controller functionality but utilizes a totally different design. This is more of a removable thumb pad that attaches to the iPad 2's screen.

The iCade accessory for iPad from Ion Audio ($99.99, www.ionaudio.com) is actually a wooden housing that your iPad 2 gets inserted into. iCade transforms the tablet into what looks like a tabletop coin-op arcade machine, complete with a full-size joystick controller and eight arcade-style buttons. It can be used to play more than 100 classic arcade games from Atari (like Asteroids, Centipede, and Battlezone), which are sold separately from the App Store.

- **Crossword Puzzles**—If you're looking for crossword puzzle challenges, the options are extensive. There's the subscription-based NYTimes Crosswords app (shown in Figure 15.5) that re-creates each day's puzzle that's published in the *New York Times* newspaper. This app also includes a massive archive of 4,000-plus past puzzles. You'll also find dozens of other crossword puzzle apps available from the App Store.

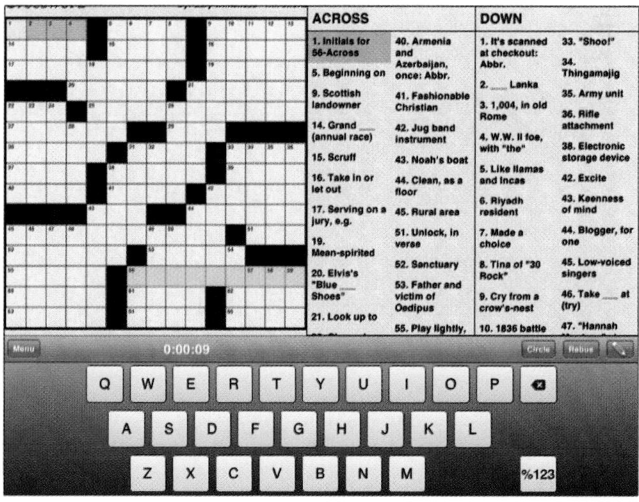

FIGURE 15.5

If you're a fan of crossword puzzles, be sure to check out the NYTimes Crosswords app. Try your hand at solving the actual puzzles that appear in the popular daily newspaper, plus access a massive archive of past crossword puzzles.

- **Simulations**—These games allow you to immerse yourself in a computer-generated, virtual world that can re-create a real-life environment or enable you to experience the most imaginative of scenarios. You can build and manage the city of your dreams by playing SimCity Deluxe for iPad, wield a mighty sword in a game like Infinity Blade, become a sniper in Super Sniper 2 HD, or help Papa Smurf build and manage a colorful Smurf village in Smurfs' Village (shown in Figure 15.6). There are also flight simulators, in which you can pilot all sorts of aircraft, or you can become the lead zookeeper of your own virtual zoo when you play Tap Zoo.

FIGURE 15.6

Smurfs' Village is an extremely popular game that's suitable for all ages. It's also an example of a free game that offers in-app purchases. As a result, it has become one of the highest-grossing iPhone and iPad apps ever. It's shown here being played on an iPad 2.

- **Sports Simulations**—These are games based on real-life sports, such as golf, baseball, basketball, football, and NASCAR. In many cases, the games re-create real-life professional athletes and/or teams using actual stats, and faithfully re-create the arenas, stadiums, courses, or tracks where the real-life sports take place. In fact, the more you know about the real-life sport when playing some of these simulations, the better you'll be at playing them. There are also less realistic sports games, like NBA Jam by EA Sports for iPad, that focus more on arcade-style action as opposed to realism.

TIP If you're an avid golfer but can't make it out to the links in person, try playing the very realistic game Tiger Woods PGA Tour 12 for iPad (shown in Figure 15.7).

FIGURE 15.7

Tiger Woods PGA Tour 12 for iPad is one of many very realistic sports simulation games you can play on your tablet.

- **Sudoku Puzzles**—Challenge your mind with the many versions of Sudoku that are available from the App Store. Also available are other types of word- and number-based puzzle challenges, like many different Word Search games. Social Sudoku is one of more than 100 Sudoku apps available for the iPhone and iPad. It's shown in Figure 15.8 being played on an iPad 2.

In each of these game categories, you'll find many different game-play experiences. Although some of the games are adaptations of popular video games originally designed for Nintendo, Sony, Microsoft, Sega, or Atari gaming systems, for example, the iOS editions of these games often take full advantage of the features and functionality that are unique to the iPhone and/or iPad.

TIP As you browse the App Store, games with titles that end with "HD" or "for iPad" are iPad-specific games. They offer enhanced graphics and make full use of the tablet's larger touchscreen. An iPhone-specific version (sold separately) might also be available.

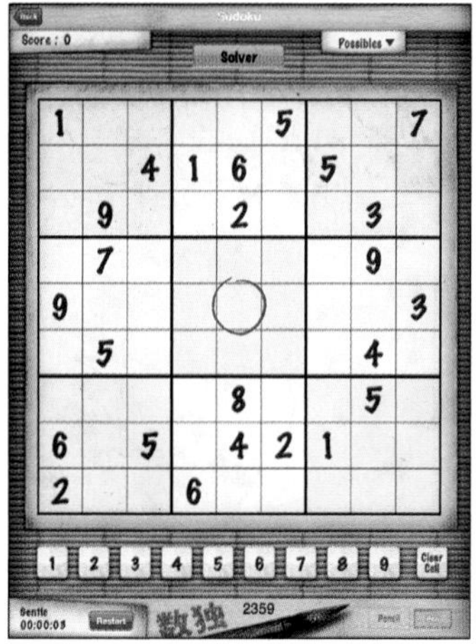

FIGURE 15.8

The Social Sudoku game is one of many Sudoku puzzle challenges available from the App Store for the iPhone and iPad.

Because your iOS device can connect to the Web, you're able to experience real-time multiplayer games and compete against friends, co-workers, your kids, or total strangers. In fact, Apple's own online-based Game Center (accessible through Game Center–compatible games, or the Game Center app that comes preinstalled on your iOS device) offers a free online forum in which you can meet and compete against others as you experience a growing number of popular multiplayer games.

Thousands of games are available from the App Store free of charge. Some are advertiser supported, whereas others offer optional in-app purchase options to access extra levels or gain special power-ups, items, or added functionality within a game. Many games are paid apps, ranging in price from $.99 to $6.99 (although occasionally you'll find a game priced a bit higher).

TIP To further enhance your game-play experience, consider investing in high-quality, noise-reduction headphones that can be used with your iPhone, iPad, or iPod touch. This will allow you to truly experience the stereo sound effects and music that often add realism and intensity to a game. Some headphones are designed to plug in directly to the headphones jack of your iOS device, and others offer wireless Bluetooth connectivity.

! CAUTION Some games are initially free of charge and offer a wonderful game-play experience. However, to access certain gaming features, obtain specific in-game items, or reach otherwise locked levels, you'll need to make in-app purchases, which over time can get expensive. These in-app purchases are typically optional but will greatly enhance your game-play experience.

In some cases, a free game will offer just one or two sample levels or just a preview of the game play, but will ultimately require you to purchase or upgrade to the paid version of the game to experience it in its entirety.

TIPS FOR FINDING GAMES YOU'LL LOVE

With literally tens of thousands of games to choose from, and more being introduced every day, there are several strategies you can use to quickly find games that'll appeal to you as you explore the App Store or Game Center.

TIP On the iPhone, to discover the hottest games divided up by genre, launch the App Store app and tap on the Categories icon that's displayed at the bottom of the screen. From the Categories screen, tap on the Games option. Then, from the Games screen, select a category, such as Action, Adventure, Board Games, Card Games, Puzzle Games, or Role Playing Games.

At the top of the Game Category screen that you select will be three tabs, labeled Top Paid, Top Free, and Release Date. Tap on either the Top Paid or the Top Free tab to see a listing of the most popular games in that genre.

On the iPad, to discover what other people are playing and what's truly popular, visit the App Store and tap on the Top Charts icon at the bottom of the screen. Then, in the upper-left corner of the screen, tap on the Categories icon. From the pull-down menu, choose Games. On the left side of the Top Charts screen will be a listing of Top Paid iPad Games, and on the right side of the screen will be a listing of Top Free iPad Games. If you scroll down, toward the bottom of the Top Charts screen, you'll discover a listing of Top Grossing iPad Games.

As you explore the App Store looking for games to purchase, download, and install, focus on the description of each game, and pay attention to its overall star-based rating as well as its detailed reviews. Chances are, a game with dozens or hundreds of four- or five-star reviews will be a top-quality game.

If you look at all versions of the extremely popular Angry Birds game, it has more than 42,000 ratings total. More than 39,000 of those ratings are four or five stars. The iPhone version of this megapopular game is shown in Figure 15.9.

FIGURE 15.9

Shown here is the iPhone version of Angry Birds. Whether you play Angry Birds HD on the iPad or this edition, you'll find yourself facing many hours worth of challenges and entertainment.

In addition to focusing on the game ratings, pay attention to the sample screenshots offered in each detailed game listing. This will give you a good idea of what the game looks like and the quality of its graphics.

Another reliable source for discovering the best iOS games is to read independent reviews from well-respected websites and publications.

After you've acquired a handful of games, from the App Store, you can seek out game recommendations from the Genius for Apps. Based on your past downloads and purchases, the Genius feature (when it's turned on) will suggest other games you might be interested in.

To access the Genius feature from an iPhone, launch the App Store app and tap on the Featured icon that's displayed near the bottom of the screen. Then, tap on the Genius tab that's displayed near the upper-right corner of the screen.

On the iPad, to access the Genius feature in the App Store, launch the App Store app, and then tap on the Genius icon that's displayed at the bottom of the screen. Then, to get game recommendations, tap on the Categories icon that's displayed in the upper-left corner of the screen, and select the Games option from the pull-down menu.

TIP In the App Store, every week Apple reviews all the latest games available for the iPhone, iPad, and iPod touch, and chooses just one to be named Game of the Week. These games tend to be the most advanced in terms of graphics, sound, and game play, and make the best use of the iOS device's features.

At the bottom of the App Store app's screen, tap on the Categories icon, and then select the Games category. The Game of the Week will be promoted in a graphic banner near the top of the screen.

EXPERIENCE MULTIPLAYER GAMES WITH GAME CENTER

Your iOS device gives you the option to play multiplayer games in several ways, depending on how the game itself is designed. When it comes to competing head-on against other human players (as opposed to computer-controlled opponents), your options typically include these:

- Multiple people can play on the same iPhone or iPad by passing the device from one person to the next in between turns.
- A direct link can be established between two or more iOS devices with the same game installed.
- Through Apple's Game Center, you can play games online with one or more other people who are located anywhere in the world. This is a safe way to interact with other gamers whenever you're looking for a competitor.

TIP Most multiplayer games also have a one-player mode, which enables you to compete against computer-controlled opponents, for example.

Apple's Game Center is a free, online-based service that is a centralized hub for multiplayer games. You can access Game Center using a compatible game app or by launching the Game Center app directly from the Home Screen. To access Game Center, your iPhone, iPad, or iPod touch must have access to the Internet via a 3G or Wi-Fi connection.

NOTE Game Center is an online-based social gaming network that's operated by Apple. It's specifically for iOS device users. The Game Center app comes preinstalled with iOS 5. You can set up an account free, using your Apple ID.

After Game Center is running, you can create an online profile for yourself (which can include your photo). To do this, tap on the Me icon at the bottom of the Game Center screen. You can also use Game Center to meet up online with friends.

The Game Center app can automatically search the iPhone field in your Contacts database for others who are active on Game Center, and it allows you to send friend requests to those people. To do this, tap on the Friends icon at the bottom of the screen, and then tap on the Get Friend Recommendations flag displayed near the center of the screen.

TIP You can also invite people you know to become your "friend" on Game Center, so you can easily challenge them on any Game Center–compatible game that you both have installed on your iOS device.

To email a friend, tap on the Add Friends flag from the Friends screen of Game Center, and then in the To field of the email message template that appears, enter the email addresses for the people you want to invite.

When you install Game Center–compatible games on your iOS device, you will have the option to turn on Game Center functionality for that game. In addition to being able to invite people to compete against, you can post your game-related accomplishments online for all to see.

Tap on the Games icon, displayed at the bottom of the Game Center screen, to see a listing of the Game Center–compatible games you currently have installed on your iOS devices, as well as your published game-related achievements for those game titles.

TIP Tap on the Games icon that's displayed at the bottom of the Game Center screen, and then tap on the Find Game Center Games flag to quickly locate games in the App Store that you might be interested in and that are Game Center (multiplayer) compatible.

Tapping the Find Game Center Games flag within Game Center will cause a special area of the App Store to load on your iOS device. It displays multiplayer games that are compatible with Game Center and your particular device. The Game Center listings are divided by game genre (as shown in Figure 15.10).

After you have established one or more online "friends" within Game Center, use the Requests feature to send or respond to game invitations and challenges involving other players. Tap on the Requests icon, displayed at the bottom of the screen, to do this.

FIGURE 15.10

From the Game Center area of the App Store (which is actually accessible from the Game Center app), you'll find a vast selection of popular, multiplayer games in all genres that are suitable for all ages.

When you're using the Game Center app, whenever you see a game app icon displayed on the screen (on the Me or Games screens, for example), it means that the featured game associated with that icon is Game Center compatible. Tap on the displayed app icon to access the App Store to read a detailed description of that game, and then download, install, and play it.

TIP Looking for new online "friends" to compete against? In Game Center, tap on the Friends icon that's displayed near the bottom of the screen. Then, on the left side of the screen, tap on the Recommendations banner. A listing of people you probably don't know, but who share your taste in games or who have comparable game skills (based on published scores), will be displayed.

Tap on the Send Friend Request icon to initiate contact with that fellow gamer. When that person accepts your request, you can play multiplayer games with them.

At the bottom of the Recommendations list, tap on Use My Contacts to search your Contacts database and find other people you know who are also registered players within Game Center.

IN THIS CHAPTER

- How to play your digital music using the Music app
- How to watch music videos, TV shows, and movies with the Videos app
- How to stream on-demand content to your iPhone or iPad from the Web with specialized apps

16

USE THE MUSIC AND VIDEOS APPS

What do eight-track tapes, vinyl records, cassettes, and most recently CDs have in common? These are all outdated methods for storing music that have been replaced by digital music players, like Apple's iPods. The music in your personal library can now be kept in a purely digital format, transferred via the Web, and listened to on a digital music player.

iOS 5 removed the older iPod app that was bundled with iPhones and iPads and replaced it with a slicker app, called Music. This app serves as your digital music player and transforms your iPhone or iPad into a full-featured iPod. However, before playing your music, you first need to load it into your iPhone or iPad. There are several ways to do this, including the following:

- Purchase digital music directly from the iTunes Store (using the iTunes app) on your iPhone or iPad. An Internet connection is required, and your purchases will be billed to the credit card linked to your Apple ID.

- You can purchase music using iTunes on your primary computer and transfer it to your iPhone or iPad using the iTunes Sync process or via iCloud.
- You can "rip" music from traditional CDs, and convert it to a digital format using your primary computer, and then transfer the digital music files to your iOS device.
- You can upgrade your iCloud account by adding the optional iTunes Match feature, for $24.99 per year, and access your entire digital music library via iCloud, whether that music was purchased from iTunes, ripped from your own CDs, or purchased/downloaded from another source.
- You can shop for and download music from another source besides iTunes, load that music into your primary computer, convert it to the proper format, and then transfer it to your iPhone or iPad using the iTunes Sync process.

NOTE Apple's iTunes Store offers an ever-growing selection of more than 20 million songs available for purchase and download, including all the latest hits and new music from the biggest bands and recording artists, as well as up-and-coming and unsigned artists/bands.

The newly designed Music app is used for playing digital music, audio books, and other audio content that you load into your iPhone or iPad. If you want to watch videos, TV show episodes, or movies that you've purchased and/or downloaded from iTunes, you'll need to use the Videos app, which also comes preinstalled with iOS 5.

Another option for watching video or listening to audio content (including music videos, TV show episodes, movies, radio stations, and so on) is to stream it directly from the Internet. For this, you'll typically need a Wi-Fi Internet connection (which is faster than 3G and has no monthly data limits). However, in some cases, a 3G connection will work.

TIP When you stream content from the Internet, it gets transferred from the Web directly to your iOS device. However, your iPhone or iPad does not save streamed content, just as your standalone television set doesn't record the shows you watch (unless you have a DVR or another recording device hooked up to it). Streaming content from the Web requires a specialized app, which is provided by the source of the content.

TIPS FOR USING THE MUSIC APP

The Music app displays the music in your digital music library that's currently stored on your device (as shown in Figure 16.1 on the iPad 2). It enables you to play one song at a time or create personalized playlists that can provide hours' worth of music listening without your having to tinker with the app.

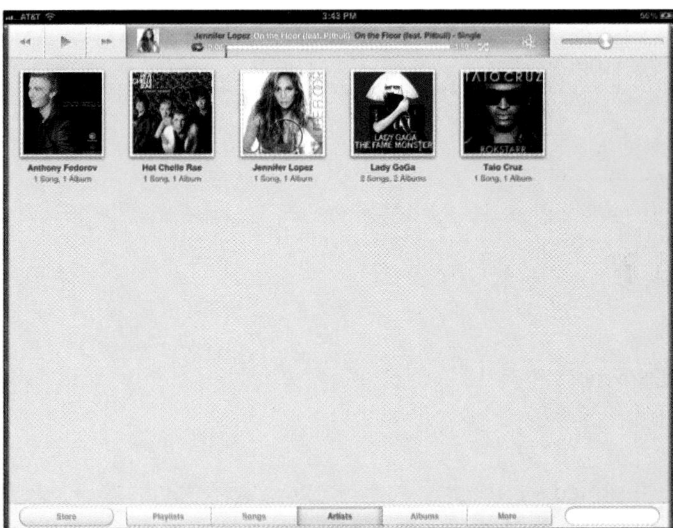

FIGURE 16.1

The main Artists screen of the newly designed Music app, which comes bundled with iOS 5.

If you have the Music app set up to work with iCloud, all the music you've purchased from iTunes (in addition to what's stored on your iOS device) will be displayed. Songs that are accessible to you via iCloud will have an iCloud displayed next to them. Tap on the iCloud icon to download the song from iCloud and store it on your iPhone or iPad. Or, tap on the song title to stream that song from iCloud and listen to it on your iOS device (without saving it).

If you'll want to listen to music in places where an Internet connection is not available (such as on an airplane), download and store your favorite music on your iPhone or iPad in advance. This takes up storage space on your iOS device, but it allows the music to be accessible anytime.

iOS 5 WHAT'S NEW The Music app works seamlessly with Siri on the iPhone 4S. You can use your voice to command Siri to play music from a specific artist, playlist, or song, just by speaking what you want. This applies to music stored on your iPhone. For example, if you want to hear, *Tonight, Tonight* from Hot Chelle Rae and it's stored on your iPhone, activate Siri and say, "Play Tonight, Tonight. " Or to play a Lady Gaga song, "Play a song from Lady Gaga."

Thanks to iOS 5's multitasking capabilities, you can play music from the Music app while using other apps on your iPhone or iPad. To play music, you don't need to launch the Music app. Instead, you can use the Music Controls accessible directly from the multitasking bar.

To access the Music Controls, double-tap on the Home screen, or on the iPad, use three fingers to swipe upward from the bottom of the screen toward the top. When the multitasking bar (shown in Figure 16.2 on an iPhone 4) appears at the bottom of the screen, swipe your finger from left to right until you see the Music Controls (shown in Figure 16.3). Tap Play (in the center of the screen) to begin playing your music library, in order.

To manage your music library, create playlists, and play songs using the Music app, launch the app from the Home Screen. Displayed along the top of the screen are various icons for controlling the music being played.

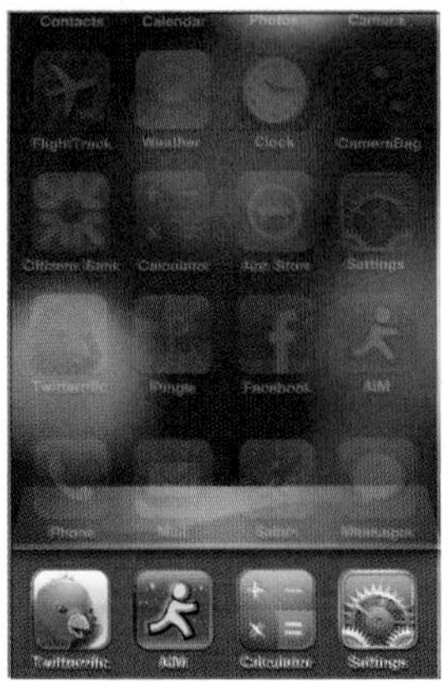

FIGURE 16.2

The multitasking bar of iOS 5. From here, access Music Controls by swiping your finger from left to right across the multitasking toolbar.

FIGURE 16.3

You can control the music playing on your iPhone or iPad from the Music Controls, accessible while you're in multitasking mode, or directly from the Music app.

MUSIC APP CONTROLS ON iPHONE

When you launch Music on your iPhone, you'll see the Store icon displayed in the upper-left corner of the screen. Tap it to access iTunes via the Web and shop for new music.

At the bottom of the screen are five command icons, labeled Playlists, Artists, Songs, Albums, and More (shown in Figure 16.4). Here's what each is used for:

- **Playlists**—Create and manage playlists within Music. A playlist is a list of songs that you manually compile from songs in your music library. It allows you to create a "digital mix tape," featuring only the music you want, in the order you want it. You can create as many separate playlists as you'd like, so you can listen to music based on what you're doing (such as jogging or working) or your current mood.
- **Artists**—View a listing of all songs stored in your iOS device, sorted by artist name.
- **Songs**—View a complete (alphabetical) listing of all songs stored in your iOS device, sorted by song title.
- **Albums**—View a complete listing of all songs stored in your iOS device, sorted by the album title from which that song was released. A thumbnail of each album cover is displayed.

- **More**—Beyond music purchased from iTunes, you can listen to audiobooks, podcasts and educational content from iTunes U by tapping on the More option. Plus, you can view a listing of songs sorted by composers or music genre, for example.

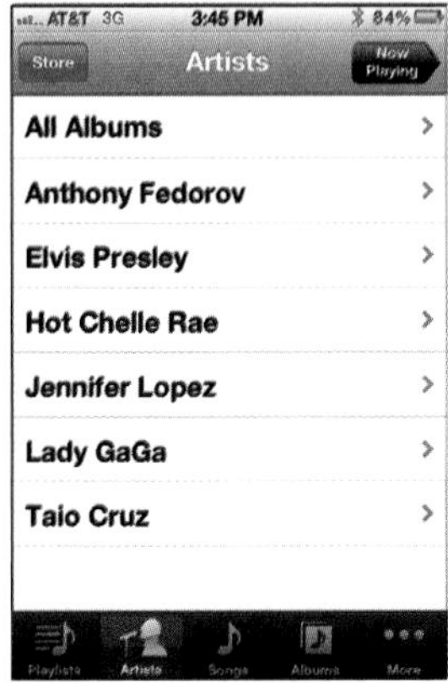

FIGURE 16.4

The main Artist screen of Music running on an iPhone 4.

CREATE A MUSIC APP PLAYLIST ON THE iPHONE

Playlists are personalized collections of songs that you can group together and then play at any time. Each playlist is given its own title and can include as many songs from your personal music collection as you wish.

You can create separate playlists for working out, to enjoy while you drive, to listen to when you're depressed, or to dance to when you feel like cutting loose. There is no limit to the number of separate playlists you can create and store on your iOS device.

> **TIP** When listening to any playlist, you can play the songs in order or have the Music app randomize the song order (using the Shuffle command). A playlist can also be put into an infinite loop, so it continuously plays until you press Pause.

1. Launch the Music app, and tap on the Playlist command icon that's displayed at the bottom of the screen.

2. To create a new playlist, tap on the Add Playlist option. Several default playlist options, such as My Top Rated, Purchased, Recently Added, and Top 25 Most Played, will be available to you right away. You can't edit these playlists, but you can create your own from scratch.
3. When prompted, create a name for your new playlist, such as Workout Music or Favorite Pop Songs, and tap the Save icon.
4. When the Songs window appears, tap on the blue-and-white plus icon associated with each song you want to add to your playlist. Tap Done to save your selections. All songs currently stored on your iPhone will be listed.
5. The Playlist window that next appears lists the name of your new playlist at the top of the screen, displays four command options (labeled Edit, Clear, Delete, and Shuffle), and then lists the individual songs in the playlist. Use the command options to manage the newly created playlist or edit an existing playlist.

   Tap the Edit command to delete songs from the playlist or change the order of the songs, and then tap the Done icon when you're finished.

   Tap the Clear icon to keep the master playlist file but remove all the songs from it. Or, tap the Delete icon to delete the playlist altogether from your iOS device.

> **TIP** Unless you tap the Shuffle option, when you opt to listen to the playlist, the songs will be played in the order displayed on the screen (that you selected). When you tap the Shuffle command, the songs from the playlist are played in a random order.

6. To listen to your newly created playlist, return to the main Playlist screen by tapping on the Playlists icon at the bottom of the screen (if you're not already there), and tap on the playlist title of your choice. Next, tap on a song from that playlist and begin listening.
7. From Music's play music screen, you'll see commands to Play/Pause the music and to skip tracks forward or backward, as well as a volume slider.

MUSIC APP CONTROLS ON iPAD

When you launch Music on your iPad (refer to Figure 16.1), you'll see the Store icon displayed in the lower-left corner of the screen. Tap it to access iTunes via the Web and shop for new music.

TIP Have you ever been listening to the radio, watching TV, or riding in an elevator and want to know the name of a song that's playing so you can purchase it? Well, there's an app for that. Download the free Shazam app from the App Store. When you hear a song you want to identify, launch the app. It "listens" to what's playing, and then identifies the song for you, complete with its title and artist. It then launches iTunes, giving you the option to purchase the song. This is one of the most popular, free iPhone apps of all time.

Also near the bottom of the screen are five command icons labeled Playlists, Songs, Artists, Albums, and More. Here's what each is used for:

- **Playlists**—Create and manage playlists within Music featuring only the music you want, in the order you want it. You can create as many separate playlists as you'd like.
- **Songs**—View a complete (alphabetical) listing of all songs stored in your iOS device, sorted by song title. Also listed along with each song is its artist, the album title it's from, and the song's length.
- **Artists**—View a listing of all songs stored in your iPad, sorted by each artist's name. The album artwork related to the artist and the album will be displayed, as well as the artist's name and how many songs from the artist's various albums you have stored on your tablet.
- **Albums**—View a complete listing of all songs stored on your iPad, sorted by the album title from which each song was released. A thumbnail of each album cover is displayed.
- **More**—View your library of songs, sorted by composer or music genre.

At the top of the Music app on the iPad, you'll see the music control icons displayed in the upper-left corner of the screen. These include the Rewind, Play/Pause, and Track Forward icons.

Near the top center of the screen are details about the song currently playing. Use the slider to move forward or backward (fast-forward or rewind) within that song. Or, tap on the arrow-shaped icon on the left side of the slider to put whatever playlist you're listing to into endless repeat mode. The other arrow-shaped icon to the right of the slider is used to put the playlist you're listening to into shuffle mode.

Also to the left and right of the slider are timers. The timer on the left shows how much of a song you've already heard, while the timer on the right shows how much of the song remains.

Tap the Genius icon to the right of the slider to access the Genius feature and discover songs you might also enjoy, based on the song you're currently playing and your past iTunes downloads.

The slider displayed in the upper-right corner of the screen is your onscreen volume control. Move it to the right to increase the volume or to the left to decrease it. You can also use the volume control buttons on the side of your iPad for this purpose, or, if applicable, the volume control buttons on the cord of your headset.

> **TIP** Quickly find any song stored on your iPhone or iPad by using a keyword search. In the search field, enter a song title (or a portion of a title), an artist's name, an album title, or any other keyword that's relevant to your music to find specific music content stored on your iOS device.
>
> On the iPhone, the Search field will appear on any screen if you swipe your finger downward, starting from the middle of the screen. Tap on the Search field to make the virtual keyboard appear. Enter your keyword or search phrase, and then tap the Search key on the keyboard to see the results. Tap on the search result of your choice to select a specific song, album, or artist.
>
> On the iPad, the Search field is always displayed as part of the Music app, in the lower-right corner of the screen. Tap on it to make the virtual keyboard appear and initiate a search.

CREATE A MUSIC APP PLAYLIST ON THE iPAD

You can create personal playlists on your iPad and then sync them for use with the iTunes software on your computer(s), or use iCloud to sync your playlists so they're available to you on your other iOS devices. Here's how to create a custom playlist on an iPad:

1. Launch the Music app, and tap on the Playlist icon that's displayed at the bottom of the screen.
2. To create a new playlist, tap on the New icon that appears near the upper-right corner of the screen, below the volume slider. Several default playlist options, such as My Top Rated, Purchased, Recently Added, and Top 25 Most Played, will be available to you right away. You can't edit these playlists, but you can create your own from scratch.
3. When prompted after tapping the New icon, create a name for your new playlist, such as Workout Music or Favorite Pop Songs, and tap the Save icon.
4. When the Songs window appears, tap on the plus icon associated with each song that you want to add to your playlist, and then tap Done (shown in Figure 16.5) to save your selections. If you want to add all the songs stored on your iPad, tap the Add All Songs icon (displayed near the top of the screen, next to the Done icon).

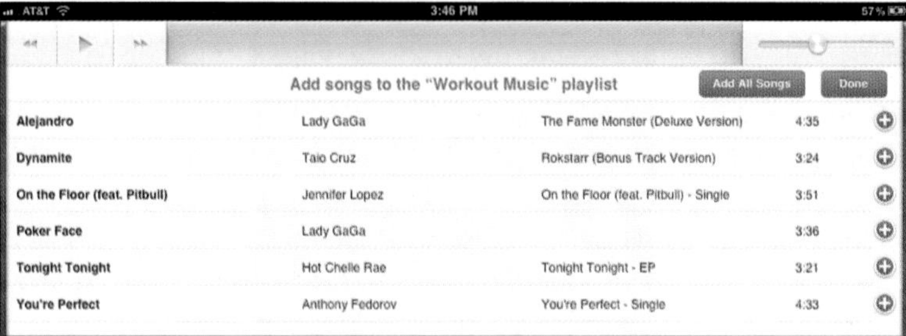

FIGURE 16.5

Choose the songs you want to add to your playlist, based on the listing of all songs stored on your iPad.

5. The Playlist window that appears next will list the name of your new playlist near the top center of the screen, and then the individual songs within that playlist.

   To change the order of the songs while accessing this screen, select a song, hold your finger on the icon that contains three horizontal lines (on the right side of the screen), and drag it upward or downward.

   To delete a song from the playlist, tap on the red-and-white minus sign icon that's displayed to the left of each song title.

   Tap on the Add Songs icon (displayed in the upper-right corner of the screen, below the volume slider) to add additional songs to your playlist.
6. Tap the Done icon, displayed in the upper-right corner of the Music app's screen (below the volume slider) to save your changes.
7. To listen to your newly created playlist, tap on any song title listed in that playlist to choose where you want to begin listening from.
8. Use the music control icons at the top of the screen to control the music you're now listening to.

MORE MUSIC APP FEATURES

After music is playing on your iPhone or iPad, you can exit the Music app and use your iOS device for other purposes. The music will keep playing. It will automatically pause, however, if you receive an incoming call on your iPhone or an incoming FaceTime call on your iPhone or iPad.

After you purchase a song from iTunes, it gets download to the computer or device it was purchased from, but is also instantly made available to all of your iOS devices via iCloud. So, you can purchase music on your primary computer, but for no extra charge also download it wirelessly to your iPhone, iPad, and/or iPod touch. Or, you can purchase a song on your iPhone, yet have it available on all of your other computers and devices that are linked to your iCloud account.

As you're looking at any song listing or album graphic in the Music app, you can delete that content from your iOS device. If it's a song listing, swipe your finger across that listing, from left to right. When the Delete icon appears (as shown in Figure 16.6) , tap on it. If it's a thumbnail for an album cover, hold your finger on that graphic until an X icon appears in the upper-left corner of the thumbnail image. Tap on the X to delete the image and all related music content.

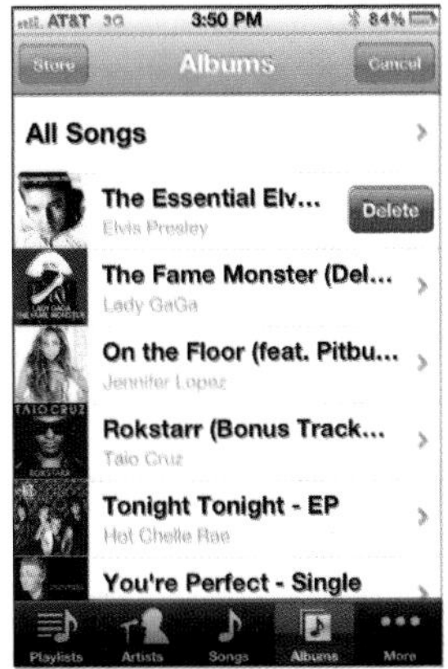

FIGURE 16.6

You can delete one song at a time, or entire albums' worth of songs, from your iOS device. In this case, to delete the one Elvis song, swipe your finger from left to right across the listing, tap on the Delete icon, and then Elvis will have left your iPhone.

TIP To introduce you to new songs, new bands, and up-and-coming artists, iTunes regularly makes certain music available for free. This free music selection changes weekly. To access free music via the iTunes Store, launch the iTunes app from your iPhone or iPad. On the iPad, for example, tap on the Music icon at the bottom of the iTunes app's screen, tap the Featured tab near the top center of the screen, and then scroll down to the Quick Links section of the Featured screen. Tap on the Free Music on iTunes option.

If you visit any participating Starbucks Coffee location, you can also preview and download featured music for free using the coffee shop's advertiser-supported Wi-Fi hotspot.

After you've downloaded a single (one song) from an artist or band, within 180 days you can purchase the entire album and get credit for the eligible song(s) you've already purchased by tapping on the Complete My Album option within iTunes. To use the Complete My Album feature of iTunes, from your iPhone, launch the iTunes app, tap on the Music icon (displayed at the bottom of the screen), and then scroll down to the Complete My Album option. Tap on it.

The Complete My Album feature can also be accessed from the iPad. To do this, launch the iTunes app and tap on the Music icon that's displayed at the bottom of the screen. Tap on the Featured icon at the top center of the screen, and then scroll down on the Featured page to the Quick Links section. Tap on the Complete My Album option.

After you tap on the Complete My Album option on your iOS device, a list of eligible albums you can purchase at a discount (based on your previous single purchases) will be displayed. Tap on your album selection, and then tap on the album description's Price icon to purchase and download the remaining songs from that album.

Apple wants you to shop for your music from iTunes, for obvious reasons. However, you do have other options. From your primary computer, you can shop for (or otherwise download) music from other sources, and then transfer that content to your iPhone or iPad by importing the music files into iTunes on your primary computer, and then performing an iTunes Sync. Or, you can upgrade to the iTunes Match service and gain access to your entire digital music library via iCloud.

Some other sources for legally buying and downloading music include the Amazon MP3 music store (www.amazonmp3.com), Napster (www.napster.com), eMusic (www.eMusic.com), and Rhapsody (www.rhapsody.com).

> **TIP** Want to sing along with your favorite songs but don't know the lyrics? No problem! Purchase and download the Lyrics ID app ($.99) from the app store. It displays the song lyrics to the songs currently stored on your iPhone as the music is playing. There are also a handful of karaoke apps available from the App Store. Use the App Store's Search feature (with the keyword Karaoke) to find third-party apps, like The Singing Machine ($.99) and Karaoke Party ($5.99).

USE THE VIDEOS APP TO WATCH TV SHOWS, MOVIES, AND MORE

After you purchase and download TV show episodes, movies, or music videos from iTunes, that video-based content can be enjoyed on your iPhone and/or iPad using the Videos app. It can also be viewed on your primary computer using iTunes and shared between devices via iCloud.

iOS 5 WHAT'S NEW Video content acquired from iTunes can be watched on your iOS device or, if you have Apple TV, streamed from your device to your home theater system.

The Videos app comes preinstalled with iOS 5. After you've downloaded or transferred iTunes video content to your iPhone or iPad, it will be accessible from the Videos app.

When you launch Videos on your iPhone or iPad, at the top center of the screen will be one, two, or three tabs, based on the content stored on your device (as shown in Figure 16.7). These tabs will be labeled TV Shows, Movies, and/or Music Videos. If you have movies rented from iTunes, as opposed to movies you own stored on your iOS device, a tab labeled Rentals will be displayed in addition to or instead of a tab labeled Movies.

FIGURE 16.7

The Videos app shows what video content you have stored on your device. Content is categorized based on whether it's a TV show episode, movie, or music video.

When you tap on the TV Shows, Movies, Rentals, or Music Videos tab, thumbnail graphics representing that video content will be displayed. To begin playing a video, tap on its thumbnail graphic.

TIP To delete video content from your iOS device, on the iPhone, swipe your finger from left to right across the listing, and then tap the Delete icon. On the iPad, tap on the Edit icon displayed in the upper-right corner of the screen. When X icons appear in the upper-left corner of each thumbnail, tap on the appropriate X icons to delete that corresponding video content from your device.

To shop for additional video content from iTunes, while in the Videos app, tap on the Store icon that's displayed in the upper-left corner of the screen.

To play a video, tap on a thumbnail representing a TV show, movie, or music video that you want to watch. If you've downloaded a TV show, for example, a new screen will appear, listing all episodes from that TV series currently stored on your iOS device (as shown in Figure 16.8). Tap on the episode of your choice to begin playing it. You can also tap on the Play icon.

FIGURE 16.8

If you have downloaded multiple episodes of a TV series, they'll be grouped together for easy access and viewing.

For music videos or movies, a similar information screen pertaining to that content will be displayed. Tap on the Play icon to begin watching your movie or music video.

> **TIP** When playing video content, you can hold your iPhone or iPad in either portrait or landscape mode. However, the video window will be significantly larger if you position your iOS device sideways and use landscape mode.
>
> By tapping the icon displayed in the upper-right corner of the screen, you can instantly switch between full-screen mode and letterbox mode as your onscreen viewing option.

While video content is playing on your iPhone or iPad, you will see that video in full-screen mode. Tap anywhere on the screen to reveal the onscreen command icons used for controlling the video as you're watching it. These controls are identical on the iPhone and iPad (shown in Figure 16.9 on an iPad 2). When a video is playing, these controls disappear from the screen automatically after a few seconds. Tap anywhere on the screen to make them reappear.

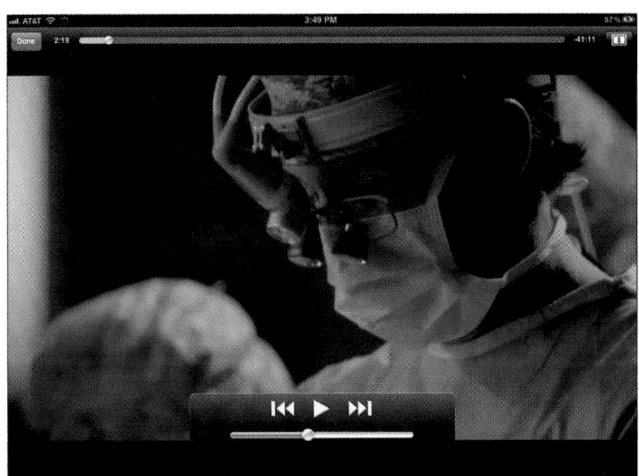

FIGURE 16.9

The onscreen icons for controlling the video you're watching on your iOS device.

Displayed in the upper left of the Videos app screen while you're watching video content is the Done icon. Tap on this to exit the video you're watching. Along the top center of the screen is a timer slider. On either end of this slider are timers. To the left is a timer that displays how much of the video you've already watched. On the right of the slider is a timer that displays how much time in the video remains.

Near the bottom center of the screen as you're watching video content are the Rewind and Fast Forward icons. Tap on the Rewind icon to move back by scene or chapter, or tap the Fast Forward icon to advance to the next scene or chapter in the video (just as you would while watching a DVD). Tap the Play icon to play the video. When the video is playing, the Play icon transforms into a Pause icon, used to pause the video.

NOTE If you pause a video and then exit the Videos app, you can pick up exactly where you left off watching the video when you relaunch the Videos app. This information is automatically saved.

Below these three icons is the volume control slider. Use it to manually adjust the volume of the audio. You can also use the volume control buttons located on the side of your iPhone or iPad, or, if applicable, the volume control buttons on the cord of your headset.

MUSIC, TV SHOWS, MOVIES, AND MORE: THE COST OF iTUNES CONTENT

The costs associated with acquiring content from iTunes are as listed here:

Content Type	Standard Definition	High Definition
Purchase Music Single (One Song)	$.69 to $1.29	N/A
Purchase Music Album	$7.99 to $15.99	N/A
Purchase Music Video	$1.99	N/A
Purchase TV Show Episode	$1.99	$2.99
Purchase Made-for-TV Movie	$3.99	$4.99
Rent TV Show Episode	No longer available from iTunes	No longer available from iTunes
Purchase Entire Season of a TV Show	Price varies, based on TV series and number of episodes. It's always cheaper to purchase an entire season than to purchase all episodes in a season separately.	Price varies, based on TV series and number of episodes. It's always cheaper to purchase an entire season than to purchase all episodes in a season separately.
Purchase Movie	$.99 to $14.99	$.99 to $19.99
Rent Movie	$.99 to $3.99 (New releases start at $3.99, with library titles available for as little as $.99 per rental.)	$1.99 to $4.99 (New releases start at $4.99, with library titles available for as little as $1.99 per rental.)
Audiobooks	$.95 to $41.95 (Unabridged audiobooks of current bestsellers tend to be among the higher priced titles. These tend to range from $14.95 to $26.95.)	N/A
Ringtones	$1.29	N/A

TIP After you've purchased one or more songs from a full-length album (but not the whole album), you can later purchase that entire album at a discount from iTunes using the Complete My Album feature. How much of a discount you're given will depend on how much music from that album you already own.

From your iPhone or iPad, launch iTunes, and tap on the Music command icon that's displayed at the bottom of the screen. Then, at the top of the screen, tap on the New Releases tab (iPhone) or the Featured tab (iPad). From the New Releases or Featured screen, scroll down to the very bottom, and tap on the Complete My Album option.

The iTunes app will analyze your music library and display the full-length albums you qualify to receive a discount on. Each listing will include the album title, artist's name, the discounted "Buy For" price, as well as the regular price of the full-length album. Tap on an album listing displayed on the Complete My Album screen to make the purchase and download the rest of the album.

QUICKLY FIND TV EPISODES YOU WANT TO PURCHASE ON iTUNES

When shopping for TV show episodes to purchase and watch using the iTunes app, tap on the TV shows icon. Shows are displayed by series name. So to see a list of episodes of *The Office*, for example, that are available, use the Search field to find *The Office*. The search will display the TV show by season number or by available episodes. For example, the listings will say *The Office Season 2, Released: September 20 2005*, or *The Office Season 8, Released September 22, 2011*.

Tap on the View icon associated with the season from which you want to purchase episodes to reveal a listing of episodes from that season, in chronological order, based on original airdate. The most recently aired episodes will be listed toward the bottom of the list, so scroll down. At the top of the screen, you'll also have the option to purchase the entire season (as opposed to individual episodes) at a discounted rate, plus be able to choose between high definition or standard definition video quality.

To save money, purchase an entire season of your favorite show's current season. Then, when a new episode airs each week and becomes available on iTunes, it will automatically be downloaded to your iOS device and made available to you via iCloud.

When you shop for TV episodes from the iTunes Store (via the iTunes app), those files get downloaded and stored on your iPhone or iPad. They're commercial free and will be available to watch whenever you wish. They're also permanently accessible via your iCloud account to be downloaded to any computer, iOS device, or Apple TV device that's linked to the same iCloud account.

NOTE Keep in mind that, without commercials, a one-hour program will appear on iTunes as being between 42 and 44 minutes long, while a half-hour program will appear on iTunes as being between 21 and 24 minutes long.

When you stream TV episodes from the Web using a specialized app, this programming does not get stored on your iOS device and is available only when your iPhone or iPad is connected to the Internet.

STREAMING VIDEO ON YOUR iPHONE OR iPAD

To stream video content to your iPhone or iPad from the Internet, you'll need to use a specialized app, based on where the content is originating from on the Web.

Whenever you're streaming video content from the Web, you can pause the video at any time. Depending on the app, you can also exit the app partway through a video and resume watching it from where you left off when you relaunch the app later.

> **CAUTION** The capability to stream content from the Web and experience it on your iPhone or iPad gives you on-demand access to a wide range of programming. However, streaming audio or video content from the Web requires a tremendous amount of data to be transferred to your iOS device. Therefore, if you use a 3G connection, your monthly wireless data allocation will quickly get used up. So when you're streaming Web content, it's best to use a Wi-Fi connection.
>
> Not only does a Wi-Fi connection allow data to be transferred to your iPhone or iPad at much faster speeds, but there's also no limit as to how much data you can send or receive. Plus, when streaming video content, you'll often be able to view it at a higher resolution using a Wi-Fi connection.

The following sections describe some of the popular apps for streaming TV shows, movies, and other video content directly from the Web.

ABC PLAYER

The ABC Player is a free, iPad-specific app from the ABC Television Network that allows you to watch full-length episodes of your favorite ABC-TV dramas, reality shows, sitcoms, game shows, and soap operas, free. The episodes are streamed to your iPhone or iPad and can be watched using this app. The shows are advertiser supported, so you'll need to watch ads during the programs you stream.

> **NOTE** When you purchase TV show episodes from iTunes, they are ad free. When you use a TV network's app to stream TV shows, you'll probably be forced to watch commercials.

The ABC Player app is separate from the free ABC News app, which allows you to watch news coverage from the network.

TIP NBC also offers a free app (called NBC) for streaming full-length episodes, seeing previews of upcoming shows, and keeping track of your favorite shows. It's equivalent to having the NBC television network in an on-demand format, so you can watch shows whenever you want.

HBO GO

If you're already a paid subscriber to the HBO cable television network, you can download the free HBO Go app and watch every episode of every HBO original series on-demand, as well as an ever-changing lineup of movies, comedy specials, sports programs, and documentaries that are currently airing on HBO.

After you set up a free online account with your local cable or satellite television provider, sign in to the HBO Go app and select the programming you want to watch. Begin playing a TV episode or movie with the tap of a finger, or create a queue of shows to watch at your leisure. Movies and TV episodes can be paused and resumed later.

One great feature of the HBO Go app is that HBO sometimes releases episodes on this app one week before they air on television. Plus, you can access behind-the-scenes content of popular HBO series, like *Game of Thrones*.

CAUTION Most of the streaming video apps for the iPhone and iPad work only in the United States. If you try to access HBO Go from abroad, for example, the app will not work.

HULU PLUS

Full-length episodes from thousands of current and classic TV series are available on your iOS device using the free Hulu Plus app. However, the majority of the content offered from this service requires you to pay a monthly subscription fee to access and view it.

Hulu Plus members can access season passes to current TV shows airing on ABC, FOX, and NBC, or pick and choose from thousands of episodes from classic TV series. All video is streamed at 720p HD resolution to your iPhone or iPad, so a Wi-Fi connection is recommended, although the app does work with a 3G Internet connection.

The *Hulu Plus* app allows you to pause programs and resume them later, plus create a queue of shows to watch on your tablet.

MORE INFO Visit www.hulu.com/plus to subscribe to the Hulu service and browse available programming.

INFINITY TV

If Infinity is your cable TV provider, you can use this app to watch a wide range of free, on-demand programming, including TV shows and movies. The free TWCable TV app from Time Warner Cable offers similar functionality. However, if you subscribe to another cable TV service, check the App Store to see whether a similar app is available.

MAX GO

This free app works just like the HBO Go app but enables you to watch Cinemax programming on demand from your iOS device. The content is free, as long as you're already a paid Cinemax subscriber. This app offers you instant access to more than 400 movies per month, plus access to Cinemax's original TV programming.

NETFLIX

Netflix is a subscription-based service that enables you to watch thousands of movies and TV show episodes via the Internet on your television, on your computer screen, or directly on your iPhone or iPad (when you use the free Netflix app). The subscription fee for Netflix starts at $7.99 per month.

You can watch as much streaming content as you'd like per month. Simply browse the Netflix Instant Watch library, and tap on the Play button when you find the movie or TV show episode you want to watch. You can also create and manage an Instant Queue.

TV.COM

The free TV.com iPhone app (which also works perfectly on an iPad) enables you to watch full episodes of your favorite TV shows from the CBS Television Network, The CW Network, Showtime, CNET TV, and a few other television networks. The app works with a 3G Internet connection, but a Wi-Fi connection is recommended to experience the highest quality video possible. All content is free of charge but is advertiser supported.

YOUTUBE

The YouTube app comes preinstalled on your iPhone or iPad and enables you to watch streaming videos produced and uploaded by everyday people, companies, television networks, and other organizations. In addition to millions of entertaining videos and video blogs, YouTube features free educational content and how-to videos. All YouTube content is free of charge to watch. Some of it is advertiser supported.

TIP In addition to streaming videos, TV shows, and movies to watch on your iPhone or iPad, you can stream audio programming from AM, FM, and satellite-based radio stations and radio networks, as well as Internet-based radio stations. Some of the apps available for doing this are Pandora Radio, TuneIn Radio Pro, Spotify, and SiriusXM.

IN THIS CHAPTER

- How to use FaceTime for videoconferencing
- How to use Skype for iPhone to make and receive voice-over-IP calls
- How to use Skype for iPad to make and receive calls, plus do videoconferencing

17

VIDEOCONFERENCING AND VOICE OVER IP (VoIP)

The Apple iPhone 4, iPhone 4S, iPad 2, and some iPod touch models, for example, all have front- and rear-facing cameras built in, which allow you to shoot digital images or video clips (using the Camera app). These same cameras, along with your device's built-in microphone and speaker, can be used for real-time videoconferencing. Unfortunately, the older iPhone 3G and iPhone 3Gs do not have the front- and rear-facing camera, and thus can't be used for videoconferencing.

iOS 5 comes with the FaceTime app preinstalled. When your iOS device is connected to the Internet via a Wi-Fi connection, the FaceTime app enables you to participate in real-time videoconferences with any other FaceTime users.

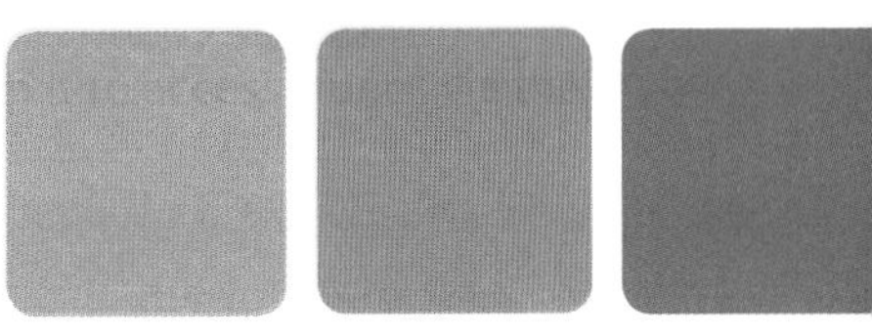

NOTE Making and receiving calls using FaceTime and participating in videoconferences is free. You can make or receive an unlimited number of calls and stay connected for as long as you'd like. FaceTime, however, does not work with a 3G Internet connection.

The first time you use FaceTime, you'll need to set up a free account. If you're using an iPhone 4 or iPhone 4S, for example, by default, your account will utilize your iPhone's unique 10-digit phone number. When you make or receive a call using the Phone app, if your iPhone determines that the person you're connecting with also has FaceTime available, simply tap on the FaceTime icon to launch the FaceTime app and convert the traditional call into a videoconference call.

When using FaceTime on an iPad, iPod touch, or Mac, however, you'll need to either link your Apple ID to your FaceTime account or link another email address that will be used as your unique FaceTime identifier (instead of a phone number).

TIP Your iPhone's phone number, the Apple ID, or the email address you link to your FaceTime account serves as your unique identifier when you're using FaceTime. It enables others to initiate a FaceTime connection with you when you both have FaceTime running on your devices. Likewise, if you want to call another FaceTime user with this app, you'll need to know the phone number or email address that the user has associated with FaceTime, or her iPhone phone number.

After this setup process is complete (it takes less than a minute), as long as you have FaceTime running on your iPad or iPod touch, and it's connected to the Internet using a Wi-Fi connection (and you remain within the Wi-Fi hotspot's radius), you will be able to initiate or receive calls and participate in videoconferences. By default, FaceTime automatically launches on your iPhone when a connection can be made with another FaceTime user.

HOW TO USE FACETIME FOR VIDEOCONFERENCING

To launch the FaceTime app, first look near the upper-left corner of your iOS device's Home Screen, and make sure that it is connected to the Web using a Wi-Fi connection. The Wi-Fi signal strength icon will be displayed if a Wi-Fi connection exists.

To turn on Wi-Fi and establish an Internet connection, launch the Settings app, and tap on the Wi-Fi option that's displayed in the main Settings menu. It's the second option, listed under Airplane Mode. From the Wi-Fi Networks screen, tap on the virtual switch associated with the Wi-Fi option to turn on Wi-Fi. Next, select the Wi-Fi network you want to join. Available networks are displayed under the Choose a Network heading.

LAUNCH FACETIME ON YOUR iPHONE

On the iPhone, FaceTime is launched through the Phone app. When you initiate a call with another iPhone user, on the main phone screen after a call is connected, the FaceTime icon will become active, meaning that if you tap on it, a videoconference connection will be made.

You can also look at the contacts listed in your Contacts database from the Phone app (by tapping on the Contacts icon). If the contact you're looking at is also able to connect to FaceTime, the FaceTime icon will become active and a video-camera icon will appear in it.

Finally, if you receive an incoming call from another FaceTime user, your phone will ring but you'll be notified that the call is a FaceTime request, as opposed to a regular incoming call. If you accept the request, a FaceTime connection will automatically be established between the two devices, and a videoconference will begin.

> **NOTE** After a FaceTime videoconference connection is made between your iPhone or iPad and another FaceTime user, the main FaceTime screen looks identical, regardless of which device you're using. See the section "Participating in a FaceTime Call."

LAUNCH FACETIME ON YOUR iPAD

As soon as the FaceTime app is launched, the device's forward-facing camera will turn on, and you should see yourself in your iPad's screen. On the right side of the screen will be a window requesting that you enter your Apple ID and password to sign in (as shown in Figure 17.1). Enter this information using the virtual keyboard, and then tap the Sign In icon that's displayed below the username and password fields. Or you can tap on the Create New Account option to set up a free Apple ID account from within the FaceTime app.

You're now ready to initiate or receive FaceTime calls and participate in videoconferences via the Web. Displayed near the lower-right corner of this app screen are three command icons labeled Favorites, Recents, and Contacts (as shown in Figure 17.2).

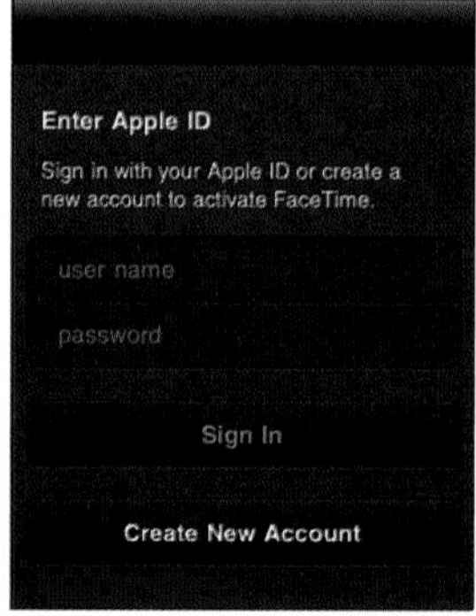

FIGURE 17.1

On the iPad, you'll need to manually launch FaceTime and sign in to your FaceTime account before a videoconference can be established. This step is not necessary when you're using FaceTime on an iPhone.

FIGURE 17.2

You can decide whom to FaceTime videoconference with using the Favorites, Recents, or Contacts icon that's displayed at the bottom of the FaceTime screen when it's used with an iPad.

CREATE A FACETIME FAVORITES LIST

A Favorites list in FaceTime is a list you can customize to include the people with whom you'll FaceTime videoconference the most. In essence, this Favorites option serves as a one-touch speed-dial list. Tap on the Favorites tab displayed at the lower-right portion of the FaceTime screen (on an iPad) to access it.

> **NOTE** On the iPhone, your Favorites List is maintained as part of the Phone app. Tap on the Favorites icon at the bottom of the Phone app's screen. This Favorites list can include a contact's phone number (to initiate a call) or FaceTime account (to initiate a FaceTime videoconference connection).

To add a contact in your Favorites list on the iPad within FaceTime, tap on the plus sign icon that's located in the upper-right corner of the Favorites window, and then select Contacts from your established contacts database (that is created and maintained using the Contacts app).

TIP In the Contacts entry for each person, if that person is an iPhone 4 or iPhone 4S user, be sure to associate his mobile phone number with the iPhone label, as opposed to the mobile phone label, so that the FaceTime app can easily identify and connect with him.

FACETIME'S AUTOMATIC RECENTS LIST

On the iPad, when you tap on the Recents icon while using FaceTime, you see a list of people with whom you've already communicated using FaceTime. Tap on any of the contacts in this list to videoconference with that person again.

NOTE On the iPhone, the Recents list pertaining to FaceTime is maintained in the Phone app. When you look at the Recents list on your iPhone, FaceTime connections are highlighted by the appearance of a small video camera icon below the contact's name.

If this is the first time you're using the FaceTime app on your iPad, the Recents window will be empty, except for the All and Missed tabs displayed at the top of the window. After you begin using the app on the iPad, the All tab displays all FaceTime videoconferences you've participated in, as well as any incoming missed calls you didn't answer. Tap on the Missed tab to see a list of just the incoming FaceTime calls you didn't answer.

CHOOSE A CONTACT FROM YOUR CONTACTS DATABASE

The Contacts icon that's displayed near the lower-right corner of the FaceTime screen (on an iPad) enables you to select and call a fellow FaceTime user who is listed in your Contacts database.

Remember that FaceTime works only with other compatible iOS devices or Mac users. When you're calling another iPad 2, iPod touch, or Mac FaceTime user, the FaceTime app or software must be running on that user's device for her to accept a call. As long as someone's iPhone 4 or iPhone 4S, for example, is turned on and connected to the Internet (via Wi-Fi), the person can automatically receive incoming FaceTime calls.

HOW TO INITIATE A FACETIME CALL FROM YOUR iPAD

To initiate a call with someone who also has FaceTime installed and operating on his computer or iOS device, select that person from your Contacts list, and tap on the email address or iPhone phone number that he used to register with FaceTime.

If a connection can be made, a FaceTime icon will automatically appear next to the person's name in the FaceTime app.

When you initiate a call, at the bottom center of the screen, the message "FaceTime with" and the person's name will be displayed. Next to this label will be the Call End icon, which you can tap at any time to terminate the connection.

PARTICIPATING IN A FACETIME CALL

When you're using a FaceTime-compatible iOS device, when a FaceTime connection is established with another party, your own image that was displayed in full-screen mode on the device's screen will shrink, and will now be displayed in the upper-left corner of the screen. The rest of the FaceTime screen will display the person you're now connected with using FaceTime.

Notice that near the very bottom of the screen are three command icons (as shown in Figure 17.3) labeled Mute, End Call, and Switch Camera. These command icons are used for the following purposes:

- Tap on the Mute button to retain the video connection but mute your iOS device's built-in microphone so that the person you're communicating with will be able to see you but not hear you.
- Tap on the End Call icon to terminate the FaceTime connection and promptly end the call.
- Tap on the Switch Camera icon to alternate between the two cameras built in to your iOS device. The forward-facing camera will be facing toward you, while the camera on the back of the device will show off whatever it's pointing at.

FIGURE 17.3

When a FaceTime videoconference is underway, your image will be displayed in a small window. The person you're talking with will be displayed in the main area of the FaceTime screen, and several command icons will display near the bottom center of the screen.

TIPS FOR IMPROVING YOUR FACETIME CONNECTIONS

Here are a few strategies for improving the quality of your FaceTime connection, which will help to ensure that you'll see and hear the person you're videoconferencing with, and that the other person will be able to see and hear you.

> **TIP** These strategies should be implemented by both you and the person you're videoconferencing with.

- Use a Wi-Fi Internet connection that has a strong signal. If necessary, move closer to the wireless Internet router.
- Participate in a FaceTime videoconference from a quiet location so that your iPhone or iPad's microphone doesn't pick up background noise that will distort or drown out your voice.
- Make sure that the primary lighting in the area is shining on your face and is not behind you. If too much light is behind you, the person you're videoconferencing with will see your silhouette (as opposed to the detail of your face). Try to position the main light source in front of you so that your face is evenly lit. A light shining from overhead, for example, will often cause shadows to appear on your face, which might make you look older or ill.
- While videoconferencing, refrain from excessive movement. The real-time video image will remain clearer if you're sitting or standing still.
- When participating in a videoconference, it's common to forget that the camera is turned on after a while. Refrain from doing anything that you don't want the other person to see and/or hear.
- The most confusing aspect of FaceTime is making that initial connection with someone else and setting your iOS device to initiate a call to the proper iPhone number, Apple ID, or email address that's associated with that person's FaceTime account. After a connection is established once, future connections can be made with a single tap on the screen.

> **TIP** When using FaceTime, you never have to pay long-distance phone charges, international calling fees, or cellphone roaming charges. Nor do you have to worry about using up your cellphone minutes or monthly 3G wireless data usage allocation from your wireless service provider. Perhaps the biggest benefit to using FaceTime is that you can actually see *and* hear the person you're communicating with.

MAKING AND RECEIVING PHONE CALLS VIA THE INTERNET USING SKYPE

Skype is a Voice over IP phone service that enables you to make and receive calls over the Web (as opposed to a cellular phone network or traditional telephone landline). The Skype service is available for PCs and Macs and requires special software to transform a computer into a virtual speakerphone, allowing users to make and receive calls that originate from the Internet.

TIP Thanks to a partnership between Facebook and Skype, in Facebook, you can now engage in a free videoconference with any of your Facebook friends who are also online. The iPad-specific Facebook app enables you to use this videoconferencing feature.

There is a free Skype app that was designed for the iPhone, as well as a separate iPad-specific Skype app (that also offers the capability to participate in real-time videoconferences with any other Skype users, including those on a PC). Both Skype apps are available from the App Store.

NOTE The Skype app takes advantage of your iOS device's Internet connection, built-in speaker, and built-in microphone (and in the case of the iPad, its built-in cameras) to transform into a full-featured speakerphone or videoconferencing tool.

Making unlimited Skype-to-Skype calls (including videoconference calls) is always free. However, there is a very low per-minute fee to make calls to a landline or cellular telephone from your iOS device using either the iPhone or iPad-specific version of Skype. This per-minute fee is typically just pennies per minute, even if you're traveling overseas and make a call back to the United States. You can also save a fortune on international calling from the United States when making calls to any other country.

NOTE Although Skype calls originate from the Internet, calls can be made to (or received from) any landline or cellphone. Thus, your iPhone or iPad, when connected to the Internet via a 3G or Wi-Fi connection, can be transformed into a full-featured speakerphone, complete with caller ID, conference calling, a mute button, and one-touch dialing.

! CAUTION Skype works much better (and with no limitations) when used with a high-speed Wi-Fi Internet connection. When used with a 3G connection, it requires a significant amount of wireless data usage and will quickly deplete your monthly wireless data allocation from your wireless service provider, or result in high international wireless data roaming fees if used abroad.

Through Skype, you can obtain your own unique telephone number (for an additional fee of $6 per month), which comes with call forwarding, voicemail, and other features, so you can manage incoming calls whether or not Skype is activated and your iPhone or iPad is connected to the Web. However, this is optional.

When you have your own Skype phone number, people without their own Skype account will be able to reach you inexpensively by dialing your unique Skype phone number, regardless of where you're traveling. You can, however, initiate calls without paying for a unique local phone number.

NOTE In terms of call quality, as long as you're within a 3G coverage area or a Wi-Fi hotspot and your iOS device has a strong web connection, calls will be crystal clear.

The Skype app is very easy to use and enables you to maintain a contacts list of frequently called people, dial out using a familiar telephone touch-pad display, and maintain a detailed call history that lists incoming, outgoing, and missed calls.

TIP For added privacy when using Skype on your iPhone or iPad (so that people around you can't listen in on your speakerphone conversations), connect a wireless Bluetooth headset to your iOS device. Version 3.5.117 (or later) of the Skype app for iPhone or Version 3.5.118 (or later) for the iPad both now support Bluetooth headsets.

Keep in mind, when using Skype with an iOS device, the quality of your phone connection will relate directly to the strength of the Internet signal your iPhone or iPad is using. If you experience poor call clarity and you're using a Wi-Fi Internet connection with your iOS device, move closer to the wireless router to enhance the signal strength and improve call clarity.

When you don't have Skype activated, you can automatically forward incoming calls to another number or have them go directly to your Skype voicemail account. On the iPad, to access the call forwarding feature, tap on your name that's displayed in the upper-left corner of the screen to reveal the My Info window. On the iPhone, tap on the My Info icon that's displayed in the lower-left corner of the Skype app's screen. Next, tap on the Call Forwarding feature to turn it on, and then enter the phone number to which you want to forward calls.

When you're online with the Skype service, you can have your status displayed so other Skype users will be able to find and call you via the Skype network. If you don't want to be disturbed by incoming calls, access the My Info screen and tap on the Status option. From the Status window, select Do Not Disturb or Invisible.

TIP Similar to the Skype app, the AT&T Call International app is available for free from the App Store. Using your iPhone or iPad, you can use it to make Voice over IP international calls for between two and four cents per minute. This optional app works whether or not you use AT&T Wireless as your wireless service provider.

IN THIS CHAPTER

- How to introduce yourself to Siri
- How to use Siri with your iPhone 4S
- How to utilize Siri with your favorite apps

18

MEET SIRI, YOUR NEW PERSONAL ASSISTANT

Even if you're a jaded iPhone user who seldom gets excited by new technological gadgets, it's virtually impossible not to be impressed by the new Siri feature incorporated into the iPhone 4S running iOS 5.

Thanks to Siri, instead of having to utilize the iPhone's touchscreen to interact with the device, and then constantly use the relatively small onscreen keyboard to enter data or information, now you can simply use your voice and speak using normal sentences. There are no commands to memorize.

> **NOTE** As of late-2011, Siri is available exclusively on the iPhone 4S; however, it will most likely be incorporated into the iPad 2 and yet-to-be released iOS devices in the future. Plus, enhancements are constantly being made to Siri for its use with an iPhone 4S.

Right from the start, you should understand that Siri doesn't know or understand everything, and it does have limitations in terms of what it can do and which apps it works with. However, you will find it to be a powerful tool that helps you utilize your iPhone, especially when you need hands-free interactivity with your iPhone.

In addition to using cutting-edge voice recognition, Siri uses advanced artificial intelligence, so it doesn't just understand what you say, it interprets and comprehends what you mean, and then translates your speech to text. And if you don't initially provide the information Siri needs to complete your request or command, you'll be prompted for more information.

WHAT YOU SHOULD KNOW BEFORE USING SIRI

For Siri to operate on your iPhone 4S, the phone must have access to the Internet via a 3G or Wi-Fi connection. Every time you make a request or issue a command to Siri, your iPhone connects to Apple's data center. Thus, if you're using a 3G connection, some of your monthly wireless data allocation is used up (if data allocation is imposed by your wireless service provider).

TIP Because a Wi-Fi connection is significantly faster than a 3G connection, you'll discover that Siri responds faster to your requests and commands when you use a Wi-Fi connection.

You should also understand that heavy use of the Internet, especially when connected via a 3G connection, depletes the battery life of the iPhone faster. So, if you constantly rely on Siri throughout the day, the iPhone's battery life per charge will be shorter.

! CAUTION If your iPhone is placed in Airplane mode (and Wi-Fi connectivity is turned off), Siri will not function. Siri will say, "Sorry, I am having trouble connecting to the network."

WAYS TO ACTIVATE SIRI

As you go about using your iPhone 4S, if you want to use the Siri feature, you first must activate it. There are three ways to do this:

- Press and hold down the Home button on your iPhone for two to three seconds.

- Pick up your iPhone and hold it up to your ear. Siri will activate automatically. (However, this feature first must be turned on from within Settings.)
- Press the Call button on your wireless Bluetooth headset that is paired with your iPhone 4S. This enables you to use your iPhone hands-free from up to 30 feet away.

When Siri is activated, the message, "What can I help you with?" is displayed near the bottom of the screen, along with a circular microphone icon (shown in Figure 18.1). You'll simultaneously hear Siri's activation tone. Do not start speaking to Siri until this tone is heard. You'll have about five seconds to speak before the microphone deactivates. To reactivate it, tap on the microphone icon or repeat one of the previously mentioned steps.

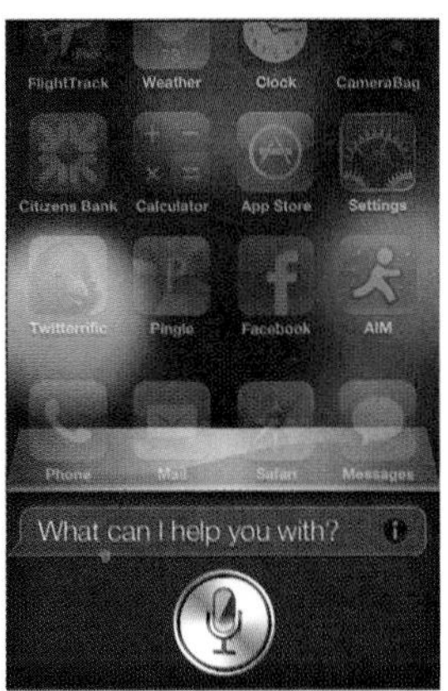

FIGURE 18.1

When Siri is activated, the "What can I help you with?" screen appears, and you hear Siri's activation tone.

As soon as you hear Siri's activation tone, speak your question, command, or request. You can either speak into the iPhone directly or into a Bluetooth wireless headset that's paired with your iPhone.

For the most accurate results when using Siri, speak directly into the iPhone or a wireless Bluetooth headset and try to avoid being in areas with excessive background noise. Speak as clearly as possible, so Siri can understand each word in your sentences.

Siri is one of the few iPhone features that works from the Lock screen. Thus, even if you have the Passcode Lock feature turned on, someone can still pick up your iPhone and send email or a text message (using your accounts), or access data from your iPhone using Siri, without your permission. To keep this from happening, set up the Passcode feature on your iPhone. Then, in the Settings app, turn off the Siri option that's offered in the Passcode Lock menu screen (shown in Figure 18.2).

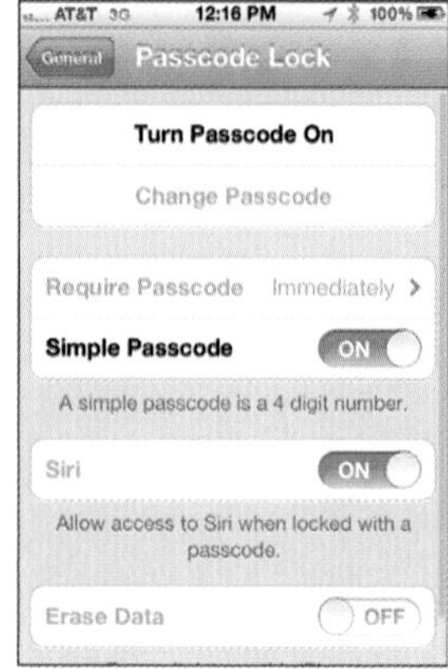

FIGURE 18.2

When you turn off the Siri option in the Passcode Lock screen, Siri will not activate from the Lock screen.

! CAUTION In the Settings app on the iPhone 4S, the Passcode Lock screen contains a Siri option that does not appear on other iOS devices. If this feature is turned on, Siri is accessible *even with the Passcode Lock feature turned on.*

SETTING UP SIRI TO WORK ON YOUR iPHONE 4S

Before you start using Siri on your iPhone 4S, you must turn it on from within the Settings app. Follow these steps to do so:

1. Launch the Settings app from the Home Screen.
2. From the main Settings menu, tap on the General option.
3. From the General menu screen (shown in Figure 18.3), tap on the Siri option.
4. When the Siri menu screen within Settings is displayed (shown in Figure 18.4), turn on the virtual switch associated with the Siri option by tapping on it. This option is displayed near the top of the screen.
5. Select your language. The default setting is English (United States). Other options include English (Australia), English (United Kingdom), French, and German. Apple reports that additional language compatibility will be added in 2012.

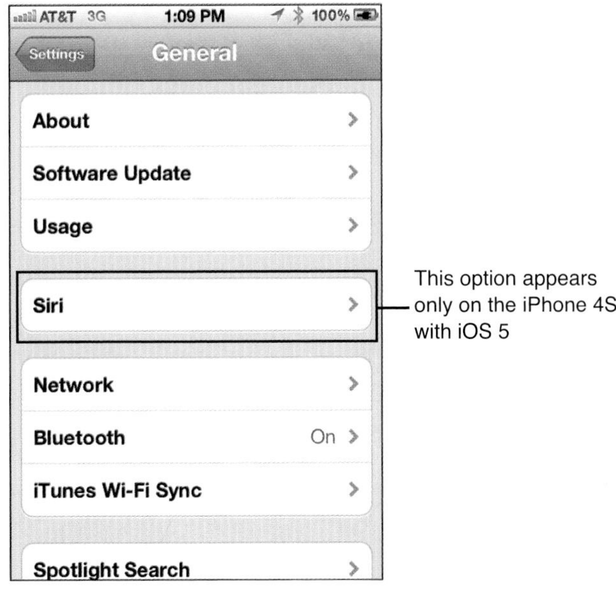

FIGURE 18.3

On the iPhone 4S, the General menu in Settings has an extra option for Siri that does not appear in the General menu if you're using any other iOS device.

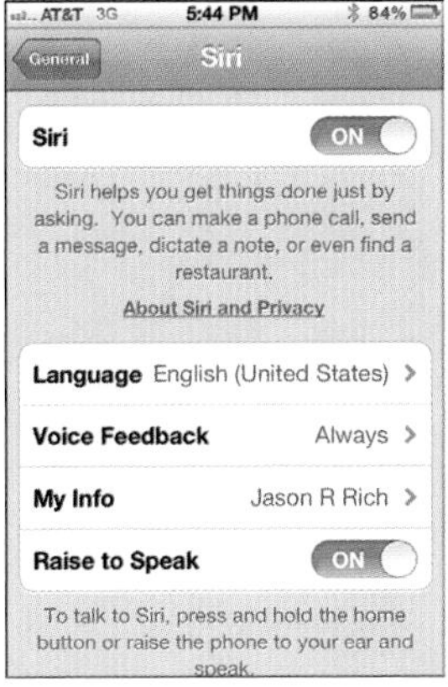

FIGURE 18.4

The Siri menu within Settings.

6. Tap on the Voice Feedback option to determine whether Siri will respond to you verbally for every request you make, or just when using the feature's hands-free mode. If Voice Feedback is turned off, text-based Siri prompts will appear on the iPhone's screen, but you will not hear Siri's voice.

7. Tap on the My Info icon to link your own Contacts entry with Siri. It's important that you create an entry for yourself in Contacts and fill in all the data fields related to your phone numbers, addresses, email addresses, Twitter username, and so on, and that you properly label each data field. For example, if your Contacts entry has three phone numbers (Home, Work, iPhone), be sure each has the appropriate label associated with it.

   Likewise, your Home and Work addresses, and the various email addresses you use, should be properly labeled with the Home and Work (or other appropriate) labels. The more information about yourself you include in your Contacts entry, the better Siri will be able to serve you.

> **TIP** Siri also utilizes information stored in the Related People fields available to you from the Add Field option as you create or edit a contact. By tapping on this field, you can add a relationship title, such as *mother*, *father*, *brother*, or *sister* to an entry. Then, when using Siri, if you say, "Call Mom at home," Siri will know exactly to whom you're referring.

   Create a Contacts entry for yourself in the Contacts app. See Chapter 14, "Strategies for Managing Calendars, Contacts, and Reminders," for information on how to do this.

8. At the bottom of the Siri menu screen, the Raise To Speak option is listed, and it's associated with a virtual on/off switch. When this switch is turned on, Siri will automatically activate when you pick up the phone and hold it up to your ear.

In addition to customizing the options offered on the Siri menu screen in Settings, it's important that you enable Siri to pinpoint your location. To do this, tap on the Location Services option in the main Settings menu.

Turn on the master Location Services option (displayed near the top of the screen) and the Location Services option specifically for the Siri app. Scroll down on the Location Services menu screen, and tap on the virtual switch associated with the Siri option. (It too should be turned on.)

After you complete this procedure, Siri has the basic information and access to content stored on your iPhone that it needs to function. As you use Siri, it will periodically ask you for additional information that you need to supply only once, and it will then be saved for future use. For example, if you activate Siri and say, "Call my mom at home," the first time you use Siri for this task, you'll be asked who your mother is. As long as you have a Contact entry for your mother stored in the

Contacts app, when you say your mother's real name, Siri will link the appropriate contact and remember this information. This applies to any nickname or title you have for other people, such as "wife," "husband," "son," "daughter, "mother," "father," "dad," "grandma and grandpa," or even "Uncle Jack."

CHECK OUT HOW SIRI CAN HELP YOU!

The great thing about Siri is that you don't have to think too much about how you phrase a command, question, or request. Siri automatically interprets what you say. However, after you activate Siri, you must wait until you hear the activation tone before you begin speaking. Siri is active only when the microphone icon appears purple. If the icon appears in just silver and gray, you must tap on it to reactivate the feature.

When you're finished issuing your command or request or asking a question, simply stop speaking. If additional information is required, Siri will prompt you for it as needed.

To get the most out of using Siri—with the least amount of frustration as a result of Siri not being able to comply with your requests—you must develop a basic understanding of which apps this feature works with, and how Siri can be used within those apps.

In general, Siri can be used with the Phone, FaceTime, Music, Mail, Messages, Reminders, Notes, Contacts, Weather, Stocks, Maps, Clock, and Find My Friends apps, plus Siri can find information on the Internet by performing web searches. You can use Siri's Dictation Mode, however, in any app where the microphone key appears on the iPhone's virtual keyboard.

> **NOTE** For additional advice about how Siri can be used, activate Siri and say, "Siri, what can you do?" or tap on the information ("i") icon next to the "What can I help you with?" message when Siri is activated.

USE SIRI'S DICTATION MODE

Even if you're using an app that Siri is not yet compatible with, chances are you can still use Siri's Dictation Mode. In many situations when the iPhone's virtual keyboard appears, you'll discover a new microphone key located to the left of the spacebar (shown in Figure 18.5).

FIGURE 18.5

Even if an app is not designed to work with Siri, such as the official Facebook app shown here, you can still use Siri's Dictation Mode to enter text using your voice, instead of typing on the virtual keyboard.

When you tap on this microphone key, Siri goes into Dictation Mode. You can now say whatever text you were going to manually type using the virtual keyboard. However, when you're finished speaking, it's necessary to tap the Done key (shown in Figure 18.6) so that Siri can translate your speech into text and insert it into the appropriate onscreen field.

For the fastest and most accurate results, speak one to three sentences at a time, and have your iPhone connected to a Wi-Fi Internet connection.

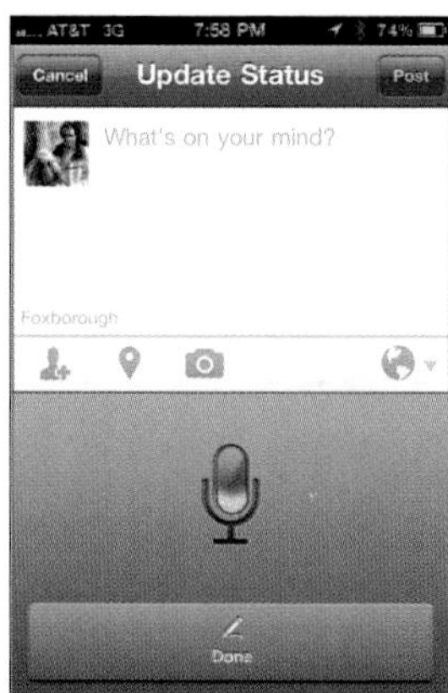

FIGURE 18.6

When using Siri's Dictation Mode, speak into the iPhone as long as the microphone appears purple. When you're finished speaking, tap the Done icon so Siri can translate your speech into usable text.

TIP While using Siri in Dictation Mode, you can easily add punctuation just by saying it. For example, you can say, "This is a sample dictation. Period," and Siri will add the period (".") at the end of the sentence. You can also use words like "open parenthesis" or "close parenthesis," "open quotes" or "close quotes," or "comma," "semicolon," or "colon" as you dictate.

TIP In most cases, you cannot ask Siri to launch an app, such as Facebook. However, you can ask Siri to use features within certain (compatible) apps. If you ask Siri to launch the Facebook app, for example, the reply will be, "I'd like to, [your name], but I am not allowed to. Sorry about that." In this case, you can often use Siri's Dictation Mode instead of manually entering text using the virtual keyboard—when updating your Facebook status, for example.

The following sections provide a sampling of what Siri can be used for and tips for how to use Siri effectively. Over time, Apple and third-party app developers will be working to upgrade Siri's capabilities, so you might discover additional functionality as you begin using Siri with various apps.

FIND, DISPLAY, OR USE INFORMATION RELATED TO YOUR CONTACTS

Your Contacts database can store a vast amount of information about people or companies. Every field within a Contact's entry is searchable and can be accessed by Siri. Or you can ask Siri to look up a specific contact for you and display that contact's Info screen on your iPhone.

Again, the more information you include in each entry stored in your Contacts database, the more helpful Siri can be. To have Siri look up and display information stored in Contacts, say something like the following:

- "Look up John Doe in Contacts."
- "What is John Doe's phone number" (see Figure 18.7).
- "What is John Doe's work address?"

TIP When Siri displays the Info screen for a Contact, it is interactive; therefore, you can tap on a displayed phone number to initiate a call, or tap on an email address to launch the Mail app to send email to that address. If you tap on a regular address, the Maps app launches, and if you tap on a website URL, Safari launches and opens that web page.

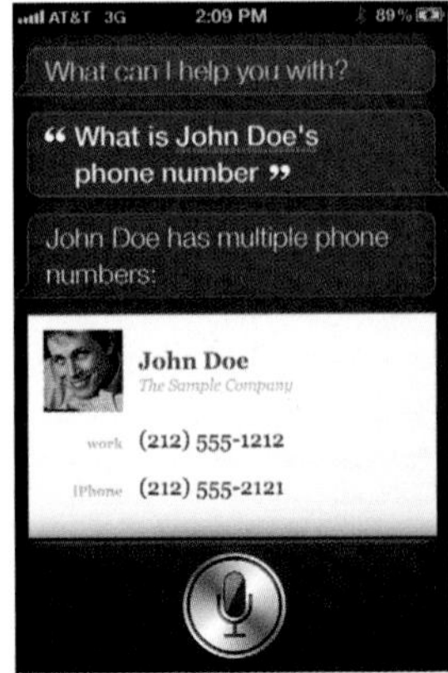

FIGURE 18.7

When you ask, "What is John Doe's phone number," the appropriate number from your Contacts database will be displayed.

Siri can also use information stored in your Contacts database to comply with various other requests, such as

- "Send John Doe a text message"—This works if you have an iPhone-labeled phone number or iMessage username or email address saved in John Doe's Contacts entry.
- "Send John Doe an email"—This works if you have an email address saved in John Doe's Contacts entry.
- "Give me directions to John Doe's home"—This works if you have a home address saved in John Doe's Contacts entry. The Maps app launches, and directions from your current location are displayed.
- "When is John Doe's birthday?"—This works if you have a date saved in the Birthday field in John Doe's Contacts entry.
- "What is John Doe's wife's name?"—This works if you have a spouse's name saved in John Doe's Contacts entry.

INITIATE A CALL

You can initiate a call by activating Siri and then saying, "Call [name] at home," or "Call [name] at work." This works if that person has a Contacts entry associated with their name, as well as a phone number labeled Home or Work, respectively. You could also say, "Call [name]'s mobile phone," or "Call [name]'s iPhone."

If you request someone's work phone number and Siri finds a contact's name but not a corresponding phone number, the response you get will be, "Sorry, there's no work number for John Doe. You can use one of these instead:" This is followed by a listing of whichever phone numbers are available for that contact (shown in Figure 18.8).

NOTE When issuing a command to Siri, you have flexibility in terms of what you say. For example, you could say, "Call John Doe at work," "Call John Doe work," or "Call the work number for John Doe," and in all these cases, Siri will initiate a call to John Doe's work number.

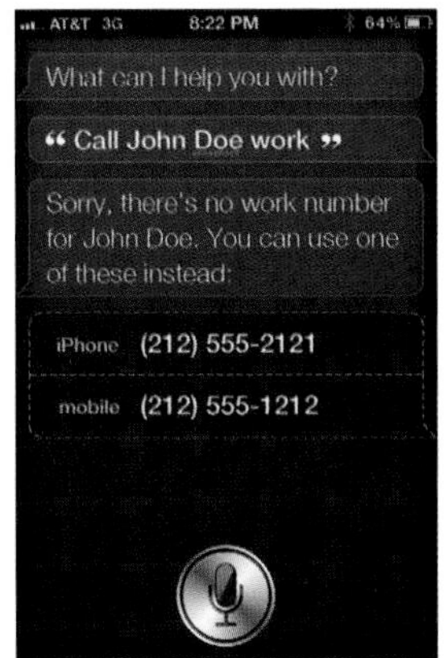

FIGURE 18.8

If you ask for a phone number, for example, that isn't stored in your iPhone, Siri will respond accordingly with available options.

Alternatively, if someone's contact information or phone number is not stored in your iPhone, you can say, "Call" or "Dial" followed by each digit of a phone number.

TIP You can also ask Siri to look up a business phone number or address by saying, "Look up [business name, such as Apple Store] in [city, state]." Or, you could say, "Look up [business type, such as a dry cleaner] in [city, state]."

When Siri finds the phone number you're looking for, Siri will say, "Calling [name] at [location]," and then automatically initiate a call to that number by launching the Phone app.

FIND YOUR FRIENDS

The Find My Friends app is available free from the App Store. If you install it and begin following friends, coworkers, or family members (with their permission), at any time, you can ask Siri, "Where is [name]?" or say, "Find [name]," and Siri will find that person and display a map showing that person's exact whereabouts. This feature is great for keeping tabs on your kids or teenagers, especially if they miss a curfew or they say they're studying at the library on a Friday evening.

For this feature to work, however, you'll need to be logged in to your free Find My Friends account via the app.

SET UP REMINDERS

If you constantly jot down reminders to yourself on scrap pieces of paper or sticky notes, or frequently manually enter to-do items in the Calendar or Reminders app of your iPhone, this is one Siri-related feature you'll truly appreciate.

To create a reminder, complete with an alarm, simply activate Siri and say something like, "Remind me to pick up my dry cleaning tomorrow at 3 PM." As shown in Figure 18.9, Siri creates the Reminder, displays it on the screen for your approval, and then saves it in the Reminders app. On the appropriate time and day, an alarm will sound and the reminder message will be displayed.

> **TIP** If you don't want to utilize the Reminders app that comes preinstalled with iOS 5, you can download a third-party app from the App Store, such as Remember The Milk (www.rememberthemilk.com), that also works with Siri.

FIGURE 18.9

Using your voice, you can create a to-do item in the Reminders app and associate an alarm with it.

TIP When creating a Reminder using Siri, you can provide a specific date and time, such as "tomorrow at 3 pm" or "Friday at 1 pm" or "July 7th at noon."

You can also include a location that Siri knows, such as "Home" or "Work." For example, you could say, "Remind me to feed the dog when I get home," or "Remind me to call Emily when I get to work." Because the Reminders app can handle location-based alerts, you can create them using Siri.

READ OR SEND TEXT MESSAGES

When you receive a new text message but can't look at the screen, activate Siri and say, "Read new text message." You'll then be given the opportunity to reply to that message and dictate your response.

Using Siri with the Messages app, you can also compose and send a text message to anyone in your Contacts database by saying something like, "Compose a text message to John Doe." You will be asked to select an email address or mobile phone number to use. To bypass this step, say, "Send a text message to John Doe's mobile phone," or "Send a text message to John Doe's iPhone." Then, Siri will say, "OK, I can send a text to John Doe for you...what would you like it to say?" (shown in Figure 18.10). Dictate your text message.

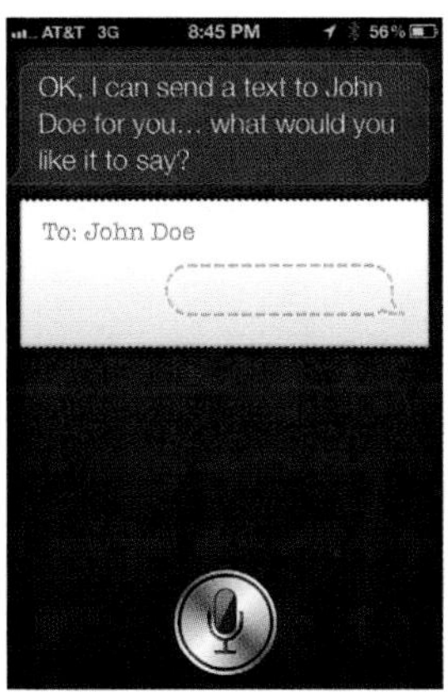

FIGURE 18.10

Siri will ask you to dictate a text message, and then display the message before it's sent.

When you're finished speaking, Siri will say, "I updated your message. Ready to send it?" The message (shown in Figure 18.11) will be displayed on the screen, along with Cancel and Send icons. You can tap an icon or speak your reply.

FIGURE 18.11

After you dictate a text message, it will be displayed on the screen for your approval.

CHECK THE WEATHER OR YOUR INVESTMENTS

The Weather app can display a current or extended weather forecast for your immediate area or any city in the world, and the Stocks app can be used to track your investments. Both apps work with Siri. However, Siri also has the capability to automatically access the Web and obtain weather information for any city or stock-related information about any stock or mutual fund, for example.

After activating Siri, ask a weather-related questions, such as

- "What is today's weather forecast?"—Siri will pinpoint your location and provide a current forecast.
- "What is the weather forecast for New York City?"—Of course, you can insert any city and state in your request.
- "Is it going to rain tomorrow?"—Siri will access and interpret the weather forecast, and then vocalize, as well as display a response.
- "Should I bring an umbrella to work?"—Siri knows the location of your work and can access and then interpret the weather forecast to offer a vocalized and displayed response.

If you have stock-related questions, you can ask about specific stocks by saying something like

- "What is [company name]'s stock at?"
- "What is [company]'s stock price?
- "How is [company name]'s stock performing?"
- "Show me [company name] stock."

As you can see in Figure 18.12, when you request stock information, you get a verbal response from Siri along with information about that stock displayed on the iPhone's screen.

FIGURE 18.12

Just by asking, Siri can tell you how a specific stock is performing.

FIND INFORMATION ON THE WEB OR GET ANSWERS TO QUESTIONS

If you want to perform a web search, you can manually launch the Safari browser, and then use the keyboard to type what you're looking for in the Search field. Or, you can active Siri and ask it to perform the search for you by saying something like the following:

- "Look up the [company] website."
- "Find [topic] on the web."
- "Search the web for [topic]."
- "Google information about [topic]."
- "Search Wikipedia for [topic]."
- "Bing [topic]." (Bing is a popular search engine operated by Microsoft.)

You also can ask a question and Siri will seek out the appropriate information on the Web.

TIP Siri is also a mathematical genius. Simply say the mathematical calculation you need solved, and Siri presents the answer in seconds. For example, say, "What is 10 plus 10?" or "What's the square root of 24?" or "What is 20 percent of 500?"

SCHEDULE AND MANAGE MEETINGS AND EVENTS

The Calendar app is also compatible with Siri, which means you can use Siri to create or modify appointments, meetings, or events by using your voice. To do this, some of the things you can say include

- "Set up a meeting at 10:30am."
- "Set up a meeting with Ryan at noon tomorrow."
- "Meet with Emily for lunch at 1pm."
- "Set up a meeting with Rusty about third-quarter sales projections at 4pm on December 12th."

Meetings you create using Siri are added to your iPhone's Calendar app. Then, if set up correctly, the scheduling data is synchronized with iCloud or your primary computer or other iOS devices.

SEND EMAIL AND ACCESS NEW (INCOMING) EMAIL

If you want to compose an email to someone, activate Siri and say, "Send an email to [name]." If that person's email address is listed in your Contacts database, Siri will address a new message to that person. Siri will then say, "What is the subject of your email?" Speak the subject line for your email. When you stop speaking, Siri will say, "Okay, what would you like the email to say?". You can now dictate the body of your email message.

When you're finished speaking, Siri composes the message, displays it on the iPhone's screen, and then says, "Here is your email to [name]. Ready to send it?". You can now respond "yes" to send the email message, or say "cancel" to abort the message. If the message isn't what you want to say, you can edit it using the virtual keyboard, or ask Siri to "Change the text to…".

SET AN ALARM OR TIMER

Siri can control the Clock app in your iPhone so it serves as an alarm clock or timer (using the functionality built in to the Clock app). You can say something like, "Set an alarm for 7:30am tomorrow" to create a new alarm. Or, to set a 30-minute timer, say, "Set a timer for 30 minutes." A countdown timer is displayed on the iPhone's screen, and an alarm sounds when the timer reaches zero.

You can also simply ask Siri, "What's today's date?" or "What time is it?" if you're too busy to look at your watch or the iPhone's screen, such as when you're driving.

GET DIRECTIONS USING THE MAPS APP

Pretty much any feature you can use the Maps app for—whether it's to find the location or phone number for a business, obtain turn-by-turn directions between two addresses, or map out a specific address location—you can access this functionality using Siri.

To use Maps-related functions, say things like the following:

- "How do I get to [location]?"
- "Show [address]."
- "Directions to [contact name or location]."
- "Find a [business type, such as gas station] near [location]."
- "Find a [business or service name, such as Starbucks Coffee] near where I am."
- "Where is the closest [business type, such as post office]?"
- "Find a [cuisine type, such as Chinese] restaurant near me."

If multiple businesses or locations are found that are directly related to your request, Siri asks you to select one, or all related matches are displayed in the Maps app using pushpins.

CONTROL THE MUSIC APP

In the mood to hear a specific song that's stored on your iPhone? Maybe you want to begin playing a specific playlist, you want to hear all the music stored on your iPhone by a particular artist, or you want to play a specific album? Well, just ask Siri. You can control the Music app using your voice by saying things like the following:

- "Play [song title]."
- "Play [album title]."
- "Play [playlist title]."
- "Play [artist's name]."
- "Play [music genre, such as pop, rock, or blues]."

You can also issue specific commands, such as "Shuffle my [title] playlist," or speak commands, such as, "Pause" or "Skip" as music is playing. However, Siri is unable to search for and display song or album listings. For example, if you say, "Show music," or "Show song playlists," you will receive a response saying, "Sorry, [your name], I can't search that content." Thus, to use Siri to control your music, you must know what music is stored on your iPhone.

FORGET STICKY NOTES—DICTATE NOTES TO YOURSELF

The Notes app that comes preinstalled with iOS 5 is used to compose notes using a text editor (as opposed to a full-featured word processor, such as Pages). Siri is compatible with the Notes app and enables you to create and dictate notes.

To create a new note, activate Siri and begin a sentence by saying, "Note that I…". You can also say, "Note: [sentence]." What you dictate will be saved as a new note in the Notes app.

When you use the command "Note," a note is created in the Notes app. It is not accompanied by an alert or alarm. However, if you use the command "Remind me…," Siri creates a reminder listing using the Reminders app, which can be associated with a time/date alarm or a location-based alarm.

TIP Siri's Dictation Mode can be used when you are word processing using the Pages app to speed up text entry without having to use the virtual keyboard. For the best results, however, dictate between one and three sentences at a time, tap Done, have Siri translate your text to speech, and then repeat the process as needed.

Using this feature to translate a significant amount of speech to text will use a lot of your monthly wireless data allocation from your wireless service provider if you're using a 3G connection. At least initially, monitor your data use carefully so you don't go beyond your monthly allocation and receive extra charges on your bill.

PRACTICE (WITH SIRI) MAKES PERFECT

Right from the start, Siri will probably understand what you say. However, as you begin using this feature often, you will become acquainted with the best and most efficient ways to communicate questions, commands, and requests to generate the desired response.

Keep in mind that Siri translates what you say phonetically, so periodically you might encounter names or commands that Siri can't understand or match up with correctly spelled information stored on your iPhone. This occurs most frequently with unusual names that sound vastly different from how they're spelled or used.

CAUTION Although Siri might seem human, in reality, it is an iPhone feature that operates using software. Before allowing Siri to send any message or text, be sure to proofread it carefully on the iPhone's screen. Keep in mind that some words sound the same when spoken, and Siri might choose the wrong word when translating your speech to text. This could lead to embarrassing situations or dramatically change the meaning of what you intended to say.

As you begin using Siri in your everyday life, you'll quickly discover this feature can streamline how you interact with your iPhone and make certain tasks much easier to accomplish. Based on the questions you ask, you'll also discover that Siri has a sense of humor. For example, try asking, "Siri, what do you look like?" or "Siri, are you attractive?"

CAUTION Theoretically, Siri can be used to control your iPhone and perform tasks hands-free while you're driving. Although using your iPhone in hands-free mode while driving might be legal in your state, if this is something you plan to do, proceed with extreme caution and don't allow yourself to be distracted from your primary responsibility, which is driving. Also, seriously consider using a wireless Bluetooth headset.

Index

A

B

C

D

E

F

N

O

P

R

S

T

U-V

W

X-Y-Z